ENGLISH AS A VOCATION: THE *SCRUTINY* MOVEMENT

English as a Vocation:
The *Scrutiny*
Movement

CHRISTOPHER HILLIARD

OXFORD
UNIVERSITY PRESS

OXFORD
UNIVERSITY PRESS

Great Clarendon Street, Oxford, OX2 6DP,
United Kingdom

Oxford University Press is a department of the University of Oxford.
It furthers the University's objective of excellence in research, scholarship,
and education by publishing worldwide. Oxford is a registered trade mark of
Oxford University Press in the UK and in certain other countries

© Christopher Hilliard 2012

The moral rights of the author have been asserted

First Edition published in 2012

Impression: 1

British Library Cataloguing in Publication Data
Data available

Library of Congress Cataloging in Publication Data
Data available

ISBN 978-0-19-969517-1

Printed in Great Britain by
MPG Books Group, Bodmin and King's Lynn

For Rose and Tess

Acknowledgements

Being in an archive is, for me, one of the defining pleasures of being a historian, and I would like to thank the staff of all the libraries and archives whose holdings I used in researching this book. I am especially indebted to Amanda Goode at Emmanuel College, Cambridge; Kate Perry and Hannah Westfall at Girton College, Cambridge; Patricia McGuire at King's College, Cambridge; Lynn Manner of the Kenyon College archives; Simon Bailey and Alice Millea of the Oxford University Archives; Verity Andrews at the University of Reading; Jacky Hodgson at the University of Sheffield Library; and Rachel Hassall of the Penguin archive at the University of Bristol. Thanks also to Helen Fraser, formerly managing director of Penguin Books, for granting me access to the collection at Bristol. The archives most important for this book have been the Downing College archives, and I am very grateful to Kate Thompson, the current archivist, Sarah Westwood, her predecessor, and David Pratt, Downing's fellow-archivist. Kate Thompson went out of her way to help me and my heroic research assistant, Benjamin Dabby. Ben combed through the Downing College matriculation registers, piecing together the data on which Chapter 3 is based. He found sources I hadn't been aware of, and I am indebted to him for his ideas and curiosity as well as for his diligence. I have since been through these materials and other records of college admissions myself, but I want to make it clear that Ben's contribution goes well beyond reconnaissance. Most of the time I was writing this book, I depended on the collections of the University of Sydney libraries, and on their interlibrary loan staff. Chris Boyd was so good at getting hold of obscure items that I began to take a mischievous pleasure in requesting ever more unlikely titles—such as the old *Doctor Who* paperbacks one of F. R. Leavis's undergraduates had written—which he duly obtained.

I thank Jacqueline Baker of Oxford University Press for believing in the project, and Jane Olin-Ammentorp, Ariane Petit, Jess Smith, Rachel Platt, Jenny Townshend, Veeralakshmy Sadayappan, and everyone behind the scenes at OUP who helped turn the manuscript into a book. OUP's formidably perceptive readers helped me to think more clearly about the scope of the book and its arguments.

Jane Grant, Ross McKibbin, Guy Ortolano, and Selina Todd read chapters of the manuscript and improved them dramatically. I really appreciate the learning and insight they brought to bear on those chapters. This time

I did *not* ask Susan Pedersen and Peter Mandler to read my work before it was published, but their training and their example guide everything I write and their continuing support means a great deal to me. Being able to talk about shared interests with Stefan Collini has been one of the privileges of working on the history of literary criticism. Nancy Walbridge Collins gave me an opportunity to clarify the direction of the project by inviting me to write an overview of it for *European Studies Forum*. For their suggestions, criticism, and encouragement, I would like to thank Laura Beers, Lawrence Black, Barbara Caine, Marco Duranti, Andrew Fitzmaurice, Margaret Harris, Kitty Hauser, Julia Horne, Chris Joyce, Jon Lawrence, Peter Marks, Tamson Pietsch, Merrilee Robb, Stephen Robertson, Brigid Rooney, Michael Saler, Robert Scoble, Glenda Sluga, Barry Spurr, Shane White, and Ken Worpole. Richard Waterhouse, Judith Barbour, Rob Jackson, Beverley Sherry, Paul Brock, Will Christie, Margaret Sampson, and Sheila Fitzpatrick helped me try to understand the Australian dimension of my subject. M. Wynn Thomas's reflections on the history of English at Swansea were enormously helpful, and not just about Swansea; I thank Dai Smith for introducing me over email to Professor Thomas. Frank Mort and James Walvin shared their memories of the University of York in the 1960s. Miles Layram not only sent me the paper he and John Roe presented at the 2010 Leavis at York conference, but also provided me with copies of the Leavis correspondence now in the University of York library—an act of wonderful scholarly generosity to a stranger.

The research for this book was generously supported by the University of Sydney and by the Australian Research Council (DP0772403). The ARC paid for time away from the classroom, for travel, and for research assistance in Britain and the United States over several years when, for two good reasons (see below), I couldn't get to the northern hemisphere. I owe an enormous debt to a succession of talented and painstaking research assistants. Ben Dabby I've already mentioned. Tobias Harper and Philippa Hetherington copied documents from the libraries of Columbia and Harvard respectively. Nathan Braccio went through Stuart Chase's correspondence in the Library of Congress for me. Peter Allender did marvellous work in the Penguin Archives at the University of Bristol. Thanks too to George Donaldson and Hugh Pemberton for leading me to Peter. In Sydney, Rhiannon Davis and Jennie Taylor have checked quotations, hunted down sources, helped with copyright permissions, and more. I value our conversations about mass culture and modern Britain over the past few years.

Robin Leavis and Kate Varney granted me access to manuscript material written by their parents and now held in archives in Cambridge and elsewhere. I owe a special debt to Robin Leavis, not only for giving me permission to quote this material, but for his searching reading of the entire text. I am grateful to Edward Thompson and Betty Thompson for permission to quote material by Denys Thompson, and I appreciate Edward Thompson's warm support of the project and the memories of his father he has shared with me. I thank the Ford family for permission to quote from Boris Ford's unpublished letters, and Tom Holbrook for permission to quote letters by David Holbrook. The extract from Ronald Bottrall's poem 'The Future Is Not for Us' is reproduced with the kind permission of Anthony Bottrall. I thank Helen Forman for allowing me to quote from John Crowe Ransom's letters. The letter from Lionel Trilling to John Crowe Ransom of 23 August 1949 is quoted by permission of the estate of Lionel Trilling. (© 2012 The Estate of Lionel Trilling. All rights reserved.) Richard Hoggart's papers are quoted with the permission of Curtis Brown on behalf of Richard Hoggart (copyright © Richard Hoggart). M. C. Bradbrook's papers are quoted with the permission of The Mistress and Fellows, Girton College, Cambridge. I am grateful to David Pratt for permission to quote the Doughty Society minute books in the Downing College archives. Material from the Oxford University archives is quoted with permission of the Keeper of the Archives, Simon Bailey. Quotations from the Penguin archive are reproduced by permission of Penguin Books Ltd, and I thank Mary Fox for her efforts on my behalf. I would also like to thank David Sutton for providing contact details for a number of rights holders.

Sarah Graham has made many specific and much appreciated contributions to the work of getting the book done, especially at crunch times, but what I really want to thank her for are all the ways, intellectual and emotional, that she actively makes it possible for me to be someone who can think and write. Our daughters, Rose and Tess, were born while I was working on this book. A book like this is not an ideal gift for two special girls, but I hope they will see the dedication as another sign, however small, of my love for them.

Contents

Abbreviations Used in the Notes

BBC WAC — BBC Written Archives Centre, Reading
Bristol — University of Bristol Library
Columbia — Rare Books and Manuscripts Library, Columbia University
CUL — Cambridge University Library
Downing — Downing College Archives, Cambridge
Emmanuel — Emmanuel College Archives, Cambridge
Girton — Girton College Archives, Cambridge
HRC — Harry Ransom Humanities Research Center, University of Texas at Austin
Kenyon — Kenyon College Archives
Leeds — Brotherton Library, University of Leeds
NL — *Downing College Association News Letter and College Record*
OUA — Oxford University Archives
Reading — University of Reading Library
Sheffield — University of Sheffield Library
Sydney — University of Sydney Archives
York — F. R. Leavis Archive, Borthwick Institute, University of York

Introduction: Pledged Intelligence

Fifteen years before he founded the Birmingham University centre that became the headquarters of cultural studies, Richard Hoggart was negotiating a different kind of encounter between literary analysis and popular culture. As an adult education tutor in Scarborough in the late 1940s, Hoggart spliced classes on Shakespeare with sessions analysing the rhetoric of advertisements and newspaper articles. Learning how such different texts worked was one of the ends of a literary training, and it was inseparable from discrimination. The students were asked to adjudicate between 'good' and 'bad' pieces of writing, stripped of their titles and authors' names. In February 1948, the class compared two descriptions of gardens, one by John Galsworthy and one by a much less popular novelist, L. H. Myers. The students' verdict, presumably reached after some prodding from Hoggart, was that the Galsworthy passage was 'a crude and blatant "build up" for a love scene, using sickening alliteration—e.g. "tiny tremors," foolish adjectives, e.g. "warm, sweet night" and the pathetic fallacy that a flower can look wistfully at a human being'. With Myers, by contrast, 'we knew well enough that this writer was not anticipating a reader with a dulled critical faculty'.[1]

The tutor's compass was the work of F. R. Leavis and his collaborators on the Cambridge journal *Scrutiny*. The students' astringent comments on Galsworthy were an unmistakable attempt at a judgement in the style already being described as 'Leavisite'—and Myers was one of the few novelists *Scrutiny* was credited with discovering and championing. Hoggart's students were being asked to respond to 'the words on the page' and not rely on background knowledge. They were learning 'practical criticism', the critical procedure associated with *Scrutiny*. When it worked, practical criticism yielded sensitive but exacting interpretations of texts. Its appeal to teachers such as Hoggart was all the greater because this mode of close reading was at the same time a mode of *teaching* close reading. It could also be used on very different material. Beginning in the early 1930s, members of the *Scrutiny* group had opened up the 'texts' of advertising

---

[1] 'Scarborough W.E.A.: Literature Class Log' (notes for 29 January 1948 and 26 February 1948), Richard Hoggart papers, 4/1/3, Sheffield.

and popular fiction, as well as canonical literature, for critical analysis. Literature was its centre, but *Scrutiny*'s province was the culture of modernity at large.

Hoggart's career as a writer as well as a teacher testifies to *Scrutiny*'s impact on British intellectual life. Leavis was a controversialist of national standing, and the terms of mid-twentieth-century debates about British culture were set in part by intellectuals whose thinking was entwined (in a fraught way) with his, such as Hoggart and Raymond Williams. *Scrutiny* and the Cambridge English school it both identified with and sniped at offered a distinctive rationale for the study of literature in universities and—as the snatches of classroom debate recorded in the logs of Hoggart's Scarborough course attest—in other theatres of intellectual activity. Leavis inspired an urgent sense of mission, and many of his own students and others who knew him only through the journal and his books became teachers and devoted their careers to what L. C. Knights, one of the editors, called 'the educational project associated with *Scrutiny*'.[2]

This book is a study of that project, of what Leavis called the *Scrutiny* 'movement'.[3] A great deal has been written about Leavis and *Scrutiny*, but the wider movement—the teachers, students, writers, and readers who made *Scrutiny* ideas and practices a significant part of twentieth-century British cultural history as well as an important episode in the development of literary criticism—has never been examined systematically or in concrete detail.[4] And most discussions of Leavis and *Scrutiny* have confined themselves to Britain, even though English departments in Colombo and Sydney were reorganized in alignment with Leavis's conception of criticism.

To examine this movement is not simply to study the 'dissemination' of *Scrutiny* approaches beyond Cambridge, nor to apply some empirical colour or ballast to a body of literary and intellectual history. It is, rather,

---

[2] L. C. Knights, 'Scrutiny of Examinations', *Scrutiny* 2/2 (September 1933): 153.

[3] F. R. Leavis to Ian Parsons, 21 August 1932, 1 October 1932, 16 September 1933, Chatto & Windus archive, CW 53/2, Reading.

[4] As Carolyn Steedman lamented in 'State-sponsored Autobiography', in Becky Conekin, Frank Mort, and Chris Waters (eds), *Moments of Modernity: Reconstructing Britain, 1945–1964* (London: Rivers Oram Press, 1999), 48. The most important books are Francis Mulhern, *The Moment of 'Scrutiny'* (London: New Left Books, 1979); Michael Bell, *F. R. Leavis* (Abingdon: Routledge, 1988); Ian MacKillop, *F. R. Leavis: A Life in Criticism* (London: Allen Lane, 1995); Guy Ortolano, *The Two Cultures Controversy: Science, Literature and Cultural Politics in Postwar Britain* (Cambridge: Cambridge University Press, 2009). Richard Storer, *F. R. Leavis* (Abingdon: Routledge, 2009), includes a useful guide to further reading (126–36). To my mind the best short introduction is Michael Bell, 'F. R. Leavis', in A. Walton Litz, Louis Menand, and Lawrence Rainey (eds), *The Cambridge History of Literary Criticism*, vol. 7, *Modernism and the New Criticism* (Cambridge: Cambridge University Press, 2000), 389–422.

to rewrite that history. The *Scrutiny* tradition was remade as well as re-housed when it was transported beyond the very distinctive setting in which it took shape, the intellectual milieu and intimate and intensive teaching practices of interwar Cambridge. The cultural critique inaugurated in and around *Scrutiny* in the 1930s provided the rationale for David Holbrook's vision of school English as creative self-exploration as well as G. H. Bantock's assault on progressive education and comprehensive schools. As an interpretation of modern cultural history and a framework for interpreting its products, that critique was awkwardly useful to Marxists, the awkwardness being not the least interesting or productive aspect of the connection. The significance of the *Scrutiny* movement is to be found in the energies it released unpredictably as well as those it channelled. Leavis is routinely caricatured as a puritan who insisted on obedience, yet the most remarkable quality of his influence is its variety. The subject thus broaches a more general problem: what becomes of a critical approach when it is transposed to new social, political, and pedagogical contexts?

Scrutiny was a self-consciously Cambridge enterprise, and its principal editor and inspiration spent his life there. Frank Raymond Leavis was born in 1895, the son of a piano retailer whose increasingly prospering business moved premises a number of times, edging closer to the collegiate centre of the town. Leavis said that his family's background was 'entirely typical of the nineteenth-century graph: Unitarian by 1820, radical reformer by 1880, and agnostic pacifist by 1914'. In the First World War, he enlisted as a non-combatant before conscription was introduced, and served with the Friends' Ambulance Service as a medical orderly. At the end of the war he returned to Cambridge to complete his degree. Leavis had read history on a scholarship at Emmanuel College briefly before beginning his war service. When he resumed his studies, he switched to the new literature course, the English tripos. He stayed on to do research on the history of the relationship between journalism and literature, receiving his PhD, still a new degree at Cambridge, in 1924. For the rest of the decade he eked out a precarious income teaching at the university.[5]

At this time, English at Cambridge did not have a faculty to administer its teaching and examining. No subject did. Before the faculties were

[5] MacKillop, *F. R. Leavis*, chs 1–3; quotation from Roger Poole, untitled essay, *Cambridge Quarterly* 25/4 (1996): 392. For further biographical information see Denys Thompson (ed.), *The Leavises: Recollections and Impressions* (Cambridge: Cambridge University Press, 1984); Ian MacKillop and Richard Storer (eds), *F. R. Leavis: Essays and Documents* (Sheffield: Sheffield Academic Press, 1995), part 4; Kate Varney and Jan Montefiore, 'A Conversation about Q. D. Leavis', *Women: A Cultural Review* 19/2 (2008): 172–87. There are several dozen essay-length memoirs by pupils and colleagues that are referred to throughout this book.

founded, only a small proportion of academics—mostly professors—had an ongoing responsibility to the university rather than the colleges for their subject. Others lectured for the university 'under a bizarre variety of ad hoc inter-collegiate arrangements'.[6] The university's lecturers and examiners were drawn from the fellowships of the colleges, whose primary teaching work was conducting weekly 'supervisions' with one or two undergraduates at a time. Supervising, too, could be farmed out to freelances or teachers on short-term appointments, if the college had a lot of students reading a subject or if it had no fellow in that subject.

These arrangements did not cease immediately on the creation of the faculties, which were established in response to the recommendations of the Royal Commission on the Universities of Oxford and Cambridge, which reported in 1922. The faculties were to exert some coordination over teaching and research, and one of the main levers would be staffing: twelve permanent university lectureships in English were established with the English Faculty.[7] Nevertheless, a great many supervisions continued to be undertaken by college teachers without university appointments. Leavis held a temporary, 'probationary' university lectureship for four years, but he also had to undertake a good deal of the irregular work customary for Cambridge teachers. He lectured for tripos papers, and he supervised at his old college, Emmanuel, assisting the director of studies, his near-contemporary Stanley Bennett. As well as teaching Emmanuel undergraduates, he did supervisions for the two women's colleges, Girton and Newnham, and supervised men at other colleges, many of them from St John's.

In 1931, Leavis's temporary lectureship expired and was not replaced with a permanent university post. When Bennett, who did have a permanent university position, broke the news to him, they quarrelled, and Leavis lost his hours at Emmanuel and St John's. All but unemployed, Leavis was now offered work at Downing College. Bill Cuttle, a classicist who knew Leavis from Emmanuel and was interested in his work, had been elected to a fellowship at Downing, and was trying to build up a college that had little in the way of funds and few undergraduates. Most Downing undergraduates were reading medicine or law. Cuttle wanted to recruit undergraduates to read new subjects, or subjects new to Downing. English would be a good fit, and the pastoral commitment Leavis had

   [6] Christopher N. L. Brooke, *A History of the University of Cambridge*, vol. 4, *1870–1990* (Cambridge: Cambridge University Press, 1993), 353.

   [7] On the Royal Commission and its consequences, see Brooke, *University of Cambridge*, 352–4, and ch. 11 generally. On the English Faculty, see Stefan Collini, 'Cambridge and the Study of English', in Sarah J. Ormrod (ed.), *Cambridge Contributions* (Cambridge: Cambridge University Press, 1998), 42–64. E. M. W. Tillyard's insider's account, *The Muse Unchained: An Intimate Account of the Revolution in English Studies at Cambridge* (London: Bowes & Bowes, 1958), is notable for its marginalization of Leavis.

demonstrated at Emmanuel, together with the examination results of the men he had taught, commended him to Cuttle.[8] The new college committed itself to Leavis and his developing 'school' incrementally over the next five years. First he was taken on as a supervisor, then appointed director of studies. The college offered support to the graduates and research students who helped with supervisions, and provided funding for scholarships. Then, in 1936, Downing's Governing Body appointed Leavis to a three-year college lectureship.[9] The hope was that Leavis would get the university lectureship that was then in the offing, in which case the English Faculty would pay Leavis a salary while leaving him able to continue supervising at Downing. In the event, the faculty advertised only a part-time lectureship. Leavis applied anyway and was successful. Downing cancelled his fixed-term college lectureship and made him a full member of the fellowship.[10]

Although the establishment of the faculties set in train a process of centralization, English remained 'largely a college-based subject' throughout Leavis's career. The faculty's curriculum was broad enough for individual colleges to retain a great deal of freedom in how they taught the subject and prepared their students for the tripos examinations.[11] At Downing, Leavis was responsible for selecting and overseeing his teaching assistants, and he was able to choose who came up to Downing to read English on the basis of their performance in examinations he had set himself. Leavis taught 335 undergraduates at Downing between the early 1930s and the early 1960s. The majority were drawn from the prosperous reaches of the middle class: they were not a phalanx of lower-middle-class and working-class 'scholarship boys', as is often thought, though those social strata were certainly represented. Leavis's Cambridge constituency extended well beyond Downing: he gave lectures for the English Faculty, and the seminars he conducted in Downing several mornings each week were attended by students from other colleges as well (not all of them with the blessing of their tutors). The Downing 'English school' was one of two complementary bases of Leavis's influence. The other, of course, was *Scrutiny*.[12]

[8] MacKillop, *F. R. Leavis*, 152–3; Stanley French, *The History of Downing College Cambridge* (Cambridge: Downing College Association, 1978), 138–9; Brooke, *University of Cambridge*, 55–6.

[9] MacKillop, *F. R. Leavis*, 153–4, 158–9.

[10] For these details and a consideration of the fairness or unfairness of the English Faculty's conduct regarding Leavis's employment, see MacKillop, *F. R. Leavis*, chs 4–5. Compare M. C. Bradbrook, '"Nor Shall My Sword": The Leavises' Mythology', in Thompson (ed.), *The Leavises*, 32–3, 34–6, 42–3 n. 6, 43 n. 10.

[11] Bradbrook, '"Nor Shall My Sword"', 38.

[12] There were exchanges between the two. Teaching for Leavis in the college provided Harold Mason, a *Scrutiny* editor from 1947 until the end in 1953, with a livelihood and a Cambridge base. Wilfrid Mellers was a Downing undergraduate when he started

Scrutiny was a product of the uncertain but germinal period immediately before Leavis found his berth at Downing. It was during these years that Leavis met and taught people who became close collaborators or forceful, though never unthinking, exponents of his ideas: Denys Thompson, L. C. Knights, D. W. Harding, and, at one remove, Raymond O'Malley and John Speirs.[13] The most enduring collaboration, of course, was with Queenie Roth, whom he met as a Girton undergraduate and whom he married in 1929. She supervised for several colleges as their children grew older, but never held a college fellowship or faculty post. She was the only woman in the group that formed the nucleus of *Scrutiny* at the beginning of the 1930s.[14] The Leavises' house was its hub. On Friday afternoons, they would host teas for F. R. Leavis's pupils and other guests. The hospitality was 'a continuing Cambridge tradition for dons' wives'.[15] It was also a recognition that the 'essential Cambridge' in which the Leavises believed was not satisfactorily embodied in the formal institutions of the university.[16] Invitations to the Friday gatherings bespoke recruitment as well as welcome.[17] Knights met Leavis to ask for advice on an essay on 'Future Developments in Literary Criticism' for a university competition. When he won the prize, the Leavises asked to see his essay. 'As a result, I was invited to their regular Friday teas and became a habitué.'[18]

Knights was one of a group of research students who congregated at the Leavises' house and talked about launching a journal.[19] He and the American Donald Culver were the 'active promoters' and official editors of

contributing articles on music to *Scrutiny*; he stayed on at the college after graduating to teach music and supervise for Leavis while continuing to write for the journal. Other Downing undergraduates wrote book reviews for the journal and a handful of articles, some of which began as essays submitted in the course of their studies.

[13] Denys Thompson was an undergraduate at St John's, Harding at Emmanuel. Speirs, *Scrutiny*'s medievalist, was taught by Leavis at Emmanuel. O'Malley was an undergraduate at Trinity College, which, in 1928, had no English fellows of its own; O'Malley's tutor acceded to his request to be supervised by Leavis. Knights was an undergraduate at Selwyn College and worked with Leavis after he became a research student. Denys Thompson, 'Teacher and Friend', in Thompson (ed.), *The Leavises*, 44; Raymond O'Malley, 'Charisma?', in Thompson, *The Leavises*, 54; Boris Ford, 'John Hastie Speirs', *Emmanuel College Magazine* 62 (1979–80): 97; Anon., 'Denys Clement Wyatt Harding', *Emmanuel College Magazine* 75 (1992–3): 197–201.

[14] Bradbrook, ' "Nor Shall My Sword" ', 34.

[15] Brian Worthington, untitled essay, *Cambridge Quarterly* 25/4 (1996): 421.

[16] F. R. Leavis, ' "Scrutiny": A Retrospect', *Scrutiny*, vol. 20, *A Retrospect, Indexes, Errata* (Cambridge: Cambridge University Press, 1963), 1.

[17] See the note to James Klugmann quoted in MacKillop, *F. R. Leavis*, 151.

[18] L. C. Knights, untitled essay, *Cambridge Quarterly* 25/4 (1996): 357.

[19] MacKillop, *F. R. Leavis*, 142–5; F. R. Leavis to Parsons, 14 February 1932, Chatto & Windus archive, CW 53/2, Reading; L. C. Knights, '*Scrutiny* and F.R.L.: A Personal Memoir', in Thompson (ed.), *The Leavises*, 70–4.

Scrutiny when the first number appeared. Alluding darkly to his situation at Cambridge, Leavis told his publisher that he thought it politic to keep his own name off the masthead at first.[20] Yet he was always the journal's principal editor, the font of ideas as well as the person to whom on-the-spot editorial decisions fell as other editors left Cambridge for jobs elsewhere.[21] He dealt with the printers and the distributors, and his wife shouldered the burden of the typing. Q. D. Leavis was intensely involved in editorial discussions, though she was never formally an editor. While the other editors' contributions were secondary to F. R. Leavis's, they were not merely nominal. The period for which the fullest collection of editorial correspondence is available, the late 1930s and early 1940s, shows Leavis consulting with other editors and, occasionally, the other editors corresponding independently.[22] Leavis told Harding that, although he wished circumstances permitted the other editors to do more, he nevertheless found in them 'an enormous source of strength'. Harding and Knights had made it possible for him to resist 'the subtle & painful pressures to which a *Scrutiny* editor is exposed'.[23]

As this comment suggests, Leavis—and other editors and regular contributors—had a strong sense of *Scrutiny*'s identity. Leavis spoke of its 'team' or 'connexion' of writers and editors, and thought of its readership as a 'public'.[24] In his valedictory editorial, Leavis remarked: 'There has never been a *Scrutiny* orthodoxy, but there has been a *Scrutiny* conception of the function of criticism at the present time, together with a corresponding one of the proper spirit of a critical quarterly.' The journal accommodated a variety of perspectives, and several of the junior editors, though not Leavis, were subjected to strong criticism in its pages: but the common understanding of the function of criticism, which included the maintenance of exigent 'standards', and the sense of responsibility to a *Scrutiny* public did have centripetal effects—the journal was never a 'miscellany'.[25] When

---

[20] F. R. Leavis to Parsons, 17 February 1932, Chatto & Windus archive, CW 53/2, Reading.
[21] F. R. Leavis to D. W. Harding, 22 May [1941]; Leavis to D. F. Pocock, 12 September 1950, F. R. Leavis papers, Col. 9.59a, Emmanuel.
[22] Leavis to Harding, 21 December [1938]; 12 April [1939?]; 7 January 1939; 18 April 1939; 3 June 1939; Knights to Harding, 4 October 1939; Leavis to Harding, n.d. [30 October 1939] (enclosing a book that Knights told him Harding would like to review for *Scrutiny*); Leavis to Harding, 16 March 1941, Leavis papers, Col 9.59a, Emmanuel.
[23] Leavis to Harding, 22 May [1941], Leavis papers, Col 9.59a, Emmanuel.
[24] Leavis to Harding, 16 March 1941; Leavis to Pocock, 18 January 1954, Leavis papers, Col 9.59a, Emmanuel; Leavis, ' "Scrutiny": A Retrospect', 21.
[25] F. R. Leavis, 'Valedictory', *Scrutiny* 19/4 (October 1953): 254; Boris Ford and Stephen Reiss, 'A Letter on the Music Criticism of W. H. Mellers', *Scrutiny* 11/2 (December 1942): 109–16; W. A. Edwards, 'Ideals and Facts in Adult Education', *Scrutiny* 3/1 (June 1934): 100–1 (on a book by Thompson).

Harding submitted an essay on F. Scott Fitzgerald in 1951, it sparked intense discussion between the Leavises and Marius Bewley, an American research student at Downing (they had not been able to consult Knights). They all agreed that 'the contemporary acceptance of Fitzgerald as a distinguished writer... ought not to be endorsed (even in appearance) by *Scrutiny*'. Harding's analysis in effect implied such acceptance, though the article did not argue any grounds for Fitzgerald's literary value. Summarizing these discussions for Harding, F. R. Leavis said: '*Scrutiny*, of course, is a forum. But we don't want to risk any misunderstanding' of the sort that would arise from Harding's long involvement with *Scrutiny*. So Leavis asked Harding's permission 'to remind the "public" of the forum aspect': by following up Harding's article with another article on Scott Fitzgerald 'from another point of view'.[26]

Everything in *Scrutiny* was within Leavis's orbit, but it was not simply, or even, a 'Leavisite' journal (he disliked the word, whose pointed suffix chimes, as Felicity Rosslyn has observed, 'with "Jacobite" and other fantasies of loyalty').[27] Among the *Scrutiny* work most valued by adult education tutors in the 1940s were Knights's articles on the relations between literature and the social. Thompson, not Leavis, was largely responsible for journal's attention to rural life and folk customs. Leavis sponsored Thompson and O'Malley's *Scrutiny* writing on schoolteaching, but his contribution to this part of the 'campaign' was not sustained or specific. Leavis described Thompson as the movement's 'magnificent propagandist'.[28] He proved a magnificent organizer as well. Thompson's journals, *English in Schools* and *Use of English*, were the platforms of *Scrutiny*'s ongoing influence among teachers. *Use of English* coordinated local discussion groups that eventually led to the National Association for the Teaching of English in the early 1960s. By the time *Scrutiny* suspended publication in 1953—getting enough contributions of sufficient standard had been a persistent problem and the non-appearance of two articles left a fatal hole in the forthcoming number—it had made a deep impact on the practice of literary criticism and on English teaching, especially in schools and the adult education movement. Leavis's celebrity dates from after *Scrutiny*'s closure, and especially from his stinging response to C. P. Snow's 'two

[26] Leavis to Harding, n.d. [January 1952], Leavis papers, Col 9.59a, Emmanuel; D. W. Harding, 'Scott Fitzgerald', *Scrutiny* 18/3 (winter 1951–2): 166–74 (the final quotation is from the editorial note at the end of this article). For more on the operation of the journal, see Ross Alloway, 'Selling the Great Tradition: Resistance and Conformity in the Publishing Practices of F. R. Leavis', *Book History* 6 (2003): 227–50.
[27] 'Atticus', 'No More Leavisites', *Sunday Times*, 28 March 1965 Felicity Rosslyn, untitled essay, *Cambridge Quarterly* 25/4 (1996): 396.
[28] Leavis to Parsons, 5 November 1932, Chatto & Windus archive, CW 53/2, Reading.

cultures' thesis, and lasted until his death in 1978.[29] He was more actively influential earlier on, when he was less famous.

This influence was never hegemonic, though since the end of the 1960s it has been common to claim that it was. 'Leavis commanded his subject, within his own generation,' Perry Anderson remarked in his still-breathtaking essay on British thought in *New Left Review* in 1968.[30] Chris Baldick, in an oft-cited book on criticism's 'social mission', asserted that the Leavises established 'a literary criticism which would dominate its century as Dryden, Johnson, and Arnold had theirs'.[31] This has become something like received wisdom. Jed Esty writes, for instance, of 'the dominant assumptions of midcentury English criticism embodied in the figure of F. R. Leavis'.[32] Leavis's career was marked by conflict with the metropolitan critical establishment of the *Times Literary Supplement* and the broadsheet press, but even among university-based critics he and his journal were never dominant. Why, then, are they so readily taken to be the reigning powers in mid-twentieth-century British literary criticism? It may have something to do with the habit of thinking about literary criticism, like literature itself, in terms of major authors. Yet critical hegemonies cannot satisfactorily be examined in this way. The prevailing assumptions of academic English were not 'embodied' in the work of an individual such as Leavis (or T. S. Eliot, or I. A. Richards, or William Empson, or G. Wilson Knight). Their provenance was less personal and more institutional. Most university English departments in Britain (and the empire) were established on the Oxford or London models.[33] Oxford and London placed more emphasis on early English language and literature, and they valued a scholarly command of literary history over individual responses to texts. The claims of 'criticism', with which *Scrutiny* and (to a lesser extent) 'Cambridge English' were identified, had much less institutional purchase.

---

[29] On this phase, see Ortolano, *Two Cultures Controversy*; Sean Matthews, 'The Responsibilities of Dissent: F. R. Leavis after *Scrutiny*', *Literature and History* 13/2 (2004): 49–66; Stefan Collini, 'The Critic as Journalist: Leavis after *Scrutiny*', in Jeremy Treglown and Bridget Bennett (eds), *Grub Street and the Ivory Tower: Literary Journalism and Literary Scholarship from Fielding to the Internet* (Oxford: Clarendon Press, 1998), 151–76.

[30] Perry Anderson, 'Components of the National Culture', *New Left Review* 50 (1968): 17.

[31] Chris Baldick, *The Social Mission of English Criticism, 1848–1932* (Oxford: Clarendon Press, 1983), 162.

[32] Jed Esty, *A Shrinking Island: Modernism and National Culture in England* (Princeton: Princeton University Press, 2003), 9.

[33] See D. J. Palmer, *The Rise of English Studies: An Account of the Study of English Language and Literature from Its Origins to the Making of the Oxford English School* (London: Oxford University Press, 1965); Jo McMurtry, *English Language, English Literature: The Creation of an Academic Discipline* (London: Mansell, 1985); Franklin E. Court, *Institutionalizing English Literature: The Culture and Politics of Literary Study, 1750–1900* (Stanford: Stanford University Press, 1992), ch. 4.

As late as the 1950s, an examiner could still decline to award a PhD because the thesis in question was 'not a contribution to knowledge, but a piece of literary criticism', and heads of department worried that a paucity of esteemed outlets for critical rather than scholarly articles hampered the careers of the critics on their staff.[34]

By 1951, when the journal *Essays in Criticism* was launched, criticism had attained a level of legitimacy in most universities, though it seldom dislodged literary-historical scholarship and philology—at least, not to the extent Leavis would have liked. At Nottingham University College, where the syllabus was set by the University of London, a 'liberal education' was compromised by the grind of studying 'Anglo-Saxon texts and philology'—or so its Professor of English, Vivian de Sola Pinto, told the literary society at Leavis's college when he visited in 1952. Once Nottingham was granted its own university charter, Pinto set about reforming the syllabus along the lines of Leavis's *Education and the University* (1943) and Knights's *Literature and the Study of Society* (1947). Pinto introduced practical criticism exercises and courses in Literature, Life, and Thought, which Cambridge had long offered. 'His aim, he concluded, was the education of the critical intelligence', not the acquisition of technical skills and facts. All the same, Pinto did not sweep away all vestiges of 'the traditional "language and literature" disciplines of Oxford and London', to the relief of his successor, a graduate of Oxford and Edinburgh who professed only 'a limited respect for notions out of Cambridge'.[35]

In the early 1960s, as new universities planned their English programmes, the journal *Critical Survey* invited representatives of most English departments in England, Scotland, and Wales to describe their curricula and disciplinary sensibilities. The impact of *Scrutiny* is visible in the number of departments that made 'practical criticism' an important part of their teaching and examining.[36] Leavis and his followers were the

---

[34] Brian Cox, *The Great Betrayal* (London: Chapman, 1992), 102; William Empson to [W. A.] Sanderson, 22 January 1958; Empson to L. C. Knights, 27 December 1966, William Empson Papers, bMS Eng 1401, Houghton Library, Harvard University, both reprinted in John Haffenden (ed.), *Selected Letters of William Empson* (Oxford: Oxford University Press, 2006), 276–8, 423–4.

[35] Doughty Society minute book, 86 (30 November 1952), DCCS/4/4/1/1, Downing; James Kinsley, 'English Studies at Nottingham', *Critical Survey* 1/2 (spring 1963): 118–22 (quotations from 118, 119).

[36] L. C. Knights, 'English at Bristol', *Critical Survey* 1/3 (autumn 1963): 180–3; Ian Watt, 'English at Norwich', *Critical Survey* 1/1 (1962): 45; David Daiches, 'English Studies at the University of Sussex', *Critical Survey* 1/1 (1962): 50–1; Clifford Leech, 'The Durham Colleges English Department', *Critical Survey* 1/2 (1963): 117; A. R. Humphreys, 'English at Leicester', *Critical Survey* 2/1 (1964): 63; G. K. Hunter, 'English at Warwick', *Critical Survey* 2/2 (1965): 131; John D. Jump, 'English at Manchester', *Critical Survey* 2/3 (1965): 188; Cecil Price, 'English at Swansea', *Critical Survey* 2/4 (1966): 255.

most active proponents of sight-reading as a means of teaching criticism, but practical criticism was Cambridge's property as well as *Scrutiny*'s. Nottingham's embrace of Literature, Life, and Thought and the decision taken by Sussex to offer courses modelled on Cambridge ones that Leavis had no hand in framing (such as its Tragedy paper) also suggest that it was Cambridge English generally, as much as Leavis's individual blueprint, that English professors looked to as they set up or reformed their curricula.[37] Several of *Critical Survey*'s respondents made oblique but unambiguous digs at Leavis and *Scrutiny* as they explained their values and aspirations.[38] Leavis taught many people who subsequently took up academic jobs, but *Scrutiny*-dominated departments were extremely rare— indeed, they only existed overseas, in the empire. Even at the University of Bristol, where Knights led the english department in the 1950s and early 1960s, practical criticism classes coexisted with compulsory linguistic work in Old English.[39]

It is telling that claims of *Scrutiny*'s dominance have tended to originate on the political left (and most discussions of *Scrutiny*'s extramural significance have come from the left).[40] *Scrutiny* occupies a much more important place in the genealogy of left literary criticism and cultural studies than it does in English studies at large. *Scrutiny*'s attraction for intellectuals on the left animated Francis Mulhern's simultaneously hostile and admiring critique of 1979. Written within the intellectual matrix of *New Left Review*, *The Moment of 'Scrutiny'* is still the most substantial and penetrating study of *Scrutiny* as a site of radical criticism of modern culture. *Scrutiny*'s appeal to critics on the left arose from the way its social criticism informed its literary criticism and vice versa: 'that complex of ideas that invests the apparently specialist procedures of "literary criticism," in the discourse on "community."' Mulhern acknowledged that this conjunction did open up 'an educational space within which the cultural institutions of

[37] F. R. Leavis's adverse judgement of those papers, or at least (in the case of Tragedy) their actual realization, is in *Education and the University: A Sketch for an 'English School'* (London: Chatto & Windus, 1943), 48.

[38] W. Moelwyn Merchant, 'English at Exeter', *Critical Survey* 1/3 (1963): 186; F. T. Prince, 'English at Southampton', *Critical Survey* 2/3 (winter 1965): 194. Both Prince and Merchant alluded to oft-quoted comments by Leavis. See also R. L. Brett, 'English at Hull', *Critical Survey* 2/1 (1964): 55.

[39] Knights, 'English at Bristol', 180–3. A dozen British university libraries held complete or nearly complete runs of *Scrutiny* before it was reissued in 1963; some, such as Manchester and Liverpool, had no holdings of it. James D. Stewart, Muriel E. Hammond, and Erwin Saenger, *British Union-Catalogue of Periodicals: A Record of the Periodicals of the World, from the Seventeenth Century to the Present Day, in British Libraries*, vol. 4, *S-Z* (London: Butterworths, 1958), 63.

[40] In addition to Baldick, *Social Mission*, ch. 7, see Janet Batsleer, Tony Davis, Rebecca O'Rourke, and Chris Weedon, *Rewriting English: Cultural Politics of Gender and Class* (London: Methuen, 1985), esp. 28.

bourgeois-democratic capitalism could be subjected to critical analysis'— by Williams, Hoggart, and others involved with the Birmingham Centre for Contemporary Cultural Studies. Ultimately, though, that complex of *Scrutiny* ideas or premises was disabling. *Scrutiny*'s criticism and 'policies' were organized around a dialectic of (genuine) 'culture' and (mechanical) 'civilization', and the '*main* and *logically necessary effect*' of that dialectic was '*a depreciation*, a *repression* and, at the limit, a *categorial dissolution* of *politics as such*. Nothing could be more disorienting for socialist cultural theory than the ingestion of a discourse whose main effect is to undo the intelligibility of its ultimate concern: political mobilization against the existing structures of society and State.'[41] *Scrutiny* did have a 'politics', but it was one in which the political in Mulhern's sense was beside the point: its central cultural questions did not have social or economic answers.

Mulhern's is a much more focused position than that of others writing in his wake about *Scrutiny* and the installation of 'English' in the education system in the first half of the twentieth century.[42] In their narrative, English functioned as an engine for managing class conflict. Through the teaching of English literature in schools, working-class children were invited into a community of common Englishness that superseded class identities and interests. If 'culture' is what makes human life most human, competing ideals like social justice are devalued or unsettled. The tendency to depreciate or dissolve 'politics as such', which in Mulhern's analysis compromised any Marxist theoretical appropriation of *Scrutiny*, was, in the literature on 'the rise of English', taken to be the dynamic of a much further-reaching ideological formation—albeit one that cannot be established satisfactorily through the almost exclusively literary source bases of these studies.[43] The first chapter of Terry Eagleton's *Literary Theory* was neither the first nor the fullest exposition of this highly questionable position, but it is by far the most influential.[44] (*Literary Theory* has sold nearly a million copies and introduced more than one generation of stu-

---

[41] Mulhern, *Moment of 'Scrutiny'*, 329–31. And, on *Scrutiny*'s appeal, see Stuart Hall, 'Life and Times of the First New Left', *New Left Review*, n.s., 61 (2010): 179.

[42] Brian Doyle, 'The Invention of English', in Robert Colls and Philip Dodds (eds), *Englishness: Politics and Culture, 1880–1920* (Beckenham: Croom Helm, 1986), 89–115; Terence Hawkes, *That Shakespeherian Rag: Essays on a Critical Process* (London: Methuen, 1986), esp. 111–12; Tom Steele, *The Emergence of Cultural Studies, 1945–65: Cultural Politics, Adult Education, and the English Question* (London: Lawrence & Wishart, 1997), ch. 3. Compare Stefan Collini, *Public Moralists: Political Thought and Intellectual Life in Britain, 1850–1930* (Oxford: Clarendon Press, 1991), ch. 9.

[43] The same objection can be made to Ian Hunter's *Culture and Government: The Emergence of Literary Education* (Basingstoke: Macmillan, 1988).

[44] Terry Eagleton, *Literary Theory: An Introduction*, 2 (1983; Minneapolis: University of Minnesota Press, 1996), ch. 1. See also Terry Eagleton, *Criticism and Ideology: A Study in Marxist Literary Theory* (1976; London: Verso, 1978), 12–17.

dents to the political history of Criticism, Inc.)[45] Although Eagleton's account is essentially a commentary on the set texts supplemented by a few biographical and historical facts (Leavis was the son of a shopkeeper, his wife the daughter of a draper, the memory of the First World War loomed large), its expansiveness and rhetorical force ensure that it is often mistaken for an explanation of an institutional and ideological process.

A more convincing account of *Scrutiny* as a movement requires an archive as well as a library. It demands research in college records and other materials to establish the social composition of Leavis's 'English school', and an examination of the materials produced by institutions—universities, teachers' organizations, publishers, the BBC—to make sense of the mechanisms by which *Scrutiny* approaches were embedded in cultural life in Britain and parts of its empire. It calls for a more nuanced understanding of the contours of twentieth-century social history than those manifested in stock judgements about the 'meritocratic' effects of the 1940s' education reforms or *Scrutiny*'s putatively 'petit-bourgeois' character. This book is therefore among other things an exercise in social and cultural history.

Yet it is also, inescapably, a study in intellectual history. It depends on reading for texture, assumptions, and procedures. Literary criticism is of course an activity as well as a complex of ideas, and the deployment of *Scrutiny*'s favoured interpretative or expository moves can be more significant than overt declarations of indebtedness or estrangement. It is also important to be able to make out what one contributor called the journal's 'watermark': its patterns of vocabulary, quotation, and allusion.[46] *Scrutiny* put into circulation an 'economy of passages'—from Pound, Eliot, Lawrence, and others—the quotation of which was a marker of affiliation.[47] As well as analysing published books and articles, this study also works with scrappier or more awkward texts such as examination papers, syllabi, and students' notes in an attempt to render legible processes of translation and adaptation that would otherwise remain abstract. This is an intellectual history concerned with intellectual *practice* as much as with 'thought'.

The book begins with an interpretation of *Scrutiny*'s literary and cultural criticism. The first two chapters introduce the ideas, styles, narratives, and analytical procedures whose appropriation and development is the main theme of the book. In the process they attempt to convey what made *Scrutiny* strike so many intelligent people at the time as exciting or revela-

[45] William Deresiewicz, 'The Business of Theory', *Nation*, 16 February 2004.
[46] Boris Ford, 'Freedom in Education: Thoughts Provoked by Mr Bantock', *Scrutiny* 15/3 (summer 1948): 162.
[47] I thank Guy Ortolano for this phrase.

tory or compelling. (Most overviews of *Scrutiny* offer readers little to help them imagine why people thought its campaign was worth dedicating their careers to.) Chapter 1 takes Leavis's college entrance examination papers as a way into understanding the sorts of criticism he sought to teach. The practice of criticism was inseparable for Leavis from the pedagogy of criticism. His teaching materials and his published manifestoes marked out a critical discipline whose concern with the texture and operations of language at once focused on the text and claimed a wider cultural jurisdiction.

Chapter 2, on the cultural criticism of the Leavises, Thompson, and Knights, argues that the importance of the 'organic community' to the movement's thinking has been vastly exaggerated (especially in the case of F. R. Leavis's own work), and that the 'undissociated' language and society of early modern England was the ideal or utopia that structured *Scrutiny* theses on culture. It also argues that the group's understanding of modernity was decisively shaped by a strand of American social science that could be accommodated to a moralist, informally ethnographic, and in some ways 'literary' mode of social commentary (the American authorities were the sociologists Robert S. Lynd and Helen Merrell Lynd and the everyman-economist Stuart Chase, whose ubiquity—if not omnipresence—in the cultural criticism of Thompson and Q. D. Leavis has been unaccountably overlooked in the scholarship on *Scrutiny*). For the *Scrutiny* group, the modern age was the machine age, and mass culture had an industrial logic that compromised humane living. Advertising and popular fiction alike were in the business of manufacturing desires. Literary studies offered access to genuine emotional experiences and ways of exposing and resisting the operations of mass culture.

The third chapter provides an anatomy of the Downing English School. It reconstructs the undergraduate population from 1932 until Leavis's retirement in 1962 using archival records and establishes the social background of these students (college records specify the schools they attended and their fathers' occupations). The chapter goes on to identify the professions in which Leavis's pupils clustered and considers the connections and disconnects between their Cambridge education and their subsequent careers. As is to be expected, the most common career choice was teaching, and significant numbers went on to become publishers, BBC staff, actors, and directors. Others made use of their training in professions alien or inimical to Leavis, such as advertising. Still others went on to careers in business or the professions. That many of Leavis's pupils had no clear or formal connection with literary studies later in life may be a banal point, but it is one easily lost sight of in discussions of so-called Leavisites.

Chapter 4 examines the *Scrutiny* movement's impact on schools. Leavis's critical approach was most directly translated for school use in the practical criticism exercises that became common in the sixth forms of grammar and public schools. Here Thompson's role was pivotal: it was chiefly through his primer *Reading and Discrimination* (1934) and a regular feature in his journal *Use of English* that practical criticism was promoted to teachers. Raymond O'Malley and Frank Whitehead as well as Thompson conducted the 'Criticism in Practice' section of *Use of English*; together with Ford and Holbrook, they were the most active organizers of 'the *Scrutiny* movement in education'. Practical criticism aside, Leavis and *Scrutiny*'s influence was often at the level of overarching vision rather than specific teaching methods. Holbrook's widely inspirational programme for English in non-'academic' secondary modern schools is a case in point. Holbrook and other teachers in the *Scrutiny* tradition were identified with 'progressive' trends in the 1950s and 1960s (while others were definitely not): but it was the triumph of progressive ideas, with their linguistic rather than literary premises, that marginalized *Scrutiny* currents in secondary education.

The heyday of Leavisism in adult education was the fifteen years after the Second World War. Chapter 5 explores the ways in which practical criticism and the example of Knights's essays and Leavis and Thompson's *Culture and Environment* (1933) shaped adult 'tutorial classes'. It traces the ways that initiatives in adult teaching informed the landmark books written in the moment of 'left-Leavisism': Hoggart's *Uses of Literacy* (1957) and Williams's *Culture and Society, 1780–1950* (1958). The latter was among other things a critique of Leavis's conception of culture; Hoggart's book turned *Scrutiny*'s critical practice against some of its guiding assumptions. This same dynamic governed early work in cultural studies around the time Hoggart established the centre at Birmingham. Chapter 6 explores these tensions, in Hoggart's plans and in the work of Stuart Hall and Paddy Whannel, as well as the last major iteration of *Scrutiny*'s cultural criticism—the volume of essays edited by Thompson that arose from the 1960 National Union of Teachers conference on 'Popular Culture and Personal Responsibility'. Scrutineers' engagements with wider publics are the subject of Chapter 7, which compares Leavis's own interventions, and his concept of 'minority culture', with the more conventional popularizing done by Thompson and especially Ford. As editor of the seven-volume *Pelican Guide to English Literature* in the 1950s and 1960s, Ford projected *Scrutiny* interpretations to a mass audience.

The final chapter moves beyond Britain to examine the movement's fortunes overseas. Chapter 8 is a necessarily selective world tour the longest stops of which are in Ceylon, Australia, and the United States. In the late 1940s and 1950s, the Kenyon School of English and Eric Bentley's anthology for American readers drew *Scrutiny* into efforts to enshrine criticism (and in particular the New Criticism) in American universities' English programmes. In Australia, more than anywhere else, university English departments were reorganized along Leavisian lines, with disruptive results. Australian literature was not a major concern for Samuel Goldberg, the architect of the 'Leavisite' experiment at the University of Sydney in the 1960s, but Goldberg's plans were nevertheless based on an interpretation of colonial culture that borrowed heavily from *Culture and Environment*. The cultural or 'sociological' interests of early *Scrutiny* writings would also function as models or suggestions for ways of writing about colonial or national literary cultures in contexts as various as India, New Zealand, and Scotland.

Organizing the book around sites or spheres of *Scrutiny*'s influence makes it possible to combine attention to intellectual practice with attention to networks and institutions. It would, of course, have been possible to write the book in other ways, and to examine the engagement between Leavis's pupils and further intellectual formations not discussed here—notably philosophy. I have said little about philosophy mostly because I am quite unqualified, but also out of doubts that the encounter between Leavisians and Wittgenstein's philosophy (and the work of Michael Polanyi and Marjorie Grene), a conjunction centred on the journal *The Human World*, has been as anywhere near as significant in its sphere as were *Scrutiny*'s contributions elsewhere.[48] Nor have I dwelt on the history of university English departments—the chapter on the empire and the United States is the only one that deals directly with universities other than Cambridge—focusing instead on *Scrutiny*'s impact in domains where its influence was most substantial and transformative. The fact that *Scrutiny* mobilized a 'public' of schoolteachers and adult education tutors more than university lecturers and metropolitan cultural workers is one of the things that makes this a distinctive episode in modern British intellectual history. These choices mean, however, that distinguished critics who wrote for *Scrutiny* but whose work was read mostly within universities—such as Harold Mason—receive little attention in this book.

Finally, this is a study of intellectual networks but not a group portrait. A lot has been written about F. R. Leavis's stormy relations with sometime

---

[48] On Leavis's own philosophical investigations, see Chris Joyce, 'The Idea of "Anti-Philosophy" in the Work of F. R. Leavis', *Cambridge Quarterly* 38/1 (2009): 24–44.

collaborators, and about both Leavises' relations with and treatment by the Cambridge English Faculty and the painful breach with the former pupils and supporters who organized the Leavis Lectureship Trust to provide a successor to F. R. Leavis on his retirement.[49] I do not want to re-litigate these disputes or reduce the project of *Scrutiny* to 'a saga of village life', as a reviewer (apparently approvingly) described Ian MacKillop's biography of Leavis. It might be objected that the movement's history cannot be understood without extensive reference to these personal conflicts. I think it can, despite the force of Leavis's personality—the fact that he was, as he described his father, 'a centre of human power'.[50] Many of Leavis's exponents did not know him personally—Hoggart had not met him, or even corresponded with him other than to ask for permission to quote him in a book, when he told Leavis: 'I have learned more from you and from *Scrutiny*—far more—than from anyone else.'[51] Moreover, the purchase of Leavis's ideas and his cause outlasted friendships. There were long periods during which Denys Thompson had no contact with the Leavises.[52] Boris Ford and Raymond O'Malley were also estranged from the couple, but both remained committed to their campaigns.[53] O'Malley wrote that 'despite some hard knocks', the effect of Leavis's initial impact on him had 'not essentially changed through contacts spread over much of a lifetime'.[54]

When O'Malley returned to Cambridge in 1959 to be interviewed for a position in the university's Institute of Education, a member of the committee asked him why Leavis affected his early pupils so powerfully. 'Was it charisma?' O'Malley's answer, formulated years after the initial question, was no. What first drew him to Leavis, in the late 1920s, he said, was a need to believe 'that somewhere there existed a scale, a grid . . . that could register both Wordsworth and the hunger marches. . . . the

---

[49] MacKillop, *F. R. Leavis*; the special issue of the *Cambridge Quarterly* (25/4 [1996]) consisting of responses to MacKillop's biography; and the 'counter-symposium' (Richard Storer's phrase in *F. R. Leavis*, 133) published by the Brynmill Press, which is directed by Leavis's former pupil (and editor of *The Human World*), Ian Robinson: M. B. Mencher (ed.), *Leavis, Dr MacKillop and 'The Cambridge Quarterly': A Brynmill Special Issue* (Denton, Norfolk: Brynmill Press, 1998). F. W. Bateson's career at Oxford bears comparison with Leavis's at Cambridge. See Valentine Cunningham, 'F. W. Bateson: Scholar, Critic, and Scholar-Critic', *Essays in Criticism* 29/2 (1979): 147–8.

[50] Michael Tanner, 'Some Recollections of the Leavises', in Thompson (ed.), *The Leavises*, 138.

[51] Richard Hoggart to F. R. Leavis, 4 May 1953, Hoggart papers, 3/9/10, Sheffield; Richard Hoggart, *An Imagined Life: Life and Times, Volume III, 1959–91* (1992; Oxford: Oxford University Press, 1993), 10.

[52] Thompson, 'Teacher and Friend', 49–51.

[53] Boris Ford, 'Round and about the *Pelican Guide to English Literature*', in Thompson, (ed.) *The Leavises*, 108–9.

[54] O'Malley, 'Charisma?', 52.

need to encounter pledged intelligence.' The 'pledged' implies charisma, but the value of the specific critical strategies of that intelligence was more impersonal. So were the ways in which they were institutionalized. Leavis's critical judgements and modes of judging could be detected decades later, O'Malley pointed out, in university and sixth-form syllabi. Leavis's human power was a big part of the experience of studying or collaborating with him, but it does not explain very much about the transmission and re-working of his ideas in schools or tutorial classes. 'Such,' as O'Malley said, 'is not the working of charisma.'[55]

---

[55] O'Malley, 'Charisma?', 52–9 (quotations from 52–3 and 59).

1

How to Teach Reading

For F. R. Leavis, the question of how to read was always entwined with the question of how to teach reading. In an early pamphlet, *How to Teach Reading* (1932), he built a case for his vision of literary study out of a critique of Ezra Pound's *How to Read* (1931).[1] Privately, Leavis remarked: 'I mean the pamphlet to be taken very seriously:... it is part of the general campaign. We're determined to make *Scrutiny* felt in the educational as well as in the literary world. The pamphlet is "literary," but moves t[owar]ds "education." It's an unprecedented combination, & has already brought results.'[2] Given this connection between the literary and the educational, it makes sense to read Leavis's programmatic statements in conjunction with the surviving traces of his teaching activities, especially the examinations he set for prospective undergraduates. The questions often included topics or passages that he and other regular *Scrutiny* contributors, such as L. C. Knights and Denys Thompson, had discussed in print. The examinations themselves became teaching texts: Cambridge University Press printed bound volumes of the entrance examinations each year for purchase by schools preparing sixth formers for Cambridge. A clear outline of a 'correct' answer was seldom implicit in an exam question, and in any case obedience pleased Leavis less than his reputation suggests (he once described a submission to *Scrutiny* from an admirer at Oxford as 'like an essay by a rather too docile pupil of mine').[3] All the same, the tone and parameters of the questions, the texts and subjects covered, and the use of

---

[1] F. R. Leavis, *How to Teach Reading: A Primer for Ezra Pound* (Cambridge: Minority Press, 1932).

[2] F. R. Leavis to Ian Parsons, 5 November 1932, Chatto & Windus archive, CW 53/2, Reading. I have added a quotation mark before the word 'education'. *How to Teach Reading* was reprinted as an appendix to his educational blueprint, *Education and the University: A Sketch for an 'English School'* (London: Chatto & Windus, 1943). Leavis told a member of the Chatto & Windus staff: 'That appendix... *How to Teach Reading*... is essential to the book... It... has *been in constant request* since it went out of print.' Leavis to Harold Raymond, 2 June 1943, Chatto & Windus archive, CW 94/17, Reading (emphasis in original).

[3] Leavis to D. W. Harding, 22 October [1940], F. R. Leavis papers, Col 9.59a, Emmanuel College, Cambridge. The submission was from D. A. Traversi, later a regular *Scrutiny* contributor.

examples and problems previously aired in the pages of *Scrutiny* or Leavis's pamphlets converged to imply certain modes of reading, or to invite examinees into exercises of judgement that were characteristic of the movement. They offer a way into understanding the force and appeal of *Scrutiny*.

Cambridge admissions were organized college by college. Candidates came to the university for a week of interviews and examinations in the subjects of their choice at the colleges to which they were applying.[4] As Downing College's director of studies in English, Leavis set examinations for young men seeking a place there to read English. He also had a hand in the entrance examination papers for the women's colleges, Girton and Newnham, in the early 1930s.[5] Leavis set his own English exams even after Downing banded together with other colleges to offer joint examinations in most subjects. In 1934, Downing's Governing Body entered negotiations to join the consortium of Clare, Corpus Christi, King's, Magdalene, Trinity, and Trinity Hall. Downing applied for membership on the understanding that it could hold separate examinations in English.[6] This was not particularly unusual. Pembroke College, too, set its own English examinations, which placed special weight on historical knowledge (political as well as literary history). Clare, Corpus Christi, King's, and the rest had no objection to Downing's holding a separate examination in English.[7] Leavis was thus able to make recommendations about admissions and scholarships based on how applicants responded to the kinds of questions he wanted undergraduates to consider, questions quite different from the ones posed by other colleges in the group.

Aspiring Downing undergraduates had to sit four English examinations: Shakespeare, English Literature after AD 1600, Practical Criticism, and Paraphrase and Comment. Leavis produced a circular for teachers explaining the 'nature and scope' of the exams.[8] For the Shakespeare paper, candidates were expected to have 'a general knowledge of Shakespeare's development, and to know well half-a-dozen of the greatest plays'. The English Literature after 1600 paper covered a vast expanse of poetry and prose,

---

[4] On the workings of the system from the 1940s to the early 1960s, see C. B. Cox, 'Cambridge Scholarships: Some Reflections', *Critical Survey* 1/1 (autumn 1960): 25–7.

[5] Leavis to Parsons, 1 October 1932, Chatto & Windus archive, CW 53/2, Reading.

[6] Downing College Governing Body minute book, 694 (17 November 1934), DCGB/M/1/7, Downing.

[7] Ibid., 701 (30 January 1935).

[8] He also gave advice about reading to prospective pupils who contacted him before they sat the entrance examinations. Leavis to R. T. Jones, 12 January 1950, F. R. Leavis papers, DCPP/LEA/15/18, Downing (Jones came up in October 1950). Leavis advised Jones to read all the fiction essays and reviews in any back numbers of *Scrutiny* that he had access to, and to seek *Scrutiny*'s guidance on Shakespeare.

but not as much as the title indicated. Questions on twentieth-century authors were unusual, rarer than they were in some other colleges' exams, and 'a candidate might reasonably devote his attention mainly to the Seventeenth Century and the Romantic period, or to the Seventeenth and Eighteenth Centuries, or to some equivalent combination. But in any case he ought to know something about the Seventeenth Century.' The literature of the seventeenth century mattered not only for its intrinsic quality, but also for its importance in T. S. Eliot's rethinking of the poetic tradition.[9]

The Practical Criticism paper was 'designed to test the quality of the candidate's reading'.[10] Candidates were presented with unattributed passages of prose or poetry. Some questions asked them to date these passages using their knowledge of the styles and themes of particular periods. Dating exercises were more or less orthodox and other colleges set them for their undergraduates too.[11] What other colleges' examinations did not do was mimic I. A. Richards's already legendary 1920s lectures in 'Practical Criticism' (kept on as an English Faculty course after Richards had left) and appraise two anonymous passages, one 'good' and one 'bad'.[12] These comparisons, Leavis's circular explained, obliged candidates to demonstrate 'critical appreciation and discrimination. Cases, for instance, of sentimentality or insincerity or mere versifying might be offered for analysis.' Denys Thompson's *Reading and Discrimination* was recommended for guidance.[13] The discriminatory powers of reading that undergraduates were expected to demonstrate were also tested by the Paraphrase and Comment paper, which included contemporary and journalistic pieces of writing. Sometimes Paraphrase and Comment questions could have been slotted into Practical Criticism papers and vice versa. 'Besides containing passages for paraphrase, and for criticism with regard to style and cogency', the Paraphrase and Comment paper was meant to 'test general intelligence, taste and cultivation in ways suggested in *Culture and Environment*, by F. R. Leavis and Denys Thompson'.[14]

[9] 'Downing College, Cambridge: Entrance Scholarship Examination in English', circular dated July 1934 and reproduced in Ian MacKillop, 'Rubrics and Reading Lists', in Ian MacKillop and Richard Storer (eds), *F. R. Leavis: Essays and Documents* (Sheffield: Sheffield Academic Press, 1995), 56.

[10] Ibid.

[11] St Catherine's and Selwyn Colleges, English Literature II examination, 1935, in *Examination Papers for Scholarships and Exhibitions in the Colleges of the University of Cambridge: December 1934–March 1935*, vol. 156, *Modern Languages, Law and History* (Cambridge: Cambridge University Press, 1935), 123. Subsequent citations treat the *Examination Papers* volumes as a serial, rather than giving the full title.

[12] I. A. Richards, *Practical Criticism: A Study of Literary Judgment* (London: Kegan Paul, Trench, Trubner, 1929).

[13] Denys Thompson, *Reading and Discrimination* (London: Chatto & Windus, 1934).

[14] 'Downing College, Cambridge: Entrance Scholarship Examination in English', 56–7.

The strictures against insincerity and sentimentality and the premium on rigorous discrimination exemplify the combativeness and moral force for which Leavisian criticism was famous.[15] It is not evident in every examination question, but on the whole there is a higher level of asperity to the Downing papers than those of other colleges, which have a magisterially relaxed air about them. Here, almost at random, are two questions from the 1935 Downing College Shakespeare exam:

> 'Two things above all he sought—a striking situation and a vivid impression of personality.' Is this an adequate account of 'what Shakespeare sought' in any ONE of the greater tragedies?
>
> What promises of the strength, and what proofs of the immaturity, of Shakespeare's genius do you find in EITHER the *Sonnets* OR one or two of the early plays?[16]

And here, equally at random, are two consecutive questions from the 1935 English Literature examination held by the consortium from which Downing had opted out:

> A friend wishes to read half a dozen novels by Scott OR by Jane Austen. Give him some reasoned advice for preferring one to the other.
>
> Tennyson has been accused of being decorative but empty; Browning of unduly energetic optimism; Arnold of pessimistic melancholy. Defend any ONE of them against these charges.[17]

Scrutiny's astringency was signalled by its title. Leavis acknowledged his debt to the *Calendar of Modern Letters*, a short-lived journal of the mid-1920s which was very different in manner and content from the later Cambridge publication, but which similarly stood for 'standards of criticism'.[18] The *Calendar* was known for its 'scrutinies', essays in the principled destruction of overrated writers.[19] The Downing examination papers that manifested *Scrutiny*'s severity most strongly were the Practical Criticism and Paraphrase and Comment papers. One Paraphrase and Comment question from 1934 served up a parliamentary speech by Ramsay

[15] For an adverse judgement from an organ of what Leavis saw as the metropolitan literary world, see L. D. Lerner, 'The Life and Death of *Scrutiny*', *London Magazine* 2/1 (1955): 68–9, 76–7.

[16] Downing College, Shakespeare examination, 1935, *Examination Papers* 156 (1935): 54. Capitals replace boldface in the original.

[17] Peterhouse, Gonville and Caius, Queen's, Jesus, Christ's, St John's, Emmanuel, and Sidney Sussex Colleges, English Literature examination, 1935, *Examination Papers* 160 (1936): 41. Capitals replace boldface in the original.

[18] F. R. Leavis (ed.), *Towards Standards of Criticism: Selections from 'The Calendar of Modern Letters', 1925–7* (1933; London: Lawrence & Wishart, 1976). See Paul Woolridge, 'The *Calendar* and the Modern Critical Essay' *Cambridge Quarterly* 40/2 (2011): 121–40.

[19] Edgell Rickword (ed.), *Scrutinies: By Various Writers*, 2 vols (London: Wishart, 1928–31).

MacDonald on the long-term unemployed and asked: 'How would you explain the following passage? What conditions or circumstances do you suppose to have produced it?'[20] The previous year in *Scrutiny*, Knights quoted Eliot's remark that 'a study of the prose styles of Mr Baldwin, Mr Lloyd George and Mr Ramsay Macdonald [*sic*] would be instructive' and added his own specific suggestion of 'half an hour's practical criticism on [Churchill's] *The World Crisis*, for example (Criticism answers the question, What kind of a mind created this?)'.[21] Candidates in 1937 were asked to 'Explain briefly the meaning of (a) *dilettantism*, (b) *cliché*, (c) *fine writing*, (d) *belles lettres*.'[22]

The connection between the Practical Criticism and Paraphrase and Comment examinations and the moral quality of Leavisian judgements is more evident in the materials offered up for appraisal than in the wording of the questions. Would-be Downing undergraduates were regularly asked to comment on the sorts of cultural document excerpted in Leavis and Thompson's *Culture and Environment*. Acknowledging receipt of a copy of *Advertising World*, Leavis remarked: 'it will be invaluable when compiling examination papers, & Thompson should do something with it for the next number of *Scrutiny*'.[23] Reflecting the *Scrutiny* interest in the cultural resources supposed to be nurtured by agricultural society, one Paraphrase and Comment paper solicited comment on passages about traditional and 'progressive' farmers in the United States and asked candidates to discuss the possibility that the illiterate 'may nevertheless reach a high level of culture' surprising to those 'who imagine that education and cultivation are convertible terms'. Thompson and Leavis made the point about education while discussing rural England in *Culture and Environment*, and the passage about American farmers appeared in a teaching exercise in the same book.[24] Late in life, Leavis would say that he did not believe in any peculiarly 'literary values': 'the judgments the literary critic

---

[20] Downing College, Paraphrase and Comment examination, 1934, *Examination Papers* 152 (1934): 62; *H. C. Deb.* 270, col. 47 (7 November 1932).

[21] L. C. Knights, 'Good Intentions in Education', *Scrutiny* 2/2 (September 1933): 218.

[22] Downing College, Paraphrase and Comment examination 1937, *Examination Papers* 164 (1937): 67. 'Meanwhile, as the corollary of discipline for discipline's sake, and equally hostile to education, we have, passing for an educated interest in literature, the elegant cult (with its token currency, and its specialized Good Form) of *belles lettres*' (Leavis, *How to Teach Reading*, 48).

[23] Leavis to Parsons, 15 February 1933, Chatto & Windus archive, CW 53/2, Reading. Denys Thompson mentioned the February 1933 issue of *Advertising World* in 'A Cure for Amnesia', *Scrutiny* 2/1 (June 1933): 10.

[24] Downing College, Paraphrase and Comment examination, 1936, *Examination Papers* 160 (1936): 60; F. R. Leavis and Denys Thompson, *Culture and Environment: The Training of Critical Awareness* (1933; London: Chatto & Windus, 1950), 104–5, 134–5.

is concerned with are judgments about life'.[25] In the 1930s, as he set out
his critical and educational programme, Leavis would not have rhetorically discounted the specifically literary quality of the modes of response,
judgement, and feeling that he was trying to cultivate, but right from the
beginning thinking about literature was intimately connected with thinking about living.

It would be hard, for instance, to have answered question 3 of 1937's
Practical Criticism paper guided only by 'literary' values, narrowly defined.
The task was to compare an unattributed first-person description of a Paris
cafe (it was by Arnold Bennett, in *Things That Have Interested Me*) and a
description of an empty kitchen (from Katherine Mansfield's short story
'Prelude').[26] The question did not show Leavis's cards ('Compare the following passages'), though candidates who had read *Culture and Environment*
could have recognized the Bennett passage as ingratiatingly scenic and redo-
lent of advertising copy with claims to sophistication ('I ordered tea on the
terrasse of the Station café within the station. It is a very good café. You
could judge by the crystalline cleanness of the decanters'). It would have
been a perversely independent examinee who declined to pass judgement
on the personal and social values projected by the Bennett excerpt. Yet the
juxtaposition of Bennett and Mansfield also nodded to a more strictly 'literary' argument, about the role of material detail in descriptive prose. The
Mansfield passage, too, is thick with it ('Nothing was left in it but a lump
of gritty yellow soap in one corner of the kitchen window-sill and a piece of
flannel stained by a blue-bag in another'). Bennett's use of quotidian detail
was widely regarded as one of his strong suits, but Virginia Woolf, in
'Mr Bennett and Mrs Brown' (1924), argued that it actually masked an essential weakness in Bennett's fiction.[27] Leavis's exam question obliquely
raised some of the same questions about surfaces and essences.

As a reviewer, Bennett turned large numbers of 'bad books...into literature'.[28] One of the exercises in *Culture and Environment* asked school
pupils to estimate 'the annual average output of "masterpieces" and "great
books"' from the evidence of a single Sunday newspaper, and to ponder
the sorts of standards implied by over-generous reviews.[29] Time and again,

[25] F. R. Leavis, 'Luddites? *or* There is Only One Culture', in *Nor Shall My Sword: Discourses on Pluralism, Compassion, and Social Hope* (London: Chatto & Windus, 1972), 97.
See also F. R. Leavis, 'The Responsible Critic: Or The Function of Criticism at Any Time',
Scrutiny 19/3 (spring 1953): 177–8.
[26] Downing College, Practical Criticism examination, 1937, *Examination Papers* 164
(1937): 63–4.
[27] Virginia Woolf, 'Mr Bennett and Mrs Brown' (1924), in *Collected Essays*, vol. 2
(London: Hogarth Press, 1966), 319–37.
[28] F. R. Leavis, 'Mass Civilisation and Minority Culture' (1930) in *For Continuity*
(Cambridge: Minority Press, 1933), 26.
[29] Leavis and Thompson, *Culture and Environment*, 119.

Scrutiny contributors deplored the quality of book reviewing in 'the Sunday papers' and the ways the Book Society, the Royal Society of Literature, and the English Association promoted the comfortably mediocre and worked to discredit 'difficult' poetry and prose.[30] In his entrance examinations, Leavis asked candidates to evaluate faulty conceptions of literature and to push back against critical valuations that he regarded as questionable or wrong. *Scrutiny* people often called these critical positions 'academic', by which they meant establishmentarian rather than scholarly, in the way people spoke of academic painters.[31]

We have already seen how Leavis's advice to teachers preparing pupils for the Downing entrance examinations implicitly licensed them to give the Victorians short shrift. Assessments of Tennyson or Browning were threads in a fabric of judgements about the English poetic tradition generally, and about the consequences of Milton's rather than Donne's being at the centre of the tradition. Leavis said that the pocket Milton he used while writing a review in *Scrutiny* was falling apart from use—it was 'the only book I carried steadily in my pocket' for the duration of the Great War.[32] Eliot's essays persuaded him that Milton's status as the canon's exemplary poet had sealed off an alternative seventeenth-century poetic tradition. Basil Willey, an English fellow at Pembroke College, recalled noticing Eliot's impact more and more with his undergraduates: 'Milton, we learned to our amazement, was a Chinese Wall blocking the onward course of English poetry.... Donne, on the other hand, was everything a poet should be; he was witty, subtle, argumentative, ironical, and had his intellect at the tips of his senses, could think passionately and feel intellectually, had a unified sensibility, and so forth.'[33]

Leavis was hardly as impressionable as Willey's undergraduates, and he dissented from Eliot's promotion of Dryden, but in *New Bearings in English Poetry* (1932) he was a powerful advocate for the work performed by Eliot's rereading, both as poet and critic, of Jacobean literature. Leavis described Eliot's accomplishment as the 'reconstitution of the English

[30] F. R. Leavis, 'What's Wrong with Criticism?', *Scrutiny* 1/2 (September 1932): 132–46; Leavis, 'Mass Civilisation and Minority Culture', 32, 37–9; Q. D. Leavis, *Fiction and the Reading Public* (1932; London: Chatto & Windus, 1965), 25, 229; Q. D. Leavis, 'The Book Society Recommends...', *Scrutiny* 1/2 (September 1932): 179–81; Leavis and Thompson, *Culture and Environment*, 45.

[31] See Leavis, 'Mass Civilisation and Minority Culture', 26.

[32] F. R. Leavis, 'In Defence of Milton', *Scrutiny* 7/1 (June 1938): 114 n.

[33] Basil Willey, *Cambridge and Other Memories, 1920–1953* (London: Chatto & Windus, 1970), 26. Eliot spoke of 'the Chinese Wall of Milton', which blocked the development of blank verse. T. S. Eliot, 'Notes on the Blank Verse of Christopher Marlowe', in *The Sacred Wood: Essays on Poetry and Criticism* (1920; London: Methuen, 1932), 87.

tradition by the reopening of communications with the seventeenth century of Shakespeare, Donne, Middleton, Tourneur and so on'. Those
poets, and Jonson and Marvell, 'seem to me...to have written good
poetry in a variety of manners. But all these manners have, in their different ways, a vital relation to speech, to the living language of the time.'
Milton, with his 'latinizing', created a 'medium' that 'denied itself the life
of the living language'.[34] The 'predominance, in various forms, of Milton'
evident in Wordsworth, Keats, and Tennyson helped explain the weaknesses of nineteenth-century poetry.[35]

A prize exhibit of this complex of judgements about the seventeenth
and the nineteenth centuries was a remark by one of Milton's contemporary champions, Professor Sir Herbert Grierson. Writing in the preface to
the *Oxford Book of Seventeenth Century Verse*, Grierson and Geoffrey Bullough cited an earlier anthologist, Francis Turner Palgrave, whose *Golden
Treasury*, first published in 1861 and reissued many times, was 'the most
influential anthology in English literary history'.[36]

> Palgrave's chief and best guide was Tennyson, on whose fine ear the metres
> of the 'metaphysicals' must have grated as did those of his friend Browning;
> and a distinguished poet of our own day has in a recent lecture indicated
> clearly that his judgement is more in agreement with that of Tennyson than
> with that of the admirers of Donne.[37]

Leavis quoted this sentence twice in the pages of *Scrutiny* and used the
first part of it, up to the mention of Browning, in his 1945 English Literature after AD 1600 examination. 'Say, from your own knowledge of
the English poetry concerned, how far you agree with the implications of
this sentence.'[38] Some of the questions he asked about Milton were
worded neutrally, at least on the surface ('Describe the nature of Milton's
originality...'), but others asked candidates to respond to negative
appraisals of Milton or to compare passages from *Paradise Lost* and
The Tempest, 'indicating the main differences in verse movement,

---

[34] Leavis, 'In Defence of Milton', 113–14.
[35] Leavis, *How to Teach Reading*, 38. F. R. Leavis, *New Bearings in English Poetry: A Study of the Contemporary Situation* (London: Chatto & Windus, 1932), 7–9, 81–2. The Eliot essay on which Leavis's argument rested also cited Tennyson in making his case that a 'dissociation of sensibility set in' some time after Donne and was 'aggravated' by the influence of Milton and Dryden. T. S. Eliot, 'The Metaphysical Poets' (1921), in *Selected Essays* (London: Faber & Faber, 1951), 287–8.
[36] Christopher Clausen, 'The Palgrave Version', *Georgia Review* 34 (1980): 275.
[37] H. J. C. Grierson and G. Bullough, preface to Grierson and Bullough (eds), *The Oxford Book of Seventeenth Century Verse* (Oxford: Oxford University Press, 1934), vii. The *Golden Treasury* did not include a single poem by Donne.
[38] Downing College, English Literature after AD 1600 examination, 1945, *Examination Papers* 207 (1946): 60; Leavis, 'In Defence of Milton', 105.

concreteness, precision, subtlety'.[39] Young men who believed in Leavis enough to want to study with him are unlikely to have given Milton higher marks for concreteness.

Milton's standing, the Leavises believed, owed something to social hierarchies. Describing the 'mode of life' documented in the posthumously published letters of George Gordon, Merton Professor of English Literature at Oxford from the early 1920s and later Professor of Poetry there, Q. D. Leavis concluded: 'its social standards and its conventional literary and cultural values are only different aspects of the same mentality'. Gordon delighted in the part undergraduates played in defeating the 1926 General Strike, and went out of his way to scorn Eliot's poetry. Q. D. Leavis concluded: 'To threaten its security in any way, by casting aspersions against the genuineness of a literary idol like Landor or Milton'—the syntax implies, fleetingly but provocatively, that the two are equivalent—'or by suggesting that the social structure needs revision, is to get the same reaction.'[40] When the *Times Literary Supplement* reviewed 'East Coker' unfavourably, Leavis remarked: 'the ancient universities are lousy with that kind of classically-trained arbiter of taste & they're now perking up again against Eliot'.[41]

Like others appointed to academic positions in English when the subject was new and there were no English graduates, Gordon's training was in Greek and Latin. 'English studies' had been, Q. D. Leavis wrote, 'apart from the linguist's claims on them, notoriously the prerogative of your classic (generally of your not-good-enough classic)'.[42] Several of the Cambridge academics against whom Leavis contended, above all E. M. W. Tillyard, were 'classics', and as well as personal conflicts their disagreements involved different understandings of what a literary education should be. Close reading and practical criticism were not the only

[39] Downing College, English Literature after AD 1600 examination, 1934, *Examination Papers* 152 (1934): 55; Downing College, English Literature after AD 1600 examination, 1936, *Examination Papers* 160 (1936): 55; Downing College, Shakespeare examination, 1935, *Examination Papers* 156 (1935): 52–3.

[40] Q. D. Leavis, 'The Discipline of Letters: A Sociological Note', *Scrutiny* 12/1 (winter 1943): 18. Gordon's inaugural lecture as Professor of Poetry in 1934 accused F. R. Leavis, along with Eliot, Herbert Read, and other critics, of blinkeredness and intolerance. 'It is the mode in such circles to speak of Milton as a minor poet, as the tiresome maestro of a backwater.' George Gordon, 'Poetry and the Moderns', in *The Discipline of Letters* (Oxford: Clarendon Press, 1946), 129, 130. Note also the sly allusion to Q. D. Leavis's piece in Terry Eagleton, *Literary Theory: An Introduction* (1983; Minneapolis: University of Minnesota Press, 1996), 31.

[41] Leavis to D. W. Harding, 24 September [1940], F. R. Leavis papers, Col 9.59a, Emmanuel.

[42] Leavis, 'Discipline of Letters', 12. See also Denys Thompson's review of Alderton Pink's *If the Blind Lead* in *Scrutiny* 2/1 (June 1933): 104–5.

Cambridge English traditions. Scholars such as Tillyard and Willey (whose background was in history, not classics) stressed the 'world pictures' of literary periods and 'background-studies', or what is sometimes called the History of Ideas', as well as, in Tillyard's case at least, close reading.[43] Tillyard believed that the first crop of Cambridge English graduates were better positioned to 'achieve an integral reading of English literature' because they began reading English after undergoing 'a solid discipline in languages or mathematics'.[44] Despite the magnanimously inclusive reference to mathematics, Tillyard believed that classics was the ideal partner to English, and that an appropriate course of study for most undergraduates would be to take Part I of the classics tripos and then switch to English (rather than doing the 'early' part of the English tripos).[45] It was not to be, at least not very often after the earliest days: many classicists distrusted the English Faculty, and the subject of English 'invaded the schools and imposed on them a premature aestheticism to the detriment of the essential linguistic discipline that Classics can best provide'.[46]

When Q. D. Leavis referred to the linguist in the same breath as the classic, it was Anglo-Saxon and philology that she had in mind. Her husband repeatedly paid homage to H. Munro Chadwick, the Cambridge Professor of Anglo-Saxon who ensured that his subject would not be compulsory for undergraduates taking the English tripos, unlike their Oxford counterparts. Anglo-Saxon should be studied 'for its own sake', wrote Chadwick and his wife N. Kershaw Chadwick in *The Growth of Literature*, 'not as ancillary to a later literature which, owing to the break in continuity, can contribute nothing to its elucidation'.[47] (In contrast, C. S. Lewis, a vigorous defender of the Oxford curriculum, made the case

[43] Willey, *Cambridge and Other Memories*, 33; Basil Willey, *The Seventeenth-Century Background: Studies in the Thought of the Age in Relation to Poetry and Religion* (London: Chatto & Windus, 1934); E. M. W. Tillyard, *The Elizabethan World Picture* (London: Chatto & Windus, 1943).

[44] E. M. W. Tillyard, *The Muse Unchained: An Intimate Account of the Revolution in English Studies at Cambridge* (London: Bowes & Bowes, 1958), 125.

[45] Many English students in the early years completed only one part of the English tripos. Knights, and, earlier, Leavis himself, completed Part I of the history tripos and then switched to English; Denys Thompson read classics before becoming Leavis's pupil; Empson started in Mathematics; D. W. Harding did Part I of the English tripos and then switched to moral sciences so he could study psychology. See Ian MacKillop, *F. R. Leavis: A Life in Criticism* (London: Allen Lane, 1995), 110, and Leavis's comment in ' "Scrutiny": A Retrospect', *Scrutiny*, vol. 20, *A Retrospect Indexes Errata* (Cambridge: Cambridge University Press, 1963), 7.

[46] Tillyard, *Muse Unchained*, 104–5.

[47] H. Munro Chadwick and N. Kershaw Chadwick, *The Growth of Literature*, vol. 1, *The Ancient Literatures of Europe* (Cambridge: Cambridge University Press, 1932), xiv–xv; Leavis, *How to Teach Reading*, 46 n; F. R. Leavis, *English Literature in Our Time and the University: The Clark Lectures 1967* (1969; Cambridge: Cambridge University Press, 1979), 12–13; Tony Inglis, untitled essay, *Cambridge Quarterly* 25/4 (1996): 354.

for Anglo-Saxon's indispensability on the grounds of continuity rather than, say, 'discipline': 'There we find the speech-rhythms that we use every day made the basis of metre; there we find the origins of that romanticism for which the ignorant invent such odd explanations.')[48] Middle English literature was noticeably absent from Downing's entrance examinations not because Leavis thought Chaucer worthless, but because at the time it was scarcely possible to read Chaucer without becoming bogged down in 'scholarship'. In the 1940s, Leavis described the Chaucer book that John Speirs was developing out of his three-part *Scrutiny* essay as 'the first real literary-critical treatment of Chaucer. And Speirs is sufficiently a scholar: the *Scrutiny* essay has had a very favourable reception, from mediaevalists among others. There is nothing else...'[49]

Though *Scrutiny* is known for its attention to the contexts of litera-ture, Leavis and Knights kept watch for encroachments from historical scholarship, which could be as 'deadening' in its own way as philology and classics.[50] When Knights read M. C. Bradbrook's *Themes and Con-ventions of Elizabethan Tragedy* in 1935, he worried that she had strayed too far from 'criticism' into research, digging up information about Eliz-abethan expectations of plot, character, rhetoric, and moral lessons. Fac-tual matter could inform interpretation, but criticism could also 'suffer a good deal from the formalizers and tabulators, pseudo-scholars who can do anything with poetry but read it'. Bradbrook was a frequent but not nuclear contributor to *Scrutiny* in its first few years and Leavis recom-mended her earlier study, *Elizabethan Stage Conditions* (1932) to school-masters coaching pupils for the Downing entrance examinations. However, Knights warned, her new book in effect encouraged 'the *substi-tution* of a form of scholarship for criticism'. 'When that happens', he went on, 'we have detached observations, made at a lower level of inten-sity and delicacy, which, instead of implicitly admitting their purely pre-liminary usefulness in the realm of objective fact, have the air of dealing with the artistic experience itself.'[51]

In the same issue as Knights reviewed Bradbrook, Leavis launched a debate with the Oxford critic F. W. Bateson concerning the place of 'liter-ary history' in the project of criticism. Any such history must be driven by 'literary values', because the works studied are 'of lasting value—of value

[48] C. S. Lewis, 'Our English Syllabus' in *Rehabilitations and Other Essays* (Oxford: Oxford University Press, 1939), 92–3.

[49] Leavis to Parsons, 16 June 1946, Chatto & Windus archive, CW 100/33, Reading.

[50] Leavis used the word 'deadening' (though in relation to other parts of the Cam-bridge English curriculum, not history) in *How to Teach Reading*, 47.

[51] L. C. Knights, 'Elizabethan Drama and the Critic', *Scrutiny* 4/1 (June 1935): 91, 93.

in the present'.[52] Leavis used a provocation from Pound's *How to Read* to make the same point in an exam question: 'When studying physics we are not asked to investigate the biographies of all the disciples of Newton who...failed to make any discovery. We apply a loose-leaf system to book-keeping so as to have the live items separated from the dead ones.'[53] (Given Leavis's opinions on the claims of science, to say nothing of accountancy, there is a wry mischievousness to this ventriloquism.) 'Literary history' in this context meant familiarity with the literature of the past as well as schol-arly efforts to chart its course. Here, as so often in the formative period of his career, Leavis's position on the relation of the past to the present ran parallel with Eliot's. 'The important critic', said Eliot in a sentence Leavis quoted approvingly, was 'absorbed in the present problems of art, and...wishes to bring the forces of the past to bear upon the solution of these problems'.[54] Leavis shared this present-mindedness with Richards, and Bradbrook, de-spite Knights's criticisms, continued to regard the proposition that 'the cru-cial test of a knowledge of the past is to be able to apply judgment in the present' as a distinctive plank of 'the Cambridge approach'.[55]

The 'theories' of literature that Leavis and collaborators such as Knights sought to dissolve were not identified with any of their academic combat-ants but part of a general Victorian patrimony shared by figures as varied as Palgrave, Matthew Arnold, and the Shakespearean A. C. Bradley. Two quotations from Arnold that found their way into Downing College en-trance examinations illustrate these conceptions of literature:

> The difference between genuine poetry and the poetry of Dryden and Pope, and all their school, is briefly this: their poetry is conceived and composed with their wits, genuine poetry is conceived and composed in the soul.[56]

---

[52] F. R. Leavis, 'Criticism and Literary History', *Scrutiny* 4/1 (June 1935): 97. See Bate-son's generous account of this debate with Leavis: F. W. Bateson, 'The Alternative to *Scru-tiny*', *Essays in Criticism* 14/1 (1964): 12–13.

[53] Downing College, Paraphrase and Comment examination, 1935, *Examination Papers* 156 (1935): 61. The quotation runs together two passages several pages apart: Ezra Pound, *How to Read* (London: Desmond Harmsworth, 1931), 5, 12. These passages are not quoted in Leavis, *How to Teach Reading*. Like most of the quotations from modern critics in the Downing examinations, this one is unattributed. Compare Leavis, 'In Defence of Milton', 110; Leavis, *The Great Tradition: George Eliot, Henry James, Joseph Conrad* (1948; London: Chatto & Windus, 1960), 3. See also A. R. Humphreys, 'A Classical Education and Eight-eenth-Century Poetry', *Scrutiny* 8/2 (September 1939): 206: 'Attention to mediocrity [me-diocre authors] is justified only if it suggests why the object of scrutiny was mediocre.'

[54] T. S. Eliot, 'Imperfect Critics' in *The Sacred Wood*, 37–8; Leavis, *How to Teach Read-ing*, 38. See also Q. D. Leavis, *Fiction and the Reading Public*, xv.

[55] M. C. Bradbrook, 'I. A. Richards at Cambridge' in Reuben Brower, Helen Vendler, and John Hollander (eds), *I. A. Richards*: Essay in His Hour (New York: Oxford University Press, 1973), 68.

[56] Downing College, English Literature after AD 1600 examination, 1935, *Examination Papers* 156 (1935): 55. See also Leavis, *New Bearings in English Poetry*, 9.

For we must never forget that Shakespeare is the great poet he is from his skill in discerning and firmly conceiving an excellent action, from his power of intensely feeling a situation, of intimately associating himself with a character; not from his gift of expression, which rather even leads him astray, degenerating sometimes into a fondness for curiosity of expression, into an irritability of fancy, which seems to make it impossible for him to say a thing plainly, even when the press of the action demands the very directest language, or its level character the very simplest.[57]

The same principles underwrote observations in popular surveys of literature, or throwaway remarks in the press, about the nature of poetry or what made a novel absorbing: the soul, an experience, or a situation was primary, and the words 'expressed' it.[58] The 'popular conception of a poet' did not give priority to 'the words on the page'.[59] Indeed, a poem was said to have an essence that existed prior to its embodiment—a common metaphor—in words.[60]

This popular conception was the antithesis of Pound's pronouncement that 'Great literature is simply language charged with meaning to the utmost possible degree'.[61] This line appeared in Pound's *ABC of Reading* (1934), but it had already done a tour of duty in *How to Read* three years earlier. In his riposte, *How to Teach Reading*, Leavis said that this was not a complete definition of literature, 'but it does at least suggest a very good corrective to the academic—and general—habit of discussing literature in terms of Hamlet's and Lamb's personalities, Milton's universe, Johnson's conversation, Wordsworth's philosophy, and Othello's or Shelley's private life'.[62]

Hamlet's personality and Othello's private life: the primary site of this 'academic—and—general habit' was Shakespeare criticism. Leavis and Knights detected two critical fallacies at work in most Shakespeare criticism written before or unheeding of Eliot's *The Sacred Wood* (1920). The first was to treat dramatic characters as if they were individuals with an

---

[57] Downing College, Shakespeare examination, 1937, *Examination Papers* 164 (197): 59.

[58] Christopher Hilliard, 'Modernism and the Common Writer', *Historical Journal* 48/3 (September 2005): 769–87; Hilliard, *To Exercise Our Talents: The Democratization of Writing in Britain* (Cambridge, Mass.: Harvard University Press, 2006), 90–7.

[59] Arthur Quiller-Couch, 'The Popular Conception of a Poet' (1894), in *Adventures in Criticism* (Cambridge: Cambridge University Press, 1926), 125; Leavis, *Education and the University*, 70.

[60] 'The History of English Literature, then, is the story of what great English men and women thought and felt, *and then* wrote down in good prose or beautiful poetry in the English language.' Stopford Brooke, *English Literature* (1876; Toronto: James Campbell & Son, 1877), 7 (emphasis added). For Arnold's approval of this remark, see 'A Guide to English Literature' (1877), in R. H. Super (ed.), *The Complete Prose Works of Matthew Arnold*, 11 vols. (Ann Arbor: University of Michigan Press, 1960–77), 8: 239–40.

[61] Ezra Pound, *ABC of Reading* (New Haven: Yale University Press, 1934), 14.

[62] Leavis, *How to Teach Reading*, 8–9.

existence of their own outside the text. The *locus classicus* was Bradley's *Shakespearean Tragedy* (1904), one of the targets of Knights's *How Many Children Had Lady Macbeth?* (1933). The famous title was borrowed from Leavis. Knights recalled: 'The phrase "How Many Children Had Lady Macbeth?" is one that F. R. Leavis used to use when I first knew him in about 1930 when he was making fun of some of the then current irrelevancies of Shakespeare criticism, such as the solemn discussion of the double time scheme in *Othello*, or Bradley's famous question "Where was Hamlet at the time of his father's murder?"'[63] The practice of interpreting Shakespearean drama through quasi-autonomous characters had a longer pedigree, however, and Knights's research supplied Leavis with eighteenth-century samples for use in examination questions.[64] Even to focus on what Hamlet or Lady Macbeth does in the play itself did not free the critic from the second fallacy: that of seeing poetic drama as essentially the same as modern realist drama, action 'with poetry and rhetoric added as ornament'. Webster's tragedies, wrote W. A. Edwards in *Scrutiny*, 'are to be read...as dramatic-poems not as historical documents, police-court evidence, or detective stories'.[65]

Leavis hammered away at this point, in his entrance examinations and in his manifestoes.[66] One of the optional questions in the 1934 Downing Shakespeare exam reads as follows:

> Scene I. [*Enter three witches.*]
> 'This scene is probably spurious. No dramatic interest or object is gained by its introduction...' [Note to Act I, sc. 1 of *Macbeth*, ARDEN edition.]
> Give your reasons for agreeing or disagreeing with this comment.[67]

---

[63] L. C. Knights to John Britton, 17 March 1957, quoted in John Britton, 'A. C. Bradley and Those Children of Lady Macbeth', *Shakespeare Quarterly* 12/3 (summer 1961): 349; F. R. Leavis, 'The Literary Mind', *Scrutiny* 1/1 (June 1932): 25.

[64] See, for instance, the passage from Maurice Morgann's *Essay on the Dramatic Character of Sir John Falstaff* (1777) discussed in L. C. Knights, 'How Many Children Had Lady Macbeth?' (1933) in *Explorations: Essays in Criticism Mainly on the Literature of the Seventeenth Century* (London: Chatto & Windus, 1946), 11–12, and quoted in Downing College, Shakespeare examination, 1936, *Examination Papers* 160 (1936): 54. The quotation from Hartley Coleridge ('Let us for a moment put Shakespeare out of the question, and consider Hamlet as a real person, a recently deceased acquaintance') employed in the 1934 Downing Shakespeare examination had also appeared in Knights's lecture: *Examination Papers* 152 (1934): 54; Knights, 'How Many Children Had Lady Macbeth?', 15.

[65] W. A. Edwards, 'Revaluations (1): John Webster', *Scrutiny* 2/1 (June 1933): 12. See also M. C. Bradbrook, *Themes and Conventions of Elizabethan Tragedy* (Cambridge: Cambridge University Press, 1935), 5, and L. C. Knights's approving comment in his review in *Scrutiny* 4/1 (June 1935): 95.

[66] See, for instance, the 1935 examination question, quoted above, about whether Shakespeare sought, above all, 'a striking situation and a vivid impression of personality'.

[67] Downing College, Shakespeare examination, 1934, *Examination Papers* 152 (1934): 54.

Those not immersed in Leavis's writings might strain to divine the wider significance of the Arden editor's note, but examinees whose teachers had read *How to Teach Reading* might have been familiar with it. The claim that *Macbeth*'s first scene had 'no dramatic interest or object' was, Leavis argued in that pamphlet, 'an appeal to a conception of "drama": *Macbeth* is a drama, and a drama is a matter of characters in action and interaction'. Aspects of the play that did not advance the plot or develop its 'scheme' had to be 'explained away'.[68] These assumptions underpinned almost everything that passed for Shakespeare criticism, he argued, and so a student probably would not notice their mischief at first—which made unprepossessing footnote a suitable hook for Leavis's argument. Knights, pressing a parallel case in 'How Many Children Had Lady Macbeth?', used another note by the Arden editor in much the same way.[69] To demonstrate what was missed or lost by treating Shakespeare simply or primarily as 'a great "creator of characters"', Leavis did some practical criticism of another part of *Macbeth*. Duncan and Banquo are talking about the air around Dunsinane. 'This castle hath a pleasant seat', says Duncan; 'the air | Nimbly and sweetly recommends itself | Unto our gentle senses'. The associations bundled into the word 'nimbly' work in concert with 'pleasant', 'sweetly', and 'gentle', noted Leavis: this is 'hill air, which is not only sweet, but fresh and vital'. Banquo observes that martlets nest in the battlements, and the choice of species is significant. Leavis remarked: 'The bird, with its swift vitality and exquisite frail delicacy, represents a combination analogous to "nimbly and sweetly".' The passage was not a celebrated one—indeed, the exercise could be repeated with any number of lines from Shakespeare—but it was 'a good instance of Shakespeare's marvellous power of using words to compel on the reader or listener a precise complex response, to evoke the combination of emotions and associations appropriate to the context'. The exchange between Duncan and Banquo has dramatic force, but not in the Arden editor's sense: the 'dramatic potency of the effect...is to a great extent independent of the speakers (though, of course, Banquo and Duncan bring in an intensifying irony)'. Focusing on character and psychology could not do justice 'to the kind of thing Shakespeare does here with words'.[70]

At points such as this, with his anticipation of the speech-act theorist J. L. Austin's deadpan title *How to Do Things with Words*, Leavis can sound as if he, too, believed that literature was 'simply language charged with

[68] Leavis, *How to Teach Reading*, 28.
[69] Knights, 'How Many Children Had Lady Macbeth?', 18 and n. See also Leavis, *Education and the University*, 68, 78, 82.
[70] Leavis, *How to Teach Reading*, 30–1. Knights mentioned the same passage, and Leavis's reading, in 'How Many Children Had Lady Macbeth?', 22.

meaning'. As we shall see, he did not, but he nevertheless insisted on the words on the page. Revisiting the concerns—and the wording—of *How to Teach Reading*, Leavis wrote in the first number of *Scrutiny* that a genuinely literary-critical approach to a Shakespeare play 'will not consider it primarily a pattern of characters (or persons), with their "psychologies," in action and interaction, but will remember that *we* form these by abstraction from Shakespeare's words—that he didn't create persons, but put words together'.[71] In great literature, the combination of words does things. 'Shakespeare's verse seems to enact its meaning, to do and to give rather than to talk about.'[72]

I. A. Richards, one of the formative influences on *Scrutiny*, also thought that literature did things with words. Yet where Leavis's analysis focused on the way the words were put together, Richards was more interested in how readers' minds 'abstracted' characters, psychologies, and experiences from those combinations of words. His *Principles of Literary Criticism* (1924) even included a 'diagram, or hieroglyph', illustrating the ways a reader's eyes and brain processed verse; and as he lectured he would turn to the blackboard to draw 'cross-sections of a reader's mind, full of springs, pulleys, and arrows indicating emotions, images and incipient impulses to act'.[73]

If these performances seem dated now, it is in part because they were so ambitious. Richards came to English teaching with a degree in moral sciences, 'engulfed in philosophical, logical, and psychological strugglings'.[74] *Principles of Literary Criticism* was an attempt to establish the psychological basis of responses to literary texts and to clarify the nature of aesthetic value; it is more a study of the fundaments of proper literary criticism than a set of principles to be applied in interpreting particular texts. Criticism was 'the endeavour to discriminate between experiences and to evaluate them', and this was impossible 'without some understanding of the nature of experience, or without theories of valuation and communication'.[75]

---

[71] F. R. Leavis, 'The Literary Mind', *Scrutiny* 1/1 (May 1932): 25. Here Leavis may have learned from some of the substantive ideas of the *Calendar of Modern Letters* group, rather than their general severity and fastidiousness. Compare the passage quoted above with C. H. Rickword's remark from 1926: ' "character" is merely the term by which the reader alludes to the pseudo-objective image he composes of his responses to an author's verbal arrangements'. Rickword, 'A Note on Fiction' in Leavis (ed.), *Towards Standards of Criticism*, 31. Leavis comments on Rickword's essay, though not this passage, in his introduction, 'The Standards of Criticism', 17, 18, 21.

[72] F. R. Leavis, ' "Antony and Cleopatra" and "All for Love": A Critical Exercise', *Scrutiny* 5/2 (September 1936): 160.

[73] I. A. Richards, *Principles of Literary Criticism* (1924; London: Kegan Paul, Trench, Trubner, 1926), 117; Willey, *Cambridge and Other Memories*, 21.

[74] I. A. Richards to John Paul Russo, 7 May 1976, in John Constable (ed.), *Selected Letters of I. A. Richards, CH* (Oxford: Clarendon Press, 1990), 198.

[75] Richards, *Principles*, 2.

Compressing his protean 1920s work into one 'position', we can say that for Richards, literature synthesized differing, opposing responses. The quality of a work was proportionate to its reconciling powers, its 'efficiency' of impulse management. Richards provokingly described Keats as 'a more efficient poet than [Ella Wheeler] Wilcox, and that is the same thing as saying that his works are more valuable'.

Even aside from such 'Benthamite' pronouncements and the occasional suggestion that texts were vehicles for the 'communication' of experiences,[76] the scientific ambitions of much of Richards's work were incongruous with the sensibilities of many who studied with him or attended his lectures—not his pupils William Empson, whose own criticism conjured with mathematics and psychology, or Charles Madge, who worked on a sort of key-to-all-metaphors while an undergraduate, but people not of a scientific bent, such as Bradbrook, for whom Richards *'was* the Cambridge English school of the late 1920s'. His Practical Criticism lectures instantly rendered 'the dreary annalist Histories of Lit…obsolete'.[77] The lectures were an academic idyll: undergraduates and other academics crowded into the hall, sat on the floor, perched on trestles; when still more people came, he lectured outside in the street. '[S]omebody said', implausibly, 'that this had not happened since the Middle Ages'.[78] Though he did not put much actual literary criticism of his own into his books, Richards was capable of arresting readings.[79] His conception of a text as a force field of impulses enabled him to read for patterns and movement in poetry that was still new and difficult: 'the central process in Mr Eliot's best poems is the same; the conjunction of feelings which, though superficially opposed,—as squalor, for example, is opposed to grandeur,—yet tend as they develop to change places and even to unite'.[80]

In the late 1920s, Leavis was Richards's junior colleague, teaching Practical Criticism classes to Girton College undergraduates in a tin

[76] Ibid., 199.

[77] John Haffenden, *William Empson*, vol. 1, *Among the Mandarins* (Oxford: Oxford University Press, 2005), esp. 106–7; Charles Madge, untitled autobiography, n.d. (*c*.1982), 26, 27, 33–6, 38–9, Charles Madge papers, box 2, folder 1, University of Sussex; M. C. Bradbrook, 'What Is Cambridge English?', n.d. (early 1970s), 3–4, M. C. Bradbrook papers, 47/429, Girton. I have silently corrected some typos. A tamer version of this passage appears in Bradbrook, 'I. A. Richards at Cambridge', 62–3.

[78] William Empson, 'The Hammer's Ring', in Brower, Vendler, and Hollanders (eds), *I. A. Richards*, 73. Compare L. C. Knights, untitled memoir, *Cambridge Quarterly* 25/4 (1996): 357.

[79] John Paul Russo, *I. A. Richards: His Life and Work* (London: Routledge, 1989), 215.

[80] Richards, *Principles*, 194–5.

hut.[81] Q. D. Leavis wrote the thesis that became *Fiction and the Reading Public* under Richards's supervision. These were working relationships rather than close friendships. All the same, Richards's writing and lectures did more to shape Leavis's project than anyone else: unlike Eliot, Richards offered a framework for a programme of training in reading. 'Training' and other words that were positive terms in Richards's writings, such as 'concrete' and 'discrimination' (though not 'efficiency') made their way into *Scrutiny* argot. He was important to Leavis and *Scrutiny* in three main ways.

First, Richards's arguments about literature working by the orchestration of complex responses showed how illuminating it could be to attend closely to 'combinations' in something like the mathematical sense of the word. Leavis's prose has none of Richards's scientific bearings nor the playful mathematics of Empson's reference to the permutations of the different senses of each element in a poem: but like theirs, Leavis's interpretations of poetry focused on the relational networks of meanings and sensations produced by 'words put together'.[82] That short piece of practical criticism of the lines in *Macbeth* about air quality around Dunsinane is characteristic of Leavis, but if we pick out the terms that suggest combinations, arrays, and ways of provoking responses from readers, it starts to sound like Richards as well. An adjective 'co-operates with' two nouns to 'evoke' 'associations'. An adverb represents a 'set of associations'. The martlet's vitality and delicacy 'represents a combination analogous to "nimbly and sweetly"'; 'all these suggestions, uniting again with those of "temple" and "heaven," evoke the contrast to "foul murder."' The passage illustrates Shakespeare's use of words to 'compel' on the listener or reader 'a precise complex response, to evoke the combination of emotions and associations appropriate to the context'.[83]

Secondly, Richards made a case for the general usefulness of a training in literary criticism. 'At present', he wrote, 'bad literature, bad art, the cinema, etc., are an influence of the first importance in fixing immature and actually inapplicable attitudes to most things.' The 'strongest objection' to a bad poem was that 'a person who enjoys it, through the very organisation of his responses which enables him to enjoy it, is debarred from appreciating many things which, if he could appreciate

---

[81] M. C. Bradbrook, 'What Is Cambridge English?', 3, Bradbrook papers, 47/429, Girton.

[82] William Empson, *Some Versions of Pastoral* (London: Chatto & Windus, 1935), 89.

[83] Leavis, *How to Teach Reading*, 30–1. For another example, see L. C. Knights's discussion of 'Shakespeare's metaphorical complexity, by means of which a new meaning emerges from many tensions', in 'Bacon and the Seventeenth-Century Dissociation of Sensibility', *Scrutiny* 11/4 (summer 1943): 276.

them, he would prefer'.[84] Good art worked only on 'the right reader':
hence the irritation and bewilderment provoked by new poetry such as
Eliot's, for which many readers were ill-equipped.[85] That modern literature required new modes of reading and that the discipline of a literary
training armed people to resist the intellectually deadening and emotionally limiting tendencies of mass culture both became animating
assumptions of *Scrutiny*.

Finally, Richards provided Leavis with a teaching method that modelled a critical method. Practical criticism was an exercise whose end
(heightened powers of discrimination) was coextensive with its means
(discriminating between good and bad writing). As Francis Mulhern
has observed, Richards's 'practical criticism' was soon detached from the
'theory of communication on which it rested, and passed into currency
as the key instrument of literary analysis in general'.[86] In *Culture and
Environment*, Leavis and Thompson glossed 'Practical Criticism' simply
as 'the analysis of prose and verse'.[87] Leavis remained a believer in practical criticism, or 'criticism in practice', as he called it later, after breaking
decisively with Richards in a review in *Scrutiny* of *Coleridge on Imagination* (1934). The book was Richards's reconstruction of Coleridge's
thought in the course of rethinking what would now be called semiot-
ics. Leavis disagreed with the specifics of his reading of Coleridge, but
the book also crystallized his misgivings about Richards's commitment
to literature. For all the rhetorical symmetry of Richards's discussion of
'science' and 'poetry' as categories of 'myth', Leavis argued, science took
priority. It had never been a secret, he said, that Richards's 'literary interests derive from an interest in theory' rather than vice versa; he was
not sufficiently interested in 'particulars' and 'the concrete' to write
good criticism. The twenty-page review concluded with a valediction:
Richards, unwilling to be 'limited...by any given discipline' now
seemed to be 'heading completely away from any useful path'. Leavis
farewelled him from 'the study of poetry'.[88]

Long after his review of *Coleridge on Imagination*, Leavis was still working on *Judgement and Analysis*, 'the book Richards sh[oul]d have written
to justify his title, *Practical Criticism*: that is, it's to be all representative

---

[84] Richards, *Principles*, 202–4. Compare Leavis, *Fiction and the Reading Public*, 77.
[85] Richards, *Principles*, 290.
[86] Francis Mulhern, *The Moment of 'Scrutiny'* (London: New Left Books, 1979), 27. See
also Stefan Collini, 'On Highest Authority: The Literary Critic and Other Aviators in Early
Twentieth-Century Britain' in Dorothy Ross (ed.), *Modernist Impulses in the Human Sciences, 1870–1930* (Baltimore: Johns Hopkins University Press, 1994), 167.
[87] Leavis and Thompson, *Culture and Environment*, 6.
[88] F. R. Leavis, 'Dr Richards, Bentham, and Coleridge', *Scrutiny* 3/4 (March 1935):
388–9, 400, 402.

analyses, theory being completely subordinate & ancillary'.[89] *Practical Criticism* reported on an experimental lecture course; *Judgement and Analysis* would draw on more than fifteen years of teaching classes around close readings of texts—Leavis spoke of having to 'pick & choose among the material I've accumulated all these years in teaching & lecturing'.[90] And insofar as *Practical Criticism* was an anthology of howlers, *Judgement and Analysis* would be a collection of model answers. Even some of the questions were the same. When Leavis realized that he would have difficulty securing permission to reproduce poems for adverse comment, he told Parsons, in 1946, 'I've used an Edna St Vincent Millay sonnet that I don't want to surrender, but suppose I shall have to—it's the one Richards uses in *Practical Criticism*.'[91] Richards's original book included the commentaries that Leavis and another don wrote in response to that sonnet, 'What's this of death, from you who never will die?'.[92] The sonnet made an appearance in Leavis's Appreciation and Analysis course in the late 1950s; he had jotted 'Practical Criticism' on the printed handout reproducing Millay's poem.[93]

In Leavis's teaching, the analysis of the poems and prose passages in the handouts was not self-contained in the way it had been in Richards's lectures: it was directed toward an encompassing understanding of literature and culture. In his lectures, a student of the 1950s remembered, 'He talked us through, in effect, a chronological history of English poetic styles based on "dating" poems on the roneo'd sheets kept in a recess by the chimney-breast, and through literary history both social and critical.'[94] Seminars using the same duplicated or printed sheets were similarly 'historical'.[95] 'History' should emerge from within literature, rather than

[89] Leavis to Parsons, 16 September 1933, Chatto & Windus archive, CW 53/2; Leavis to Parsons, 1 September 1946; Leavis to Parsons, 17 September 1946, Chatto & Windus archive, CW 100/33, Reading.
[90] Leavis to Parsons, 1 September 1946, Chatto & Windus archive, CW 100/33, Reading. Some of the lectures on which *Judgement and Analysis* would be based came from the course on Appreciation and Analysis that Leavis taught from 1937 to 1962. Three essays published in *Scrutiny* between 1947 and 1952 incorporated parts of this course's lectures, and Leavis republished them in *The Living Principle: English as a Discipline of Thought* (London: Chatto & Windus, 1975) under the title 'Judgment and Analysis'. Charles Page, ' "Cunning Passages": Leavis's Lectures on Poetry and Prose', in MacKillop and Storer (eds), *F. R. Leavis: Essays and Documents*, 92. An excerpt from the work in progress was used as an illustration in Leavis's *Education and the University*, 73–6.
[91] Leavis to Parsons, 1 September 1946; Leavis to Parsons, 17 September 1946, Chatto & Windus archive, CW 100/33, Reading.
[92] MacKillop, *F. R. Leavis*, 75; Richards, *Practical Criticism*, 62–79.
[93] Page, ' "Cunning Passages" ', 93, 118.
[94] Inglis, untitled essay, 353.
[95] Neil Roberts, ' "Leavisite" Cambridge in the 1960s', in MacKillop and Storer (eds), *F. R. Leavis: Essays and Documents*, 267.

encrust it with factual matter. In notional retirement in 1965, as he prepared courses as a visiting professor at the University of York, Leavis outlined a seminar series on ' "*Judgment and Analysis*" (Criticism in Practice)' based on 'Passages for assignment to period (etc), and for intelligent comment.' He then added a revealing gloss for his new head of department: 'This is Literary History, Cultural History, Background, as much as it is "Practical Criticism." '[96]

Reading aloud was an important aspect of Leavis's 'criticism in practice'. Richards, too, set much store in reading aloud, something that is not immediately apparent from his books.[97] His colleague Mansfield Forbes advised undergraduates to 'read slowly; aloud; tolerantly'.[98] Forbes's lectures were often organized (not always an appropriate description, it seems) around reading poems out loud, performing them, improvising.[99] He had a theory that pivotal words in a poem had a specific pitch that needed to be discovered. Forbes and Richards did an experiment using D. H. Lawrence's poem 'Piano' in a lecture (the same poem had been assigned in Richards's Practical Criticism course). Forbes's voice turned falsetto at one of the key words. The undergraduates found Richards's 'neutral' rendering more convincing.[100] On another occasion, Richards read a poem 'loudly and solemnly but quite ordinarily' while Forbes waited outside so as not to be swayed by Richards's reading before coming in to perform the poem himself. This time Richards thanked Forbes for an 'interpretation' he had not thought of before. The undergraduates stamped in approval.[101] Denys Harding, Leavis's student and a *Scrutiny* editor, recalled that Forbes 'took us with him into a poem...while he worked out the most effective rhythms and phrasings, changes of tempo, pitch of voice, all stemming from and adding to one's grasp of what the poem was doing'.[102]

As Leavis wrestled with the common privileging of imagery in poetry, he was much taken by Forbes's suggestion that the 'rhythmic groups' and

[96] Leavis to Philip Brockbank, 12 May 1965, York. I am very grateful to Miles Layram for supplying me with copies of this and other letters between Leavis and Brockbank that are now in the University of York library.

[97] See, for instance, Bradbrook, 'I. A. Richards at Cambridge', 69.

[98] Margaret Diggle, 'Mansfield Forbes on the Romantic Revival', *Cambridge Quarterly* 6/2 (1973): 108 (paraphrasing Forbes's comments in lectures).

[99] Hugh Carey, *Mansfield Forbes and His Cambridge* (Cambridge, 1984), ch. 6, esp. pp. 80–1, attempts an imaginative reconstruction of Forbes's lecturing style.

[100] Joan Bennett, '"How It Strikes a Contemporary": The Impact of I. A. Richards' Literary Criticism in Cambridge, England', in Brouwer, Vendler, and Hollander (eds), *I. A. Richards*, 47. See also Leavis, *Education and the University*, 83–4.

[101] Gwendolen Freeman, 'Queenie at Girton', in Denys Thompson (ed.), *The Leavises: Recollections and Impressions* (Cambridge: Cambridge University Press, 1984), 14.

[102] MacKillop, *F. R. Leavis*, 82. See also Keith Dobson, 'Pre-war Downing', in MacKillop and Storer (eds), *F. R. Leavis: Essays and Documents*, 242.

the 'minor suggestions of movement' in Wordsworth's 'Surprised by Joy' compensates for 'the lack of visual imagery'—and by the more general premium Forbes placed on rhythm and sound.[103] 'For Leavis', his biographer Ian MacKillop writes, 'it was *sound* that was at the heart' of Cambridge English.[104] Leavis too made the sensitive, exacting, reading of texts central to his lecturing and seminars.[105] His pupils, John Newton has recalled, heard 'much wonderful commentary on short passages of literature that was more rewarding than his printed analyses because, in his extraordinary gift for bringing out from a passage's words—apparently spontaneously on the spot—more and more of the full living spirit of its writer, the rare purity and zest of his literature were especially vivid'.[106]

Much of Leavis's criticism in the 1930s and early 1940s revolved around those poetic qualities that come to the fore in repeated, meditative readings out loud. The distinctive life of poetry was to be found in its local particulars, in the 'verse movement' at least as much as the imagery. 'Although in Shakespeare's mature style the imagery is often extremely complex, the maturity is even more a matter of an increasing subtlety of tone and rhythm.' In 1937 Downing English hopefuls were directed to analyse a speech from *King Lear* in the light of this dictum.[107] 'Milton's Verse', the essay that began with the notorious declaration that 'Milton's dislodgement, in the past decade, after his two centuries of predominance, was effected with remarkably little fuss', opened the case for the prosecution with a detailed commentary on scansion. '[R]eading *Paradise Lost* is a matter of resisting, of standing up against, the verse-movement, of subduing it into something tolerably like sensitiveness'; the reader 'is brought inevitably down with the foreseen thud in the foreseen place'.[108]

Concentrating on the rhythms of *Paradise Lost* rather than its architecture or emphasizing Shakespeare's 'increasing subtlety of tone and rhythm' did not mean that Leavis was taking the part for the whole or treating large, complex works as if they were lyric poems, two objections frequently made of practical criticism. The 'whole' was not the focus of Leavis's critical attention. The contrast with G. Wilson Knight is telling.

[103] Diggle, 'Mansfield Forbes', 111 (paraphrasing Forbes's lectures on 'The Romantic Revival' that Diggle attended as a Girton undergraduate in 1924–5); and, for the points about Leavis, MacKillop, *F. R. Leavis*, 77.

[104] MacKillop, *F. R. Leavis*, 78 (emphasis in original). See also 118.

[105] 'I *hate* "poetry-speaking"...but I think reading out very important': Leavis to Brockbank, 1 July 1966, York (emphasis in original).

[106] John Newton, 'Between Vision and Enquiry', *Times Higher Education Supplement*, 25 August 1995.

[107] Downing College, Shakespeare examination, 1937, *Examination Papers* 164 (1937): 58. See also Downing College, Shakespeare examination, 1935, *Examination Papers* 166 (Cambridge, 1935): 52.

[108] F. R. Leavis, 'Milton's Verse', *Scrutiny* 2/2 (September 1933): 123, 124, 125.

W. A. Edwards could have cited Leavis's case against 'drama'-centred approaches to Shakespeare in *How to Teach Reading* in support of his case that Webster's plays should be read as dramatic poems, but he actually invoked Wilson Knight's argument in *The Wheel of Fire* (1930) that a Jacobean play was not a 'drama' in the way that an Ibsen play was.[109] Wilson Knight's alternative was to read Shakespeare 'spatially', treating the plays as 'expanded metaphor[s]'.[110] For Leavis, by contrast, 'texture', not structure, was paramount.

Occasionally, Leavis discussed the structure of entire plays, but his favoured practice was to home in on particular passages.[111] It is significant that Newton speaks of Leavis's 'wonderful commentary on short passages of literature'. As Michael Bell observes, Leavis's 'method is far from the meticulous, exhaustive verbal analysis of, say, Cleanth Brooks'. He worked instead by 'quick, exemplary demonstration in conjunction with more general attestations'.[112] Even when circumstances invited exhaustiveness, Leavis could be unwilling to go through the motions. In 1936 he wrote a short 'critical exercise' for *Scrutiny* comparing *Antony and Cleopatra* and Dryden's version of it, *All for Love*. The superiority of *Antony and Cleopatra* 'is an immediately felt superiority in the life of the verse—superiority in concreteness, variety and sensitiveness'. The claim could be substantiated 'in spoken discussion... point by point in the least eloquent and exalted places'. However, a written illustration demanded economy, so Leavis picked the obvious example, Enobarbus's description of Cleopatra's barge. Leavis worked from details of assonance and metaphor out into 'general attestations' such as this: 'Shakespeare's superiority over Dryden is not merely an affair of metaphors; it is equally observable—if not as amenable to written commentary—in tone and movement.' The essay was lopsided because Leavis was unwilling to attempt a comparably detailed examination of Dryden's verse. He quoted a slab of it and then said: 'It should be plain that a formal comparison is hardly possible; Dryden's version offers in itself little lodgement for detailed commentary.'[113] Even in an educational demonstration of his approach, Leavis declined to spell everything out.

[109] Edwards, 'John Webster', 12.
[110] G. Wilson Knight, *The Wheel of Fire: Essays in Interpretation of Shakespeare's Sombre Tragedies* (1930 London: Routledge, 2001), 4; Knights, 'How Many Children Had Lady Macbeth?', 4–5.
[111] An exception is; F. R. Leavis, 'Diabolic Intellect and the Noble Hero: A Note on *Othello*', *Scrutiny* 6/3 (1937): 259–83.
[112] Michael Bell, *F. R. Leavis* (Abingdon: Routledge, 1988), 23–4.
[113] Leavis, '"Antony and Cleopatra" and "All for Love"', 158, 160, 161. Compare Denys Thompson on George Sturt: 'to notice his work is to quote it: one can only summarize inadequately'. Thompson, 'A Cure for Amnesia', 3.

In an earlier piece, Leavis's proselytizing reached a comparable impasse: 'My argument... will, except to those who find it obvious, seem for the most part an arbitrary tissue of arrogant dogmatisms.'[114] Other *Scrutiny* contributors and subsequent writers working within *Scrutiny's* parameters, such as Richard Hoggart in *The Uses of Literacy* (1957), habitually declared that something was obvious or hardly needed stating when from other angles it was quite contestable.[115] Writing in 1964, S. W. Dawson attributed this 'appearance of circularity' to the faulty state of critical discourse: 'The "rules" of criticism are the "rules" of conversation; certain standards of intelligence and relevance are implicit in the undertaking, as well as a reasonable minimum of common experience.'[116] Leavis's critical epistemology, Perry Anderson has observed, had as its 'crucial precondition' a shared system of values. That was the premise of Leavis's claim that a piece of literary criticism implicitly asked of its readers, 'This is so, is it not?' 'The formal circularity of the criticism of a text', Anderson writes, 'was the elliptical sign of a substantive exchange between its readers.'[117]

Yet it was a *lack* of widely accepted standards that made new initiatives in criticism important in the first place. The predicament that made *Scrutiny's* 'propaganda' work necessary made for circular or reflexive appeals. This tension between circularity and outreach ran through *Scrutiny*. Various contributors assumed readers would be familiar with Cambridge geography and the university's English curriculum, but at the same time the editors were strenuously trying to build up 'the *Scrutiny* Movement in Education', addressing and advising training college lecturers and adult education tutors and undertaking time-consuming studies of school examinations.[118] Parochial tics aside, *Scrutiny* was envisaged as a commons for that 'small minority' of people, by no means all of them Cambridge alumni, who believed that there was 'a necessary relationship between the quality of the individual's response to art and his general fitness for a humane existence'. 'The trouble is not that such persons form a minority,

---

[114] S. W. Dawson, '*Scrutiny* and the Idea of a University', *Essays in Criticism* 14/1 (January 1964): 7; Leavis, 'What's Wrong with Criticism?', 134; and Leavis's letter to Michael Black, 1 May 1962, quoted in Black, 'The Long Pursuit', in Thompson (ed.), *The Leavises*, 93. See also Bell, *F. R. Leavis*, 75; and Gary Day, *Re-reading Leavis: 'Culture' and Literary Criticism* (Basingstoke: Macmillan, 1996), 9–10.

[115] Stefan Collini, 'Richard Hoggart: Literary Criticism and Cultural Decline in Twentieth-Century Britain' in Sue Owen (ed.), *Richard Hoggart and Cultural Studies* (Basingstoke: Palgrave, 2008), 49–51; Day, *Re-reading Leavis*, 37.

[116] Dawson, '*Scrutiny* and the Idea of a University', 7.

[117] Perry Anderson, 'Components of the National Culture', *New Left Review*, 50 (1968): 52.

[118] 'The *Scrutiny* Movement in Education', August 1933, reprinted (without page numbers) in the 1963 reissue of *Scrutiny* between numbers 1 and 2 of volume 2.

but that they are scattered and unorganised.'[119] Here Leavis echoed Arnold, whom he later quoted directly: 'It is not that there do not exist in England...a number of people perfectly well able to discern what is good...from what is bad...but they are isolated, they form no powerful body of opinion, they are not strong enough to set a standard.'[120] Leavis is often casually described as an Arnoldian because they are both known to have valued seriousness and the ideal of disinterestedness, and to have believed that literature played an important role in the life of a culture. As we have seen, however, Leavis regarded some of Arnold's ideas about literature as Aunt Sallies for students to take aim at, and in a letter he described Arnold as 'the representative Victorian who tamed W.W. into a week-end nature poet'.[121] Arnold mattered as a model of critical seriousness and for his ideas concerning the relations between critics, artists, and their publics, and the standards of taste and judgement that sustained these relations.

'Where fifty poets are acclaimed by the critics the function of criticism'—Eliot's phrase as well as Arnold's—'is in abeyance, and the prospects for poetry are not good'. Candidates applying to Downing in 1945 could have chosen to spend three hours writing an essay on this proposition, which echoed Leavis's verdict in *Mass Civilisation and Minority Culture* on Sir John Squire's remark that '[s]hould our age be remembered by posterity solely as an age during which fifty men had written lyrics of some durability for their truth and beauty, it would not be remembered with contempt'.[122] Pronouncements such as Squire's, or Bennett's bracketing of R. H. Mottram with D. H. Lawrence as 'the two real British geniuses of the new age', said Leavis, 'could be made only in an age where there were no standards, no living tradition of poetry spread abroad, and no discriminating public'.[123]

The insistence on standards and discrimination ('insistence', too, was a *Scrutiny* word) goes some way to accounting for the movement's

---

[119] Both quotations from 'Scrutiny: A Manifesto', *Scrutiny* 1/1 (May 1932): 5.

[120] Leavis, 'What's Wrong with Criticism?', 146; Matthew Arnold, 'The Literary Influence of Academies' (1864), in Super (ed.), *Complete Prose Works*, 3: 242.

[121] Leavis to Parsons, 23 May 1930, Chatto & Windus archive, CW 63/12, Reading; Inglis, untitled essay, 356.

[122] Downing College, Essay examination, 1945, *Examination Papers* 207 (1946): 68; Leavis, 'Mass Civilisation and Minority Culture', 29; and see the discussion in 'The *Scrutiny* Movement in Education', which also spoke of the function of criticism being as 'in abeyance'. The Essay examination was a general paper to be sat by candidates seeking admission in a variety of subjects including English, but this question and two others are strongly literary and bear Leavis's imprint: 'The art that appeals to the "cultivated" has not always been so cut off from the life and arts of the people' and 'The language of the age is never the language of poetry'. Both questions reprised issues discussed repeatedly in the 1930s and 1940s, by Leavis and Knights, as the next chapter will show.

[123] Leavis, 'Mass Civilisation and Minority Culture', 27, 29, 30.

somewhat joyless reputation. Its personnel did not see things this way, and the phrase 'living tradition', sandwiched between 'standards' and 'discriminating public', hints at the constructive work that criticism was intended to accomplish. In the stuffily hortatory register of general-essay exam papers (in this case Downing's for 1937): 'Criticism and creation—literary history amply demonstrates it—are not the enemies they are commonly supposed to be.'[124] The production as well as the reception of art was governed by 'the prevailing standard of taste'.[125] Leavis regularly cited W. H. Auden as 'an illustration of the disastrous effect uncritical acceptance could have on a young writer of real talent', as the secretary's notes of an address to the Downing College literary society put it.[126] When Leavis wrote on the 'poetical renascence' that Auden and company were hailed as representing, he organized his assessment of particular works around a discussion of what little magazines and critical journals had to do to 'assemble the nucleus of an actively and intelligently responsive public'.[127]

Any prospect of recuperating a 'living tradition of poetry' depended on that nucleus. In *Mass Civilisation and Minority Culture*, Leavis stressed that the minority he had in mind were those capable not only of appreciating the great writers of the past but also of recognizing their contemporary successors. (How the minority was to operate in practice a later chapter will tease out.) Like Richards and other veterans of the formative years of Cambridge English, Leavis believed that a sustaining audience for modern literature could not be assumed and needed to be trained. The minority's tasks did not end there. Because they were responsible for the 'implicit standards' that 'order[ed] the finer living of an age', human consciousness depended on them. The minority were the custodians of 'the language, ... upon which fine living depends, and without which distinction of spirit is thwarted and incoherent. By "culture," ' Leavis added, 'I mean the use of such a language.'[128] *Culture and Environment* was less oblique: 'our spiritual, moral and emotional tradition', the distillate of 'the "picked experience of ages" ', was '[l]argely conveyed in language'.[129] Leavis's preoccupation with sound and verse movement was not a refinement of belletristic criticism, but a reflection of a belief that language was the site of culture as well as a metonym for it. Milton's latinizing

124 Downing College, Essay examination, 1937, *Examination Papers* 164 (1937): 67.
125 'Scrutiny: A Manifesto', 4.
126 Doughty Society minute book, (31 October 1952), DCCS/4/4/1/1, Downing.
127 F. R. Leavis, 'This Poetical Renascence', *Scrutiny* 2/1 (June 1933): 65–7.
128 Leavis, 'Mass Civilisation and Minority Culture', 14–15.
129 Leavis and Thompson, *Culture and Environment*, 81.

signalled, and enacted, an estrangement from the living language, and with that, a living culture.

Leavis and Thompson agreed with Richards's suggestion that '[a]s the other vehicles of tradition, the family and the community, for example, are dissolved, we are forced more and more to rely upon language'.[130] And as the language tended to be debased by the engines of modern civilization such as advertising, journalism, and best-selling fiction, Leavis and Thompson continued, 'it is to literature alone, where its subtlest and finest use is preserved, that we can look with any hope of keeping in touch with our spiritual tradition'.[131] To make sense of the arguments about modern civilization in play here, we need to turn from the question of how to teach reading to the question of culture and environment.

---

[130] Ibid., 81; Richards, *Practical Criticism*, 321.
[131] Leavis and Thompson, *Culture and Environment*, 81–2.

2

Culture and Environment

With *Scrutiny* up and running, F. R. Leavis began to put together an anthology that would 'impress on the world that there already is a formidable phalanx of young trained critics in the movement'.[1] *Scrutiny*, the first editorial announced, had a 'political ambition' as well as a literary one, and this volume—*Determinations: Critical Essays* was the title Leavis and his publisher Ian Parsons settled on—needed essays that spoke to the journal's cultural concerns as well as accomplished pieces of literary criticism.[2] A suitable candidate was an 'extraordinarily good essay by J. L. Russell, *The Scientific Best Seller*...which fits in very well with our purpose & our point of view—the point of view of unspecialized intelligence: our "determinations" are concerned with the "contemporary sensibility"'.[3] However, it appeared unlikely that either of *Scrutiny*'s leading writers on contemporary culture would be able to produce a contribution. Q. D. Leavis was not in a position to. As for Denys Thompson, Leavis worried: 'We've used him shamelessly for journalistic exigencies & I'm wondering whether he has done, or can do in time, anything suitable.'[4] Thompson did manage to fit an essay for *Determinations* in between his other *Scrutiny* commitments and his job teaching at a public school in Norfolk. Sardonically entitled 'Our Debt to Lamb', it traced the relationship between the genre of the light essay and the rhetorical tactics of modern advertising. The essay gathered together several threads of the *Scrutiny* project: a declinist history of modern culture; an interest in the relationship between literature and the texts of mass culture; and a conviction that literary training was a moral discipline, holding out the prospect of fortifying citizens against the seductions of mass culture, the most ominous of which was the corruption of feeling and desire.

[1] F. R. Leavis to Ian Parsons, 28 December 1933, Chatto & Windus archive, CW 53/2, Reading.
[2] 'Scrutiny: A Manifesto', *Scrutiny* 1/1 (May 1932): 3.
[3] Leavis to Parsons, 18 February 1934, Chatto & Windus archive, CW 53/2, Reading; J. L. Russell, 'The Scientific Best Seller' *Scrutiny* 2/4 (March 1934): 348–63.
[4] Leavis to Parsons, 5 November 1932; Leavis to Parsons, 2 January 1934, Chatto & Windus archive, CW 53/2, Reading.

F. R. Leavis was unmistakably the defining presence in *Scrutiny*'s literary criticism, but the group's cultural criticism was a more even collaboration. M. C. Bradbrook described the early 1930s Cambridge of Leavis, I. A. Richards, and Mansfield Forbes as 'a workshop....We lived in a small university where interchange was among people who knew each other....We were not concerned with the outside world, or with publicity...all went by talk and oral tradition.' *Scrutiny* became 'a formulation of what had before been an unfocused, a largely unestablished line of work'.[5] The closeness and reciprocity of the workshop were manifest in the pages of the journal. Claims about Jacobean writers, their language communities, and historical circumstances that were sketched in Leavis's writings recurred, more fully worked-through, in articles by L. C. Knights. The two men worked so closely together before Knights moved to Manchester in 1934 that it probably makes more sense to think of these arguments as emerging from a joint undertaking, rather than as ideas that originated with the one and were developed by the other. Knights shared empirical discoveries with Leavis, and Q. D. Leavis and Thompson exchanged documents of mass culture they had come across in the course of their research. Many of these appeared in the short book F. R. Leavis and Thompson wrote together in 1933, *Culture and Environment: The Training of Critical Awareness*.[6]

The book's subject was the troubling drift of modern civilization. 'Environment' referred to the press, advertising, commercialized leisure, and other things that people using the term culture in a more-or-less value-neutral way would describe as cultural conditions. Leavis, of course, did not use value-neutral words. He and his colleagues reserved the word 'culture' for that with real vitality, and the mass media and consumer society were mechanical, not living. Leavis had enshrined the contrast in another title: 'Mass Civilisation and Minority Culture' borrowed the German opposition between genuine *Kultur* and the more 'environmental'

---

[5] M. C. Bradbrook, 'What Is Cambridge English?', n.d. (early 1970s), 5–6, M. C. Bradbrook Papers 47/429, Girton.

[6] F. R. Leavis and Denys Thompson, *Culture and Environment: The Training of Critical Awareness* (1933; London: Chatto & Windus, 1950). In a letter to the *New Statesman* on 9 March 1957, Leavis said that he 'wrote *Culture and Environment* in a week (with Mr Thompson to advise me as to tact and tactics from the schoolmaster's point of view)'. Thompson said the same thing after Leavis's death. However, not all of the text is written in Leavis's characteristic voice, and Thompson's correspondence with Parsons when a revised edition was mooted indicates that he had more than a nominal stake in the book. F. R. Leavis, *Letters in Criticism*, ed. John Tasker (London: Chatto & Windus, 1974), 58; Denys Thompson, 'Teacher and Friend', in Thompson (ed.), *The Leavises: Recollections and Impressions* (Cambridge: Cambridge University Press, 1984), 48; Thompson to Ian Parsons, 14 March 1953; Thompson to Parsons, 18 April 1953; Parsons to Thompson, 21 April 1953, Chatto & Windus archive, CW 132/13, Reading.

category of *Zivilisation* (Coleridge had drawn an analogous distinction). While *Culture and Environment* was still a work in progress, Leavis told Parsons: 'I'm collaborating with a friend who's in a school in a book for school-use'—it was 'designed to give serious effect in the educational field to the *Scrutiny* "drive"'.[7] (Chatto & Windus obliged, posting no fewer than 4,452 promotional leaflets 'to Secondary Schools, etc.', and 3,500 copies were sold in the three years after publication.)[8] Much of the text duplicated the contents of *Scrutiny* articles or Leavis's pamphlets, and it had something of the character of an anthology in the way it served up excerpts from works of cultural criticism, advertisements, and pronouncements by culture-industry moguls, as illustrations and as specimens in exercises for sixth-form classes. Thinking about a new edition twenty years later, Thompson remarked, 'The kind of revision I contemplate would make a fuller, more consecutive work; there would be more exposition, less chucking it at the reader.'[9]

Culture and Environment no longer has the capacity to stimulate or provoke in the way that more substantial books in the *Scrutiny* canon still can. But it was a terminus or interchange for *Scrutiny* arguments about modern life, and for teachers and later writers adopting, appropriating, and arguing against *Scrutiny* modes of cultural criticism, it was *Culture and Environment* (not *Fiction and the Reading Public*) that was the key text. For both these reasons, this chapter will keep returning to it as it examines the span of *Scrutiny*'s critique of popular culture. The *Scrutiny* movement's work on the subject was the foundation of media studies in Britain and part of the patrimony of several generations of teachers and students, many of whom took positions on mass culture and modernity sharply different from those of Leavis and Thompson. Consequently, *Scrutiny*'s critical history of modernity has itself been subjected to extensive study.[10] This literature underplays several significant aspects of *Scrutiny*'s cultural criticism, above all the importance of the Leavises' and Thompson's engagement with American authorities—especially the sociologists Robert S. Lynd and Helen Merrell Lynd and the popular

---

[7] Leavis to Parsons, 21 August 1932, Chatto & Windus archive, CW 53/2, Reading.

[8] Chatto & Windus ledgers, 9/583, 10/77, Reading.

[9] Thompson to Parsons, 14 March 1953, Chatto & Windus archive, CW 132/13, Reading.

[10] On the cultural criticism, as distinct from the related question of the cultural import of literary studies, see especially Francis Mulhern, *The Moment of 'Scrutiny'* (London: New Left Books, 1979); Chris Baldick, *The Social Mission of English Criticism, 1848–1932* (Oxford: Clarendon Press, 1983), ch. 7; Gary Day, *Re-reading Leavis: 'Culture' and Literary Criticism* (Basingstoke: Macmillan, 1996), chs 1–3; Fred Inglis, *Radical Earnestness: English Social Theory 1880–1980* (Oxford: Martin Robertson with Basil Blackwell, 1982), ch. 5; and the works by Stefan Collini and David Gervais cited below.

economist Stuart Chase.[11] *Scrutiny's* 'history of the present' being a narrative of decline, an appropriate point of departure is the two at least notionally historical utopias that structured *Scrutiny's* interpretation of modernity: Elizabethan and Jacobean England, and the 'organic' rural community.

Scrutiny's attention to English rural life has attracted a volume of commentary out of proportion to its importance in the group's thinking. Rural life and customs mattered to Thompson more than to other regular contributors. It was probably Thompson who drafted the chapters of *Culture and Environment* devoted to the organic community and drawing on George Sturt's books *Change in the Village* (1912) and *The Wheelwright's Shop* (1923). Thompson believed that Sturt's books on the vanishing rural order presented valuable 'analogies for literary tradition and criticism'. Leavis later insisted that neither he nor Thompson went in for olde-England nostalgia but had been 'calling attention to an essential change in human conditions'.[12] Yet the associations with back-to-the-land sentiments proved hard to shake off, and they afforded sport for Leavis's detractors. A 'notorious colleague of mine...illustrates his gift of discreet irony in genial by-references to "the old wheelwright's shop." Everyone knows who it is he has in mind, and what kind of general smear he intends.'[13]

Rural lore was an analogy for literary tradition because both were forms of active memory, ways of keeping the experience of the past alive in the present.[14] In making this claim, Leavis and Thompson were following Richards's suggestion that both 'language' and 'the community' were 'vehicles of tradition'. Often, however, Thompson dispensed with the comparative procedure implied by 'analogy', and conflated the two sorts of tradition. After quoting Sturt's judgement that the people of 1880s Farnham inherited 'a time-honoured tradition teaching them how to go on',

---

[11] Chris Waters in 'Beyond "Americanization": Rethinking Anglo-American Cultural Exchange between the Wars', *Cultural and Social History* 4/4 (2007): 451–9, esp. 452, assigns Leavis and Thompson a prominent place in the discourse of Americanization but misses how they were thinking *with* American commentators as well as *about* America. For another interpretation of *Scrutiny* and 'America', see Genevieve Abravanel, 'English by Example: F. R. Leavis and the Americanization of Modern England', *Modernism/modernity* 15/4 (2008): 685–701. My account stresses the impact of American commentators more than Abravanel's does (she does not mention Chase). I find Abravanel's argument unconvincing because of its uncritical reliance on the notion that 'the ideology of Englishness' explains the Leavis of the *Scrutiny* years; and I think her reading of *Culture and Environment* is too superficial.

[12] F. R. Leavis, 'Luddites? *or* There is Only One Culture', in *Nor Shall My Sword: Discourses on Pluralism, Compassion, and Social Hope* (London: Chatto & Windus, 1972), 84–6.

[13] F. R. Leavis to *The Spectator*, 10 May 1963, in Leavis, *Letters in Criticism*, 100.

[14] Leavis and Thompson, *Culture and Environment*, 80–2.

Thompson skipped on to a decidedly unrustic authority: 'But the tradition was not static, taken over like a bank-balance. "You must obtain it by
great labour," as Mr Eliot has remarked in *Tradition and the Individual
Talent*, and this truth is finely exemplified by many passages in [Sturt's]
Lucy Bettesworth…in the chapter on *Our Primitive Knowledge*, for instance.' Thompson went on to say that Hardy's success as a novelist had
much to do with '[t]he tradition which Sturt recorded':

> the pleasure derived from reading Hardy's novels results not, as is commonly
> assumed, from literary art—his literary technique is naïve and clumsy—but
> from contact with the rich traditional country round of life. An understand-
> ing of this life will help to explain how Shakespeare's use of language differs
> from Milton's, in what way the idiom of newspaper and best-seller and ad-
> vertising is destructive of fine language and of fine living, and why, since
> English traditional culture is dead, it is of the first importance that tradition
> should be sustained through literature.[15]

Thompson was *Scrutiny*'s principal commentator on rural traditions.
In work published under his name alone, Leavis made reference to the
organic community only in a self-conscious and largely metaphorical way,
the exception being the end of his essay on Joyce, where he spent several
pages on the way a vanished agricultural order had nourished the English
language.[16] But his main arguments about culture did not depend on the
concept of the organic community. Although rural customs were not a
key to Leavis's own thinking, they were a recurrent concern for other
contributors to the journal and for later writers in the *Scrutiny* tradition
such as David Holbrook.

The wheelwright's shop was a utopia in the literary sense, another reality that provides a space for thinking about one's own world.[17] Elizabethan
and Jacobean England also functioned this way, and organized *Scrutiny*
thought to a much greater degree than the organic community did. Leavis
and Knights argued that Shakespeare's plays owed much of their strength
to the linguistic community of early modern England, the relative unity
of which enabled Shakespeare to conjure the learned and the demotic, the

---

[15] Denys Thompson, 'A Cure for Amnesia', *Scrutiny* 2/1 (June 1933): 5–6. Note the way
the phrase 'fine living' served to characterize both minority culture and the experience of
Sturt's Surrey villagers: ibid., 5; F. R. Leavis, 'Mass Civilisation and Minority Culture'
(1930) in *For Continuity* (Cambridge: Minority Press, 1933), 15; Leavis and Thompson,
Culture and Environment, 76, 81.

[16] F. R. Leavis, 'Joyce and "The Revolution of the Word"', *Scrutiny* 2/2 (September
1933): 199–201. For an example of his self-conscious or distancing use of the 'organic
community', see F. R. Leavis, 'Under Which King, Bezonian?', *Scrutiny* 1/3 (December
1932): 208. See also John Fraser, 'Reflections on the Organic Community', *The Human
World*, 15–16 (May–August 1974): 60.

[17] Compare Mulhern, *Moment of 'Scrutiny'*, 59.

abstract and the concrete. The dramatic achievement of the age, Knights claimed, 'was due to the bringing together and the lively interplay of different interests within a fairly homogeneous culture'. There was 'no barrier of language between higher and lower such as separates the different ranges of the contemporary reading public'.[18] Leavis made the same point: Shakespeare could not have been a 'highbrow' because the early modern public was not stratified as it was in an age of highbrow and middlebrow zones of taste (the terms became current in Britain in the 1920s). A common, living tradition made it 'possible for Shakespeare to write plays that were at once popular drama and poetry that could be appreciated only by an educated minority'.[19] Even in *Fiction and the Reading Public*, a book known for its innovative research on contemporary fiction and its marketing apparatus, Q. D. Leavis reached back to sixteenth-century prose writers such as Thomas Nashe for strained contrasts with the horizons of twentieth-century popular fiction.[20]

Best-sellers were not the only twentieth-century reference points in these arguments about early modern culture. Knights stressed the complex integrity of early modern language and culture to refute Marxist contentions that Elizabethan drama was 'the expression of a "class" culture'.[21] This was in 1936, just as British Marxists were beginning to make sophisticated contributions to literary criticism, especially in *Left Review*, which was run by Edgell Rickword, Douglas Garman, and others who, before their turns leftward, had worked on the *Calendar of Modern Letters*.[22] Four years earlier, when Leavis was pressed to specify *Scrutiny*'s political allegiances, the Marxist alternatives in English criticism were more hypothetical. Leavis could accept the idea that in the past the 'framework' of English popular culture had been 'a stylization, so to speak, of economic necessities; based, it might fairly be said, on the "methods of production"' was 'an art of living, involving codes, developed in ages of continuous experience, of relations between man and man, and man and the environment in its seasonal rhythm'. This was the case 'when England had a popular culture'. The nineteenth century destroyed that culture, and what

---

[18] L. C. Knights, 'Shakespeare and Profit Inflations', *Scrutiny* 5/1 (June 1936): 56–7; Knights, 'How Many Children Had Lady Macbeth?' (1933) in *Explorations: Essays in Criticism Mainly on the Literature of the Seventeenth Century* (London: Chatto & Windus, 1946), 5–6.

[19] Leavis, 'Mass Civilisation and Minority Culture', 38. See also Q. D. Leavis, *Fiction and the Reading Public* (1932; London: Chatto & Windus, 1965), 85.

[20] Leavis, *Fiction and the Reading Public*, 87–8, 93.

[21] Knights, 'Shakespeare and Profit Inflations', 56–7.

[22] Charles Hobday, *Edgell Rickword: A Poet at War* (Manchester: Carcanet Press, 1989), chs 6–9; Allan Young and Michael Schmidt, 'A Conversation with Edgell Rickword', *Poetry Nation* 1 (1973): 82.

remained of 'cultural tradition' surviveed '*in spite of* the rapidly changing "means of production" '.[23]

Here, it was the industrial revolution that broke the organic relationship between art and daily necessities. At this time, in the early 1930s, Leavis believed that the eighteenth century still 'enjoyed the advantages of a homogeneous—a real—culture' (one of those advantages was the 'more-than-individual judgment' of Johnson's 'common reader', who represented 'the competent, the cultivated, in general' rather than 'the great heart of the people', but was nonetheless able to maintain agreed standards because 'to be born into a homogeneous culture is to move among symbols of limited variety'; the 'circumambient confusion' of the age of the mass media stymied standards of taste).[24] As arguments about the breakdown of a unified culture and language community went through further iterations in *Scrutiny*, it became more common to date the change from the seventeenth century itself. In his 1936 essay 'Shakespeare and Profit Inflations', Knights declared: 'The advantage that Shakespeare enjoyed in being able to exploit to the full a popular idiom is paralleled by—is, in fact, part of—corresponding advantages in habits of perception and discrimination, in emotional and intellectual organization—in sensibility.'[25]

This was, of course, a reference to Eliot's assertion that a 'dissociation of sensibility' had occurred in the seventeenth century: a 'mechanism of sensibility which could devour any kind of experience' collapsed, and thought and feeling became disarticulated.[26] Leavis still regarded this as 'a fact of first importance about the seventeenth century' in the late 1950s, according to an undergraduate's seminar notes. 'There was a radical change. Compare "All for Love" and "Antony and Cleopatra." '[27] Significantly, Leavis confined himself to the evidence of literature itself, as Eliot had. But the resonant idea of a dissociation of sensibility proved hard to confine, and it lent itself to a variety of more broadly based historical arguments, some of which were made in the pages of *Scrutiny*. All these arguments treated the seventeenth century as a hinge between the pre-modern and the modern and sought to disclose what was lost in

[23] Leavis, 'Under Which King, Bezonian?', 208 (emphasis added).
[24] F. R. Leavis, *How to Teach Reading: A Primer for Ezra Pound* (Cambridge: Minority Press, 1932), 3–4; Leavis, 'What's Wrong with Criticism?', *Scrutiny* 1/2 (September 1932): 145–6.
[25] Knights, 'Shakespeare and Profit Inflations', 57.
[26] T. S. Eliot, 'The Metaphysical Poets' (1921), in *Selected Essays* (London: Faber & Faber, 1951), 287–8.
[27] Charles Winder, 'Leavis's Downing Seminars: A Student's Notes', in Ian MacKillop and Richard Storer (eds), *F. R. Leavis: Essays and Documents* (Sheffield: Sheffield Academic Press, 1995), 71, 72. See also Leavis, ' "English," Unrest and Continuity', in *Nor Shall My Sword*, 123–4.

the transition. And all of them posited some modern division of life: polite culture became divorced from plebeian culture;[28] a coherent reading public or community of taste collapsed into confusion or became stratified; *Gemeinschaft* gave way to *Gesellschaft*. As Stefan Collini has shown, the 'dissociation of sensibility' was readily conjoined to the historian R. H. Tawney's argument about the emergence of an 'economic' way of thinking independent of traditional religious or moral sanctions. Tawney's *Religion and the Rise of Capitalism* (1926) became part of the fabric of 'the *Scrutiny* programme', occupying an important place in the ideal curriculum Leavis outlined in *Education and the University* (1943).[29] Harold Wendell Smith ran the two arguments together in a series of *Scrutiny* essays late in the journal's life.[30]

A decade earlier, Knights had bedded Eliot's idea down in a detailed discussion of Francis Bacon. While Eliot had not mentioned cold rationality, growing claims for the authority of scientific reason were the most logical support for the argument that feeling and thinking became estranged on or about March 1631, when Donne died.[31] Eliot's reference to Dante and other poets in his three-paragraph disquisition on the dissociation of sensibility implied that Donne's mechanism for devouring experience was not peculiar to his own time and place, but Knights, summarizing the previous two decades' revaluation of the seventeenth century, argued that the 'literary splendours of the Shakespearean period'—and, by more or less necessary implication, that undissociated sensibility—were now 'seen as the result of Renaissance turbulence and intellectual eagerness working on traditional ways of thinking and feeling and evaluating, the reflexion of a tension that can be observed in every sphere of the national life'.[32]

---

[28] F. R. Leavis, *Education and the University: A Sketch for an 'English School'* (London: Chatto & Windus, 1943), 56. Here Leavis spoke of 'the loss remarked on by Mr Eliot and the loss entailed in a new separation between polite and popular culture'.

[29] Stefan Collini, 'Where Did It All Go Wrong? Cultural Critics and "Modernity" in Inter-War Britain', in E. H. H. Green and D. M. Tanner (eds), *The Strange Survival of Liberal England: Political Leaders, Moral Values and the Reception of Economic Debate* (Cambridge: Cambridge University Press, 2007), 262–3. See also Patrick Harrison, 'Downing after the War', in MacKillop and Storer (eds), *F. R. Leavis: Essays and Documents*, 256.

[30] Collini, 'Where Did It All Go Wrong?', 271–2.

[31] F. W. Bateson pointed out that in 'The Metaphysical Poets' '—as elsewhere in Mr Eliot's early critical writings—*feeling* means sensation. And the *sensibility* is the faculty which registers sensations.' Many misconceptions followed, Bateson said, from the assumption that 'by *feeling* Mr Eliot meant emotion'. Bateson, 'Contributions to a Dictionary of Critical Terms: II. Dissociation of Sensibility', *Essays in Criticism* 1/3 (1951): 303, 304.

[32] Eliot, 'Metaphysical Poets', 288; L. C. Knights, 'Bacon and the Seventeenth-Century Dissociation of Sensibility', *Scrutiny* 11/4 (summer 1943): 269. Explaining moments of literary transformation with reference to productive tensions in this way recalls Lukács, but his work appears to have been unknown in Britain at this time.

Unlike some optimistic British Marxist critics in the 1930s, Knights did not apply this analysis to the tensions wracking capitalist cultures in his own time. The energies of those 'traditional ways of thinking and feeling and evaluating' had been exhausted long ago. At least, this was Leavis's position. Although he always claimed developments in culture over time as part of his remit as a critic, Leavis's own historical discussions were little more than sketches. Knights and Q. D. Leavis were much more concerned to develop historical analyses of the problems *Scrutiny* grappled with. Yet there were few methodological models available in the 1930s and 1940s for the analysis of cultural transformations such as those discerned in the seventeenth century. 'Cultural history of the kind desiderated still remains to be written', Knights remarked. 'Since "facts about" a particular period can give only a vague, general impression of its life, the only start for a cultural investigation professing completeness is from literature…'[33] Most of his essay on 'Bacon and the Seventeenth-Century Dissociation of Sensibility' was therefore devoted to the close reading of Bacon's texts. 'Almost as much as his explicit philosophy,' Knights wrote, 'Bacon's prose style is an index of the emergence of the modern world.' His 'figures of speech are forensic': they do not have that 'vivid feeling for *both* sides of the analogy as we find in more representative Elizabethans'.[34] In characteristic *Scrutiny* fashion, the discussion shifted from fine-grained textual interpretation to expansive characterizations of broad swathes of cultural history, the sophistication and rigour of the textual analysis creating a momentum and authority that covered for the schematic quality of the historical interpretations.

The 'whole trend' of Bacon's work was 'to encourage the relegation of instinctive and emotional life to a sphere separate from and inferior to the sphere of "thought" and practical activity'.[35] For Knights as well as Leavis, to study the seventeenth century was to grapple with 'the characteristic problems of the modern world', and the last few pages of the essay panned forward, quoting W. B. Yeats on the desolation of the early nineteenth century, and reproducing a chunk of John Stuart Mill's *Autobiography* as an 'extreme' illustration of 'spiritual aridity'.[36] This was a stark example of the way *Scrutiny* writers, as Collini has shown, assimilated the seventeenth century of Tawney and Eliot to a longer-established critique, which ran from

[33] Knights, 'Shakespeare and Profit Inflations', 57, 59–60. F. R. Leavis later used the phrase 'facts about', in quotation marks, in *Education and the University*, 68.
[34] Knights, 'Bacon', 276.
[35] Ibid., 281.
[36] Leavis, *Education and the University*, 59 (this section of *Education and the University* first appeared in *Scrutiny* 9/2 [summer 1940]: 98–120); Knights, 'Bacon', 282 and n.

the Romantics through Carlyle, Ruskin, and Morris, of the inhumanity and bleakness of industrial society.[37] The loss of a unified sensibility in the seventeenth century was, as David Gervais has noted, analogous to the disruption of the organic community by the impersonal forces of the industrial age.[38] As Collini observes, the nineteenth century was 'always present as a negative reference point in *Scrutiny* circles'.[39] The journal's editorial collective, and later writers whom they influenced, such as Raymond Williams, David Holbrook, and E. P. Thompson contributed to the revaluation of the 'industrial revolution' as a 'catastrophe'.[40] F. R. Leavis's commitment to this interpretation of industrialization was one of the points of contention with C. P. Snow in the 'two cultures' controversy of the early 1960s.[41] Toward the end of his career, as Dickens absorbed more of his attention and he freely described cultural phenomena as Benthamite, the legacy of the first half of the nineteenth century increasingly coloured his utterances.[42]

However, in the 1930s and 1940s, when *Scrutiny* was afloat, the industrial revolution was not the focal point for Leavis and his associates that it was for Tawney, J. L. and Barbara Hammond, and Beatrice and Sidney Webb, the architects of the catastrophist historiography of industrialization. To be sure, *Scrutiny*, Leavis's pamphlets, and *Culture and Environment* quoted Cobbett on the early nineteenth century and D. H. Lawrence deploring the ugliness to which 'the moneyed classes and promoters of industry...in the palmy Victorian days' condemned the working class.[43] And *Scrutiny*'s cultural criticism similarly located industry at the centre of modern civilization. Yet references to the changes of the late eighteenth and early nineteenth centuries were far outnumbered by references to the period after 1870.[44] *Culture and Environment* was especially clear: its pages were haunted by mass education, the mass press, and Fordism. The

---

[37] Collini, 'Where Did It All Go Wrong?'; Stefan Collini, 'The Literary Critic and the Village Labourer: "Culture" in Twentieth-Century Britain', *Transactions of the Royal Historical Society* 14 (2004): 93–116.

[38] David Gervais, *Literary Englands: Versions of 'Englishness' in Modern Writing* (Cambridge: Cambridge University Press, 1993), 134.

[39] Collini, 'Where Did It All Go Wrong?', 268.

[40] Collini, 'Literary Critic and the Village Labourer'; Stefan Collini, 'Enduring Passion: E. P. Thompson's Reputation', in *Common Reading: Critics, Historians, Publics* (Oxford: Oxford University Press, 2008), 175–86.

[41] Guy Ortolano, *The Two Cultures Controversy: Science, Literature and Cultural Politics in Postwar Britain* (Cambridge: Cambridge University Press, 2009), ch. 4.

[42] F. R. Leavis, 'Why *Four Quartets* Matters in a Technologico-Benthamite Age', in *English Literature in Our Time and the University: The Clark Lectures 1967* (1969; Cambridge: Cambridge University Press, 1979), 111–32.

[43] Leavis and Thompson, *Culture and Environment*, 95.

[44] *Culture and Environment* even quoted two sources, one English and one American, that implied that it was only after the 1880s that humane constraints on competition and the profit motive slackened (62, 74–5). See also the passage quoted on ibid., 60–1.

capital of the modernity that troubled *Scrutiny*'s core contributors was not Victorian Manchester but interwar Muncie, Indiana, which became Middletown with the publication of Robert and Helen Lynd's 'community study' in 1929.[45]

America and the lessons it offered preoccupied Denys Thompson and both Leavises in *Scrutiny*'s formative years, to a far greater extent than the movement's historians to date have indicated.[46] American periodicals provided models for *Scrutiny*, quotations from American works of social criticism studded the pages of *Scrutiny* and *Culture and Environment*, and reviewers went out of their way to draw attention to novels not heavily publicized in Britain, such as James Farrell's *Studs Lonigan* trilogy set in Chicago.[47] Reviewers noted the sociological as well as literary value of American fiction. Discussing John Dos Passos's *U.S.A.*, F. R. Leavis homed in on the character of J. Ward Moorehouse, an ad man in whom 'is embodied the power that, in the general disintegration, in the default of religion, art and traditional forms and sanctions, holds society together—the Power of the Word, or, let us say, Advertising'.[48] 'Clean-cut young executive type', Ward says, appraising his own reflection. The phrase entered the *Scrutiny* repertoire, along with a cognate supplied by the popular novelist P. C. Wren, creator of Beau Geste of the Foreign Legion, who responded to Q. D. Leavis's questionnaire: 'Although I now make a good many thousands per annum, I am still not a "professional novelist," nor . . . a long-haired literary cove. I prefer the short-haired executive type.'[49] A teaching exercise in *Culture and Environment* used both expressions:

'Clean-cut executive type,' 'good mixer,' 'representative man,' 'short-haired executive,' 'regular guy' (Americanism).
Why do we wince at the mentality that uses this idiom?[50]

[45] Robert S. Lynd and Helen Merrell Lynd, *Middletown: A Study in American Culture* (New York: Harcourt, Brace, & Co., 1929).

[46] Mulhern, *Moment of 'Scrutiny'*, 125–7; MacKillop, *F. R. Leavis*, 144–5, 178; Day, *Rereading Leavis*, 34–6.

[47] Q. D. Leavis, review of *Salavin* by Georges Duhamel and *Studs Lonigan* by James Farrell, *Scrutiny* 5/4 (March 1937): 423–4. It was to American periodicals that Leavis gestured when articulating the ambitions of the young *Scrutiny*: the *New Republic*, the *Symposium*, and *Hound and Horn*. 'Scrutiny: A Manifesto', 2–3.

[48] F. R. Leavis, 'A Serious Artist', *Scrutiny* 1/2 (September 1932): 175.

[49] Leavis, *Fiction and the Reading Public*, 52.

[50] Leavis and Thompson, *Culture and Environment*, 121. 'Good mixer', also of American origin (*OED*, s.v. 'mixer', n, I.2.a), was a phrase both Leavises used pejoratively. F. R. Leavis to D. F. Pocock, 13 December 1955, F. R. Leavis papers, Col 9.59.121, Emmanuel; F. R. Leavis to Ron Gray, 25 July 1975 Leavis papers, Col 9.59a, Emmanuel; Q. D. Leavis, *Fiction and the Reading Public*, 196.

The United States was 'where the process of Western civilization has gone furthest'.[51] The American experience pointed to future developments in Britain. Thompson quoted these lines by Ronald Bottrall, a young poet highly esteemed by F. R. Leavis at the time and a contributor to *Scrutiny*:

> the close
> Of our long progress is hinted by the crass
> Fogs creeping slow and darkly
> From out the middle west.[52]

(The reference to the Midwest is important: whatever the polemical simplifications of *Scrutiny*'s discussions of America, its authors were not simply referring to some conflation of Hollywood and Manhattan.) The United States also gave rise to a body of social and cultural criticism that assisted British observers of this 'Western process'.[53] American commentaries on modern life such as Edgar A. Mowrer's *This American World* (1928), the Lynds' *Middletown*, Stuart Chase's *Your Money's Worth* (1927) and *Men and Machines* (1929), along with Jan and Cora Gordon's California travelogue, *Star-Dust in Hollywood* (1930), were positively flogged in *Culture and Environment*.[54] *The Press and the Organization of Society* (1922), by the English pacifist Norman Angell, was quoted and saluted, but Angell did not provide a key to the present in the way that Chase and the Lynds did.[55] *Scrutiny* bypassed British sociological works that examined leisure, such as the massive *Social Survey of Merseyside* (1934), at the same time as it discussed their American counterparts. Cultivating 'a familiarity with the "anthropological" approach to contemporary civilization exemplified by *Middletown*' was part of *Scrutiny*'s 'political ambition', according to the editorial manifesto in the first number.[56] Reviewing a volume of speeches by advertising and sales executives at an Atlantic City convention, Thompson remarked: 'If England is less Americanized than America, it is in the discreditable sense that less resistance to the

[51] Leavis and Thompson, *Culture and Environment*, 5; Leavis, 'Mass Civilisation and Minority Culture', 17.
[52] Denys Thompson, 'Advertising God', *Scrutiny* 1/3 (December 1932): 242. Characteristically, Thompson did not identify the poet: readers in the know would know. The same lines are quoted in Leavis's discussion of Bottrall in *New Bearings in English Poetry: A Study of the Contemporary Situation* (London: Chatto & Windus, 1932), 205.
[53] Leavis, 'A Serious Artist', 177.
[54] For instance, Chase was cited, or mention made of his books or his organization Consumers Research, on the following pages of *Culture and Environment*: 5, 19–20 (twice), 21–2, 25, 28, 29, 49–50, 65, 66, 67, 69; and then, in the 'Further Examples' of teaching exercises, 112 (twice), 113 (twice), 125, 126 (twice), 127, 130, 131, 132–3, 133–4 (twice).
[55] Leavis and Thompson, *Culture and Environment*, 36; see also Q. D. Leavis, 'A Middleman of Ideas', *Scrutiny* 1/1 (May 1932): 72.
[56] 'Scrutiny: A Manifesto', 3.

advance of civilization has been developed: no English university has produced a *Middletown*.'[57]

The eagerness with which literary critics took up a sociological study is not as incongruous as it might appear. *Middletown* was written in the register of an older moralist social criticism as much as it was within the parameters of professional social science. If no English university produced a *Middletown*, no American university did either: its authors became academics only after the publication of their book. The Lynds described a 'pecuniary society' animated by a belief in the gospel of progress and characterized by increased levels of consumption but wanting in personal fulfilment—a small city where the automobile, radio, and the movies unravelled community and individuality.[58] Formally, too, *Middletown* was not uncompromisingly sociological: it 'could also be read as a piece of descriptive literature in which census data played as large a role as quotations from the books of Sherwood Anderson'.[59] It presented an America already familiar from novels. As Sarah E. Igo points out, by focusing on a small Midwestern city without a substantial immigrant population, and by filtering out Muncie's African-American population, *Middletown* actually ran counter to contemporary social trends and presented a 'social scientific account [that] resembled contemporary fictional works such as Sinclair Lewis's *Main Street* (1920) and *Babbitt* (1922)...in its equation of white natives and American culture'. Indeed, a critic in the *New York Sun* commented that, despite the Lynds' pretensions to science, they were actually 'incapable of seeing this town except through Mr Lewis's eyes'.[60] The real-estate agent hero of *Babbitt*, with his good-mixing, regular-guy aspirations, was a familiar reference point in *Scrutiny*.[61] *Babbitt* and *Middletown* figured as different tellings of the same story.

F. R. Leavis chose 'Babbitt Buys the World', a line from Mowrer's *This American World*, as his title for a debunking of H. G. Wells's *The Work*,

---

[57] Thompson, 'Advertising God', 242. Q. D. Leavis made the same point in an appreciation of Chase, claiming that Britain had no 'middlemen of ideas' of his calibre. 'This is perhaps the measure of the difference between the U.S.A. and Great Britain: further along the road we are travelling, they have produced a conscious counter-movement.' Q. D. Leavis, 'A Middleman of Ideas', 72–3. See also Thompson's review essay of books about Andrew Mellon, John D. Rockefeller, and their ilk: 'Books of the kind under review do not seem to be written about the English counterparts of the American millionaire.' Denys Thompson, 'The Robber Barons', *Scrutiny* 5/1 (June 1936): 11.
[58] Sarah E. Igo, *The Averaged American: Surveys, Citizens, and the Making of a Mass Public* (Cambridge, Mass.: Harvard University Press, 2007), ch. 1.
[59] Wolf Lepenies, *Between Literature and Science: The Rise of Sociology*, trans. R. J. Hollingdale (1985; Cambridge: Cambridge University Press, 1988), 186.
[60] Igo, *Averaged American*, 58, 81–5, 324 n.
[61] 'Scrutiny: A Manifesto', 3; Leavis and Thompson, *Culture and Environment*, 32, 47, 66.

Wealth and Happiness of Mankind (1932).[62] The association of Wells with Lewis's hero is a sign of how seriously the Leavises and Thompson took the claim that Britain and the United States were at different points on the arc of a common 'Western process'. What Wells shared with Babbitt, to *Scrutiny* eyes, was a faith in material progress and a naïve trust in the beneficence of its corporate and bureaucratic stewards. (The later excoriation of Snow's faith in rising standards of living—more jam to go around, as he put it with an ingratiating homeliness that was bound to provoke a response—in the 'two cultures' controversy was of a piece with his criticism of Wells three decades before. Indeed, Leavis charged Snow with 'crass Wellsianism'.)[63] And the celebration of industry in Soviet propaganda tempted Leavis to regard communism as a cognate of Wellsianism, the other side of the materialist coin rather than a true alternative to capitalist civilization.[64] Wells, too, saw in the United States the shape of things to come, though he was more cheered than Leavis by the 'advance of civilization' represented by American beauty parlours. There may have been 'archness' in Wells's account, Leavis wrote, but there was no irony. Leavis could point out Wells's factual errors because he had read the *New Republic*'s exposés of the 'Beauty Racket' and Jonathan Norton Leonard's *The Tragedy of Henry Ford*, just out from Putnam and priced at three dollars—so familiar only to those who kept abreast of American developments—whereas Wells 'swallowed with completely uncritical innocence the official Ford legend'.[65]

More pernicious than any particular claim was Wells's general complacency about technological advance and economic growth. Ordinary citizens were similarly blinkered. Since 'optimism favours free spending', consumption thrived on such complacency. As a result, optimism and 'uplift' were '[t]he prevailing note of advertising', Leavis and Thompson observed in *Culture and Environment*. With the onset of the Great Depression, they wrote, optimism became a 'public duty' in the United States, making it harder to reckon with the problems of capitalism. The same pattern of self-deception worked itself out in private life, in Britain as well as America. Cheerfulness that refused to recognize reality was 'a habit of cowardice and irresponsibility taking itself for virtue, and so the more insidiously corrupting and debilitating'. The other ethos 'intimately related to the idea of Progress' was the culture of service embodied,

[62] F. R. Leavis, '"Babbitt Buys the World"', *Scrutiny* 1/1 (May 1932): 83. The quotation from Mowrer was added as an epigraph when this piece was reprinted in *For Continuity*; the title was not explained in the *Scrutiny* version.

[63] F. R. Leavis, 'Two Cultures? The Significance of Lord Snow', in *Nor Shall My Sword*, 57.

[64] Leavis, 'Under Which King, Bezonian?', 207.

[65] Leavis, '"Babbitt Buys the World"', 80, 82–3.

for instance, by Middletown's Rotary Club, which Leavis and Thompson
described as an 'attempt to give the Good-mixer-Business ethos a moral
and religious sanction in the name of "Service"'.[66]

The Rotarian good-mixer, Babbitt, and Wells were too sanguine about
the relationship between work, wealth, and happiness. Leavis thought it
quite possible that material progress hollowed out human life rather than
enriched it. Considering the problem in *Culture and Environment*, he and
Thompson quoted *Middletown* on how advertising, magazines, movies,
and radio were 'rapidly changing habits of thought as to what things are
essential for living and multiplying optional occasions for spending
money'. These changes were facilitated by '[i]nstallment buying, which
turns wishes into horses overnight'—a striking example of the way *Middletown* worked within a homiletic register as well as a social-scientific
one. In 1890, the quoted passage continued, 'Middletown appears to
have lived on a series of plateaus as regards standard of living', and there
was 'more contentment with relative arrival'; now, 'every one lives on a
slope from any point of which desirable things belonging to people all the
way to the top are in view'.[67]

Clearly, Leavis and Thompson concluded, there were problems with an
understanding of progress in which a rise in the standard of living coincided with a fall in contentment. Too many serious questions, Leavis said
more than once, were 'waived by that phrase, "the standard of living," as
the economists use it'.[68] A valid conception of the good life 'must take
account of quality of living as well as of material goods and services'.[69]
Leisure was a site where 'quality of living' could be assessed. In the Los
Angeles described by Jan and Cora Cordon, the 'social arts' had decayed to
the point that when individuals gather it is 'to escape from their loneliness
and the emptiness of their lives'. The Gordons' *Star-Dust in Hollywood* 'will
come in very useful' in explaining this point to the young, *Culture and
Environment* advised. *Middletown*, as a systematic study, bore out 'the impression conveyed by *Star-Dust in Hollywood* (and by *Babbitt*)'.[70]

As urban America exemplified the future, so Sturt's rural England
marked a wholeness that has been lost.[71] In the pre-suburban Surrey
evoked in Sturt's books, leisure was scant but unnecessary, because work
was meaningful. The wheelwrights took pride in their craft and their

---

[66] Leavis and Thompson, *Culture and Environment*, 57–9; Lynd and Lynd,
Middletown, 88.
[67] Lynd and Lynd, *Middletown*, 82–3; Leavis and Thompson, *Culture and Environment*, 62.
[68] F. R. Leavis, 'The Literary Mind', *Scrutiny* 1/1 (June 1932): 30; Leavis, 'What's
Wrong with Criticism?', 135.
[69] Leavis and Thompson, *Culture and Environment*, 62–3.
[70] Ibid., 64–6.   [71] Ibid., 3; Leavis, 'A Serious Artist', 178.

hard-won knowledge of timber and its ways. The work engaged 'their brains, imagination, conscience, sense of beauty and fitness—their personalities', Leavis and Thompson explained. Skilled workers were not the only ones whose work fulfilled them. The rural jack-of-all-trades Turner had a rich understanding of agriculture, the seasons, and wild birds and animals that enabled him to learn from and be stimulated by what he encountered on his round. In contrast, the village's young coal-carter performed only one kind of work. This 'doubles the productivity of a day's work', but that labour was monotonous, required 'but little skill' or 'local information and useful lore', and provided no opportunities for 'gather[ing] such a store for his own pleasure'. Similarly, though the old-fashioned wheelwright's work was more demanding physically, it was 'not nearly so exhausting yet tedious as machinery and "speeding-up" have since made it for his mind and temper'. Modern work made leisure 'necessary as it was not before', but at the same time incapacitated workers for recreation that would 'make them feel self-fulfilled and make life significant, dignified and satisfying (see [Stuart Chase's] *Men and Machines*, p. 181, which elucidates this point)'.[72]

As the reference to Chase suggests, Leavis and Thompson were making an argument about modern times that was also made in other modern places. For all the differences in tone and tradition, the argument in *Culture and Environment* is structurally very similar to Siegfried Kracauer's 1930 ethnography of Berlin white-collar workers' days and nights: empty leisure was the supplement of increasingly meaningless labour; there was a dialectic of standardized work and standardized leisure.[73] J. B. Priestley, the popular novelist whom *Scrutiny* counted among the enemy, observed in *English Journey* (1934) that most of the work in the 'new England' of Sloughs and Banburys 'is rapidly becoming standardized... and its leisure is being handed over to standardization too'.[74] *Middletown* made the same claim, but standardization did not become the master trope it did in Kracauer's work or *Scrutiny* cultural criticism.[75] In the writings of the *Scrutiny* circle, the term nearly always slipped its moorings and glided out into metaphor. The chapter on the subject in *Culture and Environment* started with a token example of good standardization—fire-hose couplings—then swiftly moved on to 'the possible relation between

[72] Leavis and Thompson, *Culture and Environment*, 69, 70, 71, 75, 77.

[73] Siegfried Kracauer, *The Salaried Masses: Duty and Distraction in Weimar Germany*, trans. Quintin Hoare (London: Verso, 1998), 88–9, 91–3.

[74] J. B. Priestley, *English Journey: Being a Rambling but Truthful Account of What One Man Saw and Heard and Felt during a Journey through England during the Autumn of the Year 1933* (1934; Harmondsworth: Penguin, 1977), 378.

[75] Lynd and Lynd, *Middletown*, 47, 249, 309.

standardization of commodities and standardization of persons'. That this relation existed was suggested by 'what we have seen of advertising' and, again, by Lewis's *Babbitt*, which Leavis and Thompson quoted: 'The large national advertisers fixed . . . what he believed to be his individuality. Those standard advertised wares—tooth-pastes, socks, tyres . . . were his symbols and proofs of excellence; at first the signs, then the substitutes, for joy and passion and wisdom.'[76] Edward J. O'Brien, the expatriate American whose book on the short story was often cited by the Leavises and Thompson, remarked that because industry produced objects that were 'all alike', it was in the manufacturers' interests 'that the consumers of these objects shall be all alike, as otherwise they might not choose to consume the standardized article'.[77]

The machine in an age of mass production was *Scrutiny*'s governing metaphor for modernity. The mass press and the 'best-seller' (a word that became common in the 1920s) were brought under the rubric of 'mass production' and 'the machine age', even though their emergence might have been more plausibly explained with reference to the logic of capital accumulation or the cash nexus. In *Middletown*, the Lynds emphasized the tendency of the institutions of the 'credit economy' 'to serve as a repressive agent tending to standardize widening sectors of the habits of the business class—to vote the Republican ticket, to adopt golf as their recreation, and to refrain from "queer," i.e. atypical, behavior'.[78] *Scrutiny* paid little attention to finance, relying instead on homologies between industrial production and tendencies toward 'standardization' in people's tastes and activities. This is what *Scrutiny* owes to the tradition of anti-industrial critique: not the identification of the industrial revolution of the late eighteenth and early nineteenth centuries as the fateful turning point, but the idea that the modern period—whenever one dated it from—was 'the machine age'.

That the twentieth century was 'the machine age' was a commonplace endorsed by people *Scrutiny* deplored (such as the Boston department store proprietor and credit-union promoter Edward A. Filene, whose book title *Successful Living in This Machine Age* was not meant ironically) and those it treated as authorities.[79] O'Brien's book on the short story was entitled *The Dance of the Machines: The American Short Story and the*

[76] Leavis and Thompson, *Culture and Environment*, 32.
[77] Edward J. O'Brien, *The Dance of the Machines: The American Short Story and the Industrial Age* (London: Jonathan Cape, 1929), 75. O'Brien is cited in Leavis and Thompson, *Culture and Environment*, 18, 47, 97.
[78] Lynd and Lynd, *Middletown*, 47, 278.
[79] F. R. Leavis, 'Resolute Optimism, Professional and Professorial', *Scrutiny* 1/3 (December 1932): 300.

Industrial Age; it was conceived as the first volume of a trilogy on the mechanization of American life. For O'Brien, as for the Leavises, machinery had a life of its own that became the logic of civilization at large. 'The machine imposes conformity', O'Brien wrote, 'first of all as an ideal, and then as a social necessity. Its own life depends on conformity, and it relentlessly insists on it.'[80]

The connection between cultural production and manufacturing was axiomatic: it was never spelled out what causal relationship or pattern of elective affinity might explain the purported parallels between the Model T and best-selling novels. F. R. Leavis sketched the way newspapers exemplified the processes of mass production, standardization, and 'levelling-down' by quoting Hamilton Fyfe's biography of Lord Northcliffe. The press baron, Fyfe reported, 'broke down the dignified idea that the conductors of newspapers should appeal to the intelligent few', and appealed instead to 'the unintelligent many.... He did not aim at making opinion less stable, emotion more superficial. He did this, without knowing he did it, because it increased circulation.'[81] (Fyfe's biography was 'worth reading through for its facts, which are made the more significant by the completely uncritical attitude of the author'.)[82] The success of the *Daily Mail* narrowed the horizons of other papers, Leavis argued, quoting Norman Angell—though, again, it was Fyfe who supplied the clincher: 'the *Daily Mail*...had made its way from the kitchen and the butler's pantry of the big country house up to the hall table'.[83]

The same pattern of mass production–standardization–levelling-down could be discerned in popular fiction.[84] The contention that 'mass-production conditions determine the supply of literature' recurred with only slight variations in wording in at least three works by *Scrutiny* writers.[85] The 'periodical-fiction trade' provided Q. D. Leavis in *Fiction and the Reading Public* with a clear example. 'To achieve as large a circulation as possible (to secure the advertiser) the editor sets out to satisfy the common measure of taste, and he cannot (or thinks he cannot) afford to publish any story which fails to conform to type.' Leavis's voracious research led

---

[80] O'Brien, *Dance of the Machines*, 75.

[81] Leavis and Thompson, *Culture and Environment*, 35–7 (the chapter is a redaction of pp. 18–20 of Leavis's 'Mass Civilisation and Minority Culture').

[82] Leavis and Thompson, *Culture and Environment*, 35 n.

[83] Leavis, 'Mass Civilisation and Minority Culture', 19; Leavis and Thompson, *Culture and Environment*, 35.

[84] Leavis and Thompson, *Culture and Environment*, 42–4.

[85] '[M]ass-production conditions determine the supply of literature' (Q. D. Leavis, *Fiction and the Reading Public*, 271); 'mass-production conditions now govern the supply of literature' (F. R. Leavis, 'What's Wrong with Criticism', 137); 'The supply of literature has become an industry subject to the same conditions as the supply of any other commodity' (Anon. [F. R. Leavis], 'The Literary Racket', *Scrutiny* 1/2 [September 1932]: 168).

her into the flourishing genre of guidebooks with titles like *How to Write Saleable Fiction* and *Short Story Writing for Profit*.[86] Combined with her reading of popular fiction and the extensive answers authors wrote to her survey questions, this advice literature gave her a command of the formulaic expectations of editors and publishers—though unlike others in the long line of intellectuals who studied the wares of newsagents in poorer districts, most notably George Orwell, she did not provide a detailed morphology of the cheap tale.[87] By habituating readers to 'certain limited appeals and a certain restricted outlook', periodical fiction had 'spoilt the public for fiction in book form of a more serious nature'. The argument was consistent with Richards's ideas on the consequences of bad art. Later in the book, she advised: 'The reader should have in mind throughout this chapter the account of stock responses in *Practical Criticism*, Part III. Chap. v.'[88] What made this situation different from previous centuries? Leavis did think that the popular literature of the mid-nineteenth century was less bad than 1920s best-sellers, but the essence of her case was that in the past it had been possible for diligent readers to climb the ladder of taste ('the "better" fiction' was serialized alongside sensation fiction 'in the shilling magazines and even in Dickens's twopenny weeklies'), whereas in the twentieth century, when reviewers pandered to anti-intellectual prejudices and new publishing enterprises such as the Book Society exploited the ordinary reader's fear of being confused by highbrow novels, 'the language and methods of the serious novelists are hieroglyphic to the reader of Edgar Wallace or even of Hugh Walpole'.[89]

Standardization made advertising especially important. With little to distinguish between products, advertising became indispensable to commerce.[90] That advertising 'cheats the consumer' by permitting manufacturers to lower the quality of their goods was 'only one of the many charges proved by Mr Chase's books, especially *Your Money's Worth*', Thompson wrote in *Scrutiny*.[91] Chase was sent a copy of *Culture and Environment*,

[86] Leavis, *Fiction and the Reading Public*, 27–32; Christopher Hilliard, *To Exercise Our Talents: The Democratization of Writing in Britain* (Cambridge, Mass.: Harvard University Press, 2006), 20, 83–4, 91–2.
[87] George Orwell, 'Boys' Weeklies' (1940), in *The Collected Essays, Journalism and Letters of George Orwell*, ed. Sonia Orwell and Ian Angus, vol. 1, *An Age Like This, 1920–1940* (Boston: Nonpareil Books, 2000), 460–84.
[88] Leavis, *Fiction and the Reading Public*, 32, 243 n.
[89] Ibid., 158–9; and, on the Book Society and the Book Guild, 22–6. The claim that uneducated readers could graduate from 'bad' fiction to 'good' had some empirical grounding: Leavis read a large number of working-class autodidacts' autobiographies and began writing a book about them. See Leavis, 'What's Wrong with Criticism?', 145.
[90] Leavis and Thompson, *Culture and Environment*, 30; Thompson, 'A Cure for Amnesia', 9.
[91] Thompson, 'Advertising God', 243.

'with our thanks & compliments, as being so much drawn upon'.[92] Now an obscure figure, Chase was once a well-known 'middleman of ideas' (Q. D. Leavis's phrase), brokering economics, sociology, linguistics, and other subjects to a large audience. Before he became a middleman of ideas, Chase was an accountant. In the early 1920s, the Federal Trade Commission let him go after he had investigated dubious accounting practices in the meatpacking industry too diligently (congressional Republicans had pushed for his dismissal). He co-founded the advocacy group Consumers Research; Britain's Consumers' Association, founded in 1957, claimed *Your Money's Worth* as its own point of origin.[93] The wastefulness inherent in an economy shaped by advertising and new forms of competition (the incentive to produce goods that would not last long so that consumers would have to buy replacements, and so on) was a persistent theme of Chase's early books.[94]

The first of these, *The Tragedy of Waste* (1925), was much influenced by Thorstein Veblen, the iconoclastic economist with whom Chase worked for several years after leaving the FTC.[95] *Middletown*, too, bore Veblen's imprint; the Lynds began dating after 'discover[ing] a common interest'

[92] Leavis to Parsons, 19 January 1933, Chatto & Windus archive, CW 53/2; Leavis, 'Complimentary Copies' (1933), Chatto & Windus archive, CW 53/2, Reading. Chase's papers in the Library of Congress include no letters from the Leavises or Thompson. If the archive's holdings are representative of the letters he received, he did not have a great many acquaintances in Britain. One of his British correspondents, though, was C. K. Ogden, the founder of Basic English with whom I. A. Richards collaborated after his early literary-critical phase. Chase had met Ogden earlier in the 1930s and drew heavily on *The Meaning of Meaning* (1936), by Ogden and Richards, as he wrote his popular book on linguistics, *The Tyranny of Words*. Stuart Chase to C. K. Ogden, 23 September 1936; Ogden to Chase, 26 July 1937; Chase to Ogden, 8 June 1937, Stuart Chase papers, MSS15628, box 7, Library of Congress, Washington, DC.
[93] Christopher Beauchamp, 'Getting *Your Money's Worth*: American Models for the Remaking of the Consumer Interest in Britain, 1930s–1960s', in Mark Bevir and Frank Trentmann (eds), *Critiques of Capital in Modern Britain and America Transatlantic Exchanges 1800 to the Present Day* (Basingstoke: Palgrave Macmillan, 2002), 127–8.
[94] On Chase and the 'consumer republicanism' for which he stood, see Charles McGovern, 'Consumption and Citizenship in the United States, 1900–1940', in Susan Strasser, Charles McGovern, and Matthias Judt (eds), *Getting and Spending: European and American Consumer Societies in the Twentieth Century* (Cambridge: Cambridge University Press, 1998), 50–5. See also Norman Silber, 'Chase, Stuart', in John A. Garraty and Mark C. Carnes (eds), *American National Biography*, 24 vols. (New York: Oxford University Press, 1999), 4: 745–7; William Alan Hodson and John Carfora, 'Stuart Chase: Brief Life of a Public Thinker: 1888–1985', *Harvard Magazine*, (September–October 2004, 38–9).
[95] Hodson and Carfora, 'Stuart Chase'; Silber, 'Chase', 745. Chase is not mentioned in Michael Spindler, *Veblen and Modern America: Revolutionary Iconoclast* (London: Pluto Press, 2002) or Elizabeth Watkins Jorgensen and Henry Irvin Jorgensen, *Thorstein Veblen: Victorian Firebrand* (Armonk, NY: M. E. Sharpe, 1999). John Patrick Diggins, *Thorstein Veblen: Theorist of the Leisure Class* (Princeton: Princeton University Press, 1999), 210, refers to him in passing as a writer who took up the idea of 'technocracy', with which Veblen had an attenuated connection, but there is no implication that they actually collaborated.

in his *Theory of the Leisure Class* (1899).[96] Wolf Lepenies remarks offhand-
edly in his book on the rise of sociology that *Scrutiny* treated Veblen 'as
something of a sociological guide'.[97] It took a historian of social science to
notice this, since Veblen was mentioned by name in *Scrutiny* only twice,
both times by Q. D. Leavis.[98] Thompson referred to him in his 1943
book on advertising, but in his earlier phase as an active *Scrutiny* contributor, Thompson's contact with Veblen seems to have been vicarious,
via Chase and the Lynds.[99] All the same, Thompson's cultural criticism,
like Q. D. Leavis's, recalls Veblen in its concern with the incursion of
commercial principles into ever more areas of human life; in its attention
to cultural values as an expression or 'stylization' of social status; and in its
understanding of consumption practices as a central theatre of life under
advanced capitalism, a space where modern personalities and 'modes of
life' were formed.[100]

Veblen's style in *The Theory of the Leisure Class* was to describe the dy-
namics of 'conspicuous consumption' and 'conspicuous leisure' in an in-
sistently straight-faced way. Chase, by contrast, sought to bring the reader
onside so that they could examine the irrationalities of capitalism together. His plain-dealing prose struck a very different note from that of
much *Scrutiny* writing, but he was *Scrutiny*'s most trusted guide to economics and business. More importantly, Thompson and the Leavises followed his argument that modern industry was in the business of
manufacturing demands as well as supplying products.[101] In the Wonderland of modern consumerism, Chase wrote, 'one no longer goes out to
buy as his needs arise, the market comes to him and creates needs for
him'.[102] Commenting on the ad men's speeches at Atlantic City, Thompson

[96] Igo, *Averaged American*, 32, 40. Chase reviewed *Middletown* in *The Nation*, declar-
ing: 'no such knowledge of how the average American community works has ever been
packed between the covers of one book...Who touches this book touches the heart of
America' (ibid., 23–4).
[97] Lepenies, *Between Literature and Science*, 185.
[98] Even Mulhern, who is highly attentive to questions of political economy, makes only
a few references to Q. D. Leavis's explicit mentions of Veblen. *Moment of 'Scrutiny'*, 90,
311. Leavis spoke of 'look[ing] with Veblen's eyes at this "mode of life"' in her essay on the
complementarity of George Gordon's 'social standards' and his 'conventional literary and
cultural values' (Q. D. Leavis, 'The Discipline of Letters: A Sociological Note,' *Scrutiny*
12/1 [winter 1943]: 18). Compare the treatment of 'The Higher Learning as an Expression
of the Pecuniary Culture' in Thorstein Veblen, *The Theory of the Leisure Class: An Economic Study in the Evolution of Institutions* (New York: Macmillan, 1899), ch. 14.
[99] Denys Thompson, *Voice of Civilisation: An Enquiry into Advertising* (1943; London:
Frederick Muller, 1947), 123–4.
[100] Leavis, 'Discipline of Letters', 18.
[101] Leavis and Thompson, *Culture and Environment*, 112–13.
[102] Stuart Chase and F. J. Schlink, *Your Money's Worth: A Study in the Waste of the Consumer's Dollar* (New York: Macmillan, 1927), 25. On Chase's *Alice in Wonderland* references,
see R. O'Malley and D. Thompson, *English for the Living* (London: Methuen, 1949), 21.

said that anyone who thought Britain was putting up a good fight against 'Americanization' should read the account in that volume of 'how the British public was made "raisin-conscious" '.[103]

Advertising in print media depends on images as well as words, of course, but prosy advertisements with paragraph-length appeals to consumers were common in interwar Britain, and it was these that the *Scrutiny* group examined. Apart from an occasional reference to 'pictures...of Strong Silent Vicars and Clean Sporting Aristocrats' or a classroom exercise in explaining 'the use of valets, butlers and "superior"-looking manservants in advertisements', the Leavises' and Thompson's scrutiny of advertising focused on the copy.[104] For instance:

> We have no illusions—our Beaulieu cigars are not made for the million. We do not want gigantic sales—they would make the name Beaulieu meaningless. For how can a few handcraftsmen and a small family, blessed with a genius in blending which is hereditary, hope to cater for the many? They prefer to keep their standards intact and enjoy the privilege of ministering to the perpetual pleasure of the discerning few.

This advertisement formed the basis of a teaching exercise in *Culture and Environment*. Pupils were directed: 'Classify this advertisement.'[105] The first chapter of the book identified six common types of appeal that advertisements make, and recommended teachers ask their pupils to classify and analyse particular specimens. The Beaulieu cigars advertisement was an example of category (*e*), 'Getting it Both Ways...Hobnobbing with the toffs and running with the herd.'[106] Most of the appeals Leavis and Thompson identified in this chapter involved social aspirations and anxieties: 'Fear of Social Non-conformity', ' "Good Form" Pressure', 'The Snob Appeal'.

The chapter on advertising mixed literary and cultural criticism more than the rest of the book, teasing out the effects of the self-awareness of this tobacco advertisement, for instance:

> 'Yes, it's the best I've ever smoked. But it's deuced expensive.' 'What's the tuppence extra? And anyway, you get it back—*an*' more. Burns clean and slow—that's the typical twist,—gives it the odd look. Cute scientific dodge. You see, they experimented....' 'Oh! cut the cackle, and give us another fill. You talk like an advertisement.'
> Thereafter peace and a pipe of Two Quakers.

Here, Leavis and Thompson observed, the 'self-consciousness that the educated may be presumed to have about reading advertisements seriously

[103] Thompson, 'Advertising God', 242. See also Leavis and Thompson, *Culture and Environment*, 26–8.
[104] Leavis and Thompson, *Culture and Environment*, 16, 111.
[105] Ibid., 111.   [106] Ibid., 15.

is cunningly provided for'. Appeals of 'even greater subtlety' were made in advertisements directed at 'the consciously intelligent and enlightened', the readers of *The Spectator* and *The New Statesman*.[107]

Scrutiny contributors found many connections between advertisers' prose and that of other writers. Both advertising and fiction moulded 'the standards and ideals that direct the efforts of "the man in the street"', and their styles were converging. There could be no better illustration of 'the magazine outlook of modern fiction', wrote Q. D. Leavis in a passage reprinted in *Culture and Environment*, than Arnold Bennett's *Imperial Palace* (1930), which was full of millionaires, glamorous women, and 'bluff man-of-the-world horse-sense masquerading as psychology and insight'.[108] Bennett was also on Thompson's mind when he remarked that it was 'no coincidence that novelists and journalists are often copywriters; they use the same language, *i.e.*, promote the same attitudes, the same ways of living and thinking'.[109] The parallels between fiction and advertising were partly a consequence of the commercial logic of mass culture, but they also reflected the fact that many of the tricks of advertising copy had been developed by novelists and essayists. Copywriters, Thompson reported, were encouraged to learn from the style and emotional appeal of the Bible, Robert Burns, Rudyard Kipling, C. E. Montague, and especially Robert Louis Stevenson.[110]

What lessons did Stevenson teach advertisers? Thompson explored the question in his contribution to *Determinations*, 'Our Debt to Lamb'. Stevenson, as essayist, was the inheritor of the light, jocular essay pioneered by Charles Lamb. When uneducated people tried to write impressively, they resorted to 'the affectation, archaisms, circumlocution, allusions, puns and other tokens of immaturity put into currency by Lamb'. This literary 'bag of tricks' proved helpful to writers 'who needed something impressive to conceal their own indigence of mind': Stevenson, for example, who 'drivels like this: "Cities given, the problem was to light them. How to conduct individual citizens about the burgess-warren, when once heaven had withdrawn its leading luminary?"'[111] The genre of the 'familiar' essay, as Chris Baldick calls it, with its 'nonchalantly informal, even defiantly trivial, tone', flourished in the first few decades of the twentieth century.[112] Thompson

---

[107] Leavis and Thompson, *Culture and Environment*, 16–18, 117.
[108] Leavis, *Fiction and the Reading Public*, 197–202 (quotations from 199); Leavis and Thompson, *Culture and Environment*, 53–6.
[109] Thompson, 'Advertising God', 244.
[110] Ibid., 241–2, 243–4; Denys Thompson, 'Our Debt to Lamb', in F. R. Leavis (ed.), *Determinations: Critical Essays* (London: Chatto & Windus, 1934), 210.
[111] Thompson, 'Our Debt to Lamb', 207, 209–10.
[112] Chris Baldick, *The Modern Movement*, vol. 10 of *The Oxford English Literary History*, ed. Jonathan Bate (Oxford: Oxford University Press, 2004), 254. See also Caroline

argued that the line of descent that began with Lamb and ran through Stevenson and then G. K. Chesterton, Hilaire Belloc, A. A. Milne, and E. V. Lucas and on into advertisers' prose terminated in politicians' speeches and 'schoolboy essays, which are liable to talk about the "big things of life"'.[113] This 'decay' of language was not confined to phenomena at the margins of culture (schoolboy essays, for instance). And because language was the medium or site of culture, the decay of language meant the decay of life. Hence Thompson's claim, in the cascade of contentions quoted earlier, that 'the idiom of newspaper and best-seller and advertising was destructive of fine language *and of fine living*'.[114] We come back to Pound. Thompson approvingly quoted the verdict of *How to Read*: 'When...the application of word to thing goes rotten, *i.e.*, becomes slushy and inexact, or excessive or bloated, the whole machinery of social and of individual thought and order goes to pot.'[115]

Yet our 'chief debt to Lamb', Thompson went on, was not his prose style but the bond he struck up with the reader. The *Essays of Elia* 'flatter...the man who does as he likes, reassuring him that he's right to preserve his irrationalities, foibles and prejudices', which was why they came into their own in the 'breezily democratic' twentieth century. Lamb's essays, Thompson noted, were not reprinted in his lifetime: he 'owes his canonization to the heartier journalists and professors of the last thirty years'. Thompson concluded 'Our Debt to Lamb' by placing those hearty journalistic critics in a continuum with Lamb and his epigones. Each cultivated a 'fake personality'—a jolly, anti-intellectual, materialistic persona that chummed up to readers and did nothing to ruffle their complacency. Such determined good humour discredited genuine standards and 'serious art'. The complement of the fake personality was a conception of literature as 'uplift', 'unrelated to living'.[116]

D. H. Lawrence was often waiting in the wings when Scrutineers used the words 'living' and 'life'. The depreciation of Lawrence by 'essayist' critics on the Sunday papers furnished Thompson with an illustration of the way this tradition blocked the reading public's access to serious art.

Pollentier, '"Everybody's Essayist": On Middles and Middlebrows', in Kate Macdonald (ed.), *The Masculine Middlebrow, 1880–1950: What Mr Miniver Read* (Basingstoke: Palgrave Macmillan, 2011), 119–34.

[113] Thompson, 'Advertising God', 244. See also Leavis and Thompson, *Culture and Environment*, 59; 'Criticism in Practice: V: Part "B" Set by Denys Thompson', *Use of English* 2/1 (1950): 33–4; L. C. Knights, 'Scrutiny of Examinations', *Scrutiny* 2/2 (September 1933): 155–7.

[114] Thompson, 'A Cure for Amnesia', 5–6 (emphasis added).

[115] Thompson, 'Advertising God', 244; Ezra Pound, *How to Read* (London: Desmond Harmsworth, 1931), 17–18.

[116] Thompson, 'Our Debt to Lamb', 206–7, 210–11, 212, 214.

Lawrence's writing, and his example, also informed *Scrutiny*'s analysis of the menace of mass civilization. Leavis and Thompson ended their chapter on 'Advertising, Fiction and the Currency of National Life' with a quotation from *Lady Chatterley's Lover* about the 'the way our sympathy flows and recoils'. This was what 'really determines our lives'. A good novel could lead our sympathy into new places and makes us 'recoil from things gone dead'. But it could also 'excite spurious sympathies and re-coils, mechanical and deadening to the psyche'.[117] This was the primary evil of advertising and the culture industry: the way they corroded feeling and the sorts of life people desire.

Lawrence was a touchstone for the early *Scrutiny* not so much for his novels as for the exemplary intelligence, perception, and openness of the often informal literary criticism on display in the posthumous volumes of letters, essays, and reviews—and for the fact of his existence.[118] Reviewing the *Letters*, Leavis said that they confirmed 'one's sense that Lawrence was greater than his writings'.[119] He, 'more than anyone else in our time, makes it possible to cherish some faith in the future of humanity'.[120] Law-rence 'represents the splendid human vitality, the creative faith, and the passionate sense of responsibility'—a consciousness of interconnectedness that Leavis elsewhere described as Lawrence's 'religious sense'.[121] Leavis's early pamphlet on Lawrence's work and *Culture and Environment* quoted a succession of passages, chiefly from *Lady Chatterley's Lover* and 'Notting-ham and the Mining Countryside', in which Lawrence spoke of true and false feelings. Spontaneity, genuine emotion and desires for beauty were stifled by 'mechanical' civilization and the deadening operations of its education system.[122] Leavis summed up in the emergent *Scrutiny* idiom: 'Civilised life is certainly threatened with impoverishment by education

[117] Leavis and Thompson, *Culture and Environment*, 55–6.
[118] MacKillop, *F. R. Leavis*, 183–4; F. R. Leavis, 'D. H. Lawrence and Professor Irving Babbitt', *Scrutiny* 1/3 (December 1932): 273–9; Leavis, 'The Wild, Untutored Phoenix', *Scrutiny* 6/3 (December 1937): 352–8. By 1932, Leavis was highly critical of Eliot (though still indebted to him), and his reviews of Lawrence's *Letters* and *Phoenix* contrasted Law-rence's intelligence with the limitations of some of those with more 'expensive' educations, such as Eliot and Irving Babbitt, who taught Eliot at Harvard and to some extent functioned as a rhetorical proxy for him. Leavis's *Scrutiny* reviews of both volumes had as much to say against Eliot and Eliot's views of Lawrence as they did about *Phoenix* and the *Letters*.
[119] Leavis, 'D. H. Lawrence and Professor Irving Babbitt', *Scrutiny* 1/3 (December 1932): 274–5; F. R. Leavis, 'Reminiscences of D. H. Lawrence', *Scrutiny* 1/2 (September 1932): 190.
[120] Leavis, 'Lawrence and Babbitt', 278.
[121] F. R. Leavis, 'D. H. Lawrence' in *For Continuity*, 140; Leavis, 'Lawrence and Bab-bitt', 278. See also Bernard Bergonzi, *Exploding English: Criticism, Theory, Culture* (Oxford: Clarendon Press, 1990), 35.
[122] Leavis, 'D. H. Lawrence', 137–43; Leavis and Thompson, *Culture and Environment*, 94–8.

based on crude and defective psychology, by standardisation at a low level, and by the inculcation of a cheap and shallow emotional code.'[123] Leavis made explicit the contrast between the work of the culture industry and the ideal that Lawrence embodied in his review of Dos Passos. After quoting with unaffected horror Ward Moorehouse's remark that he is running an advertising campaign 'from the human interest angle...pity and tears, you understand', Leavis exclaimed: 'can a hundred D. H. Lawrences preserve even the idea of emotional sincerity against the unremitting, pervasive, masturbatory manipulations of "scientific" Publicity, and, what is the same thing, commercially supplied popular art?'[124]

'[M]uch of modern literature, in particular the novels of D. H. Lawrence', one observer wrote in 1939, 'represents the assertion of basic human desires against the cramping defensiveness of modern life.' The sentiment would have been at home in *Scrutiny*, but in fact it was written by Robert S. Lynd. Novelists, he observed elsewhere in the same book on the place of social science in American culture, provided 'insights into our culture' that went beyond the claims of sociology and 'open up significant hypotheses for study'.[125] *Scrutiny*'s reviewer agreed.[126] In *Scrutiny*, the work of American social scientists such as Lynd provided empirical evidence and analytical frameworks for understanding modern life, but it was poets and novelists who were its ultimate interpreters, just as, for L. C. Knights, '"facts about" a particular period' could not match the depth of insight about a culture that its literature could.[127] *Scrutiny* widened the remit of literary study without decentring it—without diminishing the import of the words on the page. An 'English school' was the humane centre of Leavis's ideal university, and a training in how to read literature was the privileged way of understanding, and resisting, the modern environment.

[123] Leavis, 'D. H. Lawrence', 143.   [124] Leavis, 'A Serious Artist', 175.
[125] Robert S. Lynd, *Knowledge for What? The Place of Social Science in American Culture* (1939; Princeton: Princeton University Press, 1948), 91 n. 178.
[126] C. E. Lucas, 'Science and Values', *Scrutiny* 10/3 (January 1942): 319–20.
[127] Knights, 'Shakespeare and Profit Inflations', 57. Compare Leavis, 'Luddites?', 81: 'It is the great novelists above all who give us our social history; compared with what is done in *their* work—their creative work—the histories of the professional social historian seem empty and unenlightening'; and Q. D. Leavis to Pocock, 10 August 1971, Leavis papers, Col 9.59.121, Emmanuel. See further Ortolano, *The Two Cultures Controversy*, 154–9.

3

Origins and Destinations

In December 1954, William Walsh, a lecturer in education at the University of Edinburgh, returned to Downing College to address the Doughty Society on 'The Literary Critic and the Education of an Elite'. Like practically everyone else in attendance, Walsh had been taught by F. R. Leavis, the college literary society's de facto patron. Walsh admitted that 'the idea of an élite was, in many ways, anti-democratic', though he saw some justification for the 'common prejudice against such ideas in the existence of such an intellectual group as the "Bloomsbury" one, which, being a clique unconcerned with the general cultural situation, was a betrayal of the values of a proper élite'. He went on to outline the sort of education appropriate to an élite. Walsh characterized Leavis's 'idea of a University' as a synthesis of Arnold and Coleridge. Leavis would not have agreed, but other aspects of Walsh's talk hewed closely to his own arguments. Echoing *Education and the University*, Walsh held that literary criticism was 'the most living discipline' and that there was 'no value' in the 'idea of a "general" education'. 'The central intelligence and coordinating consciousness could only be prepared for by the discipline of literary criticism.' The discussion after the paper was largely taken up by the question of whether Arnold belonged in 'the great line of English critics', and whether there were 'any grounds for hope. Dr Leavis argued that "Scrutiny" had had a strong influence'.[1]

For thirty years Downing College was the site of Leavis's most direct and practical efforts to educate a critical élite. The college was the institution where he had the most scope to establish an 'English school' of his own design.[2] Leavis built his reputation as a teacher on his supervisions. However well he had prepared, Raymond O'Malley remembered, 'discussion brought

---

[1] Doughty Society minute book, 115–16 (1 December 1954), DCCS/4/4/1/1, Downing. Walsh's paper later formed chapter 4 of his *The Use of Imagination: Educational Thought and the Literary Mind* (London: Chatto & Windus, 1960). The statement about the 'coordinating consciousness' (ibid., 84) is from *Education and the University* and understandably misquoted in the minutes.

[2] For the phrase, see F. R. Leavis, *Education and the University: A Sketch for an 'English School'* (London: Chatto & Windus, 1943).

out implications, layers, references, ironies, simple meanings, that I had missed or misunderstood; his special capacity was always that of bringing out what is "there." . . . There was nearly always this sense of discovery, for teacher as for taught, in the supervisions.'[3] As the Downing school became established, however, Leavis entrusted supervisions to research students or *Scrutiny* collaborators, such as Gordon Cox, Geoffrey Walton, James Smith, Wilfrid Mellers, Ian Doyle, Harold Mason, Geoffrey Strickland, Morris Shapira, and John Newton (who as secretary of the Doughty Society had taken the notes on Walsh's paper). Leavis's own teaching took the form of seminars, which he led as many as four mornings every week.[4]

The seminars could be electrifying, but they were seldom reciprocal. They were billed as discussion groups but 'inclined to monologue'.[5] The notes members took read like collections of Leavis's table talk: 'Shakespeare hasn't written it all down: Dryden always does'; ' "Have read"—an instruction in the perfect imperative tense—. . . the 18th century novels (*Tom Jones, Joseph Andrews, Pamela, Clarissa*)—casually or "in your bath—don't waste time on them." '[6] One pupil of the late 1940s and early 1950s thought that Leavis's 'personal teaching. . . was not by the time I knew it particularly good. He gave no one-to-one tutorials and was not very interested in his pupils or in bringing them out or personally encouraging them.'[7] In Leavis's defence, another Downing undergraduate from the same period remarks that there is 'more than one way of being a good teacher, of which his was inspiring a life-long love of the subject and a suggestive intelligence which planted seeds which it was up to us to nurture both as students and subsequently'.[8]

As we have seen, at Downing Leavis had great latitude in deciding whom to admit to study with him. Nearly all the 335 men who read

[3] Raymond O'Malley, 'Charisma?', in Denys Thompson (ed.), *The Leavises: Recollections and Impressions* (Cambridge: Cambridge University Press, 1984), 55. See also Ronald Duncan, *All Men Are Islands: An Autobiography* (London: Rupert Hart-Davis, 1964), 86–90; D. W. Harding, 'No Compromise', in Thompson (ed.), *The Leavises*, 187–8.

[4] Tony Inglis, untitled essay, *Cambridge Quarterly* 25/4 (1996): 353.

[5] Charles Winder, 'Leavis's Downing Seminars: A Student's Notes', in Ian MacKillop and Richard Storer (eds), *F. R. Leavis: Essays and Documents* (Sheffield: Sheffield Academic Press, 1995), 71, 72; Neil Roberts, ' "Leavisite" Cambridge in the 1960s', in MacKillop and Storer (eds), *F. R. Leavis: Essays and Documents*, 267; Inglis, untitled essay, 354; Brian Cox, *The Great Betrayal* (London: Chapman, 1992), 78. See also Frank Whitehead, 'F. R. Leavis and the Schools', in Thompson (ed.), *The Leavises*, 144; O'Malley, 'Charisma?', 54.

[6] Inglis, untitled essay, 355–7 (quotations from 355); for other examples, see Roberts, ' "Leavisite" Cambridge in the 1960s', 268; Winder, 'Leavis's Downing Seminars', 72–91.

[7] Patrick Harrison, 'Downing after the War', in MacKillop and Storer (eds), *F. R. Leavis: Essays and Documents*, 258.

[8] David Matthews, *Memories of F. R. Leavis* (Bishopstone: Brynmill Press, 2010), 13.

English as undergraduates at Downing between 1932 and 1962 had
deliberately chosen Leavis and he had deliberately chosen them. 'I don't
think anyone ever went to Downing by accident', the director Trevor
Nunn told a fellow alumnus.[9] This chapter analyses the origins and destinations of these undergraduates, their paths into and out of Downing
English. The reconstruction of the cohort is based on college archives. An
admission committee's minute book and the agenda papers of Downing's
Governing Body record the names of applicants awarded places. The college archive also holds admissions books, collections of the matriculation
forms or certificates undergraduates filled out when they began their
studies. These record their names, places of birth, fathers' occupations,
character references, and other information. (The schools attended and
fathers' occupations are listed in the table in the Appendix.)[10] These
records make possible a virtually complete census of Leavis's Downing
pupils' origins. Bringing out the patterns of post-Cambridge careers is a
more impressionistic process. Careers wind across time, in contrast to the
comparatively static variables from which origins can be gauged. Partly
for this reason, the documentation on post-Downing itineraries is more
haphazard, though some of what alumni records, memoirs, letters, and
other miscellaneous texts lack in completeness and comparability they
recoup in texture and depth.

From the outset, Leavis had sought to train an intellectual élite distinct
from the social élite—the Bloomsbury–King's College nexus dependably
served as an example of the wrongness of any assumption of an easy
commerce between the two. In an essay on Leavis and his admirers entitled 'The Rise of the Provincials', Malcolm Bradbury wrote in 1956:
'Many of those who admire Leavis (among whom I count myself)...are
people who have been brought up in lower middle-class households'
characterized by a 'nonconformist strenuousness'.[11] The Oxford grandee
Maurice Bowra made a comparable estimate from a very different social
vantage point. After he finally heard Leavis lecture in 1964, all was

[9] Harrison, 'Downing after the War', 262.
[10] I have not provided omnibus footnotes for judgements involving dozens or hundreds
of individuals: the table should suffice. References to individuals cite their entries in the
admissions books, but they do not name the person in question unless the information is
already in the public domain—a restriction imposed by the Data Protection Act 1998. The
admissions books are cited by their classifications in the Downing College archives
(DCAT/5/1/6-13). Because of the Data Protection Act I was not able to consult the records
relating to men matriculating after 1957, but Kate Thompson, the Downing College archivist, very kindly extracted the relevant information from the later admissions books for me.
Citations of matriculation data from after 1957 take the form 'Admissions book (archivist),
Downing'. For further details about the source of this data, see the note in the Appendix.
[11] Malcolm Bradbury, 'The Rise of the Provincials', *Antioch Review* 6/4 (1956): 471.

revealed. 'He is what our mothers would have called CHAPEL. . . . I can now understand why our miserable undergraduates brought up in Little Bethels and Mount Zions and Bethesdas feel at home with him as with nobody else.'[12] There were indeed Downing English pupils from lower-middle-class backgrounds, and Leavis's writing, especially about the novel, bespoke a Protestant Nonconformism that resonated with some of those students and others outside Cambridge. However, the descriptions quoted are a misleading guide to the demographics of Downing English.

Nearly all of Leavis's pupils came from schools in England: just over a dozen were pupils of Welsh and Scottish schools, and most of the Scots came from the same institution, the Royal High School in Edinburgh. Classifying British schools is notoriously difficult since the school system, inasmuch as it was a system, was almost entirely decentralized until the end of the nineteenth century. Because secondary education was not compulsory until well into the twentieth century, the provision of advanced schooling was often left to wholly independent institutions, or negotiated between central or local government and schools that were largely self-funded and self-governing. Both sorts of school, the independent and the state-subsidized, could count as 'public schools'. In 1944 the Fleming committee on the public schools saw fit to remind readers of its report that the term encompassed hundreds of establishments, not just the 'small number of expensive independent boarding schools' that most people had in mind 'when they speak of a Public School'.[13] These 200-odd 'public schools' supplied Cambridge and Oxford with a majority of their undergraduates.

Downing College was no exception, though the public schools its undergraduates came from were not those famous 'expensive independent boarding schools' such as Eton, Harrow, Winchester, and so on. The only Downing English students schooled at members of the 'Clarendon nine' came from the two day schools in that list of élite public schools: Merchant Taylors', Northwood, and St Paul's, London. (The Downing undergraduate educated at the latter school was the son of Morgan Philips, the General Secretary of the Labour Party, who had started his working life as a collier: not a common profile for public-school boy's father.) It was not that the most famous boarding schools' stress on classics and 'games'

---

[12] Maurice Bowra to G. H. W. Rylands, 24 May 1964, Maurice Bowra papers, Wadham College, Oxford, quoted in Leslie Mitchell, *Maurice Bowra: A Life* (Oxford: Oxford University Press, 2009), 111.
[13] *The Public Schools and the General Education System: Report of the Committee on Public Schools Appointed by the President of the Board of Education in July 1942* (London: HM Stationery Office, 1944), 2.

precluded an interest in English or Leavis's brand of English—William Empson and Leavis's publisher Ian Parsons had been at Winchester together—but those schools tended to have connections with colleges richer and more storied than Downing. The Downing English cohort included several pupils of nineteenth-century foundations regarded as on a par with some of the older public schools: two from Marlborough, one each from Clifton and Wellington.[14] Haileybury, another boarding school founded in the nineteenth century, sent several boys to read English with Leavis.

Many more of the privately educated boys who went up to read English at Downing had come from institutions of a different order: public day schools that placed a premium on academic achievement such as Haberdasher's Aske's school and Dulwich College, and independent schools with more localized reputations, such as Sir Joseph Williamson's Mathematical School in Rochester and the Tiffin School in London. The Forest School in Walthamstow—a 'private', that is, for-profit, school—sent six pupils to Downing, making it one of the most important of Leavis's 'feeder schools'.

Such schools were in a continuum with grammar schools. At a conservative estimate, 45 per cent of Downing English undergraduates came from grammar schools or their close relatives, 'high' schools.[15] Before the reorganization of secondary education by the 1944 legislation often referred to as the Butler Act, a 'grammar school' could have been a county or borough institution administered by the local education authority, or a self-governing institution with its own endowment. Between 1902 and 1944, many of those independent schools became partly funded by central or local government ('direct-grant' and 'maintained' were the respective labels), in return for which they were supposed to offer a quarter of their places for free to poorer children who performed well in scholarship examinations. March Grammar was one such school, and six of the eight alumni it sent to Downing to read English were sons of manual workers (a slate-layer, a signalman, an agricultural labourer, a chargeman tuner, an engine driver, and a painter,

---

[14] Ross McKibbin, *Classes and Cultures: England, 1918–1951* (Oxford: Oxford University Press, 1998), 235. Leavis's pupil Brian Worthington became a teacher at Clifton, and arranged for Q. D. Leavis to visit the school regularly in the 1970s. Q. D. Leavis to Brian Worthington, 16 November 1973, Q. D. Leavis papers, GCPP Leavis 2/1/2, Girton.

[15] One hundred and forty out of 313. These figures exclude seminary graduates and those whose secondary education took place outside Britain. I have counted the Perse, Bemrose, and St Albans as 'grammar schools' because they had the word in their names at one time or another. I have also included the City of Norwich and Oldershaw schools as well. The tally would be higher if it included schools casually described as grammar schools, such as the Catholic schools John Fisher or St Illtyd's, Cardiff. As I say above, the categories were elastic.

decorator, and plumber).[16] Another government-supported school was the Perse in Cambridge, which Leavis himself attended on a local education authority scholarship.[17]

The word 'grammar' floated in and out of the name of the Perse. Schools without the phrase 'grammar school' in their names might nevertheless be regarded as such. The expression signalled academic selectivity and rigour. So did 'high school', a term sometimes used interchangeably with 'grammar school'.[18] Many girls' grammar schools were called high schools in part to distinguish them from the boys' schools, but there were also co-educational and boys-only high schools, which educated a significant number of future Downing undergraduates: Chingford County High School, West Leeds High School, Cambridge and County High School, Scarborough Boys High School, Aldershot County High School. Muriel Bradbrook described Oldershaw in Wallasey, which she had attended with her younger brothers Horace and Frank, both of whom went on to read English at Downing, as a 'northern high school'.[19] The exemplar was the Royal High School, Edinburgh. Acknowledging the paradigmatic status of The Edinburgh School, the principal secondary schools in Scottish cities were named high schools when they were founded or reorganized in the 1860s; at the same time the Nottingham Free Grammar School became the Nottingham High School.[20] Some high schools, including the Royal itself, received state funding.[21]

In 1948, after the provisions of the Education Act had been implemented, fee-paying places disappeared from most grammar schools, and places were allotted solely on the basis of results in the eleven-plus examinations. Some direct-grant schools became completely self-supporting; most grammar schools became government schools.[22] Grammar schools were depicted as the agencies of social mobility in post-war Britain, though in actuality middle-class families were the greatest beneficiaries.[23] The

---

[16] DCAT/5/1/7, pp. 50, 122; DCAT 5/1/8, p. 166; DCAT 5/1/9, pp. 57, 82; DCAT/5/1/10, p. 165, Downing. All six completed their schooling before the Butler Act's provisions affecting grammar school places came into force.

[17] Ian MacKillop, *F. R. Leavis: A life is Criticism* (London: Allan Lane, 1995), 32–3; J. M. Gray, *A History of the Perse School Cambridge* (Cambridge: Bowes & Bowes, 1921), ch. 8.

[18] See the description of Paddington and Maida Vale High School as 'a London girls' grammar school' in Richard E. Gross (ed.), *British Secondary Education: Overview and Appraisal* (London: Oxford University Press, 1965), iii.

[19] Muriel Bradbrook, untitled essay in Ronald Hayman (ed.), *My Cambridge* (1977; London: Robson Books, 1986), 39.

[20] *OED*, s.v. 'school' n¹.

[21] McKibbin, *Classes and Cultures*, 237.

[22] Frances Stevens, *The Living Tradition: The Social and Educational Assumptions of the Grammar School* (1960; London: Hutchinson, 1972), 31.

[23] The typical pattern of 'educational expansion' in Britain has been that 'though the fastest *rates* of growth almost always accrue to the working class, the greatest absolute

instrument of the eleven-plus could not render the cultural advantages of a middle-class upbringing wholly irrelevant to performance in the exams, and middle-class parents no longer had to pay for their children to get a grammar-school education. (At the same time, however, there was a movement of middle-class children into the public schools, as parents worried that an influx of working-class children would lower the social tone of the grammar schools.)[24] Nevertheless, it was the grammar school more than any other British institution that was looked to as the potential engine of what was later called 'meritocracy'.[25] The heyday of the grammar schools, from the late 1940s until their progressive replacement by comprehensives in the 1960s, is often seen as Leavis's educational moment.[26] 'The ethos of the Downing group', wrote Bradbrook, a seasoned faculty and college administrator, 'was suited to the early years of the Butler Education Act, the arrival of the meritocracy'.[27] '[M]ost of Dr Leavis's followers' at Oxford, reported an undergraduate there in the 1950s, 'seem to be grammar school boys'.[28]

Counting the number of grammar-school boys entering Leavis's English school cannot, by itself, make it possible to assess the impact of the 1944 legislation, since some grammar schools were mostly fee-paying before 1948 and free thereafter: comparing the number of grammar-school boys reading English with Leavis before and after the Butler Act is not comparing like terms. Using the records of their fathers' occupations as a proxy for social class, however, we can gauge the impact of the meritocratic moment on the undergraduate cohort. Of course, class cannot always be satisfactorily read off occupation, and blanket designations such

increments of opportunity go to the service class'. A. H. Halsey, A. F. Heath, and J. M. Ridge, *Origins and Destinations: Family, Class, and Education in Modern Britain* (Oxford: Clarendon Press, 1980), 188.

[24] McKibbin, *Classes and Cultures*, 241–3.

[25] Brian Jackson and Dennis Marsden, *Education and the Working Class: Some General Themes Raised by a Study of 88 Working-Class Children in a Northern Industrial City* (1962; Harmondsworth: Penguin, 1966); Flann Campbell, *Eleven-Plus and All That: The Grammar School in a Changing Society* (London: Watts, 1956); Stevens, *Living Tradition*.

[26] Michael Bell, 'F. R. Leavis', in A. Walton Litz, Louis Menand, and Lawrence Rainey (eds), *The Cambridge History of Literary Criticism*, vol. 7, *Modernism and the New Criticism* (Cambridge: Cambridge University Press, 2000), 392; Francis Mulhern, 'Culture and Authority', *Critical Quarterly* 37/1 (1995): 84. See also Colin Evans, *English People: The Experience of Teaching and Learning English in British Universities* (Buckingham: Open University Press, 1993), 134–5.

[27] M. C. Bradbrook, ' "Nor Shall My Sword": The Leavises Mythology', in Thompson (ed.), *The Leavises*, 36.

[28] John Vaizey, 'The Public Schools', in Hugh Thomas (ed.), *The Establishment: A Symposium* (London: Anthony Blond, 1959), 34. Vaizey was reporting what an undergraduate told him. An economist trained at Cambridge, Vaizey had been 'on the fringe' of the *Scrutiny* movement. See John Vaizey, untitled essay in Hayman (ed.), *My Cambridge*, 129; John Vaizey, 'Scrutiny and Education', *Essays in Criticism* 14/1 (1964): 36–42.

as 'civil servant' or 'clerk' can mask large differences in status.[29] Even the distinction between waged workers and such low-grade capitalists as newsagents and garage owners is complicated by the fact that the latter, too, were enmeshed in the culture of working-class communities.

The following comparison of the social origins of 1930s Downing undergraduates with their post-Butler counterparts therefore specifies occupations and explains its judgements rather than presenting unclothed numbers. (Readers can also compare the claims in the text with the table in the Appendix.) The comparison is between two groups: those who began reading English from the year Leavis arrived at Downing, 1932, until the eve of the Second World War; and those who started between 1955 and 1962, when Leavis formally retired. The Butler Act took several years to come into force, and direct-grant schools had several years to decide whether to convert themselves to fully government-funded and government-controlled schools.[30] A 'grammar-school boy' who matriculated in 1955 should have started his secondary education after the Butler Act's access and funding rules were in force.

Fifty-eight men began reading English at Downing between 1932 and 1939.[31] Eight of them had fathers in 'working-class' occupations. Five or six were skilled manual workers: a builder, a chargeman tuner, a slate-layer, a tailor, an engine-driver, and an outfitter, the last of these being a retail worker as well as—or after having paid dues as—a manual worker. (Throughout this list, one can sense the care with which their sons added the prefix 'master' to the occupation recorded on the certificate: master tailor, master butcher, master hairdresser.) One undergraduate's father was a postman who had previously worked on trams and been an enlisted soldier.[32] Another was a

---

[29] See Daniel I. Greenstein, 'The Junior Members, 1900–1990' in Brian Harrison (ed.), *The History of the University of Oxford*, vol. 8, *The Twentieth Century* (1994; Oxford: Clarendon Press, 1995), esp. 54–5 n. 36. Greenstein's forensic account of the origins and destinations of Oxford students and the massive database on which it rests unfortunately have no Cambridge equivalents. On the nature and scope of the Oxford project, see Daniel I. Greenstein, 'Standard, Meta-Standard: A Framework for Coding Occupational Data', *Historical Social Research* 16 (1991): 6–12.

[30] Thomas Hinde, *A Great Day School in London: A History of King's College School* (London: James & James, 1994), 91–2.

[31] This figure excludes several Americans who had already completed undergraduate degrees and Catholic priests enrolling for Cambridge BAs after completing their seminary training. Fathers' occupations are available for all 59 of those educated wholly or partly in Britain and reading English for their first post-secondary qualification. One matriculation document for one of these undergraduates (number 13 on the list) provides no information about his father other than that the father was dead, but this man, Ronald Duncan, wrote a memoir that goes into detail about his family. Duncan, *All Men Are Islands*.

[32] This was D. J. Enright's father. The admissions book calls him a postman; Enright elaborated on his family background in a letter to Richard Hoggart after the publication of the latter's *The Uses of Literacy*. DCAT 5/1/8, p. 134, Downing; Enright to Hoggart, 12 March 1957, Richard Hoggart papers, 3/11/313, Sheffield.

warehouseman: unskilled work, but possibly supervisory. All up, 13.8 per cent of those admitted in the 1930s were of working-class parentage.

The proportion was sharply higher in the later group. Between 1955 and 1962, ninety-three men accepted places to read English for a first degree at Downing.[33] The matriculation documents for four of those ninety-three are silent or inarticulate on the question of the father's occupation. Twenty-seven of the remaining eighty-nine undergraduates, or 30.3 per cent, had fathers employed in manual jobs or other working-class occupations.[34] Again, skilled tradesmen were represented heavily: among them were two fitters, a turner, a cabinet maker, a watchmaker, an intertype operator, a baker, a chef, a signwriter-decorator. Like the outfitter-cum-shopkeeper, a number of these men had become small businessmen and employers. Others, too, were small retailers or managers who would have qualified as 'petit bourgeois' for some observers but were nevertheless anchored in trades or institutions of local working-class life: an ironmonger and house-furnisher, the manager of a men's outfitting shop, a garage proprietor, and two grocers—one a 'master grocer', the other a 'greengrocer (shop manager)', possibly running the shop for someone else. Several had fathers in the police, armed forces, or other arms of the state. There were a few unskilled workers: a surface labourer in a colliery, a printer's machine minder. Even if we leave out the grocers, the garage owner, the outfitting shop manager who is not explicitly identified as a master of his trade, and the solitary 'music hall artiste', the proportion of undergraduates from working-class families at Downing from 1955 was still much higher than it was in the 1930s: the total falls from 27 to 22 and the percentage from 30.3 to 24.7.[35]

---

[33] Again, this figure excludes priests and people who had completed undergraduate degrees overseas (in the United States and Kenya). It also excludes the man educated at a French *lycée*.

[34] A full list (again, detached from the undergraduates' names on account of the Data Protection Act): surface labourer, colliery; printer's machine minder; master mariner; market-stall holder; warrant officer, Metropolitan Police; police sergeant; WRA HMS *Vernon*; regional fuel inspector; baker; chef; music hall artiste; armaments fitter; fitter in aircraft factory; cabinet maker; greengrocer; master grocer; ironmonger and house finisher; motor mechanic; motor trader and garage proprietor; manager of men's outfitting shop; hosiery warehouse manager; intertype operator; patternmaker; watchmaker; leathercroft instructor; turner; tool factor. I am treating 'tool factor' as a working-class job, though this is open to debate. The *OED* definition of 'factor' that seems most pertinent is a Sheffield and Birmingham usage: 'a trader who buys hardware goods from the workman or "little master" by whom they are made, usually causing his own trade-mark to be stamped upon them'. *OED*, s.v. 'factor', n, I.4.c.

[35] For comparison, 19.4 per cent of male undergraduates and research students entering all Oxford colleges between 1946 and 1967 were sons of clerks, skilled workers, small shopkeepers, and semi-skilled and unskilled workers (semi- and unskilled workers' sons amounted for 9.1 per cent of the male student population, and those of clerks, skilled workers, and small shopkeepers 10.3 per cent). Greenstein, 'Junior Members', 56. Of course, university-wide figures mask the differences between individual colleges.

The 1944 legislation meant that more working-class children could stay at school until the sixth form and thus have a chance of going to university, but the entry requirements for Cambridge and Oxford were notoriously difficult to negotiate for families without the cultural capital that went with a middle-class existence. This was one reason the most academically able grammar-school children gravitated towards provincial universities and the University of London.[36] Choosing German over Latin at the beginning of secondary schooling could render a young person ineligible to apply to one of the ancient universities several years later. '[F]ew working-class children knew what, in the long term, they were deciding when a subject was dropped; and no working-class parent ever raised objections at the time on such grounds', Brian Jackson and Dennis Marsden observed in their study of Huddersfield grammar-school children, *Education and the Working Class* (1962).[37] Sir Eric Ashby, who became Master of Clare College in 1959 after a decade as Vice-Chancellor at Queen's University, Belfast, expressed surprise at 'how few grammar schools are really trying to get their boys into Cambridge... many grammar schools would rather send their boys to a provincial university, which they know,... than risk being turned down by Oxbridge'.[38]

A majority of the working-class undergraduates beginning their studies between 1955 and 1962 arrived at Cambridge from grammar or high schools, but ten of the twenty-seven had attended church-run or Jewish independent schools and the fee-paying day schools that prepared a significant number of boys for study at Downing, such as Sir Joseph Williamson's Mathematical School (3), Tiffin (1), and Dulwich (1). The father of one of the boys who went to 'the Math', a garage proprietor, may have been prospering sufficiently in the early and mid-1950s to be able to pay the school fees comfortably. The armaments fitter who sent his son to the same school was probably not. The King's School, Pontefract, where the colliery labourer's son was a pupil when he sat the Downing examinations in 1957, was still a government-supported school in the post-war period, admitting some boys on county scholarships. The Coventry private school Bablake, which a motor mechanic's son attended, had a very

---

[36] Jackson and Marsden, *Education and the Working Class*, 164–9. See also A. H. Halsey, 'Oxford and the British Universities', in Harrison (ed.), *Twentieth Century*, 584, 585.

[37] Jackson and Marsden, *Education and the Working Class*, 115.

[38] Anthony Sampson, *Anatomy of Britain* (London: Hodder & Stoughton, 1962), 199–200. As master, Ashby supported efforts already underway at the college to recruit a greater diversity of students, with more stringent academic criteria. Previously, the college had focused its recruitment efforts on 'a number of traditional public schools'. Alan Burges and Richard J. Eden, 'Ashby, Eric, Baron Ashby (1904–1992)', *Oxford Dictionary of National Biography* (Oxford, 2004), <http://www.oxforddnb.com/view/article/50791> (accessed 10 February 2011).

small number of council-funded scholarships in the 1950s.[39] It seems that some of the working-class boys who went to independent schools in the 1950s and 1960s were 'scholarship boys' of a type that existed before the 1944 legislation. The meritocratic machinery of free grammar school places apportioned on the basis of eleven-plus performance was not solely responsible for the increasing proportion of young working-class men among Downing English undergraduates.

Despite the post-war increase in the proportion of working-class undergraduates, the student body of Downing's English school remained solidly middle class. Sons of the professional middle classes predominated. Civil servants, teachers (and nine headmasters), civil engineers, bank workers, and accountants recur over and over in the records of fathers' occupations. There were a number of doctors, solicitors, and company directors. The bulk of the undergraduate English population at Downing was, as Pat Thane observes of the backgrounds of Girton College women from the 1920s onwards, 'fairly evenly spread over the many gradations of the British middle classes', ranging from 'relatively poorly paid clerks' to 'prosperous professionals, businessmen, successful civil servants and colonial officials'.[40] As the absence of many boys from the most prestigious public schools suggests, the Downing population was not drawn to a great extent from the upper or upper middle class. David Matthews remembers Leavis asking his seminar to think on the meaning of Auden's poem 'Our Hunting Fathers' in preparation for their next meeting. 'Few of us, I think, understood them to be *our* huntin', shootin', & fishin' fathers, not having that kind of background.'[41] Among the exceptions was one fresher in 1932 who gave his father's profession as 'gentleman'.[42] Boris Ford was the son of a brigadier in the Indian Army and possessed, Leavis thought, 'that governing-class authority which is so useful in the right man'.[43]

One aspect of Downing English that seldom attracts attention is the number of Catholics studying with Leavis. No school sent Leavis more pupils (nine) than the John Fisher School in Purley. Downside, St Mary's in Crosby, and other Catholic schools also sent young men up to Downing.

---

[39] Selina Todd, 'From Scholarship Boys to Comprehensive Kids: Education, Getting on and Getting out of the Working-Class, c.1945–1970', unpublished paper, March 2009.

[40] Pat Thane, 'Girton Graduates: Earning and Learning, 1920s–1980s', *Women's History Review* 13/3 (2004): 349.

[41] Matthews, *Memories of F. R. Leavis*, 11 (emphasis in original).

[42] DCAT/5/1/6, p. 211, Downing. Other colleges probably had more sons of 'gentlemen'. At Oxford, 2.3 per cent of matriculants between 1920 and 1939 gave 'gentleman' as their father's occupation. Between 1900 and 1913 12.1 per cent did. Greenstein, 'Junior Members', 55 n. 37, 56.

[43] Leavis to Bonamy Dobrée, 13 February 1944, Bonamy Dobrée correspondence, Leeds.

A good many Catholic priests also read English. 'I have, rather to my surprise, acquired a considerable following in the Catholic educational world', Leavis told a correspondent in 1943: 'the devotion of the priests reading Arts at Cambridge is a little embarrassing'.[44] Two priests who read English with Leavis became headmasters of Catholic schools, J. N. McCarthy (who went up in 1944) at Cardinal Langley School in Manchester, and Richard Kenefeck (1935) at Cardinal Vaughan Grammar School in Kensington, where he hired another Downing English graduate (and *Scrutiny* contributor), R. C. Churchill, as a teacher.[45] When Patrick Harrison was there in the late 1940s and early 1950s, Downing had a palpable 'Catholic presence': as well as Marius Bewley and Ian Doyle, who did some college teaching, there were Maurice Hussey, Tom Birrell, Peter and Godfrey Lienhardt, John Farrelly, and Norman Henfrey, along with 'a number of Catholic-minded fellow-travelling Anglicans', one of whom was another research student who conducted supervisions, Geoffrey Strickland.[46]

The Catholic presence in Downing English highlights the triteness of the routine allegations of 'puritanism'. All the same, it is far from obvious why Leavis's way of practising criticism should appeal to Catholic laymen and priests. Leavis's bemused explanation in the letter quoted above—'my critical approach, they tell me, "integrates perfectly with Thomist philosophy"'—suggests that he did not think he fully understood it himself.[47] The Benedictine monk Sebastian Moore found in Leavis 'a teacher who, while remaining staunchly agnostic, allowed one's spiritual life to breathe in that world of great literature so long claimed for itself by a modernity impatient of the monkish'. Leavis was a principled secularist, but his principal interlocutors—for Moore, this meant Eliot and Blake, not Lawrence—were intensely concerned with the relations between religious experience, creativity, and language. Without an interpreter such as Leavis, Moore thought, 'I do not think I would have been able to open my mind to the revolution in feeling that Eliot achieves and calls for.' The pedagogy as much as Leavis's moral commitment to literature and his 'prophetic' mode of discoursing made his approach resonate with priests and monks. Leavis was a 'pastor', instilling the patience or

[44] Leavis to Raymond, 2 June 1943, Chatto & Windus archive, CW 94/17, Reading.

[45] 'Honours, Appointments, Etc.', *NL* (1960): 33 (McCarthy); 'Obituaries', *NL* (1983): 20 (Kenefeck); 'Appointments and Other News', *NL* (1942): 10 (Churchill).

[46] Harrison, 'Downing after the War', 255. The other 'fellow-travelling Anglicans' Harrison mentions were David Matthews and Eric Mathieson, about both of whom more below.

[47] Leavis to Harold Raymond, 2 June 1943, Chatto & Windus archive, CW 94/17, Reading. Sebastian Moore recalls that Leavis also joked that he had a 'large Roman clerical following... only because he had put Hopkins on the map, thus promoting "one of ours" to the top rank of English poets'. Sebastian Moore, 'F. R. Leavis: A Memoir', in Thompson (ed.), *The Leavises*, 61.

contemplativeness needed for receptivity to 'what Eliot was doing with language and therefore with consciousness itself'. Leavis's conception of critical debate as a 'common pursuit' that arrived at a 'right reading' envisaged 'a *consensus*, among hearers, *in* the poem', which was thus, Moore judged, 'a real fruitfulness of the word in the community'.[48] Of course, a theologian's response does not necessarily explain why Catholic schoolboys or their masters gravitated to Leavis. Harrison is probably right to stress the importance of the dissociation of sensibility ('best explained as R.C. propaganda', the militantly anti-Christian Empson said later) in the complex of Leavis's thought during the 1930s and 1940s.[49] The idea of an enveloping tradition and a community of language that made for experiences and judgements that transcend the individual helps explain 'how compatibility with a Catholic view of things arose'.[50]

Leavis did not have former pupils teaching in the Catholic schools that sent young men up to Downing to study English. Their teachers must have read *New Bearings in English Poetry*, *Revaluation*, *Education and the University*, or issues of *Scrutiny*. (Downside subscribed.)[51] The Catholic schools are not unusual in this respect. At least some, perhaps most, schools that sent multiple pupils to Downing did not have Downing graduates on their staff (the gaps in the information available about the graduates' careers make it impossible to be precise). This was not the case at Haberdasher's Aske's boys' school in north London. Beginning in the early 1940s, Haberdasher's Aske's sent nine pupils to read English at Downing: it and the John Fisher School were Leavis's most important feeder schools. H. L. B. Moody, who had studied with Leavis in the late 1930s, was an English master there. One of the Haberdasher's Aske's boys who went up to Downing in the 1950s was John Newton, who then became a research student, contributing to Downing's undergraduate teaching. Another was Brian Binding, who became an English teacher at Latymer Upper School in Hammersmith, where he joined another Cambridge graduate who, though not a Leavis pupil, would quote what 'the great Doctor' had said in faculty lectures.[52] Binding would circulate copies of the Cambridge

[48] Moore, 'F. R. Leavis: A Memoir', 61, 63, 64, 65–6, 67.

[49] Empson to Roger Sale, n.d. (1973), in John Haffenden (ed.), *Selected Letters of William Empson* (Oxford: Oxford University Press, 2006), 546.

[50] Harrison, 'Downing after the War', 256.

[51] In 1948 Downside School and Downside Abbey each had a subscription. *Scrutiny* trade sales ledger, 1945–9, 97, Deighton, Bell, & Co. archives, Add. 9453, B5/1, CUL.

[52] After the Butler Act, Latymer Upper became a direct-grant school and its headmaster was invited to join the Headmasters' Conference—the traditional badge of 'public school' status. J. S. Cockburn, H. P. F. King, and K. G. T. McDonnell (eds), *A History of the County of Middlesex*, vol. 1, *Physique, Archaeology, Domesday, Ecclesiastical Organization, The Jews, Religious Houses, Education of Working Classes to 1870, Private Education from Sixteenth Century* (London, 1969), 305–6.

literary magazine *Delta*, then edited by Leavis's students Strickland, Martin
Lightfoot, and Ian MacKillop. Neil Roberts, who sat his A levels in 1963,
was sold. Binding prodded him into applying to Clare College, where
Newton was by then a fellow. Roberts was successful. Having retired,
Leavis was not taking on students, but he was still leading seminars, discussing anonymous passages as he had done for decades (and using some
of the same sheets he had had printed long before). Roberts's director of
studies at Clare arranged for him to attend these seminars, which Leavis
held at home on Saturday mornings. Several of Binding's other pupils
who did not get into Cambridge went to the University of Exeter, where
Harold Mason and John Speirs lectured.[53]

Other Downing feeder schools had former pupils of Leavis's on the staff.
After R. F. Knight became an English master there in 1955, several boys
from the Tiffin School went up to Downing to read English. Knight left
five years later to become a training college lecturer, but another Downing
English alumnus, Alfred Monk, took a job teaching at the Tiffin several
years afterwards.[54] Jack Dalglish also taught there in the 1960s.[55] At Gresham's, a boarding school, Denys Thompson could provide more intimate
connections with Downing English than any other schoolmaster. When
Boris Ford went from Gresham's to Downing, he had not only read Leavis
and been taught along the lines set out in *Culture and Environment*, but
had also been introduced to L. C. Knights, who had gone to Norfolk to
visit his friend Thompson. Ford was invited 'to join them for a walk over
the sands at Wells'. He found Knights 'a rather perplexing mixture of the
severe and merry'. All the same, Ford felt pleased he had chosen a copy of
How Many Children Had Lady Macbeth? as a school prize.[56]

[53] Roberts, ' "Leavisite" Cambridge in the 1960s', 264–5, 266–7, 271. Speirs's son Logan
read English at Downing from 1957 to 1960.
[54] 'Appointments and Awards', *NL* (1955): 19; 'Appointments, Etc.', *NL* (1961): 36
(Knight); 'Appointments, Honours, Etc.', *NL* (1963): 30 (Monk).
[55] *The Teaching of English: Issued by the Incorporated Association of Assistant Masters in
Secondary Schools* (Cambridge: Cambridge University Press, 1966), xii; *Tiffnews: Newsletter
of Tiffinian Association*, no. 243 (March 2010) (unpaginated); 'Appointments, Retirements
and Distinctions', *NL* (1982): 13.
[56] Boris Ford, 'Obituary: Professor L. C. Knights', *The Independent*, 15 March 1997.
However, only one other boy came up from Gresham's while Thompson taught there to
read English at Downing. No boy from Yeovil Grammar, where Thompson was headmaster
from 1944 to 1962, read English at Downing. Thompson and Leavis were not on good
terms between 1935 and the early 1960s (for reasons Thompson describes in 'Teacher and
Friend', in Thompson [ed.], *The Leavises*, 49–50), though the break was not complete—
Thompson visited Downing College in 1937, 1948, and 1955 to address the Doughty
Society ('Chronological Record of Society Meetings', Doughty Society minute book, unnumbered pages and p. 353, DCCS/4/4/1/1, Downing). The second Gresham's alumnus
went up to Downing after the disagreement between Thompson and Q. D. Leavis. Thompson, who was not a Downing alumnus himself, may have encouraged promising sixth-
formers to apply to other colleges. See MacKillop, *F. R. Leavis*, 151.

The agents of Leavis's influence in schools were sometimes other pupils rather than masters. When Peter Matthews chose Downing, Leavis's name meant nothing to him, but he had heard that the college was strong in English. Leavis sprang out from the lines of his letters home—'Now here is the first real mind I've come into contact with, a sensitive spirit with a passion for good writing and the divine itch to exercise judgment.' These letters spurred his brother David to apply to the college. When David arrived, he was joined by two of his juniors from the same direct-grant school in south-east London, St Dunstan's (national service and the priority system for allocating undergraduate places after the war made for a student body more varied in age than was customary). As their English master coached them for the entrance examinations, Peter Matthews had given him advice about what they should read. In turn, his brother helped their cousin Geoffrey Strickland, at Farnborough Grammar School, prepare for the scholarship examinations when he was applying several years later.[57]

This was not an isolated instance but indicative of a recurring pattern. While he was at the King's School, Rochester, in the late 1930s, Geoffrey Lees was introduced to Leavis's *Revaluation* by George Greenfield, an old boy now reading English at Downing. The book made a deep impression on Lees, and he followed Greenfield to Downing three years later.[58] At the Royal High School in the 1940s, Karl Miller had an inspiring English master who bore the stamp of the same Edinburgh traditions as Muriel Spark's Jean Brodie. The person who put Miller on to Leavis, though, was Robert Taubman, who had graduated from the Royal High School early in the war and later completed a degree at Edinburgh University. He coached Miller for the Downing examinations. Correcting a mistake in a quotation, he told Miller he had better 'become word-perfect in your Eliot...before you enter the community of Little Downing'.[59]

The most intricate story of schoolboys being led to Downing by their seniors is told by Patrick Harrison. At the beginning of the Second World War, Harrison was sent to board at Lord Williams's School in Thame, at that time very much out in the country. Under the guidance of a young English master, E. A. Morley, he began to educate himself about music. One day in 1943, a sixth former, Eric Mathieson, heard him whistling *Eine Kleine Nachtmusik* on the toilet and, detecting shared interests, asked Harrison to meet him outside when he was finished. They became friends, and Harrison began to hear about Mathieson's preparations for the Cambridge scholarship exams at the encouragement of Morley, who by this time had moved on. 'It emerged that Ned Morley had been at

[57] Matthews, *Memories of F. R. Leavis*, 4, 5, 19.
[58] MacKillop, *F. R. Leavis*, 11.
[59] Karl Miller, *Rebecca's Vest: A Memoir* (London: Hamish Hamilton, 1993), 70–5, 80.

Downing, a college of which I had never heard, reading English under somebody called Leavis.' (Morley kept in touch, returning to speak to the Doughty Society on 'Shakespeare's last plays' in 1948.)[60] Mathieson did not elaborate, probably judging, 'correctly enough, that I was not ready to appreciate the message at that stage'. Mathieson won a scholarship, and on visits to the Harrisons' house in London he relayed anecdotes and did impressions of Leavis. He coached Harrison by correspondence for the examinations, there being no English master at Lord Williams's at the end of the war. The coaching included 'exercises in practical criticism and dating based largely on the Downing sheets'. By the end of 1946, Harrison had read all the published books of Leavis, Knights, and Derek Traversi, as well as much of the Downing English reading list. He was also subscribing to *Scrutiny* and buying back issues from Deighton, Bell & Co., its distributors. While waiting to be called up for national service, he in turn coached another boy at Lord Williams's, Robert Cradock. Cradock too won a place at Downing. 'So the three of us, Mathieson, Harrison, and Cradock were the product of the little cell established at Thame by Ned Morley.'[61] The teacher established it, but it was the pupils who gave it its momentum.

These stories are acutely personal. The books and the ideas acquired an exciting, transformative significance as the older boy or the teacher entrusted them to the chosen protégé. Leavis's aura was a source of some of the excitement: anecdotes about him filtered down, sometimes accompanied by impressions (mimicking Leavis appears to have been nearly irresistible).[62] But it was primarily through reading him, inhabiting his work, learning to respond in ways he and Knights and others had marked out, that they came to want to study with him. The pattern of recruitment to Downing more generally involved personal connections to a lesser extent than might be expected. The majority of men reading English arrived at Downing from schools without one of Leavis's pupils on the staff. Their teachers knew of his English school by word of mouth or through its publications.[63] At King's College School, Wimbledon, for instance, a 'Leavisite' group of sixth formers gathered around an English master, Frank Miles, who had not been through Downing himself.[64]

---

[60] Doughty Society minute book, 36 (21 May 1948), DCCS/4/4/1/1, Downing. Morley was Edward Ascroft Morley, admitted to Downing in October 1938. DCAT 5/1/8, p. 158, Downing.

[61] Harrison, 'Downing after the War', 245, 246–7, 248–9.

[62] Michael Black, 'The Long Pursuit', in Thompson (ed.), *The Leavises*, 86; Boris Ford, 'David Holbrook: A Portrait', in Edwin Webb (ed.), *Powers of Being: David Holbrook and His Work* (Madison, NJ: Fairleigh Dickinson University Press, 1995), 36.

[63] See, for instance, David Holbrook's speech at his eightieth birthday celebration at Downing College in January 2003, <http://www.dow.cam.ac.uk/dow_server/events/Holbrook80th.html>, accessed 23 March 2011. See also Black, 'Long Pursuit', 86.

[64] Roger Scruton, *England: An Elegy* (London: Chatto & Windus, 2000), 35–6. That Miles had not been one of Leavis's pupils is my conclusion, not Scruton's.

Scrutiny was intended to coordinate as a 'public' the scattered and isolated 'intelligent young men and women' who, every year, 'go down from the Universities and are swallowed by secondary and public schools'.[65] The number of 'first-generation' Downing English undergraduates is an index of the success of *Scrutiny* and Leavis's books in creating such a public.

Tracing the post-Cambridge careers of Leavis's pupils is more difficult, given the vagaries of the available evidence and the fact that a single career can involve a variety of occupations. The following account identifies those professions in which at least several of Leavis's pupils clustered and considers the relationship between their Downing education and their subsequent careers. A useful benchmark is the survey undertaken by Cambridge's English Club in 1937. When Boris Ford, Leo Salingar, Frank Whitehead, C. L. Barber, Ian Watt, and H. R. Poole canvassed undergraduates and research students in the English Faculty, one of the questions they asked was 'Are you reading English with the object of getting a job as a result?'

A majority of the 202 respondents to the questionnaire (out of about 250 students in total) answered yes. The committee's report provided a breakdown of the jobs the respondents had in mind:

Profession	No.
Teaching	68
Journalism	14
Academic	10
Ministry	10
Publishing	5
Business	3
Advertising	2
Broadcasting	2
Indian Civil.	2
Writing (x)	2
Agriculture	1
Bookselling	1
Drama	1
Films	1
Hospital Almoner	1
Law	1
Labour Management	1
Librarianship	1
Music	1
Social Work	1

[65] 'Scrutiny: A Manifesto', *Scrutiny* 1/1 (May 1932): 5.

The priceless footnote for the category 'Writing' reads: '(x both First Year)'.[66] The popularity of individual professions would vary from college to college, but this list does identify all the occupations in which groups of Downing English alumni ended up: school teaching, university teaching, journalism, publishing, librarianship, drama, law, broadcasting, advertising, and the ministry—though in Downing's case, priests already ordained outnumbered future Anglican clergymen.

The most striking thing about the questionnaire responses, of course, is the number of prospective schoolteachers. Ford and his fellows concluded: 'It is noteworthy that 68 people, or at least 27 per cent of the Faculty as a whole, intend to become Teachers.'[67] At other universities, the proportion would have been much higher. Two knowledgeable observers wrote in 1946 that the 'student community is ... much more varied at Oxford, Cambridge, and London than at the provincial Universities, where the condition of the Arts Faculty often approximates to that of the Training College, as about 90 per cent of the students are going to be teachers'.[68] There was a structural predisposition towards teaching careers. The only way many students at provincial universities could afford their studies was by committing themselves to teaching after graduation in return for a state bursary.[69] Teaching was also the only large non-scientific profession in Britain that was substantially 'graduatized' before the 1960s. Graduates of provincial universities were often caught in a circular process: the expansion of secondary education led to 'a larger university entry many of whom, when they graduated, had little option but to turn to teaching'.[70] Male Cambridge graduates customarily had more options, but schoolteaching was still a common path. A reading of the obituaries in the *Emmanuel College Magazine* reveals that many English graduates in that college, too, become schoolteachers; the Clare College alumni publication memorializes a somewhat smaller number of

---

[66] [R. B. Ford, I. Watt, C. Barber, L. Salingar, F. Whitehead, and H. E. Poole,] 'Report of a Committee of Enquiry into the Problems of Teaching in the English Faculty: February–April 1937', 2, Cam.a.937.2, CUL.

[67] Ibid.

[68] A. H. Stewart and V. de S. Pinto, 'The Training of the Teacher of English', in Vivian de Sola Pinto (ed.), *The Teaching of English in Schools: A Symposium Edited for the English Association* (London: Macmillan, 1946), 158 n.

[69] Carol Dyhouse, *Students: A Gendered History* (London: Routledge, 2006), 23–7; Richard Hoggart, *A Local Habitation (Life and Times Vol. I: 1918–1940)* (London: Chatto & Windus, 1988), 185; Bruce Truscot [pseud. E. Allison Peers], *Redbrick University* (London: Faber & Faber, 1943), 154; Stevens, *Living Tradition*, 212.

[70] Leonard Schwartz, 'Professions, Elites, and Universities in England, 1870–1970', *Historical Journal* 47 (2004): 941–62, quotation from 950–1.

teachers.[71] The general point holds: the large number of teachers among Leavis's former pupils—schoolteaching was by far the most common occupation for Downing English undergraduates about whose subsequent careers I have information—was not a peculiarity of the Downing English school.

Yet it was a significant aspect of Leavis's and *Scrutiny's* impact on British culture. The capillaries of Leavis's influence that ran through British secondary schools transformed a critical school into a cultural movement. More than a few of the schoolmasters Leavis trained moved on to become inspectors, local directors of education, and lecturers and professors in training colleges or the teacher-training institutes of education attached to universities. This last category includes Ford and Walsh, two professors of education instrumental in bringing *Scrutiny* concerns and approaches into school curricula and teacher-training. Other teachers who studied with Leavis, such as David Holbrook, Esmor Jones, and Brian Jackson (co-author of *Education and the Working Class*) at Downing, and Denys Thompson, Raymond O'Malley, and Whitehead at other Cambridge colleges, were integral to this process. (The activities of Leavis's pupils and followers in secondary education are the subject of the next chapter.)

Very few Downing English graduates worked in adult education.[72] This is curious. Many *Scrutiny* people were veterans of adult education, and *Scrutiny* contributors or fellow travellers from other colleges, such as Salingar and Lionel Elvin, worked as adult education tutors or organizers.[73] And, as we shall see in Chapter 5, *Scrutiny* was an inspiration within the Workers' Educational Association and university extramural departments after the Second World War. Many more Downing alumni became university lecturers. All up, thirty of the men Leavis taught as Downing undergraduates took up university positions in English.[74] Another,

[71] *Emmanuel College Magazine*, 1959–2008; *Clare Association Annual*, 1969–2007. Unsurprisingly, the proportions were higher for graduates of the women's colleges. Thane writes of Girton women: 'Of the graduates of the early 1920s for whom we have employment information 62 per cent became schoolteachers at some time, slightly fewer among 1930s graduates and about one-third of those who graduated in 1944–53.' Thane, 'Girton Graduates', 354.

[72] An exception was M. J. Carthew, a 'Tutor-Organiser for Industry' for the Workers' Educational Association's Eastern District. 'Appointments, Honours, Etc.', *NL* (1965): 28; 'Appointments, Honours, Etc.', *NL* (1966): 32.

[73] Lionel Elvin, *Encounters with Education* (London: Institute of Education, 1987), chs 6–7. Elvin discusses his limited and not very happy relationship with Leavis on pp. 89–90.

[74] In Britain: Frank Bradbrook (University College of North Wales, Bangor); Gordon Cox (University of Manchester); B. T. Harrison (University of Sheffield); Tony Inglis (University of Sussex); R. T. Jones (University of Natal, Pietermaritzburg, and then the University of York); Norman Henfrey (at the University of Bristol after many years teaching

Geoffrey Strickland, held academic appointments in French. This figure does not take into account those whose doctoral work Leavis supervised and those he taught informally or at other colleges. Nor does it include a dozen others who held lectureships in English at training colleges and technical colleges, some of whom had previously been schoolteachers.[75] Most of the future university lecturers Leavis taught followed fairly conventional academic career paths, an exception being Karl Miller, who, after more than two decades as an editor, joined University College London as the Lord Northcliffe Professor of Modern English Literature ('like being Mammon Professor of God', F. W. Bateson once quipped).[76]

The British universities where Leavis's pupils found positions tended to be civic universities in large industrial cities (Sheffield, Manchester, and especially Bristol) or university colleges, such as the University College of the South West of England at Exeter and the Swansea, Bangor, and Cardiff campuses of the University of Wales. A succession of Leavis's pupils and collaborators taught at what became the University of Exeter: Geoffrey Walton, one of Leavis's earliest teaching assistants; John Speirs, the *Scrutiny* regular whom Leavis supervised at Emmanuel; Harold Mason, a

in France and Canada); Philip Hobsbaum (Queen's University, Belfast, and then the University of Glasgow); G. D. Klingopulos (University College of Swansea and then Cardiff); J. C. F. (Roy) Littlewood (University of Stellenbosch and then the University of Bristol); Ian MacKillop (University of Sheffield); H. W. Mills (University of Kent); C. H. Page (University of Exeter); John Newton (Clare College, Cambridge); Ian Robinson (University College of Swansea); John Saunders (University of Newcastle); Morris Shapira (University of Kent); P. P. Tomlinson (University of Bristol); Geoffrey Walton (University College of the South West of England); Brian Way (University College of Swansea); John Worthen (University College of Swansea). Outside Britain: Marius Bewley (Rutgers University); Tom Birrell (University of Nijmegen); R. H. Crowther (St Mary's University, Halifax, Nova Scotia); D. J. Enright (multiple institutions in Egypt, West Germany, Japan, Thailand, and Singapore); R. A Fothergill (York University, Toronto); F. K. Hoyle (National University of Education, Aichiken); C. R. Levenson (Carleton University, Ottawa); Chris Terry (St Mary's University, Halifax, Nova Scotia); M. S. Vaughan (University of Natal, Durban); Geoffrey Walton (from 1949, at University College, Accra; University College of the Gold Coast; Ahmadu Bello University, Nigeria); John Wiltshire (University of Sydney and LaTrobe University in Melbourne).

[75] James Sydney Abraham at Loughborough Training College and later Hull College of Further Education; David Adams at the College of Commerce, Bristol; John Brown at Bretton Hall College of Higher Education, Wakefield; P. G. Canovan at Northern Counties Training College, Benton, Newcastle-on-Tyne; Peter Catley at Ware College, Hertfordshire; L. V. Hebblewhite at Hounslow Borough College (formerly Chiswick Polytechnic); Alan Durband at C. F. Mott College of Education; Maurice Hussey at Cambridgeshire College of Arts and Technology; J. H. Robinson at the Technical College, H. M. Dockyard, Chatham and then at H. M. Dockyard, Rosyth, Fife; M. B. Mencher at St John's College of Further Education, Manchester; J. J. Say at the College of Sarum St Michael in Salisbury (a training college for women, to staff Church of England schools); K. A. P. Smith at the Dorset Institute of Higher Education.

[76] Karl Miller, *Dark Horses An Experience of Literary Journalism* (London: Picador, 1999), 191; Frank Kermode, *Not Entitled: A Memoir* (New York: Farrar, Straus, & Giroux, 1995), 211.

Scrutiny editor and, for a time, a very close colleague of Leavis's; and
Charles Page, who arrived in 1965, possibly to replace Mason, who
returned to Cambridge that year.[77] Of the Welsh university colleges,
Swansea was the strongest Leavisian centre. G. D. Klingopulos taught
there for several years immediately after the war, and then, in the decade
after 1961, Brian Way, Ian Robinson, and John Worthen were all appointed. Robinson, who in the 1970s became the publisher of *The Human
World*, a journal sympathetic to if not centred on Leavis, formed a Leavisian caucus at Swansea along with two lecturers who had not been educated at Downing, David Sims and Sam Dawson.[78] (Looking back on his
experience of 'the hectic and crowded post-war years', Dawson would
suggest that *Scrutiny* was the only place a student 'could have gone, not
merely for reassurance, but for clarification, for education in fact'.)[79]
Worthen arrived at Swansea in 1970 with a PhD from the new University
of Kent, where the English department staff included Howard Mills and
Leavis's former deputy Morris Shapira.[80] Estranged from Leavis since the
dispute in the mid-1960s over his succession at Downing that enveloped
Mason, John Newton, and many others, Shapira was still capable of being
regarded by an unsympathetic colleague in another department as the
'last of the old-style Leavisites'.[81]

Leavis was troubled that none of his pupils received English Faculty
appointments at Cambridge over the span of his teaching career, and at
least one of them complained that he had to find work overseas because
'foreign universities were less particular or (perhaps through backward-
ness) less prejudiced against *Scrutiny*'s minor fry'.[82] While it is not usually
possible to substantiate or disprove the claims of a disappointed job candidate, there are some grounds for thinking it was not such a liability to
be regarded as a 'Leavisite', at least outside the Cambridge English Faculty. The number of Leavis pupils who got jobs in English departments

[77] 'Appointments, Honours, Etc.', *NL* (1965): 31; MacKillop, *F. R. Leavis*, 351–3.
[78] M. Wynn Thomas, email to the author, 22 March 2011; David Dykes, *The University College of Swansea: An Illustrated History* (Stroud: Alan Sutton, 1992), 187; Eric
Jacobs, *Kingsley Amis: A Biography* (1995; London: Hodder & Stoughton, 1996), 137–8;
Richard Bradford, *Lucky Him: The Life of Kingsley Amis* (London: Peter Owen, 2001),
105, 113.
[79] S. W. Dawson, '*Scrutiny* and the Idea of a University', *Essays in Criticism* 14/1 (January 1964): 8.
[80] 'Appointments', *NL* (1971): 31.
[81] Patrick Collinson, *The History of a History Man: Or, the Twentieth Century Viewed
from a Safe Distance: The Memoirs of Patrick Collinson* (Woodbridge: Boydell Press, 2011),
173. Chris Terry (1961) also completed a PhD at Kent, in 1973. 'Appointments, Retirements, Etc.', *NL* (1974): 33.
[82] Leavis to Harding, 27 November 1963, F. R. Leavis papers, Col 9.59a, Emmanuel;
D. J. Enright, *Conspirators and Poets* (London: Chatto & Windus, 1966), 34–5.

was not trivial, and professors or departments interviewing prospective lecturers had many considerations other than Downing connections to take into account.

L. C. Knights became a lecturer at the University of Manchester before he had completed his doctorate, at a time when Leavis's position was still shaky and when Leavis's broadsides and *Fiction and the Reading Public* were exciting opposition elsewhere in Cambridge. Knights later held chairs at Sheffield, Bristol, and finally Cambridge. By the time he went to Sheffield in 1947, he was well established as a critic in his own right, not just a junior partner of Leavis's (though he remained an editor of *Scrutiny*). Leavis progressively dissociated himself from Knights, withdrawing his endorsement of his critical work.[83] Knights knew that 'he thought my standards were slipping. As a head of department...I had had to work with men and women whose tastes and aptitudes differed widely from my own, and some of them I had come to like and respect.'[84] This chill did not stop Knights from appointing a Downing graduate, Peter Tomlinson, to an assistant lectureship in English at Bristol in 1955.[85] Nor did Leavis's many contemptuous dismissals of him prevent Empson's appointing Leavis's Downing pupil and admirer Ian MacKillop to a job in the Sheffield English department in 1968.[86]

Nearly half of the Downing undergraduates who became English lecturers or professors worked outside Britain—in new and longer-established universities throughout the British empire, in continental Europe, and in East Asia. For some, the move away from Britain was temporary, and they returned to jobs at the new universities founded in the 1960s. Thus R. T. Jones taught at the University of York after a period at the University of Natal and David Craig taught at the University of Lancaster after a period at the University of Ceylon followed by several years as an adult education tutor in Yorkshire. (In an academic *cause célèbre*, Lancaster later tried to sack him for fomenting rebellion among students and for letting his communism colour his teaching and

---

[83] Howard Mills, untitled essay, *Cambridge Quarterly* 25/4 (1996): 373; F. R. Leavis to the *Times Literary Supplement*, 3 March 1972, in F. R. Leavis, *Letters in Criticism*, ed. John Tasker (London: Chatto & Windus, 1974), 149.

[84] L. C. Knights, untitled essay, *Cambridge Quarterly* 25/4 (1996): 359. See also L. C. Knights, 'English at Bristol', *Critical Survey* 1/3 (autumn 1963): 182.

[85] 'Appointments and Awards', *NL* (1955): 21. Two other Downing English alumni, Roy Littlewood and Norman Henfrey, arrived at Bristol in the early 1970s after Knights had gone to Cambridge to succeed Basil Willey as King Edward VII Professor.

[86] Fred Inglis, 'Professor Ian MacKillop', *The Independent*, 3 June 2004; 'Appointments, Honours, Etc.', *NL* (1968): 40. Empson was mindful of these dismissals: Empson to [Jeffrey] Miller, 19 November 1974, William Empson papers, bMS Eng 1401, Houghton Library, Harvard University (reprinted in Haffenden [ed.], *Selected Letters of William Empson*, 594–5).

marking).[87] The overseas fortunes of Leavis's pupils and *Scrutiny* are the subject of a later chapter.

Downing English alumni also pursued academic careers in other disciplines. Mellers, *Scrutiny*'s chief music writer and a supervisor in English at Downing, taught music in the extramural department of Birmingham University for sixteen years before becoming the founding professor of music at York.[88] Michael Baxandall became a distinguished art historian. The most significant traffic between Leavis's English school and another discipline was the migration to social anthropology at the end of the 1940s. Godfrey Lienhardt, Peter Lienhardt, Paul Baxter, and Malcolm Ruel all made this switch, usually after completing Part I of the English tripos. David Pocock, a Pembroke undergraduate whose tutor sent him to Leavis's seminars, did likewise.[89] When Ruel met the eminent anthropologist E. E. Evans-Pritchard at Oxford in 1950, Evans-Pritchard asked him: 'Who is this man Leavis who is like a brick wall'—people bounced off him 'like tennis balls into social anthropology'.[90] Recalling this time in an interview, Ruel said that he was 'not sufficient of a Leavis disciple to want to do three years', and Leavis had less contact with the Lienhardts once they had left Cambridge than he seems to have wished, but Pocock remained an admirer and correspondent of both the Leavises until their deaths.[91] It seems more appropriate to see Leavis as obliquely preparing these men for social anthropology rather than driving them into it.

---

[87] 'Honours, Appointments, Etc.', *NL* (1960): 31; [Council for Academic Freedom and Democracy,] *The Craig Affair: Background to the Case of Dr David Craig and Others, Lancaster University* (London: Council for Academic Freedom and Democracy, 1972); Ian MacKillop, 'Rubrics and Reading Lists', in MacKillop and Storer (eds) *F. R. Leavis: Essays and Documents*, 65. Jones's time at Natal is discussed briefly in chapter 8. Norman Henfrey taught overseas, in France and Canada, for most of the two decades between graduating from Cambridge and joining the English department at Bristol in 1972. Norman Henfrey, 'Home and Away', *Critical Quarterly* 52/1 (2010): 17–23; 'Notes on Contributors', ibid., 128.

[88] Peter Dickinson, 'Professor Wilfrid Mellers: Musicologist and Composer', *The Independent*, 19 May 2008.

[89] David Pocock, untitled notes on letters deposited in the F. R. Leavis papers, Col 9.59.121, Emmanuel. In an interview, the anthropologist Jack Goody said that he had applied to Downing to read English and had not been accepted, though friends from school (St Albans) won scholarships. These must have included H. L. B. Moody, who went up to Downing in 1937. Goody says that he had been taught by an (unnamed) English teacher who had studied with Leavis. Goody was an undergraduate at St John's College and attended Leavis's seminars. Jack Goody, interview with Eric Hobsbawm, 18 May 1991, available at <http://www.dspace.cam.ac.uk/handle/1810/268> (accessed 4 July 2011).

[90] Malcolm Ruel, interview with Alan Macfarlane, 15 December 2002 (video at <http://www.dspace.cam.ac.uk/handle/1810/756>).

[91] Ibid.; Leavis to Pocock, 26 July 1961, Leavis papers, Col 9.59.121, Emmanuel, and Pocock's note on this letter at the end of the file (about the Lienhardts). On Pocock's debt to and enduring interest in Leavis, including his late engagement with Michael Polanyi's philosophy, see Jonathan Parry and Edward Simpson, 'David Pocock's *Contributions* and the

The kind of anthropology a literary-critical education 'prepared' them for was that articulated by Evans-Pritchard in his 1950 Marett Lecture.[92] After graduating from Cambridge, the Lienhardts, Ruel, Baxter, and Pocock all moved to Oxford to study under him. Evans-Pritchard's case against functionalism dwelt on the alternatives suggested by history, not literary criticism, but his Marett Lecture sent strong signals about the analytical affinities between anthropology and criticism. When an anthropologist did fieldwork among 'a primitive people...he learns to speak their language, to think in their concepts and to feel in their values. He then lives the experiences over again critically and interpretatively in the conceptual categories and values of his own culture and in terms of the general body of knowledge of his discipline'. At this level, Evans-Pritchard said, 'social anthropology remains a literary and impressionistic art', but it entailed more than understanding and translation: the anthropologist sought also 'to discover the structural order of the society, the patterns which...enable him to see it as a whole, as a set of interrelated abstractions'.[93] Evans-Pritchard clearly thought that discerning those patterns and wholes was beyond the remit of the literary, but *Scrutiny* critics claimed them as part of their field of study.

Leavis's pupils also went to work for agencies of the cultural establishment with which he was in chronic and periodically acute conflict.[94] The British Council, charged with projecting British culture abroad, employed a number of them. C. A. Hackett, who had studied under Leavis at Emmanuel, was the British Council's education officer in Paris immediately after the war; Leavis described him as 'a very intelligent man, very much "in" with literary circles in France (especially universities) & very enthusiastic about the "cause" (meaning me, *Scrutiny* & associated things)'.[95]

Legacy of Leavis', *Contributions to Indian Sociology* 44/3 (2010): 331–59. See also the testimony of another Cambridge-trained anthropologist of this generation, the South African David Brokensha: 'David Brokensha: Love and Work on Three Continents', part 2 (<http://www.brokiesway.co.za/university.htm> accessed 8 August 2011); David Brokensha, interview with Alan Macfarlane, available at <http://www.alanmacfarlane.com/DO/filmshow/brokensha1_fast.htm> (accessed 8 August 2011).

[92] Parry and Simpson, 'Pocock's *Contributions*', 334–5; Ruel, interview with Macfarlane. For a different but in certain respects comparable course from undergraduate literary studies to a hermeneutic anthropology, see Clifford Geertz, *After the Fact: Two Countries, Four Decades, One Anthropologist* (Cambridge, Mass.: Harvard University Press, 1995), 98, 101, 114.

[93] E. E. Evans-Pritchard, 'Social Anthropology: Past and Present: The Marett Lecture, 1950', *Man* 50/198 (1950): 118–24, quotations from 121; see also 123–4.

[94] F. R. Leavis, 'Mr Pryce-Jones, the British Council and British Culture', *Scrutiny* 18/3 (winter 1951–2): 224–8; F. R. Leavis, *Nor Shall My Sword: Discourses on Pluralism, Compassion, and Social Hope* (London: Chatto & Windus, 1972), 45, 71; Leavis to Pocock, 25 August 1952 and 5 September 1952, Leavis papers, Col 9.59.121, Emmanuel.

[95] Leavis to Parsons, 3 February 1946, Chatto & Windus archive, CW 100/33, Reading. Hackett earned a doctorate in Paris in the 1930s and became an authority on Rimbaud.

Jerry Owens was a language teacher for the council in the 1960s and 1970s, posted to Lahore, Singapore, Khartoum, Bangkok, Jakarta, and Madrid.[96] After two decades as an English master at Haberdasher's Aske's, H. L. B. Moody trained teachers at overseas institutions under the council's auspices.[97] James Smith, who assisted Leavis with teaching at Downing, worked for the British Council in Venezuela in the 1940s, though Leavis thought the council treated Smith very poorly: 'he is not a B.C. type—too genuine & for all his foibles, portentously qualified'.[98] Leavis appreciated the British Council's efforts in distributing *Scrutiny* overseas—it bought something like 10 per cent of the print run in the late 1940s—but he was understandably annoyed by its requests that the cash-strapped *Scrutiny* collective supply copies at half price.[99] The council should have been subsidizing *Scrutiny*, not vice versa, Leavis told Denys Harding.[100]

Throughout his career, Leavis suspected the BBC's motives and methods, wryly speaking of his 'anti-BBC complex'.[101] As we shall see in Chapter 7, however, collaborators such as Thompson, Ford, and Holbrook accepted the compromises that radio entailed, and three of his Downing pupils carved out sustained careers with the corporation. It may or may not be relevant that at least two of them did not go straight from Cambridge to the BBC, but spent some time teaching in schools first. The one who went directly to the BBC after graduation was Robert Cradock, the youngest member of the 'cell' at Lord Williams's School. He became Chief Producer Documentaries for BBC Radio, editing documentaries on an assortment of topics but above all on military history.[102] Derrick Amoore, several years Cradock's junior, joined the BBC in 1959 as a research assistant for the television 'magazine' programme *Tonight*.[103] The programme was still fairly new, and most of those involved, on and off camera, were

[96] 'Ronald Jerome Owens (1947)', *NL* (1996): 45.

[97] H. L. B. Moody, untitled essay, *Cambridge Quarterly* 25/4 (1996): 374.

[98] Leavis to D. W. Harding, 29 July 1947, Leavis papers, Col 9.59a, Emmanuel.

[99] Trade sales ledger, 46, Deighton, Bell, & Co. Archives, Add. 9453, B5/1, CUL. Between November 1947 and September 1948, the British Council paid for 131 subscriptions to *Scrutiny*. The journal's print run ranged from 750 to 1400 over its lifespan. As periodicals were still subject to paper-rationing in 1947–8, it is unlikely that the print run at this time was at the top of this range. L. C. Knights, '*Scrutiny* and F. R. L.: A Personal Memoir', in Thompson (ed.), *The Leavises*, 73. Compare Kerry McSweeney, '*Scrutiny*', in Alvin Sullivan (ed.), *British Literary Magazines*, vol. 4, *The Modern Age, 1914–1984* (New York: Greenwood Press, 1986), 423.

[100] MacKillop, *F. R. Leavis*, 224, 259; Leavis to Harding, 16 March 1941, F. R. Leavis papers, Col 9.59a, Emmanuel; Leavis, *Nor Shall My Sword*, 45, 71.

[101] F. R. Leavis to Philip Brockbank, 21 March 1976, F. R. Leavis papers, York.

[102] 'Obituary', *NL* (1975): 15–16.

[103] 'Obituaries', *NL* (1993): 39.

young and new to broadcasting. For many of them *Tonight* was a launching pad for 'impressive BBC careers'.[104] In 1964, Amoore became *Tonight*'s last editor. He was promoted to an administrative post but later returned to production, helping to establish *Nationwide*, a successor to *Tonight*, and directing BBC television news for five years.[105]

Amoore had taught very briefly before joining the corporation. Peter Fozzard's time as a teacher was longer and left a deep imprint on his broadcasting career. After gaining his teacher's certificate in the late 1950s, he joined the staff of the new Holland Park Comprehensive School. (Working at a comprehensive was not a common move for one of Leavis's pupils, or probably Cambridge graduates generally, given the cachet as well as the intellectual appeal of a grammar school job, but this was before grammar schools began to be dismantled and incorporated into new comprehensives, and Holland Park had a reputation as an excitingly innovative school.) Fozzard became head of the English department at Holland Park before leaving in 1970 to become a producer for BBC Schools Radio. There he 'worked on a wide range of programmes, ranging from poetry for infants, to A-Level English courses', while also working on programmes for Radio 3 and Radio 4.[106] Amoore's trajectory bears some resemblance to that of John Scupham, who moved from grammar-school teaching into schools broadcasting in the 1940s, becoming head of educational broadcasting. Scupham had read English at Emmanuel College in the second half of the 1920s, while Leavis was teaching there.[107]

At least six Downing English graduates became librarians, mostly in university libraries. The librarians who had studied under Leavis in the 1940s constitute a strikingly interconnected group. Both John Farrell and Norman Guilding worked under Philip Larkin in the Hull University Library. Guilding later moved to the Durham University Library, where the head of the library was another of Leavis's pupils, Ian Doyle. Doyle had been friends with Farrell since the age of five.[108] David Matthews, who was taught by Doyle and whom his older brother had known at Downing, worked at the National Library for the Blind, and from 1967

[104] Asa Briggs, *The History of Broadcasting in the United Kingdom*, vol. 5, *Competition, 1955–1974* (Oxford: Oxford University Press, 1995), 161–4. Though not for Karl Miller, who found BBC Television a 'brisk-to-hysterical place' and was happy to leave *Tonight* for a job on *The Spectator*. Miller, *Rebecca's Vest*, 171–2.

[105] 'Obituaries', *NL* (1993): 39.

[106] J. L. Evans, 'Peter Rathmell Fozzard (1954)', *NL* (1996): 39–40.

[107] John Cain, 'Scupham, John (1904–1990)', *Oxford Dictionary of National Biography*, <http://www.oxforddnb.com/view/article/39993> (accessed 1 December 2010); Briggs, *Competition*, 468–9.

[108] 'John Farrell (1944)', *NL* (1999): 33; 'Norman Walter Guilding (1946)', *NL* (2001): 35; A. I. Doyle, 'Memories', *NL* (2005): 22–3; Matthews, *Memories of F. R. Leavis*, 6–7.

lectured at the College of Librarianship of Wales. John Kimber, at Cambridge in the second half of the 1950s, worked in the Lambeth Borough Libraries before taking up a position at the University of East Anglia. He collaborated on a large annotated bibliography of writings by and about F. R. and Q. D. Leavis.[109] Both Guilding and Farrell became chief cataloguers, a role out of kilter with the sensibility of a teacher who described research as 'the higher navvying'. Guilding's obituary in the alumni newsletter nevertheless describes him as 'a strong follower throughout his life' of Leavis's 'teaching and thinking'.[110]

Publishing was, Fredric Warburg coyly said, 'an occupation for gentlemen', and it was not so unusual for literary-minded old boys of the public schools to ease into jobs at respected publishing houses on completing their Oxbridge degrees.[111] Downing English being less gentlemanly in style and ambition as well as social origin than some other colleges, it is fitting that Downing alumni who went into publishing worked as educational publishers. A. R. (Tony) Beal read English with Leavis between 1943 and 1948, his studies interrupted by service in the navy. After graduating he taught at a training college for a year and then took a job in the education department of William Heinemann. He and his boss, Alan Hill, turned Heinemann Educational Books into a major publisher of books for schools. They also published literary criticism and editions of modern novels (the New Windmill series) and poetry selections (the Poetry Bookshelf series). Beal himself wrote a book on D. H. Lawrence and edited a collection of Lawrence's criticism. He also helped broker a truce between Leavis and Heinemann's chairman, A. S. Frere, who was angry that Leavis had not sought copyright permission from the firm for the quotations in Leavis's *D. H. Lawrence: Novelist* (1955).[112]

Martin Lightfoot was one of the last undergraduates admitted to read English at Downing before Leavis retired from college teaching, going up in 1962. He and some Downing friends ran the university English Club, and he was thought of as a Leavis disciple.[113] Working on Cambridge literary magazines and at the Athlone Press got him interested in book design, and when he became an editor at Penguin Education in 1967, he fostered intensive collaboration between writers, editors, designers, and picture researchers, as Penguin took advantage of the new lithographic

[109] 'Obituaries', *NL* (1986): 18; M. B. Kinch, William Baker, and John Kimber, *F. R. Leavis and Q. D. Leavis: An Annotated Bibliography* (New York: Garland, 1989).
[110] 'Norman Walter Guilding', 35.
[111] Fredric Warburg, *An Occupation for Gentlemen* (1959; Cambridge, Mass.: Hutchinson, 1960); Michael Barber, *Anthony Powell: A Life* (London: Duckworth Overlook, 2004), 52–4.
[112] Jack Dalglish, 'Anthony Ridley Beal (1943)', *NL* (2004): 27.
[113] Roberts, ' "Leavisite" Cambridge in the 1960s', 273.

printing to create fresh kinds of school books. To develop the English teaching list, he worked closely with the National Association for the Teaching of English, though chiefly with those concerned with language, such as James Britton and Harold and Connie Rosen rather than former Leavis pupils in NATE such as Thompson who were wary of the turn to linguistics in school English curricula during the 1960s.[114]

All the same, Lightfoot's career in publishing reflected cultural ambitions comparable to those of Leavis pupils such as Thompson. George Greenfield's did not. Shortly after the war he stumbled into managing the house of T. Werner Laurie (he ran into an army friend outside a bookshop in Piccadilly: the friend took him to lunch, and then off to meet his father, a City potentate who had recently bought the company and needed someone to manage it).[115] Later he became a literary agent of note, and, in retirement, a historian of publishing.[116] Among his clients were explorers turned authors such as Edmund Hillary and Robin Knox-Johnson and best-selling novelists such as Sidney Sheldon, whose *Rage of Angels* (1980)—entitled 'Rape of Angels' when Greenfield first saw it—achieved excesses in excess of any best-seller deplored in *Fiction and the Reading Public*. Greenfield's autobiography devotes only a sentence to his time in the 'thin cold air' of literary criticism under Leavis's 'snipey gaze'.[117]

Greenfield was not the only Downing graduate to pursue an unexpected career in popular 'publications and entertainments'. Terrance Dicks, who went to read English with Leavis in 1954 from East Ham Grammar School, got a job at the BBC as assistant script editor on *Doctor Who*. He became the long-running science-fiction series' main writer, churning out novelizations as well as writing the scripts themselves.[118] In his writing he aimed for the un-Leavisian qualities of 'simplicity, clarity and pace'.[119] Since the 1970s, he has been a prolific writer of children's books unconnected with *Doctor Who*, their protagonists ranging from

[114] Myra Barrs, 'Obituary: Martin Lightfoot', *The Independent*, 1 June 1999. On NATE, see Chapter 4, below.
[115] George Greenfield, *A Smattering of Monsters: A Kind of Memoir* (Columbia, SC: Camden House, 1995), 43–5.
[116] George Greenfield, *Scribblers for Bread: Aspects of the English Novel since 1945* (London: Hodder & Stoughton, 1989). See also Brian Glanville, *Football Memories: Over 50 Years of the Beautiful Game* (London: Robson Books, 2004), 62–3, 125.
[117] Greenfield, *Smattering of Monsters*, 111. Another Downing English alumnus working in publishing was Anthony John Reeve (1959), who was Editing, Design and Production manager at Oxford University Press in 1970. 'Appointments, Honours, Etc.', *NL* (1970): 35.
[118] Terrance Dicks, *The Case of the Fagin File* (London: n.p., 1980), author's note; Terrance Dicks and Malcolm Hulke, *The Making of Doctor Who* (1972; London: Target Books, 1976), esp. 24.
[119] 'On Target: Terrance Dicks' (2009), in *Doctor Who: The Monster of Peladon* (BBC DVD, 2010).

cats and dogs to rookie members of the Royal Canadian Mounted Police.

Dicks was working as a copywriter before he got his break in television.[120] Several other Downing English graduates made careers for themselves in advertising and marketing, those professions most inimical to *Scrutiny*. David Brook, who came to Cambridge in 1951, was a corporate marketing manager in the 1960s (and, in the 1980s, the beloved coach of the Halifax Rugby League Football Club, further from the world of Downing English it was scarcely possible to go).[121] Richard Dyer started as a copywriter and graduated to account executive and ultimately managing director at a Johannesburg agency (he had first gone to South Africa as an RAF pilot during the war).[122] John Metcalfe, who went up in 1940, was a driving force behind the international expansion of the Dorland agency.[123] Before taking a job in advertising he had been a reviewer for *The Spectator* and the *Sunday Times* and an occasional panellist on *The Critics*, the arts programme on the BBC Home Service.[124]

If the transition from the broadsheets and the BBC to advertising might have seemed incongruous to some observers, it would not have to Leavis. The debased standards and corrupting pressures of contemporary literary journalism, as he saw it, rewarded a slick intelligence, the same cleverness unduly prized by some Cambridge colleges and tripos examiners.[125] When Karl Miller started to do well in examinations, Leavis suspected him of 'journalistic facility'.[126] Miller went on to become the most consequential literary journalist among Leavis's pupils, responsible for the literary 'back ends' of *The Spectator* and *New Statesman*, editing *The Listener*, and founding the *London Review of Books*. In the late 1950s and early 1960s, Miller brought to literary editing a seriousness or astringency consonant with a Leavisian education. Affronted senior contributors certainly saw it that way. J. B. Priestley pronounced that Miller, like Leavis, 'hated literature'.[127] Yet although Miller chose Downing so that he could

---

[120] Dicks, *Case of the Fagin File*, n.p. (author's note).

[121] 'Appointments, Honours, Etc.', *NL* (1962): 26; 'Appointments, Retirements and Distinctions', *NL* (1986): 10; 'David Brook Tributes', *Evening Courier* (Halifax), 21 November 2006. This said, R. C. Churchill, a contributor to *Scrutiny* and the *Pelican Guide to English Literature* and a schoolmaster who read English at Downing from 1935 to 1938, wrote a Penguin Special on football in the 1950s.

[122] 'Richard Andrew (Dick) Dyer', *NL* (1994): 31.

[123] 'John Metcalfe (1940)', *NL* (1994): 35.

[124] Briggs, *Competition*, 225; Humphrey Carpenter, *The Envy of the World: Fifty Years of the BBC Third Programme and Radio 3* (London: Weidenfeld & Nicolson, 1996), 250.

[125] Leavis, *Education and the University*, 43–5; Harrison, 'Downing after the War', 258; MacKillop, *F. R. Leavis*, 340.

[126] Miller, *Rebecca's Vest*, 138; Leavis, *Education and the University*, 43.

[127] Miller, *Dark Horses*, 60.

study with Leavis, he kept a certain personal and intellectual distance. In the final year of his BA, he switched supervisors to Bradbrook, in the interests of broadening his studies rather than 'defecting', he has said.[128] After establishing himself in London, Miller returned to Cambridge periodically, undefensively defending literary journalism at meetings of the Doughty Society and the English Club.[129] In the discussion following his address to the English Club, a Downing student disparaged Frank Kermode but added that in contrast with the majority of literary journalists 'at least he had a mind'. Neil Roberts, in the audience, chalked the remark up to 'naive Leavisite arrogance'. 'Miller of course took him apart.'[130]

In *Rebecca's Vest* and *Dark Horses*, Miller has written at some length about his development and about his association with Leavis.[131] Neither of these probing examinations discloses any fierce struggle between a Leavisian faith and the ways of the literary metropole. Miller conveys Leavis's bemusement or archness about his career—he recounts a series of conversations with Leavis about the competitions on literary topics that the *New Statesman* ran among its amusements, and for which Miller eventually assumed responsibility—but the overall narrative is not one of conversion or compromise.[132] It was different for John Coleman, whom Miller used as a reviewer and who was, like Miller himself, a veteran of *Granta*.[133] Coleman's school friend and Downing contemporary David Matthews thought that Coleman failed to make a 'serious contribution to literature' commensurate with his talent because he was torn between 'what FRL stood for' and his 'natural bent as a potential writer in the mould of, say, Aldous Huxley'. Others who had come to Leavis's seminars found his 'scorn... easy to imitate', and turning his style of judgement on their own verse and fiction jolted their confidence enough to make them give up writing.[135]

Nevertheless, some Downing English became published poets and novelists. Most had day jobs or other pursuits as well. Wolf Mankowitz ran an antiques business while writing novels, screenplays, and musicals, as well as editing the journal *Politics and Letters* alongside Raymond

[128] Miller, *Rebecca's Vest*, 137.
[129] Doughty Society minute book, 209, DCCS/4/4/1/1, Downing; Roberts, ' "Leavisite" Cambridge in the 1960s', 273.
[130] The critic of Kermode was Martin Lightfoot. According to Roberts, Miller warmed to Lightfoot nevertheless, and helped launch him on his publishing career. Roberts, ' "Leavisite" Cambridge in the 1960s', 273.
[131] Miller, *Dark Horses*, chs 3, 4, 7, 11; Miller, *Rebecca's Vest*, 137–47,
[132] Miller, *Rebecca's Vest*, 140–1.
[133] Miller, *Dark Horses*, 25; Harrison, 'Downing after the War', 260; Blake Morrison, *The Movement; English Poetry and Fiction of the 1950s* (Oxford: Oxford University Press, 1980), 30.
[134] Matthews, *Memories of F. R. Leavis*, 18.
[135] Cox, *Great Betrayal*, 79.

Williams and another Cambridge friend in the late 1940s.[136] Poetry and
novels account for a number of David Holbrook's scores of published
books, the others prowling through educational theory and practice, philosophy, psychoanalysis, music, and literary criticism. Ronald Duncan, a
poet and librettist as well as the founder of an agricultural commune, was
a strange temperamental fit for Downing English. The child of a wealthy
family, born overseas, taught by a private crammer; the wanderer who
strikes up friendships with Ezra Pound and Ghandi; the spontaneous
buyer of derelict cottages who lives for a time beachcombing for barrels of
wine, butter, and other goods washed up near his Devon home: these
were roles not alien to the chronicle of upper-middle-class bohemianism,
but quite out of keeping with the profile of Leavis's pupils.[137] Duncan's
father had been at Christ's College, but he opted for Downing because he
had been impressed by Leavis's interest in contemporary poetry. Duncan
said that experiencing great art caused him physical pain, and Leavis's
analyses of Hopkins's poetry were at once invaluably revealing and excru-
ciatingly moving.[138]

Leavis was not an active mentor to younger poets *as* poets after his
sponsorship of Ronald Bottrall in the early 1930s. He drew D. J. Enright,
who started at Downing in 1938, into writing essays and reviews for *Scrutiny*, but apparently kept his distance from Enright's poetry-writing.[139] As
editor of *Poets of the 1950's* (1955), Enright became a sponsor to 'the
Movement', which included several younger Cambridge students who,
though not at Downing, frequented Leavis's seminars and lectures.
Donald Davie and Thom Gunn have both attested to Leavis's influence.
Leavis's rigour, scepticism, and critique of romanticism have their echoes
in the two poets' work from the 1950s onwards, Blake Morrison has
argued in his book on the Movement.[140] The association with the Movement and the efforts of admirers such as Martin Green in *A Mirror for
Anglo-Saxons* (1960) and S. Gorley Putt in a 1961 essay to enlist Leavis as
a spokesman (the gendered term is advisable) for a putatively English

[136] 'Wolf Mankowitz (1942)', *NL* (1998): 36–7; Dai Smith, *Raymond Williams: A
Warrior's Tale* (Cardigan: Parthian Books, 2008), 240–7.
[137] Duncan's memoir, *All Men Are Islands*, may be compared with Jack Lindsay, *Fanfrolico, and After* (London: Bodley Head, 1962).
[138] Duncan, *All Men Are Islands*, 84–90, 103–5. One wonders about some of Duncan's
Leavis stories. Describing supervisions in which Leavis complained of others' failings and
slights against him, Duncan reports him as saying, 'Tom Eliot's not written anything since
the *Quartets*' (90), but Duncan began studying with Leavis three years before 'Burnt
Norton' was published.
[139] See David Holbrook, untitled essay, *Cambridge Quarterly* 25/4 (1996): 346.
[140] Morrison, *The Movement*, 31–3; and, for Enright, 2–3, 33–5. See also Donald Davie,
These the Companions: Recollections (Cambridge: Cambridge University Press, 1982), 23–4,
74–82.

plainness and decency alongside Orwell, one version of Lawrence, and C. P. Snow provided some of the impetus for Leavis to dissociate himself from Snow, which of course he did in spectacular fashion.[141]

It was through Philip Hobsbaum's translation of his teacher's practice to a writers' workshop that Leavis's English school made its most concerted contribution to creative writing. Together with Peter Redgrove, Peter Porter, Martin Bell, and Edward Lucie-Smith, Hobsbaum was a core member of The Group in London in the 1950s. Later on, Hobsbaum started similar workshops in Belfast and Glasgow when he took up academic jobs in those cities, taking a place, in Neal Ascherson's phrase, in the 'mental furniture' of Seamus Heaney, Liz Lochhead, Alasdair Gray, and other poets.[142] The London Group began meeting when formal writers' workshops along American lines, such as the already well-established programme at the University of Iowa, were unknown in Britain, and there were no ready-made models for writers' groups of comparable focus and discipline.[143] As a Downing undergraduate, Hobsbaum had organized poetry groups and edited *Delta*, sparring with members of the Doughty Society over editorial decisions. (Harold Mason, at this time a supervisor to many Downing undergraduates, 'asked whether an editor should include weaker poems in order to make the magazine sufficiently large. Mr Mason further proposed that the meeting vote on the motion, that it was not worth the editor's going into print if he had not a better collection than that in the present number of "Delta." ')[144] In 1956, Hobsbaum took over the stewardship of a London poetry group that had met at G. S. Fraser's flat until he moved to Leicester to teach. The gatherings at Fraser's had been rowdy 'bottle parties'. Under Hobsbaum, the circle became 'the sort of concerned critical group which he had had at Downing College, Cambridge, and the evenings were much more formally organized. Only one poet read each week, in the carefully-timed first half. After a break (coffee) there came a second half when you read poems you had brought'.[145]

[141] MacKillop, *F. R. Leavis*, 317. See also Martin Green, *Children of the Sun: A Narrative of 'Decadence' in England after 1918* (New York: Basic Books, 1976), 413–21; F. R. Leavis to the *Sunday Times*, 1 November 1964, in *Letters in Criticism*, 114.

[142] Neal Ascherson, 'Great Brain Spotter', *Independent on Sunday*, 28 February 1993.

[143] Mark McGurl, *The Program Era: Postwar Fiction and the Rise of Creative Writing* (Cambridge, Mass.: Harvard University Press, 2009), ch. 2; Christopher Hilliard, *To Exercise Our Talents: The Democratization of Writing in Britain* (Cambridge, Mass.: Harvard University Press, 2006), esp. ch. 8.

[144] Doughty Society minute book, 109–12, quotation from 110 (23 November 1954), DCCS/4/4/1/1, Downing. Hobsbaum presented a paper the following week defending *Delta* in more detail. Ibid., 114 (29 November 1954).

[145] Alan Brownjohn, untitled typescript, n.d., The Group papers, MS 4557/1360, Reading.

Looking back, Hobsbaum described his Group as 'an experiment in practical criticism', 'an activity derived ultimately from the practical criticism classes of Richards and Leavis'. The poems, stories, and chapters to be read were stencilled and duplicated—Hobsbaum's wife, Hannah Kelly, another Group member, shouldered that burden—and circulated to participants a week before the meeting. 'The provision of scripts meant that there was a built in aid towards relevance in discussion. Divergent opinions could always be referred back to the words on the page, and this prevented discussion from straying into the realms of metaphysics and conjecture.'[146] Lucie-Smith quipped that the Group's biggest debts were to Cambridge English and the duplicating machine: the approaches of the former could not have been put to work without the provision for making multiple copies.[147] The discussions led Hobsbaum himself back to academic work: he said later that a conversation at one meeting with Lucie-Smith and Mark Roskill was what convinced him to go to Sheffield to begin a PhD under Empson. 'I was particularly intrigued by the need to relate divergent readings of poems to each other and to the text which occasioned them.' The questions, about the ontology of the text, were Empson's and Richards's more than they were Leavis's: but it was a Leavisian procedure that had led Hobsbaum to this point.[148]

Actors and directors drew on Leavis's training in reading in less formal ways. Many Downing students were involved in Cambridge's active theatre scene, and two distiguished directors, Peter Wood and Trevor Nunn, read English with Leavis, having been introduced to his work at school.[149] Student actors and directors at other colleges also frequented Leavis's lectures and went to his seminars, including Nunn's predecessor as artistic director of the Royal Shakespeare Company, Peter Hall. Hall had resolved before he arrived at Cambridge to 'learn as much about Shakespeare as I possibly could, because I wanted to direct Shakespeare'.[150] He has described Leavis as a decisive influence on his generation of directors, counting Nunn, Richard Eyre, and Jonathan Miller as well as himself among those so indebted.[151] Wood, too, has spoken of Leavis's influence on his practice as a director.[152]

---

[146] Philip Hobsbaum, untitled typescript, n.d., The Group papers, MS 4557/1358, Reading.

[147] Edward Lucie-Smith, 'Uses and Abuses of the Literary Group', *Critical Survey*, 1/2 (spring 1963): 78.

[148] Hobsbaum, untitled typescript, n.d., The Group papers, MS 4557/1358, Reading.

[149] Harrison, 'Downing after the War', 262; Ronald Hayman, 'Peter Wood: A Partnership', *The Times*, 8 June 1974. For other Downing English undergraduates involved in theatre while at Cambridge, see 'Obituaries', *NL* (1986): 18 (John Kimber); 'Philip John Strick (1958)', *NL* (2007): 55.

[150] John Tusa, interview with Sir Peter Hall, BBC Radio 3, 2 December 2001. Available at <http://www.bbc.co.uk/radio3/johntusainterview/hall_transcript.shtml> (accessed 22 March 2011).

[151] Heather Neill, 'My Best Teacher', *Times Education Supplement*, 2 March 2001.

[152] Hayman, 'Peter Wood'.

Yet Leavis hardly ever went to the theatre and, as another seminar member from another college, Ian McKellen, has remarked, he was 'scathing about actors' interpretations of Shakespeare'.[153] His insistence on the importance of reading poetic drama as something other than realist drama in verse form did not preclude attending to dramaturgy, but in practice Leavis had little to say about the plays' theatricality. The incongruity of his theatrical influence becomes all the more pronounced when he is compared, as he usually was, with the patron of Cambridge theatre, G. H. W. Rylands: patrician, a fellow of King's, a Bloomsbury affiliate with enviable West End connections (he directed John Gielgud in *Hamlet* with Peggy Ashcroft as Ophelia).[154] 'Perhaps', Hall has said, 'our ideal was to speak like Rylands, and think like Leavis.'[155]

What did it mean to think, as a director, like Leavis? For Hall, it meant working outwards from painstaking textual analysis, puzzling over metaphor and ambiguity.[156] In the productions of Shakespeare's history plays during Hall's tenure at the RSC, the emphasis on close reading could be discerned in the acting as well. The verse was delivered with cool, rational discipline.[157] The *conception* of the productions owed far less to Leavis. A directorial version of practical criticism could lead into any number of ways of staging and directing a play. As a Shakespeare critic, Leavis did not deal in overarching interpretations of the plays as a whole—unlike Jan Kott, whose vision of Shakespeare as 'our contemporary', possessed of a sensibility compatible with existentialism and the theatre of the absurd, Hall and Peter Brook invoked in the programme notes to their productions of the history plays and *King Lear* in the early 1960s.[158] Inasmuch as Hall

[153] 'Cambridge University Undergraduate Productions', <http://www.mckellen.com/stage/index0.htm>, (accessed 23 December 2010). Another Cambridge actor who carried a debt to Leavis—and his wife—is Miriam Margolyes, who was taught by Q. D. Leavis from 1959 to 1962, when she was supervising for Newnham College. Miriam Margolyes to Kate Leavis, 8 April 1981, Q. D. Leavis papers, GCPP Leavis 1/3/4/2, Girton.

[154] Paul Edmondson, 'Rylands, George Humphrey Wolferstan (1902–1999)', *Oxford Dictionary of National Biography* (Oxford, 2004; online edn, May 2010), <http://www.oxforddnb.com/view/article/71832>, accessed 12 January 2011.

[155] Sally Beauman, *The Royal Shakespeare Company: A History of Ten Decades* (Oxford: Oxford University Press, 1982), 268.

[156] Beauman, *Royal Shakespeare Company*, 268; Tusa, interview with Hall; Neill, 'My Best Teacher'.

[157] Ibid., 268–9.

[158] Frank Kermode, 'The Shakespearian Rag', *New York Review of Books*, 24 September 1964. The essay on *Othello* (F. R. Leavis, 'Diabolic Intellect and the Noble Hero: A Note on *Othello*', *Scrutiny* 6/3 [1937]: 259–83) is a striking exception. Sir Laurence Olivier wrote to Leavis to say how the essay had affected his interpretation of Othello's character. Richard Wilson, a student at York in the 1970s, says that Leavis dined out on this story in his lectures. 'Leavis's story was that Olivier had had the temerity to write a letter of thanks to him for the influence of his essay, but that he was so appalled to be associated with such a production and film, and to be approached about it by a mere mummer, that he had not deigned to reply.' Wilson, letter to the editor, *London Review of Books*, 6 December 1990.

and Nunn were 'Leavisites' (as they have been described), it was in their processes rather than in specific visions or ideologies.[159]

All these types of career have affinities with the powers of thought and expression that literary study is supposed to develop, even if Leavis and other teachers of English would have been loath to acknowledge the usefulness of a literary training for future copywriters. Not every post-Downing career was like this. When Geoffrey Stuttard reflected on his time at Downing (he switched from English to history after Part I, on Leavis's advice or insistence), he made a point of emphasizing the diversity of 'what happened to ex-Leavis students' in later life.[160] Stuttard became an authority on industrial relations. A good many Downing English alumni took jobs in fields with only the most oblique relation to their literary training or *Scrutiny*'s preoccupations. The garage proprietor's son notified the alumni newsletter that he had become a director of his 'family business' within two years of completing his degree: for him and the man who followed his father into a managerial role in the carpet industry, the choice of English probably had no vocational consequences.[161] With the others who went into business—heading the mirror department of the Pilkington Brothers glass company, for instance, or managing retail sales for Berkertex, the clothing company best known for its bridal gowns—the mere existence of the Cambridge qualification doubtless eclipsed the fact that it was in English rather than history or some other subject.[162] For the Downing English graduates who became solicitors, the degree may have functioned as little more than a character reference. Solicitors had traditionally doubted the merits of university graduates, not least because of the strong association between Oxbridge and the bar, and graduates were underrepresented in the profession at least until the end of the 1950s.[163] British industry had a thin record of hiring arts graduates, but after the war the universities stepped up efforts to place them, which may account for the handful of Downing English graduates in industry.[164]

College traditions, too, guided graduates' paths. The available histories of Downing are patchy, but the records of the committee that oversaw

[159] Janet Watts, 'The Nunn Story', *Observer Colour Supplement*, 2 May 1982, 39, quoted in Christopher J. McCullough, 'The Cambridge Connection: Towards a Materialist Theatre Practice', in Graham Holderness (ed.), *The Shakespeare Myth* (Manchester: Manchester University Press, 1988), 113.
[160] Geoffrey Stuttard, 'Three Bites at the Cherry', *NL* (2001): 25.
[161] DCAT/5/1/13, p. 125; 'Appointments, Honours, Etc.', *NL* (1962): 29; DCAT/5/1/11, p. 358; 'Honours, Appointments, Etc.', *NL* (1960): 34.
[162] 'Appointments, Etc.', *NL* (1961): 37; 'Appointments, Honours, Etc.', *NL* (1970): 33.
[163] Schwartz, 'Professions, Elites, and Universities', 952.
[164] Ibid., 950, 952; Greenstein, 'Junior Members', 71. See also Paul Vaughan, *Exciting Times in the Accounts Department* (London: Sinclair Stevenson, 1995), 9–10.

admissions indicate that the college had reasonably strong imperial connections.[165] Alex Hill, the master in the early years of the twentieth century, was a keen supporter of imperial connections, and Henry Jackson, the tutor and thus the fellow in charge of admissions, 'admitted more men from India, Singapore and Hong Kong than was customary in other colleges'.[166] In Leavis's first few years, those reading English included a colonial official's son born in Simla and the son of a 'far Eastern merchant'.[167] Since colonial service was a traditional career choice for Cambridge graduates, it is not surprising that several of Leavis's pupils should pursue such careers, in Africa as well as on the Indian subcontinent.[168] When Eric Clegg joined the Colonial Audit Service in Hong Kong and F. C. Tinkler, the author of two *Scrutiny* essays, joined the Indian Civil Service, they were not conforming to a Leavisian pattern but following a path familiar among Downing alumni generally.[169]

The history of a college or a 'school' always threatens to devolve into particularities, but it is possible to draw some general conclusions about the social history of Downing English. Two points stand out. The first is that claims for a snug fit between Leavis's English school and the post-war meritocratic moment are exaggerated, as is the way with claims about 'the meritocracy'. The persistence of the public schools alongside non-fee-paying grammar schools, coupled with highly unstandardized conditions of university entrance, meant that Britain never had the level of coordination and state monopoly required for a stringently selective system for educating élites, such as France's.[170] As those schooled under the new dispensation entered university, the proportion of working-class students reading English at Downing increased. However, they still constituted a minority of the cohort. Moreover, nearly 40 per cent of the working-class men reading English from the mid-1950s did not take the Butler Act route to Cambridge. Either their parents could pay school fees—an instance of increasing prosperity rather than social mobility—or they won scholarships of the sort

---

[165] Selection Committee minute book, 1935–54, DCAT 9/1/2, Downing.

[166] W. O. Henderson, 'The Age of Storm and Stress, 1888–1914', in Stanley French et al., *Aspects of Downing History*, vol. 2 (Cambridge: Downing College Association, 1989), 76; French, *History of Downing College*, 139.

[167] Margaretha Sandys-Wood, 'Adrian Leslie Sandys-Wood (1934)', *NL* (1999): 38; DCAT/5/1/7, p. 59, Downing; DCAT/5/1/7, p. 11, Downing.

[168] Anthony Gregson became a chartered surveyor and worked for the War Department Lands Branch in the 1950s and 1960s, which took him to postings in East Africa. 'Anthony Thomas Reynolds Gregson (1939)', *NL* (1991): 36.

[169] 'Distinctions and Appointments of Downing Men During the Past Year', *NL* (1938): 6; 'Appointments and Other News', *NL* (1942): 10; F. C. Tinkler, 'The Winter's Tale', *Scrutiny* 5/4 (March 1937): 343–64; Tinkler, 'Cymbeline', *Scrutiny* 7/1 (June 1938): 5–20.

[170] For an anatomy, see Jean-François Sirinelli, *Génération intellectuelle: khâgneux et normaliens dans l'entre-deux-guerres* (Paris : Fayard, 1988).

that direct-grant and maintained schools had been obliged to offer since the beginning of the twentieth century.

Secondly, the commonplace that a great many of Leavis's pupils were inspired to become teachers is borne out by the evidence assembled here. That said, teaching was also the most likely career for an English graduate from Clare or Emmanuel, and still more for a Leeds or Nottingham graduate. Other Downing English graduates made use of their training, sometimes in ways that must have surprised or dismayed Leavis, in fields from advertising to the theatre. Discussions of Leavis tend to be discussions of English and criticism, and the due attention paid to the students who became teachers and critics in their own right means that the carpet manufacturers escape notice. As well as being the leader of a movement, Leavis was a college teacher like other college teachers, working with undergraduates for whom literature would not be a vocation.

4
Will Teachers Bear Scrutiny?

When the *Observer* ran a feature on Leavis's pupils in the wake of his debate with C. P. Snow in the early 1960s, it claimed to have uncovered a 'hidden network of Leavisites'.[1] Raymond O'Malley, one of those identified, wrote later, 'We were found, sinister fact, to be ensconced and "influential" in schools, colleges and universities in several continents.' It would have been strange, he added, 'if we had been found selling cosmetics. *Of course* we were in teaching.'[2] As we have seen, former pupils of Leavis's *were* selling, if not cosmetics, bridal gowns and carpet. But the ones most likely to be described as 'Leavisites' were conspicuous by their presence in educational institutions.

Most of the Leavis pupils who went on to teaching careers worked in grammar schools. Together with the public schools, grammar schools were the usual roost of the Oxbridge graduate turned schoolmaster. Before the move towards comprehensive schools in the 1960s, grammar and public schools were practically the only ones in which teachers worked with older pupils aiming for university. Through the work of David Holbrook, the *Scrutiny* movement had a far-reaching influence in the secondary modern schools established or converted after the Education Act of 1944 for less 'academic' children. Few Downing alumni taught in secondary modern schools, however. Several of Leavis's pupils rose to become school inspectors ('HMIs'), and a few had a hand in writing successive 'memoranda' on the teaching of English issued intermittently by the Incorporated Association of Assistant Masters in Secondary Schools, quasi-official volumes that articulated some of the conventional wisdom of the profession, and of grammar-school teachers in particular.[3] Denys

[1] Guy Ortolano, *The Two Cultures Controversy: Science, Literature and Cultural Politics in Postwar Britain* (Cambridge: Cambridge University Press, 2009), 243.

[2] Raymond O'Malley, 'Charisma?', in Denys Thompson (ed.), *The Leavises: Recollections and Impressions* (Cambridge: Cambridge University Press, 1984), 58 (emphasis in original).

[3] *The Teaching of English: Issued by the Incorporated Association of Assistant Masters in Secondary Schools* (Cambridge: Cambridge University Press, 1952), xi; *The Teaching of English: Issued by the Incorporated Association of Assistant Masters in Secondary Schools* (Cambridge, 1966), xi–xii: R. R. Pedley was a member of the committee that wrote the 1952 edition; Jack Dalglish of the committee that revised it in 1966. Dalglish became an HMI; so did another Downing English

Thompson became headmaster of Yeovil Grammar School and R. R. Pedley head of the City Boys' School, Leicester, then Chislehurst and Sidcup Grammar School, and then St Dunstan's, which had sent so many boys to the Downing English school in the 1940s. A headmaster spoke with authority in mid-twentieth-century Britain, though none of Leavis's pupils led a school whose headship conferred the standing in national debate that the leaders of Eton or Manchester Grammar enjoyed. Many of them, however, exercised their influence (or 'influence') in less public or official ways—in teachers' own forums (associations, journals) and as teachers of teachers.

Both training colleges—which taught aspiring teachers who had completed their secondary schooling—and institutes of education—university departments that trained students who already had degrees to be teachers—employed lecturers responsible for the subject of English. Those lecturers typically had experience as schoolteachers before they were appointed. Classroom practices that other teachers could profit from frequently paved the way to teacher-training positions. O'Malley, taught for many years at Dartington Hall, the progressive school in Devon to which the Leavises sent their first child. He and Thompson co-authored several series of English textbooks, and in 1959 he became a University Lecturer in Education at Cambridge. When Alan Durband, who went up to Downing in 1949, became a lecturer at C. F. Mott Training College in Merseyside, he was the author of three volumes of *English Workshop* for Hutchinson's educational publishing arm. He also had a record as an effective and inspiring English and drama teacher at the Liverpool Institute High School, where one of his appreciative A-level pupils was Paul McCartney.[4] Frank Whitehead, a regular at the Leavises' afternoon teas and a follower though never formally a pupil, taught in grammar schools before becoming a lecturer at the University of London Institute of Education and later at Sheffield University's Institute of Education.

Whitehead was recruited to Sheffield by Boris Ford, who was professor of education there from 1960 to 1963 before becoming a dean at the new University of Sussex. The 'governing-class authority' Leavis discerned in Ford was matched by energy and courteous persistence. He was an

graduate, Alfred Monk. 'Appointments, Retirements and Distinctions', *NL* (1982): 13; 'Appointments, Retirements and Distinctions', *NL* (1985): 12 (Monk). On the association, see Frank Moorby, 'English in the Grammar School', *Use of English* 4/3 (1953): 166. (Moorby was a Downing English graduate, going up in 1935.)

[4] 'Appointments and Awards, Etc.', *NL* (1957): 36; 'Publications', *NL* (1959): 28; 'Appointments, Honours, Etc.', *NL* (1962): 27; Dave Laing, '*Scrutiny* to Subcultures: Notes on Literary Criticism and Popular Music', *Popular Music* 13/2 (1994): 179; Bob Spitz, *The Beatles: The Biography* (New York: Little, Brown, & Co., 2005), 84.

accomplished networker and organizer.[5] During the Second World War, Ford worked for the Army Bureau of Current Affairs, developing teaching materials and instructional programmes for what was widely regarded as a significant initiative in Forces education and popular civics.[6] When the war ended, the Carnegie Trust was persuaded to fund its successor, 'a Bureau of Current Affairs, the aim of which will be to continue and extend, for the benefit of the population as a whole, the kind of service which, during the war, has been provided by the Army Bureau of Current Affairs'.[7] The bureau's director, the respected adult educationalist and future head of the Arts Council, W. E. Williams, was able to interpret 'current affairs' liberally, and Ford had the freedom to produce booklets and other material addressing more general educational and cultural questions. Several were on topics close to *Scrutiny*'s concerns and written by *Scrutiny* contributors: Ford himself on reading, W. H. Mellers on music, Thompson on 'the problem of leisure'; one of the bureau's last pamphlets, from 1951, was *Art and Painting* by the well-dead D. H. Lawrence. The bureau also published *Use of English*, the successor to the journal *English in Schools* that Thompson had been editing since 1939.[8] (He would continue to edit *Use of English* until 1969, when Whitehead took over.) Looking back, Ford acknowledged that it had been an improbable contrivance to launch such a journal from the Bureau of Current Affairs. The editorial board consisted of Thompson, Ford, O'Malley, and Holbrook, whom Ford had taken on at the BCA in 1947. It was through their meetings twice a year at Thompson's house that Holbrook formed 'close links' with Thompson.[9]

Use of English was to function as a 'workshop' for teachers, reporting on promising initiatives and providing model lessons and exercises.[10] Its contributors included many Downing English graduates. For a long time, *Use of English* was 'the only voice for English teachers'.[11] From 1963, it was complemented by the *Bulletin* of the National Association of Teach-

[5] Leavis to Bonamy Dobrée, 13 February 1944, Bonamy Dobrée correspondence, Leeds; Donald Mitchell, 'Obituary: Professor Boris Ford', *The Independent*, 27 May 1998.

[6] S. P. Mackenzie, *Politics and Military Morale: Current-Affairs and Citizenship Education in the British Army, 1914–1950* (Oxford: Clarendon Press, 1992), chs 5, 6, 8.

[7] 'Press communiqué, not to be published before the morning newspapers of Friday, 4th January 1946', typescript, ED 136/610, National Archives, Kew.

[8] Boris Ford, *The Bureau of Current Affairs 1946–1951* (London: Bureau of Current Affairs, 1951), 20, 29–30. Chatto & Windus assumed responsibility for Use of English in 1951.

[9] Boris Ford, 'David Holbrook: A Portrait', in Edwin Webb (ed.), *Powers of Being: David Holbrook and His Work* (Madison, NJ: Fairleigh Dickinson University Press, 1995), 40.

[10] Brian Jackson, 'Introduction: English versus Examinations', in Jackson (ed.), *English versus Examinations: A Handbook for Teachers* (London: Chatto & Windus, 1965), 9.

[11] David Allen, *English Teaching since 1965: How Much Growth?* (London: Heinemann, 1980), 8.

ers of English. NATE had grown out of local English teachers' groups, especially in the London area, and its *Bulletin* was intended to cover the activities and experiments of English teachers' groups around the country.[12] NATE was a broad church, but, in the 1960s at least, Thompson, Whitehead, Holbrook, Ford, and other Leavis pupils such as Esmor Jones were prominent members. *Scrutiny* voices were thus audible in English teachers' conversations, and Leavisian connections instrumental in establishing the settings in which those conversations took place.

Those conversations turned, on how English-teaching could be better: more meaningful, more relevant, more responsive, more creative. Many teachers were dissatisfied with the version of the subject they encountered at training college or in the classroom: English was bent to instrumental ends, a utilitarianism manifested in formal grammar teaching and dull composition work. An instrumental conception of English obviously did not give priority to literature. The 1952 edition of the Assistant Masters' memorandum hesitantly defined the subject as 'the English Language in all its forms'. In the list of examples that followed, literature was referred to only briefly.[13] For Leavis's pupils and collaborators, and for restless teachers who warmed to their ideas, English had to revolve around literature, and any trade-off between literature and language was spurious. It was by engaging with literature that a person truly learned the language.

For the *Scrutiny* group, schools were an object of both anxiety and hope. Schools could be a salient in the struggle against Fordist culture, but they were part of the machinery of mass civilization themselves. Documentation was provided by the responses to a questionnaire the editors sent to *Scrutiny* readers who taught in schools, asking them to comment on their training college experiences. L. C. Knights wrote up the results in an essay entitled 'Will Training Colleges Bear Scrutiny?' It was a dispiriting catalogue of authoritarianism, trust in rote-learning, and philistinism. Like so much of *Scrutiny*'s cultural criticism, Knights's essay lapsed into the metaphorical when it passed from symptoms to explanation: 'Behind the educational system stand the cinema, newspapers, book societies, and Big Business—the whole machinery of "Democracy" and standardization.' Training colleges turned out teachers

[12] 'Editorial', *NATE Bulletin: The Bulletin of the National Association for the Teaching of English* 1/2 (spring 1964), 1; James Britton, 'How We Got Here', in Nicholas Bagnall (ed.), *New Movements in the Study and Teaching of English* (London: Maurice Temple Smith, 1973), 20–1.

[13] Incorporated Association of Assistant Masters, *Teaching of English* (1952 edn), 2.

'perfectly fitted to their environment, perfectly unfitted for the work which they should do'.[14]

But what was the work they should do? *Scrutiny* principles informed some radically different philosophies of education and conceptions of its role in modern Britain. The specific teaching practices that went with these philosophies did not always have close precedents in the pages of *Scrutiny* itself. The most direct application of *Scrutiny* approaches in schoolrooms was the dissemination of the movement's version of practical criticism, which Denys Thompson developed in his sixth-form classes and promoted through *Use of English*.

Thompson's teaching at Gresham's School in the 1930s was closely connected with the problems and texts he was exploring in *Scrutiny*. (He was not alone in this regard: Mellers remarked of his music criticism, 'In *Scrutiny* I'm doing on a higher level the same kind of thing as I do in adult classes.')[15] The first 'literary' text Thompson assigned to his sixth form at Gresham's one year was Stuart Chase's *Mexico*, a comparison of pre-industrial village life with civilization of Middletown.[16] (Thompson and O'Malley also quarried Chase's works in their book on essay and précis writing, *English for the Living*.)[17] In October 1932, Thompson informed Leavis: 'I've been giving my top form an introduction to Bottrall following upon a reading of [Richards's] Science and Poetry and the relevant poems—in the form of sheets containing *Salute to Them that Know, We are the end*, and *The Future is not for Us*.' Leavis's *New Bearings in English Poetry*, published earlier in the year, had concluded with an enthusiastic discussion of Bottrall's work. Thompson added: 'Your review of Dos Passos and *The Literary Mind* I've found very useful in teaching; and I don't know what I would do without *Fiction and the Reading Public*.'[18] Leavis's piece on Max Eastman's *Literary Mind* and his essay on John Dos Passos's novels and the 'unremitting, pervasive, masturbatory manipulations' of commercial culture they depicted had also appeared in *Scrutiny* only months beforehand.[19]

[14] L. C. Knights, 'Will Training Colleges Bear Scrutiny?', *Scrutiny* 1/3 (December 1932): 259. See also Denys Thompson, 'Advertising God', *Scrutiny* 1/3 (December 1932): 247.

[15] W. H. Mellers, 'A Reply', *Scrutiny* 11/2 (December 1942): 124.

[16] Ian MacKillop, *F. R. Leavis: A Life in Criticism* (London: Allen Lane, 1995), 145.

[17] R. O'Malley and D. Thompson, *English for the Living* (London: Methuen, 1949), 20–1.

[18] Thompson to Leavis, 16 October [1932], Chatto & Windus archive, CW 53/2, Reading. Italics replace underlining in the original; Thompson also underlined the 'and' between the last two titles. 'The Future Is Not for Us' is the Bottrall poem from which Thompson quoted in the *Scrutiny* essay quoted in above.

[19] F. R. Leavis, 'A Serious Artist', *Scrutiny* 1/2 (September 1932): 175.

As *Culture and Environment* made clear, Thompson believed that practical criticism had a valuable place in schools. His next book, *Reading and Discrimination*, was an instruction manual in evaluative practical criticism that sold in large numbers. The initial print run of 2,000 sold out in two and a half years, whereupon Chatto & Windus printed another 1,500. *Reading and Discrimination* had sold 3,500 copies by 1939. Another 7,500 copies were printed and bound in the next decade. From 1949 until the final impression in 1957, Chatto printed 21,800 copies, in batches ranging from 2,500 to 6,000 copies. The consignment of 6,000 copies sold out within two and a half years. In the 1950s, some of these copies were packaged as school editions, and others bound for the general book trade.[20] The sales of *Reading and Discrimination* attest to the existence of a receptive public far larger than the networks of Cambridge alumni and *Scrutiny* readers. The spike in sales in the 1950s, nearly two decades after first publication, was probably also a consequence of Thompson's growing stature as an educationalist.

Thompson also sought to promote practical criticism in other ways. In 1948, he proposed a series of schools broadcasts aimed at 'the sixth forms of state schools and upper forms of "public" schools'. 'What I have in mind', he told the BBC, 'is the kind of thing exemplified in Boris Ford's BCA pamphlet, *The Reading Habit*.'[21] He envisaged a series of half a dozen talks with an accompanying pamphlet that would be published by *English in Schools*. After several introductory lectures on 'the need to discriminate between various types of reading matter' and 'the tools of the job', there would follow 'three or four talks ... devoted to discussion of passages of prose and verse printed in the pamphlet, and read in advance by the listeners'.[22] Nothing came of this scheme, but Thompson succeeded in establishing a programme of practical criticism teaching when *Use of English* succeeded *English in Schools* a year later in 1949.

For most of the following decade, the journal issued sheets with texts and excerpts for class use. The accompanying section of each issue of the journal bore the title 'Criticism in Practice', the phrase Leavis had come

[20] Chatto & Windus ledgers, 9/634, 10/268, 10/712, 11/148, 11/382, 11/578, 12/247, Reading. In the 1930s and 1940s especially, the printed pages were not immediately bound for sale, but demand was fairly steady, and in response the publisher would have another 100 or 250 copies bound and readied for sale: if the print runs are not a reliable proxy for sales figures, the binding orders are.
[21] Ford's pamphlet, parts of which recapitulate and even pastiche Q. D. Leavis's *Fiction and the Reading Public*, was republished in the first issue of *Use of English*: Boris Ford, 'The Reading Habit', *Use of English* 1/1 (1949): 9–14 (see esp. 13–14).
[22] Thompson to John Scupham, 1 June 1948, RCONT3: Thompson: Talks Misc. 1943–56, BBC WAC. Compare Anon., 'School Literature Broadcasts', *Use of English* 2/3 (1951): 156–7.

to prefer to 'practical criticism'.[23] Explaining the section's rationale, O'Malley wrote that, in their simplest form, impromptu comparisons of two texts of different quality 'may merely expose some of the tricks of tendentious writing', but, more positively, could jolt pupils into recognizing what good writing had to offer.[24] O'Malley and Thompson ran the section for the first few issues, and, once it was established, other teachers took turns: Whitehead, Holbrook, J. H. Walsh of Chislehurst and Sidcup Grammar, Dorothy Cooper of Scarborough Girls' High School. The format was familiar from Richards, from Thompson's *Reading and Discrimination*, and from the Downing College entrance examinations. In the selections of texts for comparison, the fix was clearly in: Donne versus Shelley; a Mark Twain description of the Mississippi versus a shampoo advertisement; John Clare versus 'a film song of some years ago'; a cornflake advertisement versus a description of grains from Richard Jefferies's *Field and Hedgerow*, 'serious in intention and honest in method'.[25] (O'Malley and Thompson also used Jeffries as a contrast with a beer advertisement's evocation of rural life in the second volume of *English for the Living*.)[26]

However, the strengths and weaknesses of the passages presented were not treated as self-evident, and the framers of the exercise provided pointers and suggestions for teachers. Moreover, teachers were encouraged to report on their experiences using the exercises in the classroom—printed sheets with the unattributed poems and prose passages for classroom use were made available by the Bureau of Current Affairs once enough teachers indicated that they would use them—and *Use of English* commented on the various reports. In this way the 'Criticism in Practice' section became an educational and critical collaboration. The series' continued success, Whitehead reminded readers when he assumed responsibility for one issue's 'Criticism in Practice' section, 'depends to a great extent upon the continuance of a "two-way traffic" in ideas and classroom experience'. Verbatim quotations from the pupils' own responses were especially valuable, he added.[27] The responses that teachers did report offer a glimpse of this *Scrutiny* pedagogy in action.

[23] Frank Whitehead, 'F. R. Leavis and the Schools', in Thompson (ed.), *The Leavises*, 147.
[24] Raymond O'Malley, 'Criticism in Practice: I', *Use of English* 1/1 (1949): 30.
[25] Ibid., 30–1, 33–4; 'Criticism in Practice: II...Report by Raymond O'Malley', *Use of English* 1/2 (1949): 93; 'Criticism in Practice: XIII...Further Work by Denys Thompson', *Use of English* 4/1 (1952): 48–9; 'Criticism in Practice: II...Further Work set by Denys Thompson', *Use of English* 1/2 (1949): 97.
[26] R. O'Malley and Denys Thompson, *English for the Living: Part II* (London: Methuen, 1952), 32–3.
[27] 'Criticism in Practice: V: Part "A" by Frank Whitehead', *Use of English* 2/1 (1950): 29.

When asked to compare Donne's 'A Valediction Forbidding Mourning' with Lord Lytton's 'Absent Yet Present', grammar school sixth formers provided evidence of 'genuine and discerning appreciation of the Donne...but, on the whole, unfavourable reactions to the Victorian poem found more coherent and quotable expression'. A number of pupils commented on the Lytton poem's emotional shallowness and 'unchanging rhythm'. Others faulted it for stringing images together without a 'unifying principle': 'one girl wrote "...there is no development of the main idea; the poet simply meanders round the main subject. The ideas have no connexion with each other and when the ideas are taken together the poem does not make sense." '[28] A lower-sixth girl offered a contrasting assessment in the Palgrave tradition: 'The first poem [Donne] is much too calculated and clever....The flow of ideas and images in B [Lytton] is typical of the rush of emotions in young people.' Such responses, Whitehead said, should be allowed to run free in classroom discussion, 'since for many adolescents they represent a necessary phase of growth'. If it was gratifying that a number of the respondents were receptive to Donne's poetic, their responses also revealed the limitations of their understanding of imagery—that its function was illustrative or mimetic. Whitehead's assignment for the next month was designed to prompt them to consider a poem in which the imagery did not depend altogether upon 'the resemblance of the things compared'.[29]

The goal of 'Criticism in Practice' was thus not simply to promote particular kinds of poetry at the expense of others, but to foster an understanding of the poetics on which those valuations rested. That tastes tended to align themselves with implicit theories of poetry was suggested by a teacher reporting on his pupils' comparison of Donne's description of the whale in *The Progress of the Soul* and Shelley's 'To a Skylark': in the responses of two 'able pupils' who preferred the Shelley he saw in references to 'caesuras and other technical preoccupations the effect of old-type academic-conventional training; he says that discussion left them unconvinced, though uncomfortable that cherished unconscious prejudices had been challenged'.[30]

The best response that O'Malley saw was the work of a girl in the upper sixth form of a school in East Anglia. He quoted it at length without further comment. The two poems raised questions that bore on the Leavisian concern with unity, with the demanding relationship between formal order and the open exploration of experience:

[28] 'Criticism in Practice: V: Part "A" by Frank Whitehead', 29–30 (ellipsis in original).
[29] Ibid., 30, 32.
[30] 'Criticism in Practice: II: Report by Raymond O'Malley', 95.

has the writer of B(i) [Donne], by his apparent complete preoccupation with the whale, in any way limited the range of his interests and the subtler possibilities of poetry? Has the poet of B(ii) [Shelley], by allowing his imagination to wander without control, succeeded in giving a more complex impression of the experience which he wishes to encompass?...[Donne's poem] incorporates in the verse structure a series of images which are extremely well adapted to show the nature of the whale, especially its size and the nature of its power.

> At every stroke his brazen fins do take,
> More circles in the broken sea they make
> Than cannons' voices when the air they tear.

It is important to notice the verse movement here: the heavy rhythm which is accentuated by both the sound and the meaning of the metallic images: 'brazen' and 'cannon', which suggest not only the colour and strength of the whale but also something of its unnaturalness—it is outside living nature in the remote, insensitive, inanimate world of metal.

The passage from imagery to 'verse movement' as the locus of a poem's more profound operations was a characteristically Leavisian move. And the Ricardian Leavis of *How to Teach Reading* haunted the pupil's sense that poetry works through coordination, by drawing in and orchestrating different effects: 'The shifting of metaphor in these first lines is remarkable—a large number of separate sensuous effects are called into play: movement, colour and substance, definition of the movement...Now two elements are called into the metaphor...'[31]

The 'Criticism in Practice' sheets were primarily intended for use with sixth-form classes, and, from 1955, *Use of English* began a new series of sheets meant exclusively for sixth forms and containing poetry only.[32] *Culture and Environment* itself was directed at the upper forms: the authors made it clear they were going out of their way when they made occasional suggestions of activities to try with younger pupils. Leavis's own attention to schools was focused on sixth forms, and in the 1960s C. B. Cox and A. E. Dyson, two English lecturers with a pronounced but far from filial allegiance to the *Scrutiny* tradition ran annual conferences for sixth formers as spin-offs from their main undertaking, the *Critical Quarterly*.[33] Interviewing grammar-school teachers in the 1950s, Frances

[31] Ibid., 95–6.
[32] 'Reading Sheet "A"—New Series', *Use of English* 5/4 (1954): 263; J. H. Walsh, 'Reading Sheets: XXV', *Use of English* 7/1 (1955): 42.
[33] Whitehead, 'Leavis and the Schools', 141–2; Brian Cox, *The Great Betrayal* (London: Chapman, 1992), 119–21. *Use of English* published an essay by a pupil at a co-educational grammar school, attesting to the enduring currency of *Scrutiny*-inflected sixth-form teaching. Bernice Reeve described how she was thrown by *King Lear* and how she outgrew the

Stevens found that they spoke with heightened enthusiasm about their sixth forms. Sixth-form teaching brought teachers who were university graduates closest to their own education, and closest to what they were best equipped to teach—literature, rather than subjects in which they usually had less formal grounding, such as composition. A headmaster told Stevens: 'We are all, at heart, university lecturers in our chosen subjects.'[34]

The romance of the old sixth form as a proto-university experience suffuses the stories of teachers and ex-pupils encouraging sixth formers to think about applying to Downing. John Charlesworth, a grammar-school teacher writing on the prospects for sixth-form teaching in 1969, confessed to sharing the nostalgia widespread among public-school boys and grammar-school children for the smaller, intimate sixth forms that were already well on the way out. At Charlesworth's school, King Edward VII School, Lytham, in 1949–51, the whole of the 'arts-sixth' was small enough to sit round a single library table. There was 'a sense of close relationship with two or three masters'. He remembered 'Friday evenings spent with discussion group or play-reading society' and a little magazine, *Synopsis*, 'laboriously hand-written and containing reams of Eliotese and reviews of Dr Leavis's latest book'.[35] He went up to Downing in 1951 to read English. One of his testimonials was from his school's head of English, Geoffrey Pellant, who had gone up to Downing to read English in 1940.[36]

The old, intimate sixth form was in decline from the beginning of the 1960s, if not before. More and more young people stayed at school past the age of sixteen. A levels had begun to function as general-purpose qualifications, so sixth forms were no longer the preserve of those aspiring to go to university. Some, such as C. B. Cox, regarded any consequent change to the existing curriculum as disastrous.[37] Charlesworth was nostalgic but not

sort of character-based criticism Knights and Leavis campaigned against. 'Relevance' and 'life', plangent words in the Leavis lexicon, went some way to describing literature's importance. Leavis himself went unmentioned. When Reeve referred to *Fiction and the Reading Public* she practised the calculated offhandedness of the initiate in not naming the author. Bernice Reeve, 'A Pupil's View', in Jackson (ed.), *English versus Examinations* (London: Chatto & Windus, 1965), 24–8.

[34] Frances Stevens, *The Living Tradition: The Social and Educational Assumptions of the Grammar School* (1960; London: Hutchinson, 1972), 80; John Charlesworth, 'The Final Years', in Denys Thompson (ed.), *Directions in the Teaching of English* (Cambridge: Cambridge University Press, 1969), 173.

[35] Charlesworth, 'Final Years', 176–7. Compare Roger Scruton, *England: An Elegy* (London: Chatto & Windus, 2000), 35–7, on 'Leavisite' sixth-form groups at King's College, Wimbledon, and the Royal Grammar School, High Wycombe.

[36] DCAT/5/1/11, p. 288, Downing; 'Geoffrey Frank Pellant (1940)', *NL* (2002): 49.

[37] Charlesworth, 'Final Years', 178–9, 181–2.

elegiac, seeing a promising model in a new Bristol comprehensive school's sixth form. In a populous sixth form, Charlesworth said, there was not enough time for the intensive eliciting of students' individual responses to literature, which had flourished in British sixth forms since the late 1940s and had an influence on A-level examinations. That sort of sixth-form English was indebted to *Scrutiny*; and the best sixth-form study, Charlesworth suggested, recognized the principle Leavis expressed in *Education and the University*: that 'literary studies lead constantly outside themselves'. What Charlesworth now proposed was that this principle be taken further, and that teachers learn from the pedagogies being developed in junior forms and even in primary schools. Teaching should work outwards from 'the prime centre of the students' own experience'; classwork had to move fluidly between writing, talk, drama, and literature, between students' personal experiences and what they encountered in literary texts. 'Themes' might be a useful way of coordinating literary study, creative writing, and other activities. Charlesworth took as his text a quotation from *Growth through English*, John Dixon's report on the Anglo-American seminar on English teaching held at Dartmouth College in New Hampshire in 1966. The lessons of Dartmouth as presented by Dixon seemed to Charlesworth 'to be as valid for 16 + English as for 12 +'.[38]

The irony of this is that the trends Dixon described and endorsed eclipsed *Scrutiny* models of teaching in schools, as literature lost its claim to centrality and became one of many language uses to be explored. Charlesworth's position reconciled *Scrutiny* premises—the importance of literature, the mission of English as a counter to the impersonality of a 'technological society'—with the sensibilities of the 'child-centred', 'progressive' educational movements that became enormously influential in the 1960s and 1970s. This accommodation may seem incongruous in the light of *Scrutiny* references to minority culture, standards, tradition, order, maturity, and the like. Perhaps the intriguing and significant aspects of *Scrutiny*'s impact on British schools was the way the *Scrutiny* tradition underwrote both 'progressive' and 'traditionalist' projects.

After the 1930s, Thompson and O'Malley withdrew from *Scrutiny*, and G. H. Bantock became the journal's main voice on educational matters. Bantock had read English at Cambridge (at Emmanuel) in the 1930s and, together with D. W. Harding, he was an advocate for the novels of L. H. Myers, which became part of the 'currency' of Downing undergraduates. He taught in London grammar schools for nearly a decade before becoming a lecturer in English at the City of Leeds Training College. Four years

---

[38] Ibid., 168–92, esp. 186–92.

later he moved to the education department of University College, Leicester, which was his institutional home for the rest of his career.[39] Bantock's misgivings about the world democracy had made ran deeper than those of most Scrutineers. Reviewing *Disagreements* (1950) by R. C. Churchill, a *Scrutiny* contributor, Downing English alumnus, and teacher in Catholic schools, Bantock was not convinced of the validity of the book's basic question: why 'culture' was disappearing, or restricted to a minority, at a time when the material preconditions for the enjoyment of the arts were more widely available. Churchill was a supporter of both 'culture' and 'democracy' (though few readers would take his book as being as enthusiastic about democracy as Bantock thought it was); Bantock said he was not sure that 'egalitarian democracy of the type we enjoy today' and 'a high state of culture' were even 'possible compatibilities'.[40]

Bantock's first book was based on a sequence of confrontational *Scrutiny* essays on post-war society (the menace of planning and technocracy) and trends in education. 'Some Cultural Implications of Freedom in Education' (1948) was immediately concerned with the consequences of the ideas of Susan Isaacs and other 'child-centred' educational theorists. These ideas underwrote an emphasis on experimentation in the classroom and teachers' unwillingness to impose a view of life on their charges. This educational theory reached beyond the school and was 'at once a reflection of and a further means of implementing the profoundly anti-rational forces' at work in contemporary society. It did not distinguish between the relative values of impulses and feelings; it encouraged the belief that the possibilities of attainment in an individual were not subject to rational analysis where children—'essentially irrational and incapable'—were concerned. The anti-rational forces with which progressive education was aligned were destroying 'the wisdom of the European tradition on which our civilisation has been built'. In his *Scrutiny* essay, Bantock quoted the dictum of the Harvard report on 'general education' that the less academically gifted were 'as worthy and as valuable democratic citizens as anyone else'. This was 'just not true, as it should hardly be necessary to insist on here', said Bantock, appealing to an implied 'us' of like-minded *Scrutiny* readers.[41]

[39] Peter Cunningham, 'Bantock, Geoffrey Herman (1914–1997)', *Oxford Dictionary of National Biography* (Oxford, 2004), <http://www.oxforddnb.com/view/article/68103>, accessed 3 May 2011; F. R. Leavis to D. W. Harding, 24 September [1940], F. R. Leavis papers, Col 9.59a, Emmanuel.
[40] G. H. Bantock, 'Better 500 Years of Hollywood?', *Use of English* 2/1 (1950): 42; R. C. Churchill, *Disagreements: A Polemic on Culture in the English Democracy* (London: Secker & Warburg, 1950).
[41] G. H. Bantock, 'Some Cultural Implications of Freedom in Education', *Scrutiny* 15/2 (spring 1948): 82–97 (quotations from 95, 96). I. A. Richards was a member of the Harvard committee.

Raymond Williams wrote two years later that when the ideas in *Mass Civilisation and Minority Culture* were taken as far as Bantock pushed them in this essay, the thesis as a whole started to look unsatisfactory.[42] In the issue after the essay on 'Freedom in Education' was published, Boris Ford, too, took it as reflective of certain aspects of the *Scrutiny* tradition. Bantock's essay was calculated to appeal to 'the *"Scrutiny* reader"', he observed: 'much of the phraseology and many of the references appear with the appropriate watermark'.[43] Bantock had referred to D. H. Lawrence, and especially to the papers collected posthumously in *Phoenix*, which have been described as 'the discourse of Downing'.[44] One footnote quoted Lawrence's fury at the endless empty talk of 'these young people', his 'horror of these little swarming selves'; another drew attention to the paradox that Lawrence's ideal of 'living spontaneous individuality in every man and woman' would require 'most careful rearing'.[45]

Bantock was unapologetically in favour of deliberate rearing and the teacher's authority: he did not worry away at this crux. William Walsh, in *The Use of Imagination*, paused over it, but only to insist—italics bore the burden of persuading—that Lawrence was not advocating anything facile or romantic or anarchic.[46] Walsh agreed with Lawrence's dictum that humans were not equal, and believed that the invocation of equality in debates over schooling distorted properly educational concerns and led to a 'debasement of standards'.[47] Subtitled 'Educational Thought and the Literary Mind', *The Use of Imagination* combined Walsh's critical interests with his educational ones, teasing theories of education out of readings of Leavis, Eliot, Coleridge, Hopkins and others (the paper on critics and the education of an élite that he read to the Doughty Society formed one chapter).

A decade later, Walsh contributed to the first of the Black Papers, the sporadic educational critiques that became a byword for reactionary sentiments shortly after they began in 1969. His appetite for ideological combat was limited, however, and he told the Black Papers' editors, Cox and Dyson of the *Critical Quarterly*, that he was bowing out after the first pamphlet was published. He had had 'all sorts of curious attributions of

[42] Raymond Williams, 'Books for Teaching "Culture and Environment"' (1950), in John McIlroy and Sallie Westwood (eds), *Border Country: Raymond Williams in Adult Education* (Leicester: National Institute of Adult Continuing Education, 1993), 177.
[43] Boris Ford, 'Freedom in Education: Thoughts Provoked by Mr Bantock', *Scrutiny* 15/3 (summer 1948): 162.
[44] MacKillop, *F. R. Leavis*, 184.
[45] Bantock, 'Freedom in Education', 92 n., 95 n.
[46] William Walsh, *The Use of Imagination: Educational Thought and the Literary Mind* (London: Chatto & Windus, 1960), 220–1.
[47] Ibid., 220.

ideas to me'—as did Cox himself.[48] Like many of the people he published
in the Black Papers, Cox was critical of the 'egalitarianism' of progressive
education. He believed it held more academically able students back, or
so frustrated them that they gave up on school. He was convinced of the
pedagogical value of streaming and selection. Cox's opposition to educational 'egalitarianism' was not articulated to a generalized anti-egalitarian
politics in which some citizens were unworthy or were so many 'swarming
selves'. He was proud of his liberal positions on many political questions,
and was surprised by how natural it was for others, allies and opponents
alike, to connect a rejection of progressive education with a scepticism
about democratic politics.[49]

Bantock and Walsh were joined on the Black Papers' roster by one
other pupil of Leavis's. Pedley, one of Leavis's earliest undergraduates at
Downing College and a frequent contributor to *Use of English*, wrote a
short essay for the first Black Paper entitled 'Comprehensive Disaster'.
It insisted on the need for 'able' students to be stimulated and motivated
by the company of their peers, as, Pedley said, happened in grammar
schools.[50] Pedley's essay prompted a letter suggesting that friends like this
could harm the cause: 'Direct Grant school heads writing on junior
schools are not going to impress the teaching profession, and this plays
into the hands of someone like the Rt. Hon Edward Short [the Labour
education secretary] who can then condemn all the articles as reactionary.'[51] (The letter was from the future Conservative cabinet minister
Rhodes Boyson, one of the illiberal figures with whom Cox and Dyson
found themselves working closely.) Cox and Dyson themselves had been
strongly influenced by Leavis at Cambridge, and their *Critical Quarterly*
published essays by people variously 'in the Leavis tradition'—Bantock,
Holbrook, D. J. Enright, Douglas Hewitt, Douglas Brown—in a symposium on criticism's 'debt to Dr Leavis'—but the jauntiness of the early
editorial statements, the focus on literature written since the war, and the
inclusion of voices hostile to Leavis, such as Helen Gardner, made it clear
that the *Critical Quarterly* was not the successor to *Scrutiny* that some

[48] Cox, *Great Betrayal*, 147.
[49] Ibid., chs 8–10. For an especially strong example of Cox's surprise at the company he
found himself keeping, see *Great Betrayal*, 211.
[50] R. R. Pedley, 'Comprehensive Disaster' in C. B. Cox and A. E. Dyson (eds), *Fight for
Education: A Black Paper* (London: Critical Quarterly Society, n.d. [1969]), 45–8. Pedley
went up to Cambridge in 1930: while he was taught by F. R. Leavis, he was admitted to the
college just before Leavis began working there. Pedley had strongly endorsed Leavisian
ideas on English teaching and the value of practical criticism, and nodded to Knights's
work on Shakespeare, in the pages of *Use of English*. See Adrian Barlow, ' "The Focus of a
Humane Culture": R. R. Pedley on Teaching and Examining English', *Use of English* 57/1
(2005): 5–17.
[51] Quoted in Cox, *Great Betrayal*, 177–8.

readers were on the look-out for in the 1950s and 1960s.[52] In an editorial in 1960, Dyson placed Leavis well down a list of critics shaping the journal's sensibility. Lionel Trilling and E. M. Forster, at the top of the list, showed that insight and discrimination were compatible with taking pleasure in literature; Leavis, in contrast, was 'unfortunately negative...his standards of excellence are such that only a few writers in any century could hope to come up to them'.[53]

Leavis himself may have agreed with some of the Black Papers' contentions—he wrote often about student unrest in the 1960s, and the Liberal Party's failure to defend grammar schools made him reconsider his vote—but the Black Papers were not a Leavisian undertaking.[54] Downing English graduates and Scrutineers were outnumbered as contributors by members of two groups Leavis took a dim view of: fellows of All Souls, Oxford (John Sparrow, Bryan Wilson) and Movement writers enjoying the role of contrarian (Kingsley Amis, Robert Conquest, Philip Larkin).[55] Yet, as Ford recognized when he identified the *Scrutiny* 'watermark' in Bantock's 1948 essay, it was possible to make strongly antiprogressive arguments in a *Scrutiny* idiom. As if to wrest that idiom from Bantock, to claim the *Scrutiny* tradition for other points of view, Ford spent some time discussing the Bantock's piece *as a Scrutiny* piece, reflecting on the self-conscious public or constituency the journal's contributors imagined. Making a case against 'imposing' views on children with reference to the open-ended discussion method he helped develop for the ABCA and to his experiments teaching Shakespeare by getting students to perform scenes, Ford appealed to *Scrutiny* arguments about the collapse of standards. 'Surely...there is something creditable in being chary of imposing a view of life at a time of uncertainty, when it is all too easy to do so.' The lack of agreed moral and cultural standards meant that individual teachers had 'no social backing' for their views ('unless they are of the crudest kind'), so attempts to exercise authority would be ineffective and counterproductive.[56] Teaching literature or music effectively required processes of experiment and dialogue rather than imposition.

---

[52] Ibid., 77–9, 121–4; C. B. Cox and A. E. Dyson, 'Foreword', *Critical Quarterly* 1/1 (1959): 3–4.

[53] A. E. Dyson, 'Editorial', *Critical Quarterly* 2/1 (March 1960): 4–5.

[54] F. R. Leavis, ' "Believing in" the University', *The Human World* 15–16 (May–August 1974): 98.

[55] Cox and Dyson (eds), *Fight for Education*; C. B. Cox and A. E. Dyson (eds), *Black Paper Two: The Crisis in Education* (London: Critical Quarterly Society, n.d. [1969]).

[56] Ford, 'Thoughts Provoked by Mr Bantock', 164, 165–8; Bureau of Current Affairs, *Discussion Method* (London: Bureau of Current Affairs, n.d.); Doughty Society Minute Book, 33 (5 March 1948), DCCS/4/4/1/1, Downing.

For David Holbrook, those processes could be transferential.[57] Holbrook's strategies for encouraging children to explore their feelings and exercise their creativity grew out of his reading in psychoanalysis, Melanie Klein especially.[58] The therapeutic and exploratory aspects of Holbrook's teaching ideals are especially clear from *English for the Rejected* (1964), a book about teaching in the 'lower streams' of secondary modern schools. The core of *English for the Rejected* was a sequence of case studies or dossiers on an English class of 'backward' children. Each case study concluded with comments from a child-psychoanalyst, and included writings from the children, Holbrook's comments on their behaviour, and snatches of practical criticism of their writing. Some of the dossiers were headed with the children's IQs and crushing comments from their primary-school teachers—'Has no originality or imagination'—which Holbrook rebutted with proportionate rage.[59] He went out of his way to praise the literary accomplishment of these children's writing, prompting Whitehead to accuse him of a 'falsification of values', confusing the quality of the child's poem with the psychological dividends of writing it. Why, asked Whitehead, 'do we (apparently) find it so difficult to believe in the importance of the latter without losing our sense of proportion over the former?'[60]

Of all Leavis's students, Holbrook was the most creative and influential exponent of teaching practices that broke with disciplinarian forms of schooling and were intended to equip children to explore their selves and their world. (Although, in this respect, Holbrook was aligned with people who welcomed the cultural changes of the 1960s, he was energetically opposed to many aspects of 'permissiveness', especially pornography.)[61] *English for Maturity* (1961) as well as *English for the Rejected* addressed teachers in the secondary modern schools. Holbrook accepted, though not without sceptical asides, that selection on the basis of academic ability was possible and legitimate, and that eleven-plus failures could not be expected to do some of the tasks grammar-school children could. Nevertheless, his books mounted a harassing critique of the lack of imagination in grammar school teaching as he catalogued its influence on secondary modern curricula. Lacking a cogent philosophy of their

---

[57] David Holbrook, *English for the Rejected: Training Literacy in the Lower Streams of the Secondary School* (1964; Cambridge: Cambridge University Press, 1968), 22.

[58] Ibid., 21–2, 38–40, 41.

[59] Ibid., 54.

[60] Frank Whitehead, *The Disappearing Dais: A Study of the Principles and Practice of English Teaching* (London: Chatto & Windus, 1966), 175–7.

[61] David Holbrook (ed.), *The Case against Pornography* (London: Tom Stacey, 1972). While a writer in residence at Dartington Hall from 1971 to 1973, he was appalled at the way 'libertarianism had progressed to outright decadence'. Holbrook to Ford, n.d., quoted in Ford, 'David Holbrook: A Portrait', 45–6.

own, secondary moderns aped grammar schools, with uniforms, Latin mottoes, and, worst of all, standardized examinations. Secondary moderns could at least claim 'parity of certification', Holbrook remarked sardonically (the claim that the new secondary modern schools would enjoy 'parity of esteem' with grammar schools proved notoriously hollow).[62] The *Scrutiny* watermark is discernible here. From Thompson's earliest reviews and Knights's article 'Scrutiny of Examinations', *Scrutiny* writers had drawn attention to the oppressive effects of external examinations on teaching, and interpreted examinations as part of the standardizing apparatus of an industrial or bureaucratic civilization.[63] The post-war extension of secondary education entrenched the importance of external examinations; abetted by the textbook industry, O levels impinged ever more on pupils and teachers.[64] The alternative to examination-driven teaching that Holbrook elaborated was also indebted to *Scrutiny*. 'The syllabus of the secondary modern school', he wrote in the *Critical Quarterly* in 1959, 'should go towards preparing three-quarters of the English population to be mature and stable beings; to be the matrix for new forms of popular culture, popular language culture above all, to replace the old dead popular culture of folksong and religious reading and drama'. English would be 'at the centre, as the source of aims and values, and of delight in the civilising word'.[65]

Holbrook followed the Leavis of *Education and the University*—written at the time Holbrook became a Downing undergraduate—in seeing English as a coordinating force as well as a supremely important subject. That an education in literature was a training for living a morally intelligent life in defiance of the modern 'environment' was of course a *Scrutiny* axiom. Absent from Holbrook's programme was the idea of minority culture. Pointedly using the *Scrutiny* language of 'training of sensibility' against that idea and against sentiments such as Bantock's dismissal of the Harvard committee's assertions about citizens' equality, Holbrook asserted: 'While sensibility is no doubt linked with intelligence, there can be no distinctions made between the needs of each individual for training of the

<hr/>

[62] Holbrook, *English for the Rejected*, 5.

[63] L. C. Knights, 'Scrutiny of Examinations', *Scrutiny* 2/2 (September 1933): 137–63.

[64] Brian Jackson, 'Introduction: English versus Examinations', in Jackson (ed.), *English versus Examinations*, 9, 11–18; A Text-book Maker, 'The Making of Text-books', in Brian Jackson and Denys Thompson (eds), *English in Education: A Selection of Articles on the Teaching of English at Different Levels from Infant School to University* (London: Chatto & Windus, 1962), 141–2 (originally published in *Use of English* 2/4 [1951]: 177–80); [Denys Thompson,] 'Editorial: The Text-Book Circle', *Use of English* 2/1 (1950): 5; Whitehead, *Disappearing Dais*, 71.

[65] 'Why Teach Literature…In the Secondary Modern School', *Critical Quarterly* 1/1 (1959): 61.

sensibility. A really civilised democratic education policy would recognise that in the needs of sensibility—of being—all men are equal, and that it is only in intelligence—or whatever the eleven-plus tests measure—that some are more equal than others.'[66]

In Holbrook's ideal programme for secondary-modern English, literature and imaginative writing were crucial. Clarity and fluency, the practical competence in the language that educational authorities and employers expected of school leavers, became possible only after children were able to delight in language.[67] This position was standard among educationalists connected with *Scrutiny*. Its point of origin was George Sampson's *English for the English* (1921), which argued that the utilitarian benefits of English teaching would accrue almost as a matter of course if literature became the main focus.[68] Ford's 1955 report on technical education provided empirical support.[69] For Holbrook as for Leavis, the local texture of the writing was the key to a student's experience of literary uses of language. The abridgements of the classics produced for schools were counterproductive because they 'destroy[ed] much of the local quality of the writing'. What was the point of a comic-book version of *Macbeth*? A ' "classic" of literature lives, surely, only in its words?'[70]

Much of Holbrook's educational writing concentrated on the personal or therapeutic value of writing for oneself, but 'making things up' also enriched students' experience of literature because it encouraged them to use for themselves 'the modes whereby others reached their "organisation of expression"'. Introducing children to literature successfully required teachers to set books that children were likely to enjoy: making them read books they were unenthusiastic about only drove them further toward rubbish like Enid Blyton or W. E. Johns in their leisure.[71] Here Holbrook amplified the argument of A. J. Jenkinson's *What Do Boys and Girls Read?* (1940), which was published with a foreword by Susan Isaacs and

[66] 'Why Teach Literature... In the Secondary Modern School', 60.

[67] David Holbrook, *English for Maturity: English in the Secondary School* (Cambridge: Cambridge University Press, 1961), 127. All references are to this edition, the first, unless otherwise specified.

[68] Denys Thompson, 'Introduction' to George Sampson, *English for the English: A Chapter on National Education* (1921; Cambridge: Cambridge University Press, 1970), 9; L. C. Knights to Denys Harding, 4 October 1939, F. R. Leavis papers, Col 9.59a, Emmanuel.

[69] [Boris Ford], *Liberal Education in a Technical Age: A Survey of the Relationship of Vocational and Non-Vocational Further Education and Training* (London: Parrish, 1955); Denys Thompson, 'What Is Literature?', *NATE Bulletin* 3/2 (summer 1966): 5–6. It has to be said that Ford's report lent more moral than empirical support to the claim for the indirect utilitarian benefits of literature teaching. See *Liberal Education*, 53–4, 73.

[70] Holbrook, *English for Maturity*, 152, 153.

[71] Ibid., 126, 151–8.

represented 'an important advance in pupil-centred studies'.[72] (Jenkinson was a pupil of Leavis's at Emmanuel College and after graduating taught at Scarborough Boys' High School and then at training colleges; a Marxist, he was not involved with *Scrutiny*.)[73] Reading literature also brought a child 'on to that traditional meeting place of minds where he can measure his own experience against the experience of "the race" and its values'.[74]

This allusion to *Mass Civilisation and Minority Culture* was one of many points where Holbrook drew on the texts and favoured terminology of *Scrutiny* writers.[75] The relation to *Scrutiny* was strongest, most productive, in Holbrook's elaboration of the context of English teaching, the 'environment' of mass culture. This was an intellectual and political affiliation that was not reinforced by strong personal bonds, at least not between Holbrook and Leavis. Holbrook's closest ties among the *Scrutiny* group were with Ford, Thompson, and Mellers, for whom he wrote libretti. When Holbrook returned to Downing after the war to finish his degree, he was an assistant editor of the relaxedly eclectic Marxist quarterly *Our Time*, which evidently made the Leavises wary.[76] Q. D. Leavis remarked later that as an undergraduate Holbrook had chosen to go for supervisions to Hugh Sykes Davies, at the time a member of the Communist Party, and so had not really been a pupil of her husband's.[77] Holbrook's later commitment to *Scrutiny* interpretations of literature and culture is especially striking because Marxism of course offered alternative explanations and because of his enduring friendship with the editor of *Our Time*, the *Calendar of Modern Letters* founder Edgell Rickword.

The 'complex within which we train reading', Holbrook remarked in *English for Maturity*, was 'both a verbal and spiritual malaise of our time'.[78] Like Thompson, Holbrook moved fluidly between the verbal and the spiritual. Euphemisms such as 'the smallest room in the house' were of a piece with 'the lifeless world of clean kitchens, and the tooth-paste smiles of the ad.-men and the magazines by which they operate'.[79] The Lawrentian

---

[72] A. J. Jenkinson, *What Do Boys and Girls Read? An Investigation into Reading Habits with Some Suggestions about the Teaching of Literature in Secondary and Senior Schools* (1940; London: Methuen, 1946); Shayer, *Teaching of English in Schools*, 130–2 (quotation from 130). See also G. G. Urwin, 'Books versus Pulp Magazines', *Use of English* 2/1 (1950): 26, 28.

[73] Keith Dobson, 'Pre-war Downing', in Ian MacKillop and Richard Storer (eds), *F. R. Leavis: Essays and Documents* (Sheffield: Sheffield Academic Press, 1995), 238.

[74] Holbrook, *English for Maturity*, 126.

[75] See also the note on further reading in Holbrook, *English for Maturity*, 244.

[76] Ford, 'David Holbrook: A Portrait', 29, 37.

[77] Q. D. Leavis to Brian Worthington, n.d. [1970s?], Q. D. Leavis papers, GCPP Leavis 2/1/2, Girton.

[78] Holbrook, *English for Maturity*, 169.

[79] Ibid., 127–8.

idea that modern civilization produced artificial and corrupting desires, which both Thompson and F. R. Leavis developed in their discussions of the culture industry, was especially important for Holbrook. He described this 'spiritual malaise' almost in parable form. Holbrook saw two fourteen-year-olds kissing and groping on the grass in front of the school offices. After a while it dawned on him that '*the caresses were not meant*: . . . they were copied from the cinema'.[80] In the second edition, published in 1967, after Holbrook's interest in psychoanalysis had deepened further, he added: 'The children were imitating behaviour they had seen on the screen—and that behaviour was sex depersonalised and de-emotionalised to a schizoid degree for the purposes of commerce.'[81] Sexuality was much more of a concern in Holbrook's writing than it was for Thompson and the Leavises in the 1930s, and while this is partly explicable by Holbrook's psychoanalytic frame of reference, the more overt sexualization of postwar mass culture must have played a part, as the emphases in Richard Hoggart's writing and teaching in the 1950s attest.[82]

When he was not examining sexuality and violence in cinema and pulp fiction, Holbrook's tone and terminology were recognizably close to those of *Culture and Environment*. In *English for Maturity*, for instance, he contrasted 'the popular songs of the old rural England' with 'the highly accomplished popular songs written for commercial distribution nowadays'. The contrast was an instance of and an analogy for the difference between 'indigenous culture' and 'commercial culture'. 'The "experience"—if one can call it that—in the latter has to be manufactured to fit a lowest common denominator of popular "wisdom." ' The levelling-down logic of commercial culture meant that its forms could provide no 'felt wisdom', compromising our ability to live fully.[83] The hope was that the exploratory work of creative writing and of reading literature could provide some of the personal resources that traditional popular culture once had.

Holbrook's course of treatment emphasized writing in a way that *Culture and Environment* did not, but he shared the diagnosis that Leavis and Thompson, relying on Richards, outlined there: as other vehicles for 'tradition' disintegrated, language and literature became even more important.[84] The switch between literary tradition and rural tradition, common in Thompson's writing, recurred in Holbrook's as well. Holbrook pursued

[80] Holbrook, *English for Maturity*, 170.
[81] David Holbrook, *English for Maturity: English in the Secondary School*, 2nd edn (Cambridge: Cambridge University Press, 1967), 172.
[82] See below, 171–2.
[83] Holbrook, *English for Maturity*, 52.
[84] F. R. Leavis and Denys Thompson, *Culture and Environment: The Training of Critical Awareness* (1933; London: Chatto & Windus, 1950), 81–2; I. A. Richards, *Practical Criticism: A Study of Literary Judgment* (London: Kegan Paul, Trench, Trubner, 1929), 321.

the subjects of rural life and folk culture beyond mere analogy. In this respect, he worked within a tributary of *Scrutiny* to which Thompson was the formative contributor. Holbrook illustrated the familiar *Scrutiny* argument that Shakespeare's poetry drew vigour from 'the common people's tongue' by comparing quotations from the plays with bits of East Anglian dialect. Holbrook listed a number of Shakespearean coinages that metaphorically applied concrete words to abstract or moral phenomena: 'It *beggar'd* all description', 'ensconce', 'mind's eye'. These coinages were an extension of a demotic practice of metaphor-making, one still extant in the rural communities of East Anglia that Holbrook knew.[85] (Marvellously for someone in the *Scrutiny* tradition, Holbrook was descended from wheelwrights on both his mother's and his father's side.)[86] 'Metaphor is essentially a moral process in language', Holbrook wrote: 'it endeavours to extend our experience over the abstract, the spiritual, the intractable, starting from the known.' The metaphorical quality of rural sayings 'embod[ied] a moral wisdom'. Rural speech and other manifestations of 'indigenous culture' such as folk song were the products of moral and imaginative exploration, their continuity with past discoveries and observations sustaining the mental lives of people born centuries later. A folk song did have an original author, but once it was made up, the song was sung by others, and they modified it: 'thus a song was formed which reflected the taste and outlook of the whole community'.[87]

Holbrook devoted a chapter of *English for Maturity* to folk song, which other teachers involved with *Use of English*, such as O'Malley, thought a valuable means of teaching children who were stifled by the BBC's Light Programme and comics 'what real, fresh experience is'.[88] Holbrook argued that their lyrics' combination of simplicity and subtlety offered children a way into poetry: a child accustomed to the language of 'The Seeds of Love' would intuitively respond to Lear's 'I am bound | Upon a wheel of fire'.[89] How exposure to the residues of a living traditional culture would affect children went unexplained. Although Holbrook supplied a long list of suitable records and analysed exemplary songs, the chapter was uncharacteristically light on practical guidance and ideas for lessons—as if the discussion of folk song really belonged in the first part of the book, where Holbrook outlined his vision of teaching and the 'environment' teachers

---

[85] Holbrook, *English for Maturity*, 70–1 (Holbrook's italics).

[86] Holbrook to Richard Hoggart, 10 April 1963, Richard Hoggart papers, 7/Holbrook/1, Sheffield.

[87] Holbrook, *English for Maturity*, 70, 71, 99.

[88] Raymond O'Malley, 'Folk-Songs in the English Room', *Use of English* 4/3 (1953): 169.

[89] Holbrook, *English for Maturity*, 102.

had to work within and against. Folk song was an example, perhaps an unfeasibly allegorical one, of how the creative and the traditional could be reconciled; how the artistic could be 'socialized' in a non-Marxist way.[90] Invested as the *Scrutiny* movement was in individual experiences and judgements on the one hand and to tradition and some form of order on the other, any cultural or educational programme along *Scrutiny* lines would be beset by paradox. Holbrook did not quote the thorny sentence of Lawrence's that Bantock and Walsh did, but his championing of creative writing and his copious suggestions how to incorporate it into teaching amounted to a demonstration of how to rear spontaneity. Another admirer of Leavis's, at least, saw the challenge of teaching writing in Lawrence's terms. Discussing *Free Writing* by Dora Pym and L. V. Southwell in *Use of English*, Douglas Brown finished his review with Lawrence's words. He did not feel the need to say who he was quoting.[91]

At the close of the 1960s, the head of English at an independent school in Somerset declared that there was now, undoubtedly, a 'New English'. Parsing, 'writing for an undefined audience in an artificial way with the aim of avoiding mistakes', and all that, were out, 'and "creative" English is in'. The 'New English' could be traced, L. E. W. Smith suggested, to *Culture and Environment*: 'the young men who studied this in their sixth-form days have now become heads of department and writers of English books'. It was more than just chance, Smith added, that Holbrook, 'whose books have been most influential in the Secondary Schools', and Esmor Jones, the first secretary of NATE, 'were both at Downing College, Cambridge, when Dr Leavis was English Tutor there'.[92]

One of the things that this judgement glosses over is the fact that *Scrutiny* ideas were nearly always coupled with, and modified by, other bodies of thought and practice. Holbrook's conceptions of literature and culture were shaped and tinctured by work in the *Scrutiny* tradition, but his teaching tactics originated elsewhere—in his reading of psychoanalysis and his experiments in secondary modern schools and Bassingbourn Village College. This institution was one of the chain of village colleges

---

[90] Compare Holbrook's struggle with this problem elsewhere in the book: 'The tendency [in commercially produced pop music] is not towards what seems unique although it is universal, but towards the more than universal or too common (demand must just exceed supply to make commercial culture work) and the non-unique.' Ibid., 52.

[91] Douglas Brown, 'Free Writing', in Jackson and Thompson (eds), *English in Education*, 175.

[92] L. E. W. Smith, 'Creative Writing and Language Awareness', *English in Education* 4/1 (1970): 4, 8 n.

established by the Cambridgeshire education secretary Henry Morris.[93] When Holbrook began work at Bassingbourn in 1954, he taught Cambridge extension classes to adults. One of them was the primary-school teacher Sybil Marshall, whose 'symphonic method' of integrating subjects as different as music and home economics in a single lesson greatly impressed Holbrook (he recommended her to the BBC repeatedly and probably played some part in her appointment by Ford to a lectureship at Sheffield's Institute of Education, where she published a book about her teaching methods that was taken up enthusiastically by teachers).[94] Holbrook was also assigned the 'bottom stream' children to teach and told to teach them however he liked.[95] It was here that the experiments that led to *English for the Rejected* began; the scraps of rural lore Holbrook's pupils possessed registered in the book's pages.

Frank Whitehead was an articulate exponent of *Scrutiny* positions in debates within and around NATE in the 1960s and 1970s, but it was his tutors at the London Institute of Education, rather than Leavis, who equipped him to 'think coherently and critically about aims and methods in the teaching of English'.[96] Returning to the Leavises' house for one of their Friday gatherings while he was doing his teacher training in 1938–9, Whitehead had an awkward conversation with F. R. Leavis about his London tutor Peter Gurrey. The latter's book *The Appreciation of Poetry* (1935) referred favourably to *How to Teach Reading*, and Whitehead formed the 'uncomfortable impression that Leavis's real interest was in learning whether Gurrey either was or might become a "disciple"'.[97] Gurrey came to observe a fourth-form grammar-school class Whitehead taught during his teaching practice. He had taken a pair of prose passages, one good and one bad, from E. G. Biaggini's *The Reading and Writing of English*—an Australian book based on experiments similar to Richards's Practical Criticism course, with a preface by Leavis—and was trying to

[93] Harry Rée, *Educator Extraordinary: The Life and Achievement of Henry Morris, 1889–1961* (London: Longman, 1973), chs 3, 4,6, 7, and esp. pp. 28–32.

[94] David Holbrook, 'Marshall, Sybil Mary (1913–2005)', *Oxford Dictionary of National Biography* (Oxford: Oxford University Press, 2009; online edn, January 2011), <http://www.oxforddnb.com/view/article/96053>, accessed 28 April 2011; Sybil Marshall, *An Experiment in Education* (1963; Cambridge: Cambridge University Press, 1966); Holbrook to Dick Keen, 26 January 1956; Holbrook to Miss Fulloon, 5 September 1958, RCONT 1: David Holbrook: Talks: File 1: 1949–62, BBC WAC.

[95] Ford, 'David Holbrook', 38; 'Poet Elected to Research Fellowship at King's College Cambridge', n.d. (c.1962), RCONT 1: David Holbrook: Talks: File 1: 1949–62, BBC WAC.

[96] Whitehead, *Disappearing Dais*, 9.

[97] Whitehead, 'Leavis and the Schools', 144. Leavis had included Gurrey in a list of people to be circularized about *Culture and Environment* but not sent a free copy. Leavis to Parsons, 23 January 1933, Chatto & Windus archive, CW 53/2, Reading.

draw out his pupils' judgements.[98] The class did not go well, but all Gurrey would say after shaking his head was that Whitehead had not 'got it' yet. After watching Gurrey and his colleague Maura Brooke Gwynne teach different classes, Whitehead concluded that 'it' was 'something to do with the unsuspected ability of pupils to read, respond, write and act out of their own powers and volition if given opportunity, encouragement and the right stimulus'. He saw his subsequent career as an attempt to combine this 'fostering of the young person's innate creativity' with *Scrutiny's* concern for 'standards of discrimination'. Though he admired Leavis greatly, Whitehead suspected he would not have really grasped 'Gurrey's "it" '.[99]

Though not a 'disciple', Gurrey was an admirer of Leavis, and over the years 'a steady stream of students came from undergraduate studies with Leavis to professional training at the [London] Institute English Department'.[100] Extremely influential on the teaching of writing in British schools, Gurrey was interested in linguistics and the philosophy of language.[101] This brings us to another problem with Smith's attribution of the 'New English' to the *Scrutiny* tradition: it ignored linguistics and psychology. The move towards more open and child-centred English teaching was part of a wider shift in the teaching of many subjects and in the ways schools were run. This transformation was driven by the theories and findings of developmental and educational psychologists, such as Piaget and Isaacs. The examples set by early twentieth-century British educationalists such as Margaret McMillan and Caldwell Cook and (for the teaching of English in particular) E. A. Greening Lambourn were also an inspiration.[102] Many of the 1960s innovations in English teaching were

[98] E. G. Biaggini, *The Reading and Writing of English* (London: Hutchinson, 1936). See also Ernest Gordon Biaggini, *English in Australia: Taste and Training in a Modern Community* (Melbourne: Melbourne University Press in association with Oxford University Press, 1933), 11.

[99] Whitehead, 'Leavis and the Schools', 144–5.

[100] James Britton, 'Professor P. Gurrey', *ELT Journal* 35/3 (1981): 352–3.

[101] J. H. Walsh, 'The Teaching of Writing', in Thompson (ed.), *Directions*, 108, 109.

[102] David Shayer, *The Teaching of English in Schools, 1900–1970* (London: Routledge & Kegan Paul, 1972); Allen, *English Teaching since 1965*; Margaret Mathieson, *The Preachers of Culture: A Study of English and Its Teachers* (London: Allen & Unwin, 1975), chs 5, 8; Carolyn Steedman, 'State-sponsored Autobiography', in Becky Conekin, Frank Mort, and Chris Waters (eds), *Moments of Modernity: Reconstructing Britain, 1945–1964* (London, 1999), 41–54; Carolyn Steedman, *Childhood, Culture, and Class in Britain: Margaret McMillan, 1860–1931* (London: Virago Press, 1990). As early as 1932, the Association of Assistant Mistresses' *Memorandum on the Teaching of English* warned that Caldwell Cook's *Play Way* was, like Lambourn's *Rudiments of Criticism*, a 'suggestive and inspiring book' that 'may become a fetish': *Memorandum on the Teaching of English: Drawn up by the English Panel of the Association of Assistant Mistresses, 1932* (London; Association of Assistant Mistresses in Secondary Schools, [1932]), 2.

responses to research on language acquisition and sociolinguistics, to ideas about language originating with philosophers and psychologists. References to L. S. Vygotsky's theories of the relations between language development and thought were ubiquitous.

In the introduction to a 1969 collection of essays, Thompson even tried to argue for a convergence between Leavis's thinking and Vygotsky's, quoting a late Leavis dictum about language as 'a vehicle of collective wisdom and basic assumptions, a currency of criteria and valuation collaboratively determined'.[103] But Thompson resisted the territorial claims of linguistics, and was clear about his priorities. 'Literature is the one thing worth teaching English for', he told the 1966 NATE conference. 'I believe most people in this hall will accept that assertion, but outside there are wide divergences.'[104] There were divergences inside the hall too, and the decline of the *Scrutiny* tradition in schools was proportionate to the ascendancy of teaching methods informed by linguistics.

Linguistics' most unwelcome intrusion into English in schools was in the form of the O-level 'Use of English' papers. Prominent members of NATE described these examinations as 'disastrous' and said that there was 'no bigger blockage to the serious teaching of English'.[105] The language papers were a focus for grass-roots discontent as well: a NATE study group in Birmingham made a critical study of the 1965 papers against the stated criteria, which led some GCE authorities to invite NATE to nominate members to their boards.[106] For Thompson, the new linguistics prompted the same objections as the discredited teaching of formal grammar and stale exercises in letter- and report-writing. The crucial question, Thompson said, was 'Which brand of linguistics, if any, helps a child speak and write better, leaves him keener and the more able to read good literature and to see through an advertisement?'[107]

Clearly, the expected answer was 'none' (and the aspirations of English teaching were those of *Culture and Environment* and *Mass Civilisation and Minority Culture*: training in reading good literature and the ability to 'see through' mass culture). For Leavis through the decades, the idea of language was enormously significant, but linguistics was not. Since, for

---

[103] Denys Thompson, 'Introduction', in Thompson (ed.), *Directions*, 7–8; F. R. Leavis, 'The Pilgrim's Progress', in *Anna Karenina and Other Essays* (London: Chatto & Windus, 1967), 41.

[104] Denys Thompson, 'What Is Literature?' *NATE Bulletin* 3/2 (1966): 5.

[105] Frank Whitehead, 'Examinations and the Teaching of English', *NATE Bulletin* 1/2 (spring 1964): 10–13; Whitehead, *Disappearing Dais*, 71; Jackson, 'Introduction', 12; Thompson, 'What Is Literature?', 7; Thompson, 'A Reflection', in Thompson and Jackson (eds), *English in Education*, 228–9.

[106] 'Report of Secretary of Studies', *NATE Bulletin* 3/2 (summer 1966): 64.

[107] Thompson, 'What Is Literature?', 7.

Leavis and his followers, literature was the best or the only way into an understanding of these operations of language, to separate 'literature' and 'language' into discrete parts of the curriculum made for an impoverished place for literature as well as a crabbed approach to language. It assumed that literature could be, as Whitehead put it, 'segregated as an optional subject, an academic subject which treats books that have no real impact on the living human concerns of the pupil; a subject, moreover, in which the pupil's own creative writing plays no part'.[108]

When they expressed these views, Whitehead was chairman of NATE and Thompson was still editor of *Use of English* and a respected senior figure in British education. This eminence did not mean that they spoke for all English teachers, of course, or even all members of NATE, which was a federation of local groups. Many of Thompson and Whitehead's positions were accepted by NATE members who were not identified with Leavis or *Scrutiny*. The belief that schooling should 'provide a healthy counterbalance' to the influence of cinema and commercial television was widespread, especially among grammar-school teachers.[109] John Dixon felt the numbing effects of O-level language examinations, deplored a narrow 'skill model' for English, agreed that English should arm children against advertising, and saw the larger mission of the subject as to foster personal growth.[110] But by the mid-1960s, when he was a lecturer at Bretton Hall College of Education in Wakefield, he no longer shared the Leavisian belief in the centrality of literary study. On the evidence of A-level curricula and, by extension, university study, Dixon remarked in 1969, criticism seldom lived up to its claim to be—he quoted Leavis—a discipline 'whose boundaries cannot be drawn', whose ambition was 'an interest in man, society, and civilisation'. For his generation of teachers, literary criticism had been the means of achieving the 'special attention to language and experience' that had generated the most valuable innovations in school English. He doubted that would remain the case much longer.[111]

Dixon was an important exponent of English teaching concerned with 'language in operation', a rubric that subsumed literature as one sort of language use among many. *Growth in English*, his account of the Dartmouth

[108] Frank Whitehead, 'Examinations and the Teaching of English', *NATE Bulletin* 1/2 (spring 1964): 11.

[109] Stevens, *Living Tradition*, 108–9; Mathieson, *Preachers of Culture*, 202–3.

[110] John Dixon, 'English Renewed: Visions of English among Teachers of 1966', *English in Education* 43/3 (2009): 242; John Dixon, *Growth through English: A Report Based on the Dartmouth Seminar 1966* (1967; [Reading]: National Association for the Teaching of English, 1969), 2; Simon Clements, John Dixon, and Leslie Stratta, *Reflections: An English Course for Students Aged 14–18* (1963; Oxford: Oxford University Press, 1966), 26, 27, 29.

[111] John Dixon, 'A New Tradition in the Teaching of English', *English in Education* 3/2 (1969): 57.

conference, was an influential case for a pedagogy in which talk figured as the primary form of language and the teacher's priority was the pupils' own use of language to express themselves and explore their world. The British contingent at Dartmouth included many Leavis pupils and associates and *Scrutiny* editors—Thompson, Whitehead, Ford, Holbrook, Harding, and Esmor Jones—and Dixon's report tended to marginalize their views.[112] Whitehead believed Dixon's book changed the course of English teaching in Britain for the worse.[113] The linguistic turn did not originate with Dixon's report, however, and what proved destructive to the claims of *Scrutiny* approaches to English teaching from the mid-1960s onwards was less Dixon's specific programme than the assumptions underlying it.

These assumptions and something of their attendant sensibility came through clearly in the paper James Britton read at Dartmouth. A professor at the London Institute of Education, Britton was probably the most influential broker of linguistic research to British teachers in the post-war period.[114] After a discussion of close reading and practical criticism exercises, Britton ventured an 'unorthodox way of defining literature which has the advantage of placing it among linguistic activities generally'. We all use language, Britton wrote, 'to get things done in the outer world and to manipulate the inner world. Action and decision belong to the former use; freedom from them in the latter enables us to attend to other things— to the forms of language, the patterns of events, the feelings. We take up as it were the role of spectators: spectators of our own past lives, our imagined futures, other men's lives, impossible events. When we *speak* this language, the nearest name I can give it is "gossip"; when we *write* it, it is literature.' By these lights, 'literature is not simply something that other people have done. What a child writes is of the same order as what the poet or novelist writes and valid for the same reasons.'[115] Literature was a mode of expression or exploration not radically different from other 'linguistic activities'; and questions of value of the sort raised by practical criticism, while not dismissed, were not a priority.

The implications for the classroom were not obviously linguistic. British children were not given substantial courses in Chomskyan transformational grammar as their contemporaries in some American states were.[116] Britton's linguistic arguments undergirded a conception of

[112] Allen, *English Teaching since 1965*, ch. 2. There is a list of the conference participants in Dixon, *Growth through English*, 115–17.
[113] Whitehead, 'Leavis and the Schools', 150–1.
[114] Allen, *English Teaching since 1965*, chs 4–5.
[115] James Britton, 'Response to Literature', in *Prospect and Retrospect: Selected Essays of James Britton*, ed. Gordon M. Pradl (Montclair, NJ: Boynton/Cook, 1982), 36–7.
[116] Esmor Jones, 'American Visit', *NATE Bulletin* 3/2 (summer 1966): 58.

English as the study of language in use: classes would, as Dixon put it, 'move freely' between the various modes of language use—talk, writing, drama—and, coming in after a semi-colon, literature.[117] 'Themes'—such as home, work, or the natural world—proved a popular organizing principle for English courses (and course books) based on this premise. As David Shayer observed in 1972, a thematic approach assumed 'the unity of the subject, bringing prose, poetry, reading, comprehension, talking and writing together'. It also recognized the pupil's experience as the point of departure for English studies.[118] Some curriculum boards took up thematic approaches, and an accumulation of published courses or teachers' manuals exemplified them: *Reflections* (1963), the English course devised by Dixon, Leslie Stratta, and Simon Clements; *English through Experience* (1963) by A. Rowe and P. Emens; Geoffrey Summerfield's *Topics in English* (1965), *Impact One* and *Two* (1967) by R. H. Poole and P. J. Shepherd, *Themes* (1967) by E. M. Hunnisett, *The Oxford English Source Books* (1968) by Britton's Institute colleague Nancy Martin, *Aspects of English* (1970) by D. S. Higgins. By the early 1970s, a 'somewhat standardised pattern' was emerging.[119]

Reflections, which had sold 200,000 copies by 1968, was 'organiz[ed] . . . around themes directly related to life': the mass media; family, community, and work; and 'Questions of Our Time'.[120] The advice to the teacher tackling the issue of 'work' illustrates the approach well. Parents usually wanted a safe or steady job for their children, Clements, Dixon, and Stratta wrote, and they seldom thought seriously about whether a particular job was really suited to an individual child. Children had few defences against the pressure their parents, friends, and community brought to bear on them, and had little opportunity to think of work as creative or purposeful. 'These are the limited horizons we hope to expand.' Clements, Dixon, and Stratta suggested several ways of opening up the topic. Pupils with part-time jobs could be asked to provide detailed descriptions of what they did, and the rest of the class could give their reactions; children could interview their parents, possibly asking questions drafted by the class as a whole; or photographs, poems, and prose extracts reproduced in *Reflections* could be used to stimulate discussion. One of the prose excerpts was drawn from the American sociologist C. Wright Mills's *White Collar*. The other, a picture of 'work that is boring and noisy and

---

[117] Dixon, *Growth through English*, 13.
[118] Shayer, *Teaching of English in Schools*, 170.
[119] Ibid. The idea predated the 1960s. See A. E. Smith, *English in the Modern School* (London: Methuen, 1954), 45–6.
[120] Clements, Dixon, and Stratta, *Reflections*, 3. The sales figure comes from Fred Inglis, *The Englishness of English Teaching* (London: Longman, 1969), 36 n. 13.

monotonous', came from Alan Sillitoe's *Saturday Night and Sunday Morning*. The novel's title 'itself suggests the pattern of Arthur's life', a different kind of escapism from that contemplated in the Philip Larkin poem reproduced alongside the passage from Sillitoe's novel. Classes would lead on to creative writing (imagine 'a nurse or miner or docker…starting the day's work or ending the day's work') or 'argumentative' essays ('What is the point of having Unions in various trades and professions?') and factual exercises ('Collect statistics and information on the pay and prospects for a group of trades, crafts, professions…').[121]

Here the principle of 'relevance' to schoolchildren's own lives was pushed so far that English shaded into Social Studies, and literature functioned scarcely even as a mode of language use as opposed to a vehicle for perspectives. In *Growth through English*, Dixon had stated: 'In English, pupils meet to share their encounters with life…literature, by bringing new voices into the classroom, adds to the store of shared experience.'[122] Assessing the quality of *Saturday Night and Sunday Morning* or Larkin's poem *as literature* was not the point. In principle, a thematic approach did not necessarily downgrade literature. Introducing his *Topics in English*, Summerfield said that poems and short stories should not be used invariably as jumping-off points for children's own writing: 'we should be prepared to let literature *be*, rather than reduce it to the subsidiary role of stimulus'; literature was 'the most important part of any English scheme of work, after the attainment of literacy'.[123] In practice, the irreducible, 'literary' aspects of a poem or novel were often subordinated to an extractable theme. Texts became documents.[124] Of course, it was *Culture and Environment*, more than anything else, that had made a place in English classes alongside literature for the products of the media and entertainment industries.[125] But it did so in order that their dangers could be recognized, not to have them naturalized alongside literature. Whitehead was dismayed by comprehension exercises on 'dull and worthless journalism' and activities where pupils tried their hands at writing advertising copy or tabloid news stories.[126]

---

[121] Clements, Dixon, and Stratta, *Reflections*, 22–4 (ellipses in original).

[122] Dixon, *Growth through English*, 13.

[123] Geoffrey Summerfield, *Topics in English: For the Secondary School* (London: B. T. Batsford, 1965), 16 (emphasis in original).

[124] Allen, *English Teaching since 1965*, 47.

[125] Peter Hollindale, 'Why Have Things Gone Wrong?', *Use of English* 23/4 (1972): 336.

[126] Whitehead, 'Examinations', 11; Whitehead, 'Leavis and the Schools', 146. In fact some of his adversaries clung to the some of the ideas of *Culture and Environment*: *Reflections* lamented the limitation of children's experiences by the hold the *Mirror* or the *Sketch* had on their households and recommended classroom exercises to help them 'overcome' those limitations; Clements, Dixon, and Stratta also alluded to Leavis and Thompson's

These developments did not go unchallenged. Fred Inglis, whose book *The Englishness of English Teaching* (1969) acknowledged its 'allegiance to the premises of that great English course book *Culture and Environment*', argued forcefully at the 1971 NATE conference against Dixon's *Growth through English* and *Language in Use* (1971), by Peter Doughty and others with the Nuffield Programme in Linguistics and English Teaching. Inglis knew, he said, that to 'offer…a critique of language study' and reassert the value of literature and the particular qualities of literary criticism invited the retort that one was 'Luddite, Leavisite, irrationalist'.[127] Individual teachers remained committed to an English with literature at its centre and believers in Leavisian objectives. But the curricula and the examination regimes had shifted decisively away from a *Scrutiny* conception of English in schools. We can point to several reasons for this change.

First, the new approaches were closely associated with comprehensive schools, whereas the grammar schools were the strongholds of *Scrutiny*-inspired teaching (and Holbrook's approach was most influential in the secondary moderns). Stratta suggested that a thematic approach was an appropriately flexible way of organizing courses for student bodies with a wide range of abilities.[128] When he and Dixon and Clements produced *Reflections*, they were all teaching at Walworth, the pilot comprehensive school in south London, and 'many of the principles' in their book came from 'the traditions of Walworth school'.[129] Harold Rosen, a prominent member of NATE and a founder of the London association that was its core, had been head of the English department at Walworth before he moved into teacher education. He took up a lectureship at the London Institute of Education alongside his own teachers, Britton and Nancy Martin, who were also the teachers and chief enablers of the *Reflections* team.[130] Other early exponents of theme-based English, such as Summerfield and Anthony Adams (author of *Team Teaching and the Teaching of English* and another Dartmouth participant), had experience teaching in

schema of advertising 'appeals' and recommended comparing ads with the appraisals in the Consumers' Association magazine *Which?*. Clements, Dixon, and Stratta, *Reflections*, 26, 27, 29. Both Smith, 'Creative Writing and Language Awareness', 4, and Inglis, *Englishness of English Teaching*, 36 n. 13, described *Reflections* as a descendant of *Culture and Environment*.

[127] Inglis, *Englishness of English Teaching*, 36 n. 13 (see also pp. 3, 177); Fred Inglis, 'How to Do Things with Words: A Critique of Language Studies', *English in Education* 5/2 (1971): 75; Allen, *English Teaching since 1965*, 56–9.

[128] Leslie Stratta, 'Underprivileged Children: English for Whom?', *NATE Bulletin* 2/3 (autumn 1965): 20; Dixon, 'English Renewed', 243.

[129] Clements, Dixon, and Stratta, *Reflections*, 4.

[130] John Richmond, 'Harold Rosen', *The Guardian*, 4 August 2008; Clements, Dixon, and Stratta, *Reflections*, 4; Steedman, 'State-sponsored Autobiography', 50.

comprehensives. As Labour policy in the 1960s and 1970s lent central government support to a form of school that had previously been supported only by a handful of local education authorities, comprehensives steadily replaced grammar schools and secondary moderns. Inevitably, teaching practices developed for comprehensives came to dominate secondary education.

Secondly, the newer approaches carried the considerable authority of social science. Thompson might point to the similarities between statements by Leavis and Vygotsky, but the real authority of *Scrutiny*-inspired educational thought was moral and artistic (and years of experience teaching in schools of a type that was being phased out). Lecturers in training colleges and institutes of education were more likely to look to psychology and linguistics for guidance on pressing questions. Rosen remarked in 1970 that fashioning new and satisfactory teacher-training models would entail 'ransacking the work of philosophers, anthropologists, psychologists, linguists and others. For we can no longer believe that Richards, Leavis and Eliot will see us through however rewarding they may continue to be.'[131]

The *Scrutiny* legacy in teaching was also a victim of the larger transformation of cultural and social authority in the 1960s and 1970s. The moralist register of cultural criticism lost some of its resonance with the breakdown of what Callum Brown has called 'discursive Christianity' (as distinct from formal religious observance, which had been declining for much longer).[132] Even Scrutineers and *Scrutiny* followers who urged 'that we restore the pleasure principle in our English periods' (such as Thompson) and embraced a permeable canon (most conspicuously, Whitehead) remained committed to notions of discrimination, and ideas about what counted as art, that were jolted by 'the Sixties'.[133] The continuing condemnation of a generalized 'pop' could appear dated and inadequate. The aesthetic innovations of late 1960s popular culture struck older Scrutineers (though not Mellers, who wrote seriously and technically about the Beatles' music and saw them as capable of originality and art despite the fallen nature of commercial music) as so much noise or doodling, no more complex than 1930s dance bands or advertisements, but younger teachers did not necessarily see things this way.[134] Increasingly, supporters of literature-led teaching found themselves arguing against claims that the

---

[131] Harold Rosen, 'The Professional Education of the Teacher of English', *English in Education* 4/2 (1970): 71.

[132] Callum G. Brown, *The Death of Christian Britain: Understanding Secularisation, 1800–2000* (2001; Abingdon: Routledge, 2009), ch. 8.

[133] Thompson, 'What Is Literature?', 4; Whitehead, *Disappearing Dais*, ch. 2.

[134] Wilfrid Mellers, *Twilight of the Gods: The Beatles in Retrospect* (London: Faber & Faber, 1973), 17, 33. Compare Anon., 'Pop into Revolt', *The Human World* 2 (February 1971): 62–73, esp. 65.

canon was a repository of middle-class culture that working-class children should not have foisted upon them. 'As developments in wider society have diminished the status' of canonical works of art, Margaret Mathieson observed in the mid-1970s, 'Leavisite' teachers who had once played the role of critical outsider had been 'accommodated' by schools as supporters of 'traditional values'.[135]

The juxtaposition of poems and reportage in classrooms and the reluctance to continue asserting the claims of a 'correct' or 'good' English in contradistinction to regional, class, and ethnic variations bespoke a more pluralist educational sensibility than the *Scrutiny* or grammar-school ethos. Looking back on the late 1960s and early 1970s, Whitehead remarked: 'the English-teacher's sense of the necessity for *resistance*, generated so inexorably by *Culture and Environment*, was gradually and insidiously eroded'.[136] In a circular soliciting support for the organization The Responsible Society, Holbrook remarked that 'most young people in responsible positions, like young teachers, no longer seem to feel the need for discrimination—of the kind people used to concern themselves with in the days of *Culture and Environment*'.[137]

In her study of the diffusion of Cousinian psychology through the French *lycée* system, Jan Goldstein likens the work of Victor Cousin's students and disciples to the Calvinist ministers of Max Weber's *Protestant Ethic*. Because Calvin had not given his followers advice about how to cope with lay people's fears that they were not among the elect, 'it fell to Calvinist ministers, who encountered the distressed parishioners face to face, to formulate that necessary, practical aspect of the doctrine'. Manuals of pastoral care were a better guide to quotidian theology than Calvin's own writings. And, as Goldstein observes of her nineteenth-century subjects, the gap between the master's thought and the needs of its disseminators meant that much Cousinian pedagogy was to a large extent the creation of his disciples.[138]

Scrutiny ideas and practices, too, could not always be 'applied' in straightforward fashion in schools. Holbrook's programmes for creative writing took some of their inspiration and much of their rationale from *Scrutiny*'s interpretation of modern civilization, but their practical techniques and their psychological basis originated elsewhere. School

[135] Mathieson, *Preachers of Culture*, 209.
[136] Whitehead, 'Leavis and the Schools', 146.
[137] David Holbrook, circular (this copy addressed to Denys Thompson), 26 October 1971, Penguin Archives, A640, Bristol.
[138] Jan Goldstein, *The Post-Revolutionary Self: Politics and Psyche in France, 1750–1850* (Cambridge, Mass.: Harvard University Press, 2005), 195–6.

English was closest to Cambridge English in sixth forms. Practical criticism proved a pedagogy capable of travelling without much adaptation for sixth-form use. In the case of the *Scrutiny* movement, the space between the centre and the schools was especially significant, because *Scrutiny* thinking, unlike Cousinian, was an unstable solution. It held together elements that could authorize educational programmes with conflicting aims, from Holbrook's creative liberation to Bantock's defence of traditional authority against 'egalitarian democracy'. It also introduced a teaching practice, the analysis of the media and mass culture, that remained entrenched in English teaching long after its rationale of discrimination had corroded. This pattern, of a critical instrument being detached from its *Scrutiny* context and redeployed in the service of a radically different cultural politics, was also the pattern of 'left-Leavisism'.

5

Adult Education and 'Left-Leavisism'

Scrutiny took an interest in adult education, and adult education an interest in *Scrutiny*, from the journal's earliest days.[1] L. C. Knights, Denys Thompson, W. A. Edwards, and W. H. Mellers taught adult education classes, and the journal reviewed new books in the field. Although *Culture and Environment* was 'designed for school use', one of the 'incitements' to writing it was Thompson's experience working for the Workers' Educational Association.[2] Leavis asked Chatto & Windus to send presentation copies to R. H. Tawney, 'being a power in the W.E.A.', and to others in the organization's hierarchy, including W. E. Williams.[3] As editor of the WEA journal *The Highway*, Williams had written to Leavis after only two numbers of *Scrutiny* had been published, 'beg[ging] me to write as drastically as possible for it on adult education'.[4] (This was the first of many times Williams provided a platform for *Scrutiny*-related initiatives, including *Use of English* and the *Pelican Guide to English Literature*.)[5] But it was in the fifteen years after the Second World War that the *Scrutiny* influence on adult education was most pronounced and most productive. Adult education was the hub of post-war 'left-Leavisism'.

The popular progressive current of British culture during and immediately after the Second World War prepared a younger generation of university graduates for induction into the movement. So, more practically,

---

[1] Tom Steele, *The Emergence of Cultural Studies, 1945–65: Cultural Politics, Adult Education, and the English Question* (London: Lawrence & Wishart, 1997), 81–4. This chapter was drafted before I read Steele's book. Our interpretations coincide at a number of points, most of them to do with Richard Hoggart, even though our source bases are quite different.

[2] F. R. Leavis and Denys Thompson, *Culture and Environment: The Training of Critical Awareness* (1933; London: Chatto & Windus, 1950), vii.

[3] Leavis to Ian Parsons, 19 January 1933; Leavis to Parsons, 3 January 1933; Leavis, 'Complimentary Copies' (1933), Chatto & Windus archive, CW 53/2, Reading.

[4] Leavis to Parsons, 31 December 1932, Chatto & Windus archive, CW 53/2, Reading.

[5] On Williams see also Stephen Woodhams, 'Adult Education and the History of Cultural Studies', *Changing English* 6/2 (1999): 244–5.

did the teaching opportunities that Forces life offered to graduates. In occupied Naples, Richard Hoggart had run an army arts club that received the support of a major in the Education Corps (the club formally became an Army Education Centre).[6] The Army Bureau of Current Affairs was primarily concerned with education for citizenship, organizing lectures and discussions about reconstruction and international politics, but it also provided an umbrella for classes in less demonstrably civic subjects, such as literature.[7] Civilian interest in questions of reconstruction fuelled a boom in classes offered by the partnership between the University of Oxford Delegacy for Extra-Mural Studies and the WEA, which ran courses in East Sussex, Lincoln, and the industrial towns of north Staffordshire as well as in and around Oxford.[8]

Towards the end of the war, the new Ministry of Education provided additional funding for adult education, and, over the term of the 1945–51 Labour government, the University Grants Committee trebled its funding for the universities' extramural teaching. Their number of 'grant-aided full-time tutors and organizing tutors...leaped from forty-three in 1944 to 260 in 1951'.[9] The Hull committee that appointed Hoggart in 1946 also appointed five of the other men and women it interviewed the same day.[10] The growth of adult education in the 1940s is of a piece with other cultural developments during the War and the Attlee years. As with the reorganization of the BBC, which built on the success of armed forces broadcasting, and the development of the Council for the Encouragement of Music and the Arts into the Arts Council, a wartime initiative was the impetus, and in some respects a model, for extensions to the public infrastructure of culture under Labour.[11]

[6] Richard Hoggart, *A Sort of Clowning: Life and Times, Volume II, 1940–59* (London: Chatto & Windus, 1990), 52–75, esp. 53. For similar stories, see John McIlroy, 'Teacher, Critic, Explorer', in W. John Morgan and Peter Preston (eds), *Raymond Williams: Politics, Education, Letters* (Basingstoke: Macmillan, 1993), 14; Jack Woolford, 'Tony McLean: A Memoir', in Workers' Educational Association South Eastern District, *Adult Education and Social Change: Lectures and Reminiscences in Honour of Tony McLean* (n.p., n.d. [1984?]), 4–5.

[7] S. P. Mackenzie, *Politics and Military Morale: Current-Affairs and Citizenship Education in the British Army, 1914–1950* (Oxford: Clarendon Press, 1992); T. H. Hawkins and L. J. F. Brimble, *Adult Education: The Record of the British Army* (London: Macmillan, 1947), 207–11.

[8] Lawrence Goldman, *Dons and Workers: Oxford and Adult Education since 1850* (Oxford: Oxford University Press, 1995), 233.

[9] John A. Blyth, *English University Adult Education, 1908–1958: The Unique Tradition* (Manchester: Manchester University Press, 1983), 222.

[10] Hoggart, *Sort of Clowning*, 75.

[11] Asa Briggs, *The History of Broadcasting in the United Kingdom*, vol. 4, *Sound and Vision* (Oxford: Oxford University Press, 1979), part 1, chs 2–4; F. M. Leventhal, ' "The Best for the Most": CEMA and State Sponsorship of the Arts in Wartime, 1939–1945', *Twentieth Century British History* 1/3 (1990): 289–317; Janet Minihan, *The Nationalization*

Adult education is rightly thought of as an engine of cultural democratization akin to the BBC or Penguin, but taking a train or bus to another town to contend with students' ideas and preconceptions was a more interactive and, in a modest and personal way, risky sort of outreach.[12] The life of the tutor could be spartan and isolating. Tutors were often responsible for a patch of territory and had to go on circuit, travelling to another town on successive evenings.[13] Working between Middlesbrough and the north Yorkshire coast, Hoggart would stay in the hotels favoured by commercial travellers, and his memoir evokes the curious shabby glamour of that salesmen's world.[14] The chilliness of church halls and the distractions of cafés in which classes met have their place in adult education folklore.

The central institution of literary education for adult students was the 'tutorial class', a WEA innovation of the early twentieth century that swiftly displaced the 'peripatetic university' arrangement, whereby scholars from Oxford and Cambridge toured the country delivering lectures.[15] The tutorial class was a three-year programme, meeting weekly except in the summers. Each session would last two hours, usually beginning with a more or less formal lecture and then an hour's discussion.[16] Tutorial classes were arranged jointly by university extramural departments and local WEA branches.[17] After 1945, the bonds between the WEA and the universities slackened as the latter sought more freedom to experiment with different course formats and more vocational content.[18] The majority of tutorial classes remained organized through the WEA,[19] but the

of Culture: The Development of State Subsidies to the Arts in Great Britain (New York: New York University Press, 1977), ch. 7; Andrew Sinclair, *Arts and Cultures: The History of the Fifty Years of the Arts Council of Great Britain* (London: Sinclair Stevenson, 1995).

[12] See W. A. Edwards, 'Ideals and Facts in Adult Education', *Scrutiny* 3/1 (June 1934): 95.

[13] Hoggart, *Sort of Clowning*, 75–6; Dai Smith, *Raymond Williams: A Warrior's Tale* (Cardigan: Parthian Books, 2008), 304–5.

[14] Hoggart, *Sort of Clowning*, 75–80, 85–6.

[15] J. W. Saunders, 'University Extension Renascent', in S. G. Raybould (ed.), *Trends in English Adult Education* (London: Michael Joseph, 1959), 53; Edwin Welch, *The Peripatetic University: Cambridge Local Lectures, 1873–1973* (Cambridge: Cambridge University Press, 1973). The term 'adult education' encompassed a variety of classes and institutions besides joint WEA-university tutorial classes. For an anatomy, see John Lowe, *Adult Education in England and Wales: A Critical Survey* (London: Michael Joseph, 1970), chs 3–9.

[16] Fred Inglis, *Raymond Williams* (London: Routledge, 1995), 123.

[17] Until 1945, all tutorial classes in England were joint WEA–university undertakings. S. G. Raybould, *University Extramural Education in England, 1945–62: A Study in Finance and Policy* (London: Michael Joseph, 1964), 62.

[18] Blyth, *English University Adult Education*, 160.

[19] Raybould, *University Extramural Education*, 62. This is why the log book from Hoggart's class has 'Scarborough W.E.A.' on its title page, even though Hoggart was paid by Hull University College. 'Scarborough W.E.A.: Literature Class Log', Richard Hoggart papers, 4/1/3, Sheffield.

changes in funding meant that the dominant players in adult education were university extramural departments—bodies whose members worked at some remove from 'internal' departments organized by discipline— rather than trade unions and voluntary organizations concerned with working-class education—which, in practice, had usually meant working-class men's education.

The constituency of adult education, at least in the humanities, was also becoming more middle-class—and more feminine. In its annual report for 1946–7, the Oxford delegacy's Tutorial Classes Committee provided a breakdown of student occupations that included few unskilled workers, but many skilled workers such as toolmakers and a number of draughtsmen (the occupation of the grammar-school-educated miner's son in Stan Barstow's topical 1960 novel *A Kind of Loving*), and a large number of schoolteachers, who brought a 'vocational purpose' that sat uneasily with the Oxford–WEA tradition.[20] Already in 1946–7, the occupations represented most heavily were teaching and (for women) domestic duties.[21] 'Housewives' and members of the 'lower professions', especially schoolteachers, predominated in literature tutorial classes in the 1950s. Stephen Coltham described his group in Lincoln in 1946–7 as 'including a larger proportion of working-class students than the average Literature class contains'. His report, like all the others that year, provided an occupational classification of the student body. The seven men in the class were a metal dresser, an advertising assistant in an engineering firm, a machine tool fitter, a mechanical engineer, an electrical engineer, an agricultural engineer, and an aircraft electrician: skilled technical or white-collar workers. Of the twelve women, six did 'home duties', one was a mailing clerk, two were shorthand typists, one was a teacher, another a library assistant, and one, curiously, was described as a 'Companion'. If this was a literature class with more working-class participants than usual, the average literature course was not very working class.[22]

For S. G. Raybould, the professor in the extramural department at the University of Leeds, the decline in the proportion of manual workers in tutorial classes 'meant that the W.E.A. was turning its back on its historic

[20] *Tutorial Classes Committee Report for the Year 1949–50* (Oxford: University of Oxford Delegacy for Extra-Mural Studies, 1950), 7; Oxford University Tutorial Classes Committee, 'Oxford University Tutorial Classes Committee: Annual Report for the Year 1946–47: C—Reports of Full-Time Tutors on their work other than that of Tutorial Classes', 33, Department of Continuing Education Papers, CE 3/61/34, OUA.

[21] *Tutorial Classes Committee Report for the Year 1946–47: Tutorial Classes and Summer School* (Oxford: University of Oxford Delegacy for Extra-Mural Studies, 1947), 3.

[22] Stephen Coltham, table and tutor's report, 'Literature II', Lincoln, in 'Oxford University Tutorial Classes Committee: Annual Report for the Year 1946–47: B—Tutorial Class Reports' (May 1947), 83, 85, Department of Continuing Education papers, CE 3/61/34, OUA.

mission to aid the "educationally underprivileged"'.[23] Rank-and-file
tutors, too, questioned the justice of providing equally for middle-class
students and those with fewer advantages.[24] Others complained about the
tone that better-off students set in their classes. A tutor in Kent described
one of his classes in the mid-1940s as 'dilettante, middle-class par excellence'.[25] Here, as in a complaint about students who turned classes into
'a socialite occasion', reservations about channelling effort and resources
towards the comparatively privileged have a palpable undertow of sexism.[26]
Teaching women and training-college graduates was not quite the cause
that some men, energized or radicalized by their war experiences, had
signed up for.

Yet for teachers of literature, adult education had never primarily been
workers' education. It was not that literature courses were becoming more
middle class and female: it was that a subject with a substantial middle-
class and female public was overtaking subjects with a stronger masculine,
labour-movement pedigree, such as economic history.[27] In the 1930s, literature had been the Cinderella of the curriculum, the Oxford delegacy
reported, using a metaphor dear to educationalists of the time. By 1947,
it accounted for the largest number of tutorial classes offered in the Oxford
system.[28] The influx of middle-class women and men into literature
courses is consistent with the remarkable proliferation of amateur theatri-
cals, film societies, and arts clubs in provincial towns and cities in the
1940s and 1950s. Popular desires for more active participation in the arts
and education exceeded the organized opportunities available.[29]

The people who crowded into evening classes after the war did not
necessarily value literature in the same ways as their teachers did. Tutors
were in the business of educating students' desires as well as satisfying
them. In practical criticism, literature tutors—some of whom, like Hoggart,
knew Leavis and other *Scrutiny* authors only through their writing—had

[23] Blyth, *English University Adult Education*, 183.

[24] 'Oxford University Tutorial Classes Committee: Annual Report of Organizing Secretary:
Session 1949–50', 5, Department of Continuing Education papers, CE 3/61/37, OUA.

[25] 'Oxford University Tutorial Classes Committee: Annual Report for the Year 1946–
47: C—Reports of Full-Time Tutors on their work other than that of Tutorial Classes', 33,
Department of Continuing Education papers, CE 3/61/34, OUA.

[26] Raymond Williams, report on Literature class at Cuckfield, in Oxford University
Tutorial Classes Committee, 'Annual Report for the Year 1947–8: B—Tutorial Class Reports', May 1948, 26, Department of Continuing Education papers, CE 3/61/35, OUA.

[27] *Tutorial Classes Committee Report for the Year 1948–49* (Oxford: University of Oxford
Delegacy for Extra-Mural Studies, 1949), 3.

[28] *Tutorial Classes Committee Report for the Year 1947–48: Tutorial Classes and Summer
School* (Oxford: University of Oxford Delegacy for Extra-Mural Studies, 1948), 4.

[29] Christopher Hilliard, *To Exercise Our Talents: The Democratization of Writing in Britain* (Cambridge, Mass.: Harvard University Press, 2006), chs 2, 8.

a mechanism for piercing students' romantic notions and assembling new conceptions of literature by grappling with the words on the page.[30] Moreover, the *Scrutiny* tradition offered ways of 'reading' mass culture and making connections between novels and their 'environment'. This enabled tutors to accommodate some of the vocational demands of their constituents.

Tutors in the Oxford system were acutely aware of its tradition of education and political commitment symbolized above all by R. H. Tawney's early classes in Rochdale. *Scrutiny*'s vision of literary criticism could also be a cause, and one that turned out to be capable of being combined with a Labour or communist commitment to workers' education. The Raymond Williams of the 1940s and 1950s was at once a Marxist and a follower of Leavis. And while he and other socialists in the Oxford delegacy valued their connection with F. W. Bateson, who was one of the Oxford academics who worked with the extramural tutors during their summer schools, Bateson's writings had nothing like the impact Leavis and Knights did on their thinking about the relations between literature and society.[31] 'The immense attraction of Leavis lay in his cultural radicalism', Williams recalled. '...It was the range of Leavis's attacks on academicism, on Bloomsbury, on metropolitan literary culture, on the commercial press, on advertising, that first took me.... Finally, there was Leavis's great stress on education. He would always emphasize that there was an enormous educational job to be done.'[32] And, crucially, there was no body of British Marxist literary and cultural criticism—Christopher Caudwell, Edgell Rickword, Philip Henderson, and Jack Lindsay notwithstanding—that could compete with *Scrutiny* at this time.[33] In the work of 'left-Leavisites', *Scrutiny*'s pedagogical and analytical practices were regularly in tension with *Scrutiny*'s principles. Much of what is significant and fascinating about this post-war episode in politics, letters, and education arose from this tension.

This chapter follows the careers of *Scrutiny* criticism and teaching styles in adult education through two main archives: Richard Hoggart's papers and the records of the Oxford delegacy. The huge archive of the Oxford

---

[30] Richard Hoggart to F. R. Leavis, 4 May 1953, Hoggart papers, 3/9/10, Sheffield; Richard Hoggart, *An Imagined Life: Life and Times, Volume III, 1959–91* (1992; Oxford: Oxford University Press, 1993), 10.

[31] Inglis, *Raymond Williams*, 133; Smith, *Raymond Williams*, 359–60.

[32] Raymond Williams, *Politics and Letters: Interviews with New Left Review* (London: New Left Books, 1979), 66–7.

[33] Raymond Williams, 'Books for Teaching "Culture and Environment"' (1950), in John McIlroy and Sallie Westwood (eds), *Border Country: Raymond Williams in Adult Education* (Leicester: National Institute of Adult Continuing Education, 1993), 177; Stuart Hall, 'Life and Times of the First New Left', *New Left Review*, n.s. 61 (2010): 179.

delegacy reveals a great deal about the evolving practice of Williams and makes it possible to see how a number of lesser-known tutors in the Oxford extramural system experimented with courses on *Scrutiny* lines and debated the value of practical criticism, '"Culture and Environment" studies', and courses in applied critical literacy that at once built on and dissented from the early work of the Leavises and Thompson. Hoggart's class logs, which provide glimpses of student perspectives (which often elude historians of education), show how the lessons of *Scrutiny*, *Culture and Environment*, and *Fiction and the Reading Public* were translated into classroom practice. And Hoggart's 1957 book *The Uses of Literacy* was a Leavisian case against Leavisian premises.

The reception and development of *Scrutiny* in the Oxford system is not an Oxford-versus-Cambridge story. The delegacy employed graduates of Cambridge and Swansea as well as Oxford. In any case, the literature tutors with Oxford degrees were not necessarily agents of the Oxford English Faculty. While senior members of the Oxford faculty were hostile to Leavis's critical approach, their students were often more open to Leavis and *Scrutiny*. 'Dr Leavis is anathema to virtually all the lecturers at Oxford, and they don't conceal the fact; but Bateson has invited Leavis to lecture at Oxford two years running, and on each occasion the meeting was crowded out and enormously enthusiastic.'[34] Bateson was one of the sponsors of the Oxford University Critical Society, most of whose members were students. Bernard Bergonzi, one of its members, recalls that the society 'used Leavis as a kind of patron, and he came once a year from Cambridge at the Society's invitation to lecture to a large audience'.[35]

All the same, in the years after the Second World War, literature teaching in the Oxford Delegacy still inclined to literary history and surveys rather than the concentration and close reading that characterized Leavis's variant of Cambridge English. Writing in the Oxford extramural journal *Rewley House Papers*, Williams claimed to have seen a tutorial-class syllabus that included this extraordinary feat of compression:

[34] Boris Ford to Alan Glover, 27 March 1953, Penguin archives, 0290.0, Bristol.
[35] Bernard Bergonzi, *Exploding English: Criticism, Theory, Culture* (Oxford: Clarendon Press, 1990), 6–7; David Matthews, *Memories of F. R. Leavis* (Bishopstone: Brynmill Press, 2010), 20–1; A. Alvarez, *Where Did It All Go Right? A Memoir* (New York: William Morrow, 1999), 115, 127–8. However, see also Kenneth Trodd, 'Report from the Younger Generation', *Essays in Criticism* 14/1 (January 1964): 23. In the late 1940s, Blackwell's bookshop on Broad Street ordered more copies of new issues of *Scrutiny* than Leavis's Cambridge haunt, Heffer's (though Galloway and Porter in Cambridge ordered more than Blackwell's). *Scrutiny* trade sales ledger, 1945–9, 29–32, 51–3, Deighton, Bell, & Co. archives, Add. 9453, B5/1, CUL.

LECTURE THREE: James Joyce—Irishman, poet, dramatist, novelist, exile; the nature of his experiments; readings from *Dubliners, Portrait of the Artist, Ulysses, Finnegans Wake,* and *Pomes Penyeach.* To be followed by discussion.

This lecture, if it actually took place, was exceptional, but the syllabi that survive in the Oxford Extra-Mural Delegacy's archive support Williams's contention that tutorial classes covered more novels, plays, and long poems than could be examined in any detail in an academic year or weekly meetings. By trying to cover too much ground, Williams wrote, 'most Literature courses... proposed an examination of literature at the rate, and with the generalizations, of orthodox literary history'.[36]

Williams illustrated the problem with a pastiche of a class discussion of George Eliot's *Felix Holt*: 'it was sub-titled *Portrait of a Radical*—an interesting link with life there; Chartism!—and then it followed that the name of George Eliot was really Marian Evans, and that she had lived, unmarried, with George Henry Lewes, and was a leading member of that group of neo-Comtist thinkers of the 1850's...'.[37] The people who collected 'marginal facts' about literary works were often 'unable to read intelligently an unnamed piece of verse or prose that might be set before them'.[38] The promise of practical criticism was that scrutinizing a text without the crutches of context or conventional valuations opened up opportunities for genuine critical analysis and serious personal engagement with poetry or prose. The discipline of close reading could liberate the mind from mechanical thinking and potted literary histories. However, as students became more familiar with the procedure, they began reflexively hunting ambiguities and objective correlatives. This did not mean that one should renounce 'Leavis and all his works'. Williams responded by incorporating textual analysis into a programme of set texts rather than stand-alone 'exercises'. Given the time constraints of the tutorial class, sessions would be based on one or two short poems, for instance, or 'one crucial chapter, or two or three crucial paragraphs, from a novel'.[39]

Practical criticism was not Leavis's invention, of course, but to advocate practical criticism in the terms Williams did, and at the time he did, was

---

[36] Raymond Williams, 'Some Experiments in Literature Teaching' (1948–9) in McIlroy and Westwood (eds), *Border Country*, 148.

[37] Ibid., 147. For a similar example (but a very different judgement) see the passage from 'Roger Dataller' quoted in Jonathan Rose, *The Intellectual Life of the British Working Class* (New Haven: Yale University Press, 2001), 427.

[38] Williams, 'Some Experiments in Literature Teaching', 148.

[39] Ibid., 148, 149, 150. Compare Richard Hoggart, 'Teaching Literature to Adults: Notes on Extra-Mural Teaching' (1959), in *Speaking to Each Other: Essays*, 2 vols (London: Chatto & Windus, 1970), 2: 236–7.

to follow Leavis more than it was to follow Richards.[40] The imprint of *Scrutiny* was especially clear in Williams's *Reading and Criticism* (1950), a book intended for adult education tutors that had much to say about the importance of value judgements and slack reviewing in the newspapers, and which included sample exercises in comparing good novels with bad best-sellers.[41] *Reading and Criticism* built on an earlier exercise in brokering *Scrutiny* to teachers and their pupils: Thompson's *Reading and Discrimination*. Thompson read Williams's manuscript for the publishers and recommended publication.[42]

The book appeared in a series intended for adult education teachers (it was edited by Thomas Hodgkin, Secretary to the Oxford Extra-Mural Delegacy).[43] Like Williams's essay in *Rewley House Papers*, it was debated in the adult education journals that gathered geographically scattered tutors into disciplinary and pedagogical conversations. Writing about *Reading and Criticism* in the pages of *Adult Education*, T. W. Thomas of the Swansea Joint Tutorial Classes Committee remarked that Williams's book reflected the efforts of 'various critics' over the last few decades 'to discourage us talking "about" literature and to get us to read the text as our sole source and authority'. This might now be a commonplace in the universities, he said, but 'one can still find in the adult education movement surprising reluctance to approach literature through the critical reading of texts': *Reading and Criticism* was an attempt to overcome that reluctance, 'a case for practical criticism in the extra-mural class'. Thomas professed enthusiasm for Williams's argument, but his praise was vague while his reservations were specific. 'We all know how easy it is to dissect a poem and leave it a heap of dismembered parts.' While close reading rightly focused on what texts do with words, it did so at the risk of 'losing sight of the whole'. The method was especially weak for making sense of novels. Responding to Williams's article in *Rewley House Papers*, Thomas questioned how much difference there was between Williams's experiments with the impromptu criticism of passages on duplicated sheets and his subsequent concentration on a crucial chapter or several crucial paragraphs: did this really amount to abandoning 'exercises'? 'Reading extracts,

---

[40] Williams's *Rewley House Papers* essay mentioned Richards but took Leavis as its primary reference point. Williams, 'Some Experiments in Literature Teaching', 148, 150.

[41] 'Mr F. R. Leavis has been largely responsible for the intelligent development of critical analysis as an educational discipline, and to his work, and that of *Scrutiny*, I am indebted.' This acknowledgement might 'ensure that this book is labelled "partisan," and assigned to its "school"'. Not so, said Williams: 'As an independent student I have found the work of these critics valuable because it insisted on "the text as the starting-point of criticism."' Raymond Williams, *Reading and Criticism* (London: Frederick Muller, 1950), ix–x.

[42] Williams, *Reading and Criticism*, x; Inglis, *Raymond Williams*, 126.

[43] Inglis, *Raymond Williams*, 311 n.

however intensively, is not reading the novel', said Thomas, 'and as a method of class study I have not found it satisfactory since it obliges the student to rely on the tutor's interpretation which determined the selection.'[44]

Nevertheless, *Scrutiny* approaches made their way into adult education classes at this time, and not only by people whom colleagues regarded as followers of Leavis. John McIlroy notes that one Oxford tutor who began using practical criticism in his classes in the mid-1940s, Stephen Coltham, was not a literature specialist, which suggests that the method could help tutors as well as students get their bearings.[45] The same could be said of D. C. Bryson, a philosopher who taught a literature class in north Staffordshire in 1947–8.[46] Albert Emery, a tutor in the Potteries who had been an 'internal' adult student at Balliol College before the First World War, was another non-specialist—he taught politics, economics, and history as well as literature—who incorporated the new criticism into his teaching in a different way.[47] A 1936 syllabus on the modern novel presented *Principles of Literary Criticism* as the orthodoxy of contemporary critical theory; Emery quoted and paraphrased Richards on the objectives of criticism (distinguishing between experiences, understanding the harmony of 'responses'). However, there was no indication that practical criticism would play a part in the course: the overviews of each session signalled a thematic history-of-literature approach. Emery's response to Richards appears to have been the inverse of the Leavisian one, holding to Richards's general theory but not taking up his teaching method.[48]

Leavis and *Scrutiny* are usually thought of in for-or-against terms, but these tutors' syllabi show that it was possible to pick and mix. Reading lists that included books by *Scrutiny* contributors also included the highly teachable *Elizabethan World Picture* (1943) by Leavis's enemy E. M. W.

[44] T. W. Thomas, 'Practical Criticism and the Literature Class', *Adult Education* 24/2 (1951): 20, 23–4, 25.

[45] McElroy, 'Teacher, Critic, Explorer', 24 and 44 n.; S. W. Coltham, report on Modern Literature course, Lincoln, 1950–1, in 'Oxford University Tutorial Classes Committee: Report on the Work for the Year 1950/51: Tutorial Class Reports', Department of Continuing Education papers, CE 3/61/38, OUA.

[46] 'Writers do not merely reveal the state of society and of themselves. They create values—they can make us think and feel in new ways.... That is finally a matter of personal response.... And so the method adopted will be to read as intensively and carefully as possible a small number of representative and important works by modern authors.' D. C. Bryson, syllabus on 'Literature and the Modern World', Burton, north Staffordshire, 1947–8, Department of Continuing Education papers, CE 3/60/30, OUA.

[47] On Emery's career, see Goldman, *Dons and Workers*, 10, 140, 142, 146.

[48] A. E. Emery, 'Syllabus of a Course of Study on ... Literature and the Modern World', part 1, 'The Novel' (North Wingfield, 1936); Emery, 'Syllabus of a Course of Study on ... Modern English Writers', part 3, 'The Modern Novel' (Stafford, 1936), Department of Continuing Education papers, CE 3/60/18, OUA.

Tillyard.[49] Some tutors, of course, never recommended works by *Scrutiny* authors. B. S. Dudman did, but she also shadow-boxed with *Scrutiny*. Teaching in Stafford in 1947–8, she said in her syllabus: 'To know *why* [a reader] enjoys both "Tess of the D'Urbervilles" and "Cold Comfort Farm" is to begin to be aware of different "values."' The distinction between kinds of reading pleasure did not hold for Thompson and the Leavises: one could not appreciate the good and still enjoy the bad. Dudman, dissenting from the *Scrutiny* insistence on standards, suggested that 'the positive use of criticism' was 'not to establish "standards" of "good" and "bad," but to help readers find their way about among the standards established by the creative writers'.[50]

The Oxford tutors who came closest to endorsing the *Scrutiny* programme were Williams, Douglas Hewitt, and Graham Taylor. Hewitt had read English at Pembroke College, Basil Willey's college, and he was a firm believer in the intellectual-history aspect of Cambridge English as well as Leavis's approach.[51] People taking tutorial classes, he wrote in the *Critical Quarterly* in 1959, 'hope to establish some discussable principles of judgment; they hope to gain some idea of the growth and development of our literature; they hope to understand the relationship of this literature to the society in which it was—and is—written and to the values of society. One is inclined to say that they are all Cambridge men and women at heart.' Hewitt added that the tripos papers on Life, Literature, and Thought would appeal to them. As we have seen, Leavis's dating and practical criticism classes were 'historical', tracing 'the growth and development of our literature', albeit in a less direct way than other members of the English Faculty did. Hewitt regarded close reading as the best means to all three of the ends he listed. 'The starting point, therefore, for most classes is, or should be, the detailed critical study of texts and the attempt to express general critical principles—practical criticism.'[52]

Hewitt's syllabus for a course on Literary Taste and Judgment in 1961–2 put this understanding of the ends and the means of criticism into practice. The class would consider the basis of value judgements and proceed 'by the detailed study of a number of very varied poems and passages of prose... These will, so far as possible, be presented in such a way that our minds are not made up for us before we start thinking about them by

[49] 'Enemy' is Leavis's word: Leavis to Parsons, 10 November 1973, Chatto & Windus archive, CW 541/6, Reading.
[50] B. S. Dudman, 'Background to Modern English Literature' (Stafford, 1947–8), Department of Continuing Education papers, CE 3/60/30, OUA.
[51] *The Cambridge University List of Members 1973–1974* (Cambridge: Cambridge University Press, 1974), 534.
[52] Douglas Hewitt, 'Why Teach Literature... in Adult Education', *Critical Quarterly* 1/1 (March 1959): 54.

knowledge of who wrote them and what is the accepted opinion about them. We should find ourselves considering the nature and function of certain literary techniques and, more generally, the manner in which language achieves its effects.' Before getting to the three texts the students would study intensively—*King Lear, Pride and Prejudice*, and Iris Murdoch's *The Bell*—they would spend a term on 'reading matter... provided in the form of duplicated sheets, by the tutor'.[53]

The brevity of Williams's syllabi was notorious among his colleagues, but he could bring himself to spell out a very *Scrutiny* creed:

The assumptions this course sets out to substantiate are the following:
1. That a work of literature—poem, play, or novel—exists only in a settled organization of words; and that all understanding, and all judgement, of that work must be related to the words themselves for justification. Consequently, such counters as 'plot', 'character', 'action', [and] 'style' must depend for their sanction on primary analysis of the word-organization which is the only fact in the work.
2. That there is good writing, and bad writing.
3. That it is possible to demonstrate the difference between the two by analysis, without having to rely on 'hunches'.
4. That reading of the kind which this course attempts to encourage, reading, that is, where the maximum intelligence, sensibility, and honesty is brought to bear on the text, does not decrease the 'pleasure' of reading any work which has any value; but will rather make it more conscious, less arbitrary, and longer lasting.[54]

'Discrimination' was alive and well. The first year of the course would stress that literature was 'the exact expression of realized values. Reading extends, refines, and co-ordinates sensibility. Criticism is reading of that order in its most conscious form.' Accurately reading the values expressed in literature 'will depend on the full exploration of the words in the text. "Nothing exists in literature but in language." ... Analysis of the quality of a writer's language is also, necessarily, analysis of the quality of his thought, feeling, and perception.'[55] The syllogistic sharpness was Williams's own, but the precepts and terminology ('sensibility', 'values', 'co-ordinates', 'organization') were *Scrutiny*'s. The statement about critical 'counters' such

[53] Douglas Hewitt, 'Literary Taste and Judgment', Maidenhead Sessional Class, 1961–2, Department of Continuing Education Papers, CE 3/60/44, OUA.
[54] Raymond Williams, 'Syllabus of a Course of Study on Literature: Together with that of an Alternative Course on Culture and Environment' (Brighton and Cuckfield, 1947), 3, Department of Continuing Education Papers, CE 3/60/30, OUA; Inglis, *Raymond Williams*, 122–3.
[55] Williams, 'Syllabus of a Course of Study on Literature: Together with that of an Alternative Course on Culture and Environment' (Brighton and Cuckfield, 1947), 6, Department of Continuing Education Papers, CE 3/60/30, OUA.

as character and plot was a rewriting of a sentence in L. C. Knights's *How Many Children Had Lady Macbeth?*.[56] 'Exact expression of realized values' was silently quoted from Knights's 1939 essay pleading for 'correlation' between the teaching of English and history.[57]

This was one of a cluster of essays—others include the *Scrutiny* pieces on the dissociation of sensibility and the relation of Shakespearean drama to economic forces ('profit inflations')—in which Knights considered the relationship between literature and culture. For tutors who believed that literary criticism had a 'social function', Knights's ideas clearly appealed. Graham Taylor, a Swansea graduate, quoted the same line about 'realized values' as Williams had in the syllabus for the course on Elizabethan drama that he taught in Lincoln in 1951–2. From drama, students could glean 'valuable, and otherwise unavailable, evidence about Elizabethan sensibility and characteristic Elizabethan moral attitudes to the problems of living, and about the relations of "culture" and "environment" during the period'. This was possible because those exactly expressed values 'are never purely personal'. Unlike Williams, Taylor quoted Knights's essay at length: 'The discipline of strict literary criticism is the only means we have of apprehending these embodied values with sureness and subtlety.' Here we reach the same sort of 'correlation' favoured in Knights's other meditations on literature and its contexts: 'in an attempt to understand the quality of living in a past period—to understand, that is, all those intangible modes of being which are only hinted at in the documents on which economic and political history is based—the study of that period's literature is central, and some degree of *critical* ability is indispensible to the historian of culture'.[58] The argument ramified further than it should have, since all Knights's case studies derived from the early modern period, the culture of which was supposed to manifest a unity denied to other times and places. Taylor, in his syllabus, repeated the *Scrutiny* commonplace that the Elizabethan age 'nourished a healthy, integrated culture, which found its finest expression in drama'.[59]

[56] 'In the mass of Shakespeare criticism there is not a hint that "character"—like "plot," "rhythm," "construction" and all our other critical counters—is merely an abstraction from the total response in the mind of the reader or spectator, brought into being by written or spoken words; that the critic therefore—however far he may ultimately range—begins with the words of which a play is composed.' L. C. Knights, 'How Many Children Had Lady Macbeth?' (1933) in *Explorations: Essays in Criticism Mainly on the Literature of the Seventeenth Century* (London: Chatto & Windus, 1946), 4.

[57] L. C. Knights, 'The University Teaching of English and History: A Plea for Correlation' (1939), in *Explorations*, 193.

[58] Knights, 'The University Teaching of English and History', 193–4; all quoted in G. Taylor, 'Elizabethan Life and Literature', Lincoln, 1951–2, Department of Continuing Education papers, CE 3/60/34, OUA.

[59] Taylor, 'Elizabethan Life and Literature', Lincoln, 1951–2, Department of Continuing Education papers, CE 3/60/34, OUA.

Taylor, Williams, and Hewitt further demonstrated their adherence to the *Scrutiny* project in the way they broadened the scope of literature teaching to encompass the concerns of *Culture and Environment*. This was also a response to their teaching situation: 'Adults asked, usually by implication, what does this study really mean to me as a person, and to my life in the everyday world; how does it connect with that life outside books?'[60] When Williams proposed a course with the title 'Culture and Environment' in 1947, it was envisaged as a first-year course for students who had no previous experience with literary study: after taking Culture and Environment, they would move on to 'the literature course proper'.[61] Williams's rubric, again, was indebted to Knights's articulation of the relationship between literature and society as well as to Leavis and Thompson's demarcation of the territory.[62] 'The Study of Culture and Environment is one of applied sociology; but the application is based on the methods of literary criticism. The culture of a society, in its broadest meaning, is the index of the quality of living within the society. Its assessment is the social function of the literary critic.' Williams followed the Leavises and Thompson is seeing literary criticism as a means of 'applying' social science. The topics to be covered included advertising, newspapers, radio, cinema, 'the problem of a community', as well as subjects not treated in Leavis and Thompson's primer, such as political speeches. The reading list was a patchily updated version of the bibliography in *Culture and Environment*. The 'essential' books included Leavis's *Education and the University* (first on the list, not in alphabetical order), *Culture and Environment*, Thompson's books on advertising and newspapers, and such Thompson touchstones as George Sturt's *Change in the Village*, R. H. Tawney's *The Acquisitive Society*, the Lynds' *Middletown*, and Stuart Chase's *Your Money's Worth*. Significantly, Thorstein Veblen's *Theory of the Leisure Class* was there too: Williams must have recognized its affinity with the other works in the *Culture and Environment* orrery.[63]

---

[60] Hoggart, *Imagined Life*, 92–3.

[61] Raymond Williams, 'Syllabus of a Course of Study on Culture and Environment', in 'Syllabus of a Course of Study on Literature: Together with that of an Alternative Course on Culture and Environment' (Brighton and Cuckfield, 1947), 12, Department of Continuing Education papers, CE 3/60/30, OUA.

[62] L. C. Knights, 'Shakespeare and Profit Inflations', *Scrutiny* 5/1 (June 1936): 57, 59–60; L. C. Knights, 'Bacon and the Seventeenth-Century Dissociation of Sensibility', *Scrutiny* 11/4 (summer 1943): 268–85. Williams's 'Culture and Environment' syllabus makes a reference to Bacon's ideas about language and the 'dissociation of sensibility' that would seem quite incongruous if the syllabus were not read alongside Knights's essay on Bacon.

[63] The recommended reading included more books by Leavis, Thompson, and Knights; T. S. Eliot, Norman Angell, Edward O'Brien, and Robert S. Lynd; and a sole Marxist, Christopher Caudwell. Raymond Williams, 'Syllabus of a Course of Study on Culture and

Q. D. Leavis's *Fiction and the Reading Public* was noticeably absent in a course that covered 'FICTION. As a business. Best-sellers, book societies, and reviewers.'[64] Recommending 'Books for Teaching "Culture and Environment"' in *Use of English* in 1950, Williams said that Q. D. Leavis's book was, 'of course, the standard work' on popular fiction, but his judgement on *Culture and Environment* itself suggests what reservations he had about *Fiction and the Reading Public*.[65] While Leavis and Thompson had opened up an important field of study, their own interpretations of modern culture were unsatisfactory. 'I feel myself that the assertion of a "minority" is by now largely irrelevant and, in certain social terms, idle and harmful.' (This was in the passage where he criticized G. H. Bantock.)[66] Q. D. Leavis spoke to (and sought to construct) a critically 'mature' minority, explaining the cultural implications of the best-seller. She was not trying to persuade the Book Society's members that the institution was a dangerous portent. Engaging with people who enjoyed best-sellers or Hollywood films was part of an adult education tutor's job.

Moreover, many tutors held political views that made them uncomfortable with the ease with which ideas about 'the masses' and 'herd instincts' were used in *Scrutiny*. Williams's list of questions to be considered in a course taught in Battle in 1949–50 tellingly deploys the first-person plural:

> Why is Culture a word we prefer not to use?
> Is there a 'Problem of Leisure'?...
> Is there a difference between art and entertainment?
> What is a highbrow?
> Who are the masses?
> Is 'I know what I like' the last word?...
> Why we 'never read' advertisements...
> Are best-sellers born or made?
> Why is modern art 'difficult'?
> Is the artist one of the 'useful people'?[67]

Environment', in 'Syllabus of a Course of Study on Literature: Together with that of an Alternative Course on Culture and Environment' (Brighton and Cuckfield, 1947), 13–14, Department of Continuing Education papers, CE 3/60/30, OUA.

[64] In its place, Williams recommended Stanley Unwin's *The Truth about Publishing* (first published in 1926 but subsequently revised) and the book Unwin wrote with George Stevens, *Best-Sellers: Are They Born or Made?* (1939). Raymond Williams, 'Syllabus of a Course of Study on Culture and Environment', in 'Syllabus of a Course of Study on Literature: Together with that of an Alternative Course on Culture and Environment' (Brighton and Cuckfield, 1947), 12, Department of Continuing Education papers, CE 3/60/30, OUA.

[65] Williams, 'Books for Teaching "Culture and Environment"', 176.

[66] Ibid., 177.

[67] Raymond Williams, 'What Is Culture?', Battle, 1949–50, Department of Continuing Education papers, CE 3/60/32, OUA.

The content of the questions, too, pointed to a politics different from that of the founding documents of ' "Culture and Environment" studies',[68] a politics Williams would elaborate in the final chapter of *Culture and Society, 1780–1950* (1958), where he wrote: 'There are in fact no masses; there are only ways of seeing people as masses.'[69] That the category 'the masses' might be as much of an ideological artefact as 'the highbrow' was not a possibility entertained by Thompson or the Leavises.

In the early 1950s Williams campaigned—within the Oxford delegacy and in the pages of *The Highway*—to apply the insights of culture-and-environment teaching to the everyday uses of literacy of the 'useful people'. His courses on Public Expression were an attempt to occupy a territory between culture-and-environment studies and the skills training (report writing, public speaking, 'clear thinking', and so on) provided by trade union and Labour College courses: courses of this sort might enable the delegacy to reach the manual workers disappointingly underrepresented in tutorial classes.[70] In Hastings over the 1951–2 academic year, Williams's class dealt with how to prepare to write reports and letters to newspapers, how to read newspapers 'intelligently', and the tricks and traps of emotive words, analogies, statistics, and quotations.[71] Some of Williams's colleagues thought that Public Expression breached the WEA principle of 'liberal', non-vocational education.[72] Williams's case for Public Expression based its liberal credentials on its development of the *Scrutiny* tradition of cultural analysis. The experience of Culture and Environment and Literature and Society courses had shown that 'the teaching of "successful" expression must inevitably raise important questions, such as can only be handled in "liberal" terms'. Since the 1930s, many in adult education had acknowledged that 'students must be helped, not only with the reading of poems, plays and novels, but also with the reading of material with which they are probably more familiar, and by which their habits of reading may have

---

[68] Williams, 'Books for Teaching "Culture and Environment" ', 174.

[69] Raymond Williams, *Culture and Society, 1780–1950* (1958; Harmondsworth: Penguin, 1963), 289.

[70] McIlroy, 'Teacher, Critic, Explorer', 35–9. On the Labour Colleges, see Margaret Cohen, 'The Labour College Movement between the Wars: National and North-West Developments', and John McIlroy, 'The Demise of the National Council of Labour Colleges', both in Brian Simon (ed.), *The Search for Enlightenment: The Working Class and Adult Education in the Twentieth Century* (1990; Leicester: National Institute of Adult Continuing Education, 1992). By the second half of the 1940s, the Labour College activities detailed in the journal *Plebs* were overwhelmingly 'practical'.

[71] Raymond Williams, 'Public Expression', Hastings, 1951–2, Department of Continuing Education papers, CE 3/60/34, OUA.

[72] McIlroy, 'Teacher, Critic, Explorer', 36.

been greatly affected: material such as newspapers, magazines, pamphlets, advertisements, etc.'[73]

Public Expression had its origin, Williams said, in such Leavisian teaching and in popular books on reasoning such as R. H. Thouless's *Straight
and Crooked Thinking* (1930) and Susan Stebbing's *Thinking to Some Purpose* (1939).[74] Stebbing and Thouless only went so far, however. Their
books were useful in getting students as far as analysing newspapers and
advertisements 'on a "sense or nonsense" level', but many mass-cultural
texts could not be 'faulted on the score of logic' and required the ability
to read for 'tone, method, and effect'. This was what Thompson did in his
books on newspapers and advertising, and it was this that the culture-
and-environment tradition brought to the teaching of practical cultural
literacy.[75] His case for Public Expression struck at least one sceptical contemporary as a Leavisian case. Geoffrey Gough, the Oxford-WEA organizer for mid-Cornwall, wrote to Frank Pickstock, the delegacy's secretary,
concerned that the 'Cambridge Newer Criticism' was 'clearly the spear-
head of this movement'. Its brand of 'Close textual criticism . . . is far from
being an accomplish[men]t general among English graduates, never mind
philosophers, historians etc. . . . One approves the critical standards of
most of the better products of whichever university one's prejudices direct
one's attentions towards. But that especial kind of critical training is central to Raymond's whole conception of P[c]. Ex[n]. which was generally endorsed.' There would not be enough tutors qualified to teach such
courses.[76]

Gough was responding to the argument Williams had set out in 1954
at a conference on Public Expression at Wedgwood Memorial College
in Barlaston, which was in the Oxford delegacy's catchment. Williams
was 'Director of Studies' for the meeting, which was 'partly a conference
about the scope of the subject and its place in adult education; partly a
course on methods based on the experience of those who have conducted classes'.[77] The other speakers included Graham Taylor and Williams's Cambridge friend Clifford Collins, who had been taught by
Leavis (in the Downing seminars, presumably), and Arthur Marsh, the
economics tutor who was the Oxford delegacy's other main advocate of

[73] Raymond Williams, 'Conference on "The Teaching of Public Expression": Barlaston,
7th–9th May 1954', 16 May 1954, 2, Department of Continuing Education papers, CE
3/271/18, OUA.
[74] Ibid., 1.
[75] Williams, 'Books for Teaching "Culture and Environment"', 175–6.
[76] Geoffrey Gough to Frank [Pickstock], 13 May 1954, Department of Continuing
Education papers, CE 3/271/18, OUA.
[77] [Pickstock] to Williams, 7 February 1954, Department of Continuing Education
papers, CE 3/271/18, OUA.

Public Expression.[78] As Marsh's field suggests, not all Public Expression classes were indebted to *Culture and Environment*. Students could be coached with reference to standard authorities on English usage such as Fowler, as well as Thouless and Stebbing.[79] Moreover, while the culture-and-environment aspects of Public Expression meshed with the more circumscribed practicalities of report writing and other 'communication' skills, the latter were the priority of adult education's trade union partners, and communications courses offered by unions *and* by adult education bodies that had previously been staunchly 'liberal' were usually separated from the framework of cultural analysis that Williams and others had developed out of the work of Thompson and the Leavises.[80]

At the same time as he campaigned for Public Expression, Williams remained a forceful advocate of practical criticism in adult education, and an exponent of close textual analysis in his own critical work. His book *Drama from Ibsen to Eliot* (1952) was assailed by another extramural tutor as a fanatical application of practical criticism at the expense of drama's non-textual elements.[81] After the mid-1950s, however, his literature syllabi made more acknowledgement of history and context, and acting and production received more attention in his drama courses.[82] Formal analysis also played a diminished role in Williams's writing. *The Long Revolution* (1961) and *Communications* (1962) register the shift in Williams's interests first worked through in Culture and Environment and Public Expression teaching. While *Culture and Society* focused on the texts of a tradition of cultural criticism, rather than the social and economic transformations that structure its historical narrative,[83] that book is a history of ideas in which Edmund Burke's political positions count for much more than his rhetorical strategies.

With *Culture and Society*, Williams shifted away from the *Scrutiny* tradition on matters of principle as well as critical practice. He pointedly rewrote Leavis's assertion that human consciousness rested with, or was constituted by, the minority who could appreciate 'Dante, Shakespeare Donne, Baudelaire, Hardy' and recognize their contemporary successors.

---

[78] 'Outline of Programme of Lectures and Discussions', n.d. [1954], Department of Continuing Education papers, CE 3/271/18, OUA; E. F. Bellchambers to Pickstock, 23 March 1954, CE 3/271/18, OUA; Smith, *Raymond Williams*, 210. Collins had been an undergraduate at King's College (ibid., 241).

[79] R. Goodman, 'Public Expression', Hastings, 1954–5, Department of Continuing Education papers, CE 3/60/37, OUA.

[80] McIlroy, 'Teacher, Critic, Explorer', 38–9.

[81] Smith, *Raymond Williams*, 354.

[82] McIlroy, 'Teacher, Critic, Explorer', 27.

[83] See Stefan Collini, 'The Literary Critic and the Village Labourer: "Culture" in Twentieth-Century Britain', *Transactions of the Royal Historical Society* 14 (2004): 109–10.

Williams kept Shakespeare, but for Dante and company he substituted 'the English common law, Lincoln Cathedral, committee procedure, Purcell, the nature of wage-labour, Hogarth, Hooker, genetic theory, Hume'. Appreciating them and their successors or contemporary equivalents constituted human consciousness.[84] The concluding chapter argued at length that 'a culture is not only a body of intellectual and imaginative work; it is also and essentially a whole way of life'.[85] Leavis had never argued that literature and art were the sum total of culture, but rather that they were its essence or distillate: hence Knights's claim that literature expressed 'realized values', and that a culture (at least an 'integrated' one such as that of early modern England) could be known through its literature—more than, say, through its laws or its organization of labour. To unsettle literature's centrality was to break with a fundamental tenet of the *Scrutiny* tradition. Richard Hoggart's career as an extramural tutor and cultural critics followed this same trajectory, but in a more contradictory way, for Hoggart's analytical method and his moral authority remained profoundly Leavisian even as he, too, dislodged literature from the centre of culture.

Hoggart opened the class 'with Christian resignation. Othello, he felt, was not going well with one or two students, and we were not getting out of it what we should.' The 1950–1 Shakespeare class was the fourth year-long course he had taught with the same group of students in Scarborough, but, five weeks in, it seemed 'as if our tutor could see the things he gave three years to, broken, and had to stoop to build 'em up with outworn tools'. (The recorder for the evening was Harry Bottomley, who regularly tried to inject some humour into the log.) Hoggart had decided that 'The general questions...would have to come later, since the first concern was to be sure we knew, as a group, how to read, and get hold of, a section of the play, so as to bring out properly the dramatic relations and movement.'[86] However, reading two key scenes all the way through over two successive meetings did not stop the students from discussing the play in terms of characters and their motivations; one member of the class wondered 'how the character of Iago would appear upon examination by Freud!'[87] Several weeks earlier, when the class's resident defender of Iago speculated about his motives, 'Mr Hoggart replied by saying that we must

[84] Williams, *Culture and Society*, 247, 249; F. R. Leavis, 'Mass Civilisation and Minority Culture' (1930) in *For Continuity* (Cambridge: Minority Press, 1933), 14–15. On such lists, see Peter Mandler, *The English National Character: The History of an Idea from Edmund Burke to Tony Blair* (New Haven: Yale University Press, 2006), 206–7.

[85] Williams, *Culture and Society*, 311.

[86] 'W. E. A. Scarborough Branch. Literature Class. Tutorial—4th Year. Tutor:—R. Hoggart. M.A. Log Book', entry for 9 November 1950, Hoggart papers, 4/1/4, Sheffield.

[87] Ibid., 9 November 1950. The scenes were III. iii and V. ii.

try not to bring our C20 psycho-analysis to bear too minutely on the play—we must bring to it a willing acceptance in belief of poetic drama & not to expect too cut [and] dried [a] characterisation.'[88]

Evidently anticipating responses like these, Hoggart had begun the course by emphasizing the problems of interpreting Shakespeare plays in terms of character:

> The tutor mentioned Bradley[']s interpretation of the plays, a major critic, he talks of them in character[,] the approach is psychological we must re- member Shakespeare wrote his plays in a hurry, characterisation not to[o] important but merely an expediency for play, some characters were merely stage machinery to produce effect on audience. Bradley went beyond Eliza- bethan requirements. Shakespeare used dramatic contrasts for effect, charac- ter is not to be taken seriously.[89]

The notes are garbled, but we can still make out an argument that echoed those of Leavis and Knights in their early 1930s pamphlets, *How to Teach Reading* and *How Many Children Had Lady Macbeth?* Bradley's *Shake- spearean Tragedy* was only the most fully realized statement of the idea that Shakespeare's plays were, above all else, dramas, and 'a drama is a matter of characters in action and interaction'.[90] Treating Shakespeare's characters as people with lives of their own independent of the text was, as we have seen, common among lay readers as well as 'academic' critics.

Hoggart's alternative here was not Leavis but G. Wilson Knight.[91] While Shakespeare's characters were 'human enough in many respects', Hoggart told the class, they were nevertheless 'still images, representative of one aspect of personality in the main, but not stereotyped'. Conse- quently, the plays could be 'regarded as extended metaphors'.[92] Here Hoggart paraphrased the prolegomenon to Knight's *The Wheel of Fire* (1930), a book to which he and his students referred repeatedly.[93] L. C.

[88] Ibid.

[89] Ibid., 29 September 1950.

[90] F. R. Leavis, *How to Teach Reading: A Primer for Ezra Pound* (Cambridge: Minority Press, 1932) 28.

[91] Knight taught at the University of Leeds, but not until 1946, after Hoggart had fin- ished his MA there.

[92] Scarborough log, 19 October 1950, Hoggart papers, 4/1/4, Sheffield.

[93] G. Wilson Knight, *The Wheel of Fire* (1930; London: Routledge, 2001), 11–14. For instance: 'The imagery here, as elsewhere in the play, Mr Hoggart continued,...was not or- ganically part of the play; it was not fused into the text, as in "King Lear"'. Knight had argued that *Othello* was full of 'solid gems of poetry which lose little by divorce from their context: wherein they differ from the finest passages of *King Lear* and *Macbeth*, which are as wild flowers not to be uptorn from their rooted soil if they are to live' (Compare Knight, *Wheel of Fire*, 110). Margaret Crowther, taking her turn with the class log, summarized Hog- gart's version of the argument: 'There is a balance in the lines—a dignified conventionalism in the whole passage—a finish & serenity that is entirely lacking in the plays of Macbeth & Lear. It has a detached, perfected style which while beautiful in itself does not seem to be

Knights and W. A. Edwards invoked it in *Scrutiny* in the 1930s, though Wilson Knight's concern with structure, and the stress he laid on patterns of imagery, were at some remove from Leavis's own concern with sound and movement and with the local workings of the poetry rather than the architecture of the plays.[94] As a Shakespeare teacher, Hoggart was not pressing a *Scrutiny* line. (In any case, Leavis never wrote a book on Shakespeare that could be taken as an authoritative and teachable statement, in the way *New Bearings* was for poetry and *The Great Tradition* was for the novel.) What stamped Hoggart as a Leavisian teacher was the tone of his judgements, the qualities he prized and deplored, and his procedure for getting students to compare the good with the bad.[95]

In February 1948, he set his Scarborough class a written exercise comparing Shakespeare's sonnet 71 ('No longer mourn for me when I am dead') and Christina Rossetti's sonnet 'Remember me when I am gone away'.[96] The exercise recalls the comparisons in the Downing College entrance examinations and the 'Criticism in Practice' section of *Use of English*; one of Rossetti's other poems was among the cannon fodder in Richards's Practical Criticism course.[97] Hoggart returned the students' work and gave feedback before they went on to do some practical criticism in class. '[We] were interested', wrote the secretary, 'in the point that the difference between these sonnets is that of one age opposed to another.' This was one of the rationales for 'dating' exercises, and it interlocked with the Leavisian or Knightsian idea that the evidence necessary for interpreting a literary text in its cultural context was already there inside the text, not buried in an archive or among a scholar's accumulated 'facts'. The report of the verdict on the two sonnets distilled various *Scrutiny* statements into classroom cliché:

united with and connected with the play. It stands isolated & it is this that gives it a certain artificiality & remoteness—a characteristic very much contrary to the spontaneous & passionate utterances in Macbeth & King Lear.' (Scarborough log, 9 November 1950, Hoggart papers, 4/1/4, Sheffield.) The repeated comparison of *Othello* with *Macbeth* and *King Lear* is also of a piece with Knight.

[94] W. A. Edwards, 'Revaluations (1): John Webster', *Scrutiny* 2/1 (June 1933): 12; Knights, 'How Many Children Had Lady Macbeth?', 4–5.

[95] Steele, *Emergence of Cultural Studies*, 124, quotes a letter from Hoggart to his teacher at Leeds, Bonamy Dobrée, in 1946, criticizing the excesses of young 'Leavis boys' in adult education who 'insist, rather too completely for me, that all we can do is attack debased language & sentiment by a series of set exercises designed to debunk the mass of suggestive material which conditions *all* adult students'. Criticizing 'Leavisites' is not the same as criticizing Leavis, of course. I think the discussion that follows shows Hoggart was a strongly Leavisian teacher in the late 1940s and early 1950s.

[96] Scarborough log, 26 February 1948, Hoggart papers, 4/1/3, Sheffield.

[97] I. A. Richards, *Practical Criticism: A Study of Literary Judgment* (London: Kegan Paul, Trench, Trubner, 1929), 32–41.

In criticising the Rossetti sonnet, we traced a tendency to sympathise more with Victorian sentiment than with Elizabethan robustness. An outstanding point was that many young ladies had found Christina Rossetti more 'human' than Shakespeare and had been persuaded by her gentle, conventionally poetic euphemisms and her narcotic rhythms.[98]

Q. D. Leavis in particular haunted these sentences: *Fiction and the Reading Public* insisted on the narcotic quality of commercial fiction, and, as we have seen, routinely contrasted it with the 'robustness' of Elizabethan prose. Her book was also hard on undiscriminating young women (E. M. Hull's *The Sheik* 'was to be seen in the hands of every typist and may be taken as embodying the typist's day-dream').[99]

The class moved on. 'Next, we tried out a new scheme in criticism, writing down our considered opinions on two passages of prose which dealt with the liberty of the individual. Mr Hoggart summarised for us, after which we tried to look pleased or silently crumpled our pages.'[100] D. H. Lawrence's *Letters*, which Leavis treated as exempla of vital, open intelligence, supplied one of these passages.[101] The terms of appraisal recalled Leavis ('taut and nervous in its style') if not Lawrence himself ('we felt it to be the language of a man speaking to men').[102] The class log does not identify the author of the second excerpt on individual liberty, but the comparison was clearly between different registers rather than between 'good' and 'bad', as the final contrast of the evening was. This was the juxtaposition of passages from Galsworthy's *The Patrician* (1911) and Myers's *The Orissers* (1922) mentioned at the beginning of this book.[103] The revelation that the 'crude and blatant' scene was by Galsworthy appears to have jolted Mr Bottomley.[104]

Every few weeks in this 1948 course a session was given over to this sort of 'discriminating' practical criticism. The specimens analysed one

[98] Scarborough log, 26 February 1948, Hoggart papers, 4/1/3, Sheffield.

[99] Q. D. Leavis, *Fiction and the Reading Public* (1932; London: Chatto & Windus, 1965), 138.

[100] Scarborough log, 26 February 1948, Hoggart papers, 4/1/3, Sheffield. For some second thoughts, put down in writing in 1951, see Richard Hoggart, 'Teaching Literature to Adults: English Studies in Extra-Mural Education', in *Speaking to Each Other*, 2: 222.

[101] Ian MacKillop, *F. R. Leavis: A Life in Criticism* (London: Allen Lane, 1995), 183–4; F. R. Leavis, 'D. H. Lawrence and Professor Irving Babbitt', *Scrutiny* 1/3 (December 1932): 273–9.

[102] Scarborough log, 26 February 1948, Hoggart papers, 4/1/3, Sheffield.

[103] At least two other *Scrutiny*-minded adult education tutors, Raymond Williams and Graham Taylor, set or recommended novels by Myers: G. Taylor, 'Modern Literature', Lincoln, 1951–2, Department of Continuing Education papers, CE 3/60/34, OUA; Inglis, *Raymond Williams*, 124.

[104] Scarborough log, 26 February 1948, Hoggart papers, 4/1/3, Sheffield.

winter evening were advertisements, pep talks, parliamentary speeches, and the species of essay from which, Thompson argued, copywriters learned their craft. The lesson was heavily indebted to *Culture and Environment*. Indeed, the first advertisement Hoggart handed out was recycled from its pages (and so had not appeared in a newspaper for more than fifteen years). The text began:

> In this wonderful London of ours perhaps there is to-day no more wonderful thoroughfare than Bond Street, and here is to be found no more wonderful shop than the establishment of Kenneth Greene. It is (as it were) a Sartorial Temple where the earnest seeker may find all that he desires— things both inner and intimate for his personal comfort, and things outer for the gracious off-setting of his person and delectation of the world in general, from the shoe upon his foot to the hat wherewith he crowns his manhood.

Culture and Environment noted that ' "[s]tyle" of this kind may be very commonly found in the work of contemporary essayists...enjoying high repute'. The more important point, said Leavis and Thompson, was the way 'style' like this cheapened the language and emotional life, and sustained 'accepted ideas about the "standard of living"'.[105] Hoggart pressed their first point but not the wider indictment, which was, arguably, a reason for teaching students about objectionable styles, rather than a moral to be taught directly. Hoggart's students 'agreed that it [the advertisement] was in the essayist style imitative of Addison or Lamb. It was an advertisement to attract the attention of young men desiring to be well-dressed, or perhaps middle-aged dandies, to the sartorial necessities to be found in this high-class establishment. We concluded that the example was written in an immature and childish manner.'[106] The lesson was not completely absorbed, as the note-taker's merry reference to 'sartorial necessities' shows. Developing the brief remarks in *Culture and Environment* into a general argument about advertising and popular writing in 'Our Debt to Lamb', Thompson had declared: 'the uneducated when they wish to be impressive in writing will resort to the affectation, archaisms, circumlocution, allusions, puns and other tokens of immaturity put into currency by Lamb'.[107]

The lessons from 'Our Debt to Lamb' and *Culture and Environment* continued as the class read a piece by Charles Morgan. They were nearly out of time, and could only glance at it. 'In a rapid survey the majority of

---

[105] Leavis and Thompson, *Culture and Environment*, 52–3.
[106] Scarborough log, 29 January 1948, Hoggart papers, 4/1/3, Sheffield.
[107] Denys Thompson, 'Our Debt to Lamb', in F. R. Leavis (ed.), *Determinations: Critical Essays* (London: Chatto & Windus, 1934), 207.

the class considered it to have a tranquil, soothing effect and to be well-written.' Then 'Mr Hoggart exploded a bombshell by condemning it as a piece of fake writing...pretentious, high-class blurb'.[108] They returned to Morgan at the beginning of the next class. The tutor backed up his claims. 'Mr Hoggart told us that although being well read and having a wide vocabulary, Chas Morgan faked his writing by purloining phrases from other works, To say what he wanted[,] Morgan laboured through pages & pages of writing which was flowery, blown up & over rhythmised, even at times archaic....To sum up, we found that Chas Morgan "spoke a lot but said nowt."'[109] Someone might have been playing a role Hoggart later described as the stagey northerner.[110]

Morgan was a Book Society favourite. In *Scrutiny*'s second issue, Q. D. Leavis had said that admiration of his work 'comes easily to those who find "modern" novels distasteful'; and that 'Conviction that [Morgan's] *The Fountain* is a beautiful piece of fiction' precluded the appreciation of more demanding novels.[111] Richards had argued that familiarity with bad art made it harder to appreciate the good. In *Principles of Literary Criticism* this was an argument about individuals' reading. The *Scrutiny* group developed it into a thesis on the tendency of modern culture generally. Popular taste had an institutional apparatus (the press, advertising, cinema, the Book Society, and so on) whose commercial and cultural dynamic was one of levelling-down. Thompson and both Leavises had emphasized the ways that publicity and what was effectively 'the same thing, commercially supplied popular art', corroded emotional life as well as taste.[112]

Like the authors of *Culture and Environment*, Hoggart was interested in the ways the culture industry sought to manipulate emotion, and discussed them with his students. They read an advertisement 'appealing to the emotion of mother-love. It was written in a style reminiscent of a sensational Hollywood film, flashing from scene to scene in a dynamic fashion. We concluded that this style of psychological advertisement meets with the desired response as shown by the enormous sums charged for newspaper and magazine space.'[113] The inference from the cost of advertising space as much as the identification of a psychological 'appeal' places these remarks within the framework of *Culture and Environment* and *Fiction and the Reading Public*. Hoggart then delivered a firmly

---

[108] Scarborough log, 29 January 1948, Hoggart papers, 4/1/3, Sheffield.
[109] Ibid., 5 February 1948.
[110] Hoggart, *Sort of Clowning*, 109.
[111] Q. D. Leavis, '"The Book Society Recommends..."', *Scrutiny* 1/2 (September 1932): 181.
[112] F. R. Leavis, 'A Serious Artist', *Scrutiny* 1/2 (September 1932): 175.
[113] Scarborough log, 29 January 1948, Hoggart papers, 4/1/3, Sheffield.

Leavisian case against the corrupting tendencies of mass culture. His class analysed a lurid newspaper report of a crime. It was 'a badly-written, crude piece of work. Such a writer could have no real values in life or he would not misuse images to gain his effect. It was evidently written to stir up crude emotions.... Mr Hoggart stressed the point that the reading of crude and sensational literature, as published by some of the press, may make people incapable of appreciating real literature.'[114]

These ideas about writing and emotional well-being were part of the currency of left-Leavisism. In *Reading and Criticism*, Williams had quoted Eliot's dictum that 'every vital development of language is also a development of feeling' and said that the converse also seemed true: 'The crude or vague language, the pompous and mechanical rhythms, which we have discerned in these extracts, subsist—there is no other explanation—on crudity and imprecision of *feeling*.'[115] Hoggart was perhaps at his most Leavisian in the final comment recorded by the student on duty that night: if people become habituated to the manipulations of the press and unable to appreciate real literature, 'the management of their own lives might be affected'.[116] For the Hoggart of the 1940s and early 1950s, the early work of the *Scrutiny* group offered not only a teaching method and critical exercises: it made a case for studying and teaching English in which literary judgements were also 'judgements about life'.

The Uses of Literacy explored the ways in which 'the new mass art' and the climate of post-war prosperity were 'unbending the springs' of a working-class culture forged in urban Britain from the late nineteenth century onwards.[117] Hoggart's fellow tutors immediately recognized it as a book that spoke to, and was shaped by, the adult education movement. 'We are all of us in great debt to you', wrote Frank Pickstock from Rewley House in Oxford.[118] An invitation came to address the Manchester University extramural department's annual tutors' weekend.[119] Tutors from

[114] Ibid.
[115] Williams, *Reading and Criticism*, 17 (emphasis in original).
[116] Scarborough log, 29 January 1948, Hoggart Papers, 4/1/3, Sheffield.
[117] On the book's cultural critique, see Sue Owen, '*The Abuse of Literacy* and the Feeling Heart: The Trials of Richard Hoggart', *Cambridge Quarterly* 34/2 (2005): 147–76; the essays by Stuart Hall, Stefan Collini, and David Fowler in Sue Owen (ed.), *Richard Hoggart and Cultural Studies* (Basingstoke: Palgrave Macmillan, 2008); Stefan Collini, *English Pasts: Essays in History and Culture* (Oxford: Oxford University Press, 1999), 225–7; and for the social and cultural context, Peter Mandler, 'Two Cultures—One—or Many?' in Kathleen Burk (ed.), *The British Isles since 1945* (Oxford: Oxford University Press, 2003); Stephen Brooke, 'Gender and Working Class Identity in Britain during the 1950s', *Journal of Social History* 34/4 (summer 2001): 773–95.
[118] Pickstock to Hoggart, 10 April 1957, Hoggart papers, 3/11/301, Sheffield.
[119] Ron D. Waller to Hoggart, 10 July 1957, Hoggart papers, 3/11/306, Sheffield.

Derbyshire and Swansea wrote to tell Hoggart of experiments that resonated with his call for new ways of bringing ideas to a mass audience or about their plans to discuss the book in their own extramural classes.[120] John Levitt, an Oxford Delegacy tutor in Staffordshire, had been looking forward to *The Uses of Literacy* since he and Hoggart discussed it on a trip to West Germany the previous year. The book surprised him. 'I had imagined it to be something rather different—an astringent, consciouslyminority sort of thing like *Culture and Environment*, for instance.' What Hoggart had produced was 'something…far more valuable and much more human than that'. It might, Levitt thought, 'become a classic like *Change in the Village*'.[121] The reference points remained *Scrutiny* ones despite Levitt's reservations about 'minority culture'.

The Uses of Literacy recalls *Scrutiny* in a way that Williams's work from the same period does not: its interpretation of changes in working-class culture rested heavily on the textual analysis of popular literature. Hoggart's book has often been seen as a successor to *Fiction and the Reading Public*. Q. D. Leavis's book was the unmistakable object of his reproach that 'books on popular culture often lose some of their force by not making sufficiently clear who is meant by "the people," by inadequately relating their examinations of particular aspects of "the people's" life to the wider life they live, and to the attitudes they bring to their entertainments'.[122] Hoggart's partly autobiographical essays on working-class life in the first part of *The Uses of Literacy* were to provide a framework for the interpretation of pulp fiction, magazines, and popular songs in the second part. Williams observed in his review of *The Uses of Literacy*: 'It is fair to say of Mrs Leavis's admirable book that the reading public is really only present in the title; the documents in the case are her real centre of attention. Hoggart, similarly, attends to the documents, but he also seeks to see the reading public as people, and to judge the documents with this reference.'[123]

Even in 'the more specific literary analysis' of the second part of the book, though, Hoggart's critical procedure was notably different from Q. D. Leavis's.[124] *Fiction and the Reading Public* had lots of quotations, lists, and summary judgements, but not much in the way of plot summaries or descriptions of settings and situations. *The Uses of Literacy* did, and, in its description of the content of fiction and attention to the

[120] Gerald Walters to Hoggart, 14 July 1957, Hoggart papers, 3/11/328; Gwyn I. Lewis to Hoggart, 7 May 1957, Hoggart papers, 3/11/323, Sheffield.
[121] John Levitt to Hoggart, 20 February 1957, Hoggart papers, 3/11/322, Sheffield.
[122] Richard Hoggart, *The Uses of Literacy: Aspects of Working-Class Life, with Special References to Publications and Entertainments* (London: Chatto & Windus, 1957), 11.
[123] Raymond Williams, 'Fiction and the Writing Public' (1957) in McIlroy and Westwood (eds), *Border Country*, 106.
[124] Hoggart, *Uses of Literacy*, 11.

'attitudes' it played to or cultivated, Hoggart's book resembled Leavis's less than it did George Orwell's *Horizon* essays, 'Boys' Weeklies' (1940) and 'The Art of Donald McGill' (1941).[125] Long afterwards, Hoggart named both essays as he recalled the writings that made the deepest impression on him in his early years as an adult education tutor.[126] And in the 1960s, surveying the 'use of literary criticism in understanding popular art, mass art and some other forms of mass communication', he remarked that the British pioneers included 'Dr and Mrs Leavis and Denys Thompson; and, from a different angle, George Orwell'.[127] Appropriately, one of the early essays Hoggart submitted to *Tribune*—not long after Orwell had given up its literary editorship—was a piece on railway station bookstalls.[128] Both the Orwell essays mentioned above begin with evocations of comparably 'low' vendors of reading matter, the cheap stationer and the newsagent's shop in a working-class neighbourhood. Hoggart's ventriloquizing of working-class 'attitudes' also had some affinity with Orwell's sketches of the mentality of the unemployed. If *The Uses of Literacy* was, as Stefan Collini describes it, a 'version of *Sons and Lovers* interwoven with an up-dating of *Fiction and the Reading Public*', it was also an updating of *The Road to Wigan Pier* interwoven with a version of 'Boys' Weeklies'.[129]

Yet *The Uses of Literacy*, as Collini has demonstrated, is a work of cultural criticism deeply influenced by *Scrutiny*—in its narrative of cultural decline; in its conflation—or correlation, we might say after Knights—of the literary and the cultural at crucial points in its argument; and in the consensus about values that it assumes with its anticipated readership.[130] Like F. R. Leavis especially, Hoggart prosecuted his case in a way that

[125] George Orwell, 'Boys' Weeklies', in *The Collected Essays, Journalism and Letters of George Orwell*, ed. Sonia Orwell and Ian Angus, 4 vols (Boston: Nonpareil Books, 2000), 1: 460–84; Orwell, 'The Art of Donald McGill', in *Collected Essays*, 2: 155–65.

[126] Hoggart, *Sort of Clowning*, 91.

[127] Hoggart, 'Literature and Society' (1966), in *Speaking to Each Other*, 2: 31 and n. See also the comment that 'Orwell did some good early work here [on popular fiction] and a few others have followed him', in Hoggart's inaugural lecture at Birmingham University, in effect a manifesto for the Centre for Contemporary Cultural Studies. Richard Hoggart, 'Schools of English and Contemporary Society' (1963), in *Speaking to Each Other*, 2: 257 and n.

[128] Richard Hoggart, *Sort of Clowning*, 86.

[129] Stefan Collini, 'Richard Hoggart: Literary Criticism and Cultural Decline in Twentieth-Century Britain' in Owen (ed.), *Richard Hoggart and Cultural Studies*, 53. See also Steele, *Emergence of Cultural Studies*, 125–6.

[130] There was even the odd in-joke. Discussing newspaper columnists' back-scratching criticisms of 'any kind of authority', Hoggart wrote: 'If major examples do not come along often enough, there is usually some headmaster or headmistress in Warrington or Derby or Yeovil whose decision about school-clothing or speech-day pronouncements about "the younger generation" can be given a national castigation in the interests of the free and right-thinking parent.' (Hoggart, *Uses of Literacy*, 153.) Denys Thompson was the headmaster of Yeovil Grammar School.

assumed a high level of assent from its (minority) audience. Quotations from Austen or references to Defoe were assumed to be self-evident. 'We all know only too well'; 'I need hardly say'.[131] He took pains to explain working-class customs to his readers, but it was unnecessary to spell out what lesson to draw from a mention of a literary figure. Although Hoggart envisioned his audience as 'the serious "common reader" or "intelligent layman" from any class', he nevertheless proceeded from the Leavisian assumption that 'certain standards of intelligence and relevance are implicit in the undertaking [of criticism], as well as a reasonable minimum of common experience'.[132]

There was, as Collini writes, 'a classic Leavisian rhythm' to Hoggart's staggered story of cultural decline. The community of language and culture that obtained in Elizabethan England had fractured by the nineteenth century, but its remnants persisted; then, with the expansion of the reading public and the commercialization of literature and the press from the end of the nineteenth century, the surviving aspects of the common culture were obliterated. Elizabethans such as Thomas Nashe, whose prose was compared unfavourably with 1930s best-sellers in *Fiction and the Reading Public*, were pressed into similar service against the 'new-style publications' of the 1950s in *The Uses of Literacy*.[133] Cultural change was persistently figured as cultural loss in Hoggart's book. And the character of that loss was described in terms transposed from Leavisian *literary* analysis, such as 'concreteness' and 'felt discrimination'.[134] The affinities between Hoggart's terminology and argumentative strategies and that of the Leavises and Thompson were 'systemic'.[135]

Yet Hoggart dissented from a premise of *Scrutiny*'s criticism: the relationship between crudity of language and crudity of feeling. The key passage is the discussion of 'story papers', especially those directed at working-class women such as *Peg's Paper* and *Red Letter*, in part one, the part of *The Uses of Literacy* that is not primarily literary-critical.[136] Looking closely at the stories, 'we'—the in-group 'we'—'are reminded at once of the case against "stock responses": every reaction has its fixed counter for presentation'.[137] Richards's chapter on stock responses was part of

[131] Collini, 'Richard Hoggart', 50–1.
[132] Hoggart, *Uses of Literacy*, 11; S. W. Dawson, '*Scrutiny* and the Idea of a University', *Essays in Criticism* 14/1 (January 1964): 7.
[133] Collini, 'Richard Hoggart', 43, 44, 50.
[134] Ibid., 46.
[135] Ibid.
[136] On these periodicals see Billie Melman, *Women and the Popular Imagination in the Twenties: Flappers and Nymphs* (Basingstoke: Macmillan, 1988); Joseph McAleer, *Popular Reading and Publishing in Britain, 1914–1950* (Oxford: Clarendon Press, 1992), ch. 6.
[137] Hoggart, *Uses of Literacy*, 106.

Scrutiny's patrimony: Q. D. Leavis's readers, too, were told that they should keep it in mind as they read part of her book.[138] Having made the point, though, Hoggart paused and, using *Scrutiny* patois asked what the manipulation of stock responses really indicated. 'That the writers use cliché, and that the audience seems to want cliché, that they are not exploring experience, realising experience through language?'[139] Yes: and reading *Peg's Paper* was unlikely to lead on to reading 'anything that could be called serious literature'. However, '[i]f we regard them as faithful but dramatised presentations of a life whose form and values are known, we might find it more useful to ask what are the values they embody. There is no virtue in merely laughing at them: we need to appreciate first that they may in all their triteness speak for a solid and relevant way of life.' The story papers presented a 'limited and simple' world 'based on a few accepted and long-held values'. This world was often 'childish and garish', one where 'the springs of the emotions work in great gushings. But they do work: it is not a corrupt or a pretentious world.'[140]

Working-class culture was to be located in values, and even bad art could function as a space for those values.[141] In the passage from Leavis's own criticism to 'left-Leavisite' criticism, its moralist mode became independent of its original assumptions. The moral authority of post-Leavisian criticism rested on the sensibility and concreteness of the manner of passing judgement, not the principled foundation of the judgements. The usefulness and power of Leavisian practice as well as Leavisian precepts meant that the *Scrutiny* tradition underpinned quite different projects, in adult education as in other spheres. As we have seen, classes in Public Expression and Culture and Environment developed the practice of *Scrutiny's* cultural criticism to a point where it served ends very different from the training of a minority. 'Left-Leavisism' was not a synthesis of *Scrutiny* and Labour or Marxist politics: it was a process of working with or working through the assumptions and analytical practices established by *Culture and Environment* and arriving at a point where that book's governing principles no longer held.

---

[138] Leavis, *Fiction and the Reading Public*, 243 n.

[139] Hoggart, *Uses of Literacy*, 106.

[140] Ibid., 107.

[141] See Steele, *Emergence of Cultural Studies*, 28. Malcolm Pittock, too, says that Hoggart '[came] to question Leavisian assumptions about the correlation between social attitudes and quality of reading', though he presents this as a conclusion Hoggart reached much later, in the 1990s. Pittock's essay, which seems largely animated by a desire to resurrect old arguments that Hoggart was no match for Raymond Williams as either a theorist or a socialist, confines its discussion of the Leavises to their overt political declarations and so can say little about how their critical *practice* could be inhabited by someone like Hoggart who 'was...hardly a natural supporter of Leavisian elitism'. Pittock, 'Richard Hoggart and the Leavises', *Essays in Criticism* 60/1 (2010): 51–69 (quotation from 57).

6

Discrimination and the Popular Arts

The Uses of Literacy was a contribution to a renewed debate on the cultural effects of 'periodicals and entertainments' in the late 1950s and early 1960s.[1] Like his *Scrutiny* predecessors, Hoggart was most concerned with print, but he examined a different sort of 'abuse of literacy' (that was his original title) from those Q. D. Leavis and Denys Thompson had. The forms of emotional debasement that concerned the *Scrutiny* writers were daydreaming, sentimentality, and the exaltation of material luxuries. Hoggart continued in this vein, but, like other post-war critics, had more to say about exploitation fiction. After the Second World War, frank representations of sex, violence, and sexual violence were increasingly commonplace in periodical fiction and pulp paperbacks. A turning point may have been the enormous wartime popularity of James Hadley Chase's *No Orchids for Miss Blandish*, which was read, if apologetically, by soldiers and civilians who would never have thought of buying gangster fiction from a back-street newsagent.[2] Chase's books were among the objects of Hoggart's hardest judgements in *The Uses of Literacy*, and a reason Chatto's lawyers demanded Hoggart replace his quotations with pastiches.[3] Again, Orwell pointed the way. Writing in *Horizon* in 1944, Orwell identified Chase as a portent, the corrupted world of his fiction 'a day-dream appropriate to a totalitarian age'. In E. W. Hornung's Raffles stories, written at the beginning of the twentieth century, there were still gentlemen and taboos, even though Raffles himself had no moral code; in Chase's books,

---

[1] See Lawrence Black, *Redefining British Politics: Culture, Consumerism and Participation, 1954–70* (Basingstoke: Palgrave Macmillan, 2010), ch. 5; and, for earlier surveys, Robert Hewison, *Too Much: Art and Society in the Sixties, 1960–75* (London: Methuen, 1986), ch. 1; Harry Hopkins, *The New Look: A Social History of the Forties and Fifties in Britain* (London: Secker & Warburg, 1963), chs 21, 30.

[2] On the popularity of *No Orchids for Miss Blandish*, see Joseph McAleer, *Popular Reading and Publishing in Britain, 1914–1950* (Oxford: Clarendon Press, 1992), 92. For a glimpse of post-war pulp fiction and its distributors see Steve Holland, *The Trials of Hank Janson* (Tolworth: Telos, 2004).

[3] Sue Owen, '*The Abuse of Literacy* and the Feeling Heart: The Trials of Richard Hoggart', *Cambridge Quarterly* 34/2 (2005): 166–76.

'Emancipation is complete, Freud and Machiavelli have reached the outer suburbs.'[4]

While publications consumed more of Hoggart's attention than other entertainments, he did write about pop songs. The conspicuous provision of entertainment for an 'affluent' youth market was one catalyst for the intensified discussion of mass culture in Britain. Another was the advent of commercial television. *The Uses of Literacy* referred occasionally to BBC television, but the manuscript went to the publishers in 1955, the same year as ITV began broadcasting. While television sets settled into more and more houses over the course of the 1950s, many of the popular periodicals that had been profitable in the interwar period ceased publication—less because of falling circulations, in the case of some titles, than because of the pressures the concentration of ownership put on profitability.[5] Later critics examined an array of cultural products markedly different from the sorts covered in *Scrutiny* and even *The Uses of Literacy*.

Centre 42, the arts hub that the playwright Arnold Wesker worked to establish in the early 1960s had its origins not only in efforts to get the labour movement to take the arts more seriously (at the 1960 conference of the Trades Union Congress, Wesker 'persuaded the Association of Cinematography, Television and Allied Technicians...to move Resolution 42, which called on trade unions to participate in the cultural life of the country', whence the number in Centre 42's cryptic name),[6] but also in a critique of commercial entertainment broadly consonant with that of the *Scrutiny* group. 'Too much that is good...is being cheapened and vulgarised by the purveyors of mass entertainment'; 'Our classical culture seems to be largely in pawn to commercial interests', and the alternative was 'the American derived but anonymously cosmopolitan "Popular" culture we have spread over England in recent years'; 'An ugly world is dangerous for people become what they see'.[7] At the PEN Congress in London in 1956,

[4] George Orwell, 'Raffles and Miss Blandish' (1944), in *The Collected Essays, Journalism and Letters of George Orwell*, ed. Sonia Orwell and Ian Angus, 4 vols (Boston: Nonpareil Books, 2000), 3: 223, 224.

[5] Richard Findlater, *What Are Writers Worth?* (London: Society of Authors, 1963), reproduced in Peter Davison, Rolf Meyersohn, and Edward Shils (eds), *Literary Taste, Culture and Mass Communication*, 14 vols (Cambridge: Chadwyck-Healey and Teaneck, NJ: Somerset House, 1978–80), 10: 302–3; Richard Hoggart, *The Uses of Literacy: Aspects of Working-Class Life, with Special References to Publications and Entertainments* (London: Chatto & Windus, 1957), 274.

[6] Patricia Hollis, *Jennie Lee: A Life* (1997; Oxford: Oxford University Press, 1998), 253.

[7] Ralph Bond, quoted in [Arnold Wesker], 'Two Snarling Heads', typescript, 14 September 1960, Arnold Wesker papers, box 136, folder 9; Henry Anderson, Gerald Dillon, Stanley Pinker, Ken Turner, Sally Anderson, *Resolution 42: A Declaration on the Visual Arts from the First Group* (London, 1961), 8, copy in Wesker papers, box 136, folder 9; Clive Barker, untitled report and recommendations on policy for Centre 42, 26 August 1961, p. 3, Wesker papers, box 147, folder 2, HRC.

there was 'much talk about the existence of a sort of cultural Gresham's Law'.[8] Just as the circulation of bad coin debased the currency, the proliferation of trash made it hard for good art and literature to get a hearing. Leavis had borrowed the idea from Norman Angell; Raymond Williams observed in 1958 that the phrase had become quite common 'as Leavis's influence has grown'.[9]

Leavis himself had much to say about the cultural drift of the 1960s. His retirement from college teaching coincided with an explosion of invited lectures and other interventions (the contrast between Leavis's own public performances and those of his followers is discussed in the next chapter). As Guy Ortolano shows in detail in his book on the 'two cultures' controversy involving Leavis and C. P. Snow, Leavis's public comment touched on a wide range of contemporary issues, from working-class consumerism to 'development' in the Third World. These statements reprised the questions of 'materialism' and the distortions induced by the idea of a 'standard of living' that had exercised *Scrutiny* in the 1930s.[10] Leavis also commented on student protest and took the opportunity to deplore the 'highly amplified, tortured sounds' Jimi Hendrix wrung from his guitar, 'which he handled with strong sexual overtones' (the quoted authority is Hendrix's obituary in *The Times*).[11] Leavis's primary concern, however, was the irresponsibility of élites rather than 'permissive' behaviour itself. Technocrats such as Snow who were unwilling to give non-economic values due recognition, and other establishment figures, such as Lord Annan and Lord Robbins, who were too easily sanguine about cultural change, especially where university standards and access to higher education were concerned, were Leavis's main targets. They formed a complex he sardonically called 'enlightenment'.[12] Leavis's *Aufklärer* turned out in force as expert witnesses for Penguin Books in its obscenity trial for

[8] Hopkins, *New Look*, 236.
[9] F. R. Leavis, 'Mass Civilisation and Minority Culture' (1930), in *For Continuity* (Cambridge: Minority Press, 1933), 19–20; F. R. Leavis and Denys Thompson, *Culture and Environment: The Training of Critical Awareness* (1933; London: Chatto & Windus, 1950), 36; Raymond Williams, 'A Kind of Gresham's Law' (1958), in John McIlroy and Sallie Westwood (eds), *Border Country: Raymond Williams in Adult Education* (Leicester: National Institute of Adult Continuing Education, 1993), 85. See also Raymond O'Malley, *One-Horse Farm: Crofting in the West Highlands* (London: Frederick Muller, 1948), 135–6.
[10] Guy Ortolano, *The Two Cultures Controversy: Science, Literature and Cultural Politics in Postwar Britain* (Cambridge: Cambridge University Press, 2009), esp. chs 2, 5, 6; F. R. Leavis, 'Two Cultures? The Significance of Lord Snow', in *Nor Shall My Sword: Discourses on Pluralism, Compassion, and Social Hope* (London: Chatto & Windus, 1972), 54, 57.
[11] Leavis, 'Pluralism, Compassion, and Social Hope', in *Nor Shall My Sword*, 189.
[12] See the essays in Leavis, *Nor Shall My Sword*; F. R. Leavis, *Anna Karenina and Other Essays* (London: Chatto & Windus, 1967).

publishing an unexpurgated edition of *Lady Chatterley's Lover* in 1960.[13] (Leavis, who had defied the Home Office's ban on the importing of *Ulysses* in the 1920s and been an early defender of Lawrence's novel, declined to testify and said afterwards that Allen Lane had not done 'a service to literature, civilization or Lawrence in the business of *Lady Chatterley's Lover*'.)[14]

The *Scrutiny*-inspired critiques of popular culture in the 1960s were the work of other hands. A germinal moment was the conference on 'Popular Culture and Personal Responsibility' organized by the National Union of Teachers in 1960. The conference itself was not organized by pupils or associates of Leavis's, but it resulted in two publications that renewed the precepts and arguments of *Culture and Environment* in contrasting ways. *Discrimination and Popular Culture* (1964), a collection of essays edited by Denys Thompson and published by Penguin, was more an updating of the 1930s *Scrutiny* case than an adaptation of it. Stuart Hall and Paddy Whannel's *The Popular Arts* (also 1964) attempted to specify the sorts of genuine art and valid aesthetic experiences possible within 'mechanical' forms. Together, they constitute the last significant episode in the *Scrutiny* tradition of cultural criticism.

The NUT conference and the publication of these two volumes also coincided with Richard Hoggart's founding of the Birmingham University centre that launched British cultural studies. Hoggart's vision, articulated in his inaugural lecture at Birmingham, was of a programme of study along the lines of Hall and Whannel's book: an enterprise critical of the *Scrutiny* tradition but still operating within some of its parameters. (And one subject to fierce criticism along *Scrutiny* lines from David Holbrook.) In the event, the Centre for Contemporary Cultural Studies, with Hall as its de facto head, quickly moved away from the forms of inquiry that Hoggart had advocated and that *The Popular Arts* epitomized. *Culture and Environment* and *Fiction and the Reading Public* no longer provided models for new work, or even genuine foils for new approaches (although a ritual of disowning persisted for a long time). Cultural studies' debts to *Scrutiny* were, after the mid-1960s, historical and infrastructural.

The NUT conference reflected something of the political mix of the teachers' union. The NUT had more connections with the Labour Party

---

[13] See H. Montgomery Hyde (ed.), *The Lady Chatterley's Lover Trial (Regina v. Penguin Books Limited)* (London: Bodley Head, 1990).

[14] MacKillop, *F. R. Leavis*, 304–9 (quotation from 309). On Leavis, *Ulysses* and the authorities, see Alistair McCleery, 'Naughty Old Leavis', *Times Higher Education Supplement*, 13 September 1991.

than with the Conservatives, but its refusal to affiliate with the Trades
Union Congress and insistence on calling itself a 'teachers' professional
organisation' rather than a 'trade union' led 'many socialists to look upon
its leaders as sympathizers with the Conservative Party, and lacking in
progressive ideas'. Communists were influential in some local branches.[15]
The conference had its origin in a resolution passed at the union's annual
meeting earlier in 1960, a resolution whose language inclined toward the
less 'progressive' elements of the membership. The motion called upon
parents and 'those who use and control the media of mass communication', to help teachers in their efforts to 'counteract the debasement of
standards which result from the misuse of the press, radio, cinema and
television; the deliberate exploitation of violence and sex; and the calculated appeal to self-interest'. Teachers alone could not maintain 'the moral
and cultural standards of the nation and its children'.[16]

The NUT was not as implacable as these quotations suggest, however. The resolution acknowledged that 'today more young people than
ever before are actively engaged in intellectual pursuits'. The special
conference's active participants included people (such as Whannel and
Hall) who were film and jazz buffs as well as concerned teachers.[17] The
conference attracted a diverse crowd: teachers and educational officials,
members of parliament, child welfare workers, clergy and members of
religious organizations, representatives of women's groups, and assorted
academics and freelance intellectuals, including Wesker and Raymond
Williams; the novelist Marghanita Laski; Hilde Himmelweit, the social
psychologist whose research into television's effects on children was
heavily cited in 1960s commentaries on the mass media; and the historian Eric Hobsbawm, present in his capacity as a jazz critic.[18] Publishers
and broadcasters sent scores of delegates, and the conference was
launched by the Home Secretary and sponsor of the 1944 Education

[15] Walter Roy, *The Teachers' Union: Aspects of Policy and Organisation in the National Union of Teachers 1950–1966* (London: Schoolmaster Publishing, 1968), 102, 112.
[16] Quoted in Stuart Hall and Paddy Whannel, *The Popular Arts* (London: Hutchinson, 1964), 23.
[17] See Colin MacCabe, 'An Interview with Stuart Hall, December 2007', *Critical Quarterly* 50/1–2 (2008): 18.
[18] Hilde T. Himmelweit, A. N. Oppenheim, and Pamela Vince, *Television and the Child: An Empirical Study of the Effect of Television on the Young* (London: Oxford University Press, 1958); *Popular Culture and Personal Responsibility: A Conference of Those Engaged in Education Together with Parents, Those Directly or Indirectly Concerned with the Welfare of Children and Young People, and People Involved in the Mass Media Themselves, to Examine the Impact of the Media of Mass Communications on Present-Day Moral and Cultural Standards: Held at Church House, Westminster, 26th to 28th October 1960: Verbatim Report* (London, n.d.) (hereafter *Verbatim Report*), 123–4; Eric Hobsbawm, 'Diary', *London Review of Books*, 27 May 2010, 41. At the end of the conference report is a list of all who registered for the conference and their institutional affiliation, if any: *Verbatim Report*, 341–8.

Act, R. A. Butler. A handful of Downing English graduates attended—
R. R. Pedley, who later contributed to the first Black Paper, represented
the Incorporated Association of Headmasters, and R. F. Knight was one
of five training college delegates.[19]

Despite the invocation of 'personal responsibility', most of the community groups represented favoured or countenanced further public reg-
ulation of advertising and television programming. On the first morning,
Williams summarized the history of mass communication in Britain and
concluded by arguing that personal responsibility was no substitute for
public policy. The audience members who asked questions approved of
Williams's plea for measures to shore up independent publishing against
the operations of the market, though a representative from the Ministry
of Education pointed out the contradiction between this appeal and
Williams's negative judgements on the paternalism of the BBC, 'the only
organ of public responsibility that has so far been created in broadcasting
fields'. Williams retorted that this was 'a contradiction of the society not
of me'. 'I think that the very survival of the idea of defence of minority
culture was extremely damaging, although unintentionally so, to the creation of a good majority culture.'[20]

This was one of the few allusions recorded in the conference proceed-
ings to the Leavises' and Thompson's ideas. (Several speakers, though,
mentioned Gresham's Law.)[21] The language of 'standards', 'debasement',
and 'counteracting' mass culture's effects was not the exclusive property
of Scrutineers and Leavis pupils. It reflected widely diffused attitudes to
the media and the entertainment industry shared, among others, by clergymen and consumer activists. Both groups were out in force at the NUT
conference. Lawrence Black has observed of the Consumers' Association's
organizers that, 'like many on the unaligned political left', they spoke in
the tones of *Scrutiny*.[22] The language of the NUT resolution also reflected
widely held beliefs about the moral authority and responsibilities of
schoolteachers.[23] The fifty-page study outline on popular culture that the
NUT produced in the wake of the conference was written by Brian

[19] *Verbatim Report*, 341, 342. Knight had recently been appointed a lecturer in speech
and drama at Bede College, Durham. Previously he had been an assistant master at Tiffin
School. 'Appointments and Awards', *NL* (1955): 19; 'Appointments, Etc.', *NL* (1961): 36.
[20] *Verbatim Report*, 19–20, 21–2. Compare Raymond Williams, 'Books for Teaching
"Culture and Environment"' (1950), in McIlroy and Westwood (eds), *Border Country*,
177.
[21] *Verbatim Report*, 31, 66. One participant said, accurately, that Richard Hoggart
would 'probably end up as one of the most quoted writers and thinkers at this Conference'.
Verbatim Report, 112.
[22] Black, *Redefining British Politics*, 23.
[23] Frances Stevens, *The Living Tradition: The Social and Educational Assumptions of the
Grammar School* (1960; London: Hutchinson, 1972), 108–9.

Groombridge, an adult educationalist involved in consumer activism and campaigns to improve and democratize broadcasting, but not someone with personal or ideological investments in the *Scrutiny* movement.[24] The favoured *Scrutiny* term 'discrimination' was lodged in the working title of the Penguin volume before Thompson was appointed editor.[25] The titles Thompson himself suggested exhibit the same facility for sloganeering against sloganeers he displayed in the 1930s: 'The Media and the Masses: How not to be a victim'; 'Mugs or Men? How not to be mass-minded'; 'Minds for Sale? How to cope with the Mass Media'; 'Mass Produced Minds'; 'Made for Masses'.[26] His editor at Penguin, Dieter Pevsner, told him that a paperback's title needed to be very precise, and thus 'something much more stodgy than those you are suggesting. We felt the best would be *Discrimination and Popular Culture*.'[27]

The semi-official book of the conference was thus not a *Scrutiny* undertaking from the beginning: it became one only gradually. The book was Pevsner's idea. The son of the architectural historian, Pevsner had joined Penguin straight from university and was overseeing an array of new Penguin Specials and Pelicans.[28] He planned 'a series of books on contemporary Britain' and was interested in the work the NUT had started to do with the 1960 conference. He and Penguin's chief editor, Charles Clark, had represented the firm at the conference.[29] Clark wrote to the NUT's head of public relations, Fred Jarvis, to sound him out about a book on the subject.[30] Jarvis met with colleagues and reported to Pevsner that they believed there was 'a very real need for a publication which could take the form of a compendium on discrimination and the mass media and popular culture'. They envisaged an audience of teachers, 'intelligent parents

[24] On Groombridge see Matthew Hilton, 'The Polyester-Flannelled Philanthropists: The Birmingham Consumers' Group and Affluent Britain', in Lawrence Black and Hugh Pemberton (eds), *An Affluent Society? Britain's Post-war 'Golden Age' Revisited* (Aldershot: Ashgate, 2004), 155. See also Groombridge's later Penguin Education Special, *Television and the People: A Programme for Democratic Participation* (Harmondsworth: Penguin, 1972).

[25] 'Memorandum of Meeting Held at the N.U.T.', 29 June 1961, Penguin archives, A640/1, Bristol. The provisional title was 'Discrimination in the Mass Media'.

[26] Thompson to Pevsner, 11 August 1962, Penguin archives, A640/1, Bristol.

[27] Pevsner to Thompson, 28 August 1962, Penguin archives, A640/1, Bristol. Thompson did not protest at the latter phrase, despite his insistence in the 1930s that the products of the mass media and the entertainment industry did not qualify as 'popular culture'.

[28] Jeremy Lewis, *Penguin Special: The Life and Times of Allen Lane* (London: Viking, 2005), 307.

[29] *Verbatim Report*, 347. Penguin was the only publisher of books other than educational books to send delegates, though representatives of magazine interests were numerous.

[30] Charles Clark to Fred Jarvis, 5 January 1961, Penguin archives, A640/1, Bristol. After the 1964 election, Jarvis joined the staff of the Labour Party's Planning group (which handled strategy and marketing). Black, *Redefining British Politics*, 191.

who are concerned about what their youngsters should read and watch', university students, and sixth formers. The NUT did not assert ownership of the idea, and Jarvis did not name any preferred contributors ('we felt there would be no great difficulty in selecting these...some of them would probably be drawn from those who assisted us in the mass media conference'). If Penguin was not interested, 'I think we should consider doing something of the kind ourselves, but possibly by means of separate booklets rather than a combined volume.' The NUT's representatives 'would all much prefer that your people did it, for we feel that would be the way of creating maximum impact'.[31]

Three months later Pevsner and Clark met with Jarvis and others from the NUT at the union's headquarters in London. Groombridge, Whannel, and Hall were present; so was Hilde Himmelweit.[32] Contributors were mooted, 'but it was decided not to tie our thinking too closely to contributors before fixing on a general editor in order not to tie the editor's hands in advance'. The 'favoured candidate for the editorship' was Hoggart, a figure of standing within Penguin Books after his testimony in the *Lady Chatterley's Lover* trial. As a member of the Pilkington Committee on the future of broadcasting, however, he would be 'effectively gagged' as a commentator on television and radio for the near future. It was at this point that Thompson was put forward as a possible editor. Groombridge's name was also floated, but Penguin—Pevsner, Clark, and Alan Glover—opted for Thompson, 'the man who, with Leavis, did *Culture and Environment* in the thirties'.[33] Although the decision was Penguin's, and although the publisher was taking 'full responsibility for the book', it was left to Jarvis to approach Thompson about the editorship. Thompson accepted, and began discussing possible contributors with both Jarvis and Pevsner.

Thompson and the NUT representatives had different ideas about contributors, but there was also a level of agreement. Thompson invited Stuart Hall to write on the press after Jarvis had recommended him. 'He made a very good speech at our mass media conference, takes a great interest in the mass media and has had a certain amount of teaching experience in a secondary modern school. He could probably write about one or two of our topics.'[34] (In the end, Graham Martin, an English lecturer

[31] Jarvis to Pevsner, 29 March 1961, Penguin archives, A640/1, Bristol.

[32] Pevsner, 'Memorandum of Meeting Held at the N.U.T.', 29 June 1961, Penguin archives, A640/1, Bristol.

[33] Pevsner, 'Memorandum', 29 June 1961; Pevsner to Glover, 26 January 1962, Penguin archives, A640/1, Bristol. The original actually has 'in the thirties' as well as the book title in all caps.

[34] Jarvis to Thompson, 6 February 1962, Penguin archives, A640/1, Bristol.

at Bedford College, London, wrote the chapter on the press.) Both Thompson and Jarvis wanted Hoggart to write the chapter on magazines. As an alternative, Jarvis recommended Edward Blishen, one of the NUT members whom Pevsner met to discuss the idea of a book on the mass media. Blishen had written a novel, *Roaring Boys* (1955), based on his experience teaching tearaways in a north London secondary modern school.[35] Thompson seems to have been cooler about Blishen, and after Hoggart declined, he made an unexpected suggestion: David Holbrook.[36] Thompson appears to have chosen Holbrook on the strength of his standing with teachers and the power of his writing.[37] Pevsner replied drily that it was not clear 'whether he in fact knows anything about magazines'.[38] (He had, in fact, written about children's periodicals in *English for Maturity*, which was published the year before this correspondence.) Nevertheless, Pevsner did not veto Thompson's choice, and the *Scrutiny* character of the volume became more pronounced. With Holbrook on board, half of the eight contributors were former pupils or friends of Leavis's. In the foreword Thompson thanked Raymond O'Malley above all others for his advice.[39]

Michael Farr, who wrote the chapter on industrial design, had read English at Downing after being demobbed from the RAF at the end of the Second World War. Inspired by Nikolaus Pevsner's Slade lectures at Cambridge in 1948, Farr went to work as an editor and information officer for architectural and design organizations. His book *Design in British Industry* (1955) was a successor to Pevsner's *An Enquiry into Industrial Art in England* (1937), and written under Pevsner's supervision. He remained an admirer of Leavis and held to a belief in the importance of education as a means of resisting mass production's threats to taste and good design.[40] Farr's thoughts on design in *Discrimination and Popular Culture* owe much more to Pevsner and the Bauhaus group than to any extrapolation from *Scrutiny*, though he did include a quasi-ritualistic quotation from

[35] Edward Blishen, *Roaring Boys: A Schoolmaster's Agony* (1955; Bath: Chivers, 1974); Nicholas Tucker, 'Obituary: Edward Blishen', *The Independent*, 16 December 1996.
[36] Thompson to Jarvis, 22 January 1962; Thompson to Pevsner, 12 March 1962, Penguin archives, A640/1, Bristol. Thompson had published Blishen in *Use of English*: Edward Blishen, 'English in the Modern School', *Use of English* 10/4 (1959): 219–24.
[37] Thompson to Pevsner, 12 March 1962, Penguin archives, A640/1, Bristol.
[38] Pevsner to Thompson, 19 March 1962, Penguin archives, A640/1, Bristol.
[39] Denys Thompson, 'Foreword' to Thompson (ed.), *Discrimination and Popular Culture* (Harmondsworth: Penguin, 1964), 7. The others thanked were Jarvis, Pevsner, Holbrook, and Brian Jackson (the pupil of Leavis's who co-wrote *Education and the Working Class* and edited two anthologies of articles from *Use of English*).
[40] Gillian Naylor, 'Good Design in British Industry 1930–56', in Peter Draper (ed.), *Reassessing Nikolaus Pevsner* (Aldershot: Ashgate, 2004), 177–94.

Sturt's *The Wheelwright's Shop* on traditional relationships between crafts-men and their customers.[41] *Discrimination and Popular Culture* probably covered design because the NUT conference had dealt with it, in a session dominated by a debate between the chair, Sir Herbert Read, and the pre-senter, Richard Hamilton, an artist and design teacher who had been active in the Independent Group during the 1950s.[42] The influence of the earlier work of Thompson and the Leavises was unsurprisingly more in evidence in the chapters on topics of recurrent concern in *Scrutiny*, adver-tising and periodicals.

The advertising chapter was the work of Frank Whitehead, whom Thompson expected to 'deal radically' with the subject.[43] Whitehead had attended the NUT conference, representing the journal *Use of English*: he was the only contributor to *Discrimination and Popular Culture* to have registered for the conference.[44] Whitehead was one of the founders, in 1958, of the Advertising Inquiry Council. It was led by a consumer affairs journalist, Elizabeth Gundrey, and two lawyers, and other consumer or-ganizations supported it.[45] The involvement of teachers in the consumer advocacy groups founded in the 1950s reflects the expectation that teach-ers should defend society against psychological manipulation; and, in the case of those aligned with *Scrutiny*, an admiration for American debun-kers and consumer advocates such as Stuart Chase. Holbrook as well as Whitehead was involved in the AIC (he was on its Education Commit-tee), and the council went as far as to entitle its newsletter *Scrutiny*.[46]

It is not exaggerating much to say that Whitehead's chapter reads like a conspectus of *Scrutiny* arguments about advertising from thirty years before, with Vance Packard's *The Hidden Persuaders* (1960) and Martin Mayer's *Madison Avenue U.S.A.* (1961) replacing the works of Chase and the Lynds as American authorities. The standardization of goods effected by mass production meant that advertising was needed to create illusory differences, a distinctive 'emotional aura' for each brand (of cigarettes, for instance). Advertising demanded 'universality of appeal' from the news-papers and magazines in which it appeared, and this 'need to approach us all as units in a mass involves inevitably a levelling-down in the general

[41] Michael Farr, 'Design', in Thompson (ed.), *Discrimination*, 178.
[42] *Verbatim Report*, 135–55; Tilman Osterwold, *Pop Art* (Köln: Taschen, 2003), 211–18.
[43] Thompson to Jarvis, 22 January 1962, Penguin archives, A640/1, Bristol.
[44] *Verbatim Report*, 347.
[45] Matthew Hilton, *Consumerism in Twentieth-Century Britain: The Search for a Histori-cal Movement* (Cambridge: Cambridge University Press, 2003), 189, 200; Black, *Redefining British Politics*, 192.
[46] Holbrook to Hoggart, 17 November 1963, Richard Hoggart papers, 7/Holbrook/4, Sheffield; Hilton, *Consumerism*, 201.

standard of taste—a studied avoidance of the areas of experience in which we live most fully'. Advertising encouraged people to define the good life in materialistic terms. Advertising pandered to bad desires and manufactured new ones. It traded on 'the range of human infirmities' (here Whitehead quoted Thorstein Veblen). The 'main types of appeal in use today remain very much the same as those which were anatomized by F. R. Leavis and Denys Thompson in *Culture and Environment*—'Fear of Social Non-conformity', ' "Good Form" Pressure', 'The Snob Appeal'.[47] The discussion concentrated on print media and on prose-heavy advertisements just as *Culture and Environment* did: Whitehead acknowledged the migration of advertising budgets from print to television since 1955, but the evanescence of the medium in the decades before videotape meant he could not discuss television advertisements with much specificity.[48]

The proximity of Whitehead's chapter to familiar *Scrutiny* arguments did not trouble Penguin, though a decade later when Holbrook rewrote his contribution for a new edition of the book, his editor complained of Leavisian clichés—'very familiar stuff (ever since Leavis and Thompson in the 30's and 40's)'—and accused him of using 'Q. D. Leavis's trick of comparing today's average with yesterday's best. People once had also spurious criminal confessions, gory "police reports" and a mass of now forgotten penny and sixpenny street literature of neither more nor less merit than today's commercial publishing.'[49] Both the 1964 and 1973 versions of Holbrook's chapter occasioned heated and protracted exchanges over libel risks and what the Penguin staff and Thompson regarded as rhetorical excess and lack of analytical focus.[50] Penguin's main objection to the first edition of *Discrimination and Popular Culture* as a whole was that it provided little guidance about discriminating between popular culture's offerings. 'Can there be a good television serial? If so, how do you tell it from a bad one?' Pevsner asked of one draft chapter. 'What does responsible news look like?'[51] Another in-house reader complained that the book 'has virtually nothing to do with discrimination & seems yet another catalogue of why the mass media are as they are'. Most of the

[47] Whitehead, 'Advertising', 25, 27, 29, 35, 40; Leavis and Thompson, *Culture and Environment*, 11–25.
[48] Whitehead, 'Advertising', 33–4.
[49] James Cochrane to Holbrook, 6 January 1972, Penguin archives, A640/2, Bristol. Compare Barbara Hardy, 'The Teaching of English: Life, Literature and Literary Criticism', *English in Education* 2/2 (June 1968): 10.
[50] Pevsner to Thompson, 16 November 1962; Thompson to Pevsner, 11 February 1963 and 29 March 1963; Michael Rubinstein to Pevsner, 28 April 1964; James Cochrane to Holbrook, 3 November 1971, Penguin archives, A640/1; and the file dedicated to Holbrook's contribution to the second edition, Penguin archives, A640/2, Bristol.
[51] Pevsner to Thompson, 28 November 1962, Penguin archives, A640/1, Bristol.

contributions, he elaborated, 'tell us what is wrong, how it got like that and sometimes hint at why it must stay like that—but they dont attempt to give me, let alone average teenagers in grammar schools, any rough and ready guides to help me discriminate.' For Thompson, there were few audiences more important than grammar-school children. 'I know most of the guff in here,' the reader added; 'I also know I cant do much about it: I want to be told how to live with it and remain a sensitive human being.'[52]

Hall and Whannel's *The Popular Arts*, the other book produced in response to the NUT conference on mass culture, was an attempt to provide such guidance, to articulate criteria for comparing good and bad television serials or (to use one of their examples) understanding what made *The Goon Show* superior to run-of-the-mill radio comedy. 'It is … on a training in discrimination that we should place our emphasis. We should thinking of this as a training for greater awareness.' Both 'training' and 'awareness' replicated terms in the subtitle of *Culture and Environment*. Even G. H. Bantock, writing in 1967 when his position as a fierce opponent of progressive education and the 'vulgarized cultural order' of the 'industrial-bureaucratic state' was assured, recognized the connection between *The Popular Arts* and *Scrutiny*: 'Whatever shortcomings such a book may have, it introduces the analytical procedure in a sphere where it has, in general, been lacking (with the exception of Orwell's work) and offers a number of particularised judgements in the Leavisian spirit (that is so, isn't it?) within the field of mass civilization itself. Though most of mass culture can be dismissed as uncreative and deadening, qualitative discrimination reveals some genuine features. Who will deny the greatness of Chaplin, for instance?'[53]

Chaplin often lent himself to claims for the artistic potential of twentieth-century art forms. Hall and Whannel found him helpful as they advanced a distinction between 'mass art' and 'popular art'. Both could be made within mass-cultural forms and genres. Popular art 'in its modern forms exists only through the medium of a personal style'. The tendency of mass art, in contrast, was to suppress individuality and idiosyncrasy. The style of a popular artist like Chaplin 'develops out of his grappling with the experiences of his audience through the material and creations of his art'; in contrast, 'the mass style develops as a set of technical tricks for

---

[52] Peter [Wright] to Pevsner, 3 April [1963], Penguin archives, A640/1, Bristol.

[53] G. H. Bantock, *Education in an Industrial Society* (London: Faber & Faber, 1963), 202; G. H. Bantock, *Education, Culture and the Emotions* (London: Faber & Faber, 1967), 162; Dave Laing, '*Scrutiny* to Subcultures: Notes on Literary Criticism and Popular Music', *Popular Music* 13/2 (May 1994): 187.

projecting an image'. Conjuring with Eliot's ideas concerning tradition and impersonality—or perhaps Keats's 'negative capability'—Hall and Whannel said that the popular artist had 'the capacity... to lose himself in his material', and was therefore 'closer to the high artist' than others employed by the culture industry.[54]

This was not a possibility considered in *Culture and Environment, Fiction and the Reading Public*, or Thompson's essays in *Scrutiny*. It would have been preposterous to look for art in Hollywood's output. 'All that can be done, it must be realized', Q. D. Leavis had written, 'must take the form of resistance by an armed and conscious minority.' Hall and Whannel countered that such defensive thinking failed to acknowledge the creative potential of 'mass' art forms, cinema especially. No one needed defending from Antonioni.[55] Re-creating 'a genuine popular culture' necessitated a search for 'the points of growth within the society that now exists', not in one that had disappeared. At least some of those opportunities lay in 'creative uses of the media'. The forms of mass communication deplored by Thompson and the Leavises 'might be made to provide a range of imaginative experiences which could help young people to grapple with some of the problems they face'.[56]

I. A. Richards was not cited often in *The Popular Arts*, but his first few books informed Hall and Whannel's assumptions about how art worked: in the 'experiences' texts and images could provide or the responses art elicited. 'Responses' was a word Hall and Whannel used often, as were *Scrutiny* keywords such as 'values' and 'continuity' (as well as 'discrimination').[57] However, premises that went without saying in *Scrutiny* were disregarded in *The Popular Arts*, or replaced with new ones that were equally axiomatic. For instance, *Culture and Environment* presupposed that the aesthetic and emotional experiences provided by mass culture were mechanical and devoid of life; Hall and Whannel worked from the assumption that recorded music or cinema could create spaces for creativity and originality, and move their audiences to responses that were not stock ones. Hall and Whannel held to the *Scrutiny* tradition's valued aesthetic or cultural qualities and broke with the social diagnoses or historical narratives that the Leavises and Thompson had constructed in relation to those qualities.

The work of the concept of 'continuity' illustrates the point. Continuity with tradition was a marker of artistic vitality for Hall and Whannel as well as for Leavis. For Thompson and the Leavises, it had been all but destroyed by mass civilization: only in literature could continuity (and communion)

---

[54] Hall and Whannel, *Popular Arts*, 68.
[55] Ibid., 39.
[56] Ibid.
[57] Ibid., esp. 33, 36.

with 'the "picked experience of ages"' be maintained.[58] For Hall and Whannel, continuity helped distinguish valuable popular art from pernicious entertainments: a song derived some of its artistic power from its audience's living tradition. Thus the histrionic actors of the late eighteenth and early nineteenth centuries 'used Shakespeare's plays as personal vehicles for a style of acting which embodied certain shared values, a certain structure of feeling in their audience, as clearly as the art of Marie Lloyd did for her audience at the end of the century'.[59] The music hall performer Lloyd, as Hall and Whannel were well aware, enjoyed a certain high-cultural credibility as a result of T. S. Eliot's 1923 essay about her.[60] Lloyd, they wrote, 'worked back within [her]self to a more immediate and direct continuity between art, audience, and experience'.[61] Chaplin's films, too, drew their artistic energy from continuity with social traditions and values.

This argument ran counter to the *Scrutiny* contention that Britain no longer had a popular culture. The time when literature and popular culture were most productively interrelated was, of course, the Elizabethan period. Although F. R. Leavis and L. C. Knights regarded the organic relations between high art and popular tradition in the early modern period as irretrievably lost, Hall and Whannel ventured to draw some generalizable lessons about 'possible connections between the popular and the serious in art' from the *Scrutiny* group's work on Elizabethan drama, and in particular Knights's *Drama and Society in the Age of Jonson* (1937).[62] They conceded that 'one of the great—perhaps tragic—characteristics of the modern age had been the progressive alienation of high art from popular art. . . . Nevertheless, the connection between the two cannot be denied.'[63] To say that popular art and serious or 'high' art were connected was not the same as saying that high art drew its strength from popular culture: but popular art was often first to register changes in popular culture—'profound modifications . . . in social life and in the "structure of feeling" in society', Hall and Whannel put it, again invoking Williams's concept.[64]

Consequently, the fortunes of high art were bound to those of popular art, and to the state of culture at large. '[W]hen we look at the new media . . . we are showing a proper concern, not only for the moments of

[58] Leavis and Thompson, *Culture and Environment*, 81.

[59] Hall and Whannel, *Popular Arts*, 66–7.

[60] T. S. Eliot, 'Marie Lloyd' (1923), in *Selected Essays* (London: Faber & Faber, 1951), 456–9.

[61] Hall and Whannel, *Popular Arts*, 56–7, 67.

[62] Ibid., 81–4.

[63] Later, they returned to this argument (quoting L. G. Salingar's account in the *Pelican Guide to English Literature*) but did not even trouble to say that its declinist history was invalid. Hall and Whannel, *Popular Arts*, 376–7.

[64] Hall and Whannel, *Popular Arts*, 82, 83.

quality in the popular arts, but for the condition and quality of imaginative work of *any* level, and thus for the quality of the culture as a whole.'[65]
Here Hall and Whannel made the characteristic diagnostic manoeuvre of
Scrutiny criticism, sliding from art to 'the culture as a whole'.[66] With the
reference to the 'quality' of culture and living, Hall and Whannel wound
up at *Culture and Environment*'s starting point. Fittingly, they closed this
pivotal chapter on 'Popular Art and Mass Culture' by quoting the same
paragraph from Pound's *How to Read* as Thompson did while discussing
advertisers' prose in *Scrutiny* in 1932: 'literature... has to do with the clarity of "any and every" thought and opinion....When...the application
of word to thing goes rotten, *i.e.*, becomes slushy and inexact, or excessive
or bloated, the whole machinery of social and of individual thought and
order goes to pot.'[67] Hall and Whannel remarked that if 'imaginative
work' were substituted for 'literature', Pound's dictum could serve as an
epigraph for their book.[68] Thus *The Popular Arts* folded the *Scrutiny* tradition of cultural criticism in on itself: discrimination, training, values, and
continuity were the currency of an argument against the diagnosis and
prognosis set out in *Mass Civilisation and Minority Culture*.

While they wrote *The Popular Arts*, Whannel was head of the British Film
Institute's education department and Hall, who had come to Oxford from
Jamaica as a Rhodes Scholar in 1951, was teaching in south London and
editing *New Left Review* outside school hours.[69] In the year *The Popular
Arts* was published, he moved to Birmingham to become Hoggart's deputy
at the university's new Centre for Contemporary Cultural Studies. Hoggart had not long left adult education to become an 'internal' senior lecturer in the English department at the University of Leicester before he
was encouraged to apply for a chair in English at Birmingham. He accepted Birmingham's offer on condition that he would be able to establish
a postgraduate centre. It would have been a waste, he felt, 'not to use a
professor's position to try to advance the interests which had emerged in
the writing of *The Uses of Literacy*'. The Vice-Chancellor agreed. The rank
of professor brought freedom as well as authority. It did not, however,

[65] Ibid., 85 (emphasis in the original).
[66] Something like a *locus classicus* is Leavis, 'Mass Civilisation and Minority Culture',
30 and n. (quoting I. A. Richards, *Practical Criticism: A Study of Literary Judgment*
[London: Kegan Paul, Trench, Trubner, 1929], 319–20).
[67] Ezra Pound, *How to Read* (London: Desmond Harmsworth, 1931), 17–18; Denys
Thompson, 'Advertising God', *Scrutiny* 1/3 (December 1932): 244.
[68] Hall and Whannel, *Popular Arts*, 85.
[69] MacCabe, 'Interview with Stuart Hall', 12, 18–19. On the BFI education department, see Colin McArthur, 'Two Steps Forward, One Step Back: Cultural Struggle in the
British Film Institute', *Journal of Popular British Cinema* 4 (2001): 113–17.

come with money for a research centre. Hoggart secured the majority of the seed funding from Penguin. He met with Allen Lane and W. E. Williams, who talked Lane into it. (' "Oh, give him what he asks, Allen. You've made a fortune by riding cultural change without understanding it." ')[70] Hoggart had administrative obligations to the School of English and the university as a whole, and he was not closely involved in the day-to-day work of postgraduate supervision and the centre's research projects. Hall quickly became the centre's guiding intellectual presence. Within a few years, the centre's focus, and Hall's own concerns, shifted away from the questions Hoggart had explored in *The Uses of Literacy*. However, the arguments and assumptions of *The Popular Arts* were consistent with the programme for the centre that Hoggart had outlined in his inaugural lecture at Birmingham, which was published in *Use of English*.[71]

Cultural studies had many progenitors, Hoggart stated, 'but Dr Leavis in his culture and environment work and Mrs Leavis in her studies in popular fiction are more important than most'.[72] English was 'important at any time': studying literature deepened respect for language, and it led reader and student into a deeper apprehension of 'experience', its textures, and its values.[73] But in this mode of cultural criticism, which Hoggart shared with *Scrutiny*, the present was always a critical time. Hoggart turned from the claims of literary studies to the predicament of language in 1960s Britain. Words were becoming emptied out and unusable. Mass culture used language instrumentally, for 'persuasion and manipulation' rather than 'exploration', a word with some *Scrutiny* freight.[74] Hoggart wondered whether in any earlier period so many words had been used 'inorganically', in the commercial or political interests of parties other than the writer. His manifesto had none of the embattled sensibility of' *Mass Civilisation and Minority Culture*, but it subscribed to the belief Leavis expressed there that a culture's life depended on its language.[75] The line of descent

---

[70] Richard Hoggart, *An Imagined Life: Life and Times, Volume III, 1959–91* (1992; Oxford: Oxford University Press, 1993), 76–8, 90.

[71] Richard Hoggart, 'Schools of English and Contemporary Society', *Use of English* 15/2 (winter 1963): 75–81 and 15/3 (spring 1964): 167–74. Subsequent references are to the version in *Speaking to Each Other: Essays*, vol. 2, *About Literature* (London: Chatto & Windus, 1970), 246–59.

[72] Hoggart, 'Schools of English', 255.

[73] Ibid., 246–9.

[74] Ibid., 251–2. Earlier in the lecture, Hoggart had said that literature 'explores human experience' (247). Leavis prized literature's 'critical-exploratory' use of language; Knights entitled his collection of essays *Explorations*, though Knights used the word to refer to the function of criticism rather than that of literature itself: 'literary criticism is a form of disciplined exploration'. L. C. Knights, *Explorations: Essays in Criticism Mainly on the Literature of the Seventeenth Century* (London: Chatto & Windus, 1946), ix.

[75] Leavis, 'Mass Civilisation and Minority Culture', 14–15. See also Leavis and Thompson, *Culture and Environment*, 81.

from *Scrutiny* was manifest in Hoggart's quotation of the same irresistible passage from Pound about slushy language.[76]

The *Culture and Environment* response to the challenge of mass civilization's corruption of the machinery of thought and order was to advance ways of fortifying young people. Hoggart, at least by 1963, was much more accommodating. Each year, he said, English graduates went down from university to become schoolteachers—the passage echoed *Scrutiny's* opening manifesto—and found that their charges were primed to listen to 'voices very different from the voices heard in that high art they are now trained to teach'.[77] Jane Austen 'does not speak with the accents of *Honey*, and *Honey* is much read even in girls' grammar schools'. (The first draft of Holbrook's contribution to *Discrimination of Popular Culture* advanced a case against *Honey*. As he and Pevsner 'de-libell[ed]' it, Thompson remarked: 'I suppose the name of the magazine could be replaced by a made-up name—*Cherry*, *Poppet*, or something equally inane.')[78] Before they went to university, those teachers might have read magazines like *Honey* themselves, and might still have been attuned to its accents, but few of them resolved this split, and they resented their unresponsive students. 'It would be better', Hoggart concluded, 'if more of us were informed, if we sought more relevance and connection, if we encouraged a stronger sense that the life of the imagination has always to be fought for.'[79]

Knowing more about the 'mass or popular arts' would enable the champions of literature to engage better with those they sought to win over. It was impossible to say much of value about films or thrillers 'unless you know how these things work as art, even though sometimes as "bad art"'.[80] Devising more probing modes of formal analysis should be the top priority of cultural studies, Hoggart declared. (The Birmingham centre started, after all, as a cell within an English department.) The researchers might even enjoy it. Popular art was not all bad. Even as soap operas, westerns, and 'offbeat commercials' became 'increasingly machine-tooled', they nevertheless opened up 'spaces between the brittle voices in which a gesture sets you thinking in a new way about some aspect of human experience'.[81]

---

[76] Hoggart, 'Schools of English', 250.

[77] 'Every year... intelligent young men and women go down from the Universities and are swallowed by secondary and public schools': 'Scrutiny: A Manifesto', *Scrutiny* 1/1 (May 1932): 5. Hoggart was well aware that most English graduates (certainly from provincial universities such as Birmingham) went into teaching; and of course the lecture was published in a journal for teachers.

[78] Thompson to Pevsner, 12 March 1962, 31 October 1962, Penguin Archives, A640/1, Bristol.

[79] Hoggart, 'Schools of English', 253. Compare Hall and Whannel, *Popular Arts*, 37, and Himmelweit, Oppenheim, and Vince, *Television and the Child*, 51.

[80] Hoggart, 'Schools of English', 257.

[81] Ibid., 'Schools of English and Contemporary Society', 258.

Frank Whitehead later accused Hoggart and the Centre for Contemporary Cultural Studies of blunting *Scrutiny*'s cultural critique, of eroding teachers' 'sense of the necessity for *resistance*'.[82] The collapse of the ideal of 'discrimination' among younger teachers in the 1960s was, as we have seen, one of the reasons for the decline in the *Scrutiny* movement's influence in schools. This change preoccupied Holbrook as well as Whitehead. Holbrook and Hoggart conducted an intermittent but vigorous correspondence about the consequences of taking mass culture seriously as a species or art or self-expression over the course of the year after Hoggart delivered his inaugural lecture—a 'crucial statement of your Birmingham policy'.[83] Holbrook took Hoggart to task for claiming that mass art could reflect a truly popular culture or express genuine feeling. 'There is no doubt in my mind (and in Denys Thompson's, with whom I've discussed this,—D.T. said "I've just been seeing some telly, and R.H. has no excuse...") that in the inaugural...you suggest that somehow in television one may discover the aspirations and vitality of "the people."'[84] He said Hoggart wanted to see in television a 'warm, thriving, human nature such as Dickens (or Priestley) see in human beings'.[85] Holbrook insisted that television, like 'pop' at large, is 'never disinterested. That is, it must serve the acquisitive impulse, both by keeping its content well below the level of taste, and so making money, and making taste worse. And also by fortifying the acquisitive *myth*, that possessions make for success, and this makes for happiness.'[86]

Holbrook's indictment reiterated two of Leavis and Thompson's arguments against commercial culture. In the entertainment business and the mass media, products that catered to the lowest common denominator made it harder for quality work to be supported (the 'Gresham's Law' argument). Secondly, mass art that converged with the forms and assumptions of advertising cultivated an acceptance of material definitions of 'standards of living'. Holbrook's case against 'pop', in his letters to Hoggart and in published writings, also bore the imprint of his increasingly intense engagement with psychoanalysis, not a body of thought explored

[82] Frank Whitehead, 'F. R. Leavis and the Schools', in Denys Thompson (ed.), *The Leavises: Recollections and Impressions* (Cambridge: Cambridge University Press, 1984), 146 (emphasis in original).
[83] Holbrook to Hoggart, 8 May 1963, Hoggart papers, 7/Holbrook/3, Sheffield.
[84] Holbrook to Hoggart, 21 April 1964, Hoggart papers, 7/Holbrook/7, Sheffield. Holbrook's misgivings about Hoggart's position on television had been building since Hoggart's time on the Pilkington Committee, much of whose report Hoggart wrote. Holbrook evidently thought that the report's strictures on television's 'triviality' did not go far enough.
[85] Holbrook to Hoggart, 26 March 1964, Hoggart papers, 7/Holbrook/5; Holbrook to Hoggart, 8 May 1963, Hoggart papers, 7/Holbrook/3, Sheffield.
[86] Holbrook to Hoggart, 26 March 1964, Hoggart papers, 7/Holbrook/5, Sheffield.

much in *Scrutiny*.[87] Where Thompson and the Leavises in the 1930s habitually treated standardization and other negative processes of mass civilization as functions of the logic of *industry*, Holbrook emphasized the 'commercial impulse' and the desires produced by advertising, television, and magazines. 'In "pop" a dreamworld is created which is a substitute for actual living, and also a projection of inward myth-hallucinations.'[88]

There was a class edge to this argument. The working class—'our culture', Holbrook told Hoggart, one scholarship boy to another—had an enduring taste for hallucination. He drew Hoggart's attention to the treatment of Methodism in E. P. Thompson's recently published *Making of the English Working Class*, a book aligned with *Scrutiny's* critique of the acquisitive society as well as Tawney's.[89] (In a phrase that was always going to be quoted, Thompson characterized Methodism's combination of self-repression and sabbath-day intensities as 'a ritualized form of psychic masturbation'.)[90] Yet if Methodism was more or less indigenous to the English working class, mass culture was not. The sort of person who kept the 'hallucination factory' running was 'the middle-class type, often from Oxbridge, often connected with advertising, with a split conscience, and a dream drive, often with deep psycho-pathological elements'.[91]

Too many '"pop" chasers', Holbrook warned Hoggart, were themselves hypnotized by the hallucination. 'They must be "with it," but critically with it. The result is often that they are simply swallowed up, and find a fringe job actually in the belly of the whale—I always think Whanel [*sic*], Alloway and them are like that.' (The theorist of pop art Lawrence Alloway was another alumnus of the Independent Group.)[92] The implication was that to be the director of a Centre for Contemporary Cultural Studies was also to be inside the whale. Pop chasers, said Holbrook, 'haven't the courage to belong to a minority that stands out of the herd'.[93]

---

[87] David Holbrook, 'What New Sensibility?' *Cambridge Quarterly* 3/2 (1968): 154; Francis Mulhern, *The Moment of 'Scrutiny'* (London: New Left Books, 1979), 159.

[88] Holbrook to Hoggart, 26 March 1964, Hoggart papers, 7/Holbrook/5, Sheffield.

[89] See Meredith Veldman, *Fantasy, the Bomb, and the Greening of Britain: Romantic Protest, 1945–1980* (Cambridge: Cambridge University Press, 1994); Stefan Collini, 'Enduring Passion: E. P. Thompson's Reputation', in *Common Reading: Critics, Historians, Publics* (Oxford: Oxford University Press, 2008), 175–86; and E. P. Thompson, *The Making of the English Working Class* (1963; Harmondsworth: Penguin, 1980), 488, where Thompson concludes part 2 of the book with quotations from Blake and the same passage of the same Lawrence essay ('Nottingham and the Mining Countryside') as Leavis and Thompson quote in *Culture and Environment*, 95.

[90] Thompson, *Making of the English Working Class*, 405.

[91] Holbrook to Hoggart, 26 March 1964, Hoggart papers, 7/Holbrook/5, Sheffield.

[92] Peter Stanfield, 'Maximum Movies: Lawrence Alloway's Pop Art Film Criticism', *Screen* 49/2 (2008): 179–93, esp. 185; Anne Massey, *The Independent Group: Modernism and Mass Culture in Britain, 1945–59* (Manchester: Manchester University Press, 1995).

[93] Holbrook to Hoggart, 26 March 1964, Hoggart papers, 7/Holbrook/5, Sheffield.

These terms were used freely in the first decade of *Scrutiny*, but to speak of a 'minority' and 'the herd' in 1964 was to be discomfitingly forceful. Holbrook realized that there was an untimely quality to his contentions. 'Of course when I see old Leavis walking along Trumpington Street with a glazed look of denying the rest of the world on his face, then I recognize the dangers.' This was as far as his ambivalence ran. He added: 'But that man who escaped from the whale's belly was all bleached and pitted, half-digested, and hideous, and this is what we shall look like by the time we're finished.'[94]

Holbrook's case against 'pop' may have been untimely, but, as it turned out, Hoggart's vision of cultural studies did not have much of a future itself. By the mid-1960s, a programme based on formal analysis could no longer accommodate the energies and pressures of the field. Researchers at the Birmingham centre quickly decided that the study of media required 'a theoretical understanding of culture and society beyond the scope of literary criticism'. Not satisfied with the models provided by 1950s American sociology, they began to engage with the work of Max Weber, Emile Durkheim, Karl Mannheim, and other German and French sociologists.[95] Then there was a more decisive break, as the centre's work was transformed by the theoretical frameworks of 'western Marxism'—especially the work of Louis Althusser and Antonio Gramsci—which Perry Anderson, Tom Nairn, and other members of the editorial collective of *New Left Review* brokered to and 'naturalized for' publics in Britain.[96]

Before the middle of the decade, Hall's own work, at least, had moved along the arc of left-Leavisism, stretching the Leavises' and Thompson's arguments, critical procedures, and favoured quotations onto a politics alien to *Scrutiny*. There had been a degree of continuity across political and generational divides. The *New Left Review* of Anderson and the others—Hall resigned from the editorship in 1961—moved to confront existing intellectual traditions rather than bend them to its own purposes. In Anderson's 'Components of the National Culture' (1968), the very fact

[94] Holbrook to Hoggart, 7 April 1964, Hoggart papers, 7/Holbrook/6, Sheffield.
[95] Dennis L. Dworkin, *Cultural Marxism in Postwar Britain: History, the New Left, and the Origins of Cultural Studies* (Durham, NC: Duke University Press, 1997), 120–4. On the new directions taken after the mid-1960s, see also Stuart Hall, 'Cultural Studies and the Centre: Some Problematics and Problems', in [Centre for Contemporary Cultural Studies], *Culture, Media, Language: Working Papers in Cultural Studies, 1972–79* (London: Hutchinson, 1980), 16–38.
[96] Madeleine Davis, 'The Marxism of the British New Left', *Journal of Political Ideologies* 11/3 (2006): 335–58, esp. 341, 348; Dworkin, *Cultural Marxism*, 134–41; Perry Anderson, *Considerations on Western Marxism* (London: New Left Books, 1976).

that, in *Scrutiny*, literary criticism could sustain such far-reaching ambitions was a function of a debilitating peculiarity of the English. Anderson argued that Britain, unlike France, Germany, and Italy, had never developed a 'totalizing' critique, whether sociological or Marxist, of capitalist modernity. In no other country could a literary critic claim that English was the 'chief of the humanities', as Leavis did.[97] That Leavis could make this assertion was 'a symptom of the objective vacuum at the centre of the culture. Driven out of any obvious habitats, the notion of the totality found refuge in the least expected of studies'. When British philosophy devolved into the ' "technical" ' after Wittgenstein, 'a displacement occurred and literary criticism became "ethical" '.[98]

Literature and the arts were not irrelevant in this intellectual constellation, as is clear from the rise of 'theory' in university departments of English in the 1970s, and the work of the Birmingham centre's Literature and Society and English Studies groups during the same period.[99] But western Marxism and structuralism problematized or disavowed the *category* of art. 'To deprive the bourgeoisie not of its art but of its concept of art, this is the precondition of a revolutionary argument': the epigraph to Geoffrey Wall's 1978 translation of Pierre Macherey's *Theory of Literary Production* could serve as an epigraph of the Althusserian moment generally.[100] A conception of art as a special and privileged form of cultural artefact or activity was as central to *The Popular Arts* as it was to *Mass Civilisation and Minority Culture*. Although literary critics and practitioners of cultural studies never gave up arguing about Leavis, by the end of the 1960s nearly all of them had stopped arguing on Leavis's terms.

[97] F. R Leavis, *Education and the University: A Sketch for an 'English School'* (London: Chatto & Windus, 1943), 33.
[98] Perry Anderson, 'Components of the National Culture', *New Left Review* 50 (1968), 84–5.
[99] *Culture, Media, Language*, 227–68.
[100] Geoffrey Wall, 'Translator's Preface', in Pierre Macherey, *A Theory of Literary Production*, trans. Wall (1966; London: Routledge & Kegan Paul, 1978), vii.

7

Minority Culture and the Penguin Public

By the early 1960s, the author of *Mass Civilisation and Minority Culture* was being profiled in national newspapers and Penguin was paperbacking his books.[1] Many of his followers collaborated on the seven-volume *Pelican Guide to English Literature*, which presented '*Scrutiny*' interpretations of authors from Chaucer to Dylan Thomas to tens of thousands of 'general readers' and a swelling student readership in an age of university expansion. Their modes of criticism had hitherto been practised in intimate teaching situations (in adult education tutorial classes and sixth forms as well as Cambridge supervisions and seminars) and in a journal with a print run of 750 to 1400.[2] What was entailed in transposing *Scrutiny*'s form of criticism to the Penguin public? It was in the activities of Leavis's pupils that these compromises were worked out. However, Leavis himself did not shun the metropolitan press of which he was so fierce a critic. The nature of his media interventions and his conception of the relationship between critic and public bring into relief the differences between his principle of minority culture and the more missionary assumptions of nearly all his pupils and collaborators.

Leavis's relative celebrity in the decades after he lost his primary platform, *Scrutiny*, in 1953, was not just a function of his eminence or notoriety among literary critics, but also a consequence of a moment when the BBC's Third Programme, television, the expanded arts coverage of the Sunday papers, changes in secondary education, and the Arts Council's promotion of high culture dramatically extended the reach of intellectuals' voices.[3] This was a moment both of cultural democratization and of

[1] F. R. Leavis to *The Guardian*, 12 April 1960, in Leavis, *Letters in Criticism*, ed. John Tasker (London: Chatto & Windus, 1974), 74.

[2] L. C. Knights, '*Scrutiny* and F. R. L.: A Personal Memoir', in Denys Thompson (ed.), *The Leavises: Recollections and Impressions* (Cambridge: Cambridge University Press, 1984), 73. Compare Kerry McSweeney, '*Scrutiny*', in Alvin Sullivan (ed.), *British Literary Magazines*, vol. 4 *The Modern Age, 1914–1984* (New York: Greenwood Press, 1986), 423.

[3] Stefan Collini, *Absent Minds: Intellectuals in Britain* (Oxford: Oxford University Press, 2006), chs 6, 7, 16, 17; Kate Whitehead, *The Third Programme: A Literary History* (Oxford: Clarendon Press, 1989); Andrew Sinclair, *Arts and Cultures: The History of the Fifty Years of the Arts Council of Great Britain* (London: Sinclair Stevenson, 1995).

persistent 'cultural deference' that was, as Stefan Collini writes, 'hard to disentangle from forms of social deference'. When the philosopher A. J. Ayer became a star of the television version of *The Brains Trust*, the old Etonian's 'clipped upper-class accent, conservatively cut three-piece suits, and general air of social confidence and savoir-faire were not insignificant elements in his authority'.[4] At the same time, the founding of new universities both before and after the Robbins Committee on Higher Education reported in 1963 and the massive extension of secondary education along stratified lines after 1944 credentialled new writers and commentators as well as enlarging their audience.[5] Reflecting on the constituency that the grammar schools of this period created for *Scrutiny* approaches to culture, Michael Bell has remarked that Leavis's time was 'one in which the older hierarchical assumptions of social leadership overlapped with a new openness as to who might perform this function'.[6]

Leavis exercised his cultural authority in print rather than on the radio, let alone television.[7] He was willing to send essays to *The Spectator* and the *Times Literary Supplement*, and they were willing to publish them, despite a record of hostilities between Leavis and the latter paper, especially under the editorship of Alan Pryce-Jones in the late 1940s and 1950s. Pryce-Jones, whose first editorial gig was on the *London Mercury* during the cricket-loving and Eliot-loathing reign of Sir John Squire, exemplified for Leavis a governing-class dilettantism.[8] When Arthur Crook succeeded Pryce-Jones as *TLS* editor in 1959, Leavis sent him (and others) 'a lengthy mimeograph giving an account of the misunderstandings, insults and neglect' that he and *Scrutiny* had suffered under the previous regime. Several years later, the *TLS* published as an article a long letter that Leavis had sent.[9] If the *TLS*, the Sunday newspapers, and the literary and political

---

[4] Collini, *Absent Minds*, 399, 402, 421.

[5] *Higher Education: Report of the Committee Appointed by the Prime Minister under the Chairmanship of Lord Robbins, 1961–1963* (London, 1963: HM Stationary Office); Carol Dyhouse, *Students: A Gendered History* (London: Routledge, 2006), chs 4–5.

[6] Michael Bell, 'F. R. Leavis', in A. Walton Litz, Louis Menand, and Lawrence Rainey (eds), *The Cambridge History of Literary Criticism*, vol. 7, *Modernism and the New Criticism* (Cambridge: Cambridge University Press, 2000), 392.

[7] On Leavis's mistrust of the BBC, see Ian MacKillop, *F. R. Leavis: A Life in Criticism* (London: Allen Lane, 1995), 267–8, 282.

[8] Alan Pryce-Jones, untitled memoir in William Plomer et al., *Coming to London* (London: Phoenix House, 1957), 118–27; Derwent May, *Critical Times: The History of the Times Literary Supplement* (London: HarperCollins, 2001), 298–300.

[9] May, *Critical Times*, 363; F. R. Leavis, 'Mr Pryce-Jones, the British Council and British Culture', *Scrutiny* 18/3 (winter 1951–2): 224–8. The mimeograph was probably one that Leavis had produced a decade earlier in response to the *TLS*'s treatment, or non-treatment, of *Scrutiny* in a comprehensive survey of contemporary British writing for overseas readers. [F. R. Leavis,] ' "Literary Periodicals" and the *Times Literary Supplement*', n.d. (1950), copy in F. R. Leavis papers, Col 9.59.121, Emmanuel.

weeklies all failed to meet their critical responsibilities, they could not simply be written off.[10] In a debate with F. W. Bateson in 1953, Leavis asked rhetorically whether Bateson agreed with one of his *Essays in Criticism* contributors that 'it doesn't matter what the reviewing in the weeklies or the Sunday papers is like; or how the B.B.C. uses its immense resources, and its formidable powers of literary influence'. Did Bateson think that, provided *Essays in Criticism* and *Scrutiny* carried on, 'the function of criticism in this country is being pretty well provided for? If so, I cannot take seriously his idea of the function of criticism, or his interest in literature.'[11]

During the bitter dispute over Leavis's succession at Downing College in the mid-1960s, his name was often in the national newspapers. The undergraduates' 'well organised set of "stringers"' supplied the newspapers with copy, and the Sundays 'chased up academic rows and made stories out of the little that could be gleaned'.[12] Leavis obliged 'Atticus' in the *Sunday Times* with comments on Downing's behaviour.[13] The writer of the *Sunday Telegraph*'s Mandrake column traded on his own association with Leavis in the 1930s, reporting the advice Leavis had given him—'prowling round the room in his open-necked shirt'—about how to get a First.[14] (His subsequent career doubtless lent further support to Leavis's belief that success in examinations was sometimes a sign of 'journalistic facility'.)[15] Commenting on the Downing imbroglio and an unrelated incident at another college reported by the *Observer*, Karl Miller remarked in the *New Statesman*: 'It used to be lost causes—now the ancient universities seem to have been made the home of the pseudo-event, by courtesy of Astor and Atticus.'[16]

[10] Stefan Collini, 'The Critic as Journalist: Leavis after *Scrutiny*', in Jeremy Treglown and Bridget Bennett (eds), *Grub Street and the Ivory Tower: Literary Journalism and Literary Scholarship from Fielding to the Internet* (Oxford: Clarendon Press, 1998), 159.

[11] F. R. Leavis, 'The Responsible Critic: Or The Function of Criticism at Any Time', *Scrutiny* 19/3 (spring 1953): 179–80.

[12] M. C. Bradbrook, '"Nor Shall My Sword": The Leavises' Mythology', in Thompson (ed.), *The Leavises*, 39; Karl Miller, 'Cambridge Diary', *New Statesman*, 28 May 1965, 836.

[13] 'Atticus', 'No More Leavisites', *Sunday Times*, 28 March 1965.

[14] 'Sunday Morning with Mandrake', *Sunday Telegraph*, 10 October 1965, 6; see also Bradbrook, '"Nor Shall My Sword"', 38. The Mandrake column was at this time written by Lionel Birch, a sometime Labour parliamentary candidate and veteran of the left-leaning *Picture Post* now thriving in a different political and journalistic environment. Birch had read English at Clare College under Mansfield Forbes. Duff Hart-Davis, *The House the Berrys Built* (London: Hodder & Stoughton, 1990), 241; Hugh Carey, *Mansfield Forbes and His Cambridge* (Cambridge: Cambridge University Press, 1984), 3 n. 2, 133.

[15] Karl Miller, *Rebecca's Vest: A Memoir* (London: Hamish Hamilton, 1993), 138.

[16] Miller, 'Cambridge Diary', 836.

In this climate, and given his standing as a critic, Leavis probably would not have had trouble placing articles in substantial London publications. Most of his contributions to newspapers and periodicals after the end of *Scrutiny*, however, took the form of letters to editors. (The majority of the longer pieces from this phase of campaigning were written as lectures.) He frequently attempted, by rhetorical gestures that were unexpected and sometimes deceptively awry, to wrest the terms and tone of debate away from those of the host, and to prise his own arguments out of the boxes that a reader's passing acquaintance, or the claims of his detractors, had lodged them in.[17] Leavis's dealings with metropolitan publications were guided by a conviction that their interests were basically incompatible with his. As Collini suggests, his contributions constituted a sort of guerrilla warfare, 'a strategy of small, nagging engagements that slowly undermine the position of an enemy much stronger in conventional terms'.[18]

Leavis usually looked to smaller, local journals, especially ones with which he had a personal connection and which appeared sympathetic to him. The *Cambridge Quarterly* had the promise of being such a journal, but in the dispute over the Leavis Lectureship at the same time as the *Cambridge Quarterly* was founded Leavis and the students and admirers who edited it parted company painfully and permanently. In the 1970s, *The Human World*, edited by Leavis's former pupil Ian Robinson, published a number of his late essays.[19] Pondering where to publish a piece on *Lady Chatterley's Lover* in 1961, Leavis considered the *Cambridge Review*, but expected his treatment of Noël Annan, Joan Bennett, and Graham Hough, each of them Cambridge witnesses for Penguin at the trial, would make him unwelcome there. As his biographer writes, 'It is curious to think of the literary critic, now in his prime, considering this local journal as his first port of call.'[20]

The work that made Leavis known to thousands of people who would not usually have attended to the utterances of a literary critic, his polemic against C. P. Snow's 'two cultures' thesis, was swiftly published in *The Spectator*, but even in this case, the initial audience was very local indeed:

[17] Collini, 'Critic as Journalist', 166–9.
[18] Ibid., 165.
[19] Ibid., 155–6; and, on the Leavis Lectureship and the *Cambridge Quarterly*, see MacKillop, *F. R. Leavis*, ch. 10; and the responses by John Newton, R. D. Gooder, and L. G. Salingar in the *Cambridge Quarterly* 25/4 (1996); and M. B. Mencher (ed.), *Leavis, Dr MacKillop and 'The Cambridge Quarterly': A Brynmill Special Issue* (Denton, Norfolk: Brynmill Press, 1998). Leavis also published articles in the *Universities Quarterly*, which Boris Ford edited.
[20] MacKillop, *F. R. Leavis*, 308.

one that gathered in the junior common room of Downing College.[21] The occasion for the case against Snow was the Richmond Lecture, which commemorated a former master of the college. The lecture was advertised, and a representative of the BBC approached Leavis seeking permission to record and broadcast his lecture. He replied emphatically: 'There can be no question of recording my lecture, or using it for any BBC purpose.' Within a day or two of the Richmond lecture, however, Leavis had spoken on the telephone to Ian Hamilton of *The Spectator*, and they had agreed that the full text of the Richmond lecture would appear in *The Spectator* the following Saturday. (Hamilton had his assistant editor, a friend of Snow's, take the text round to him; though hardly pleased with the contents, he agreed not to sue.)[22] The speed with which these arrangements were made indicates that Leavis's choice to present his case to a Cambridge audience—one that included supporters of Snow's such as the historian J. H. Plumb—before making it to a national readership was a gesture of respect for Cambridge rather than a judgement that Cambridge people were the ones he most needed to address.[23]

There was doubtless an element of parochialism in Leavis's preference for Cambridge audiences, as there was in his tendency to make Cambridge a figure for 'the university' generally. But a theory of the 'public' was also in play. Drawing on Jürgen Habermas's thinking on the public sphere, scholars of modernism such as Mark S. Morrison and Patrick

---

[21] See Ortolano, *Two Cultures Controversy*.

[22] MacKillop, *F. R. Leavis*, 317–18, 322.

[23] The lecture took place on 28 February 1962; *The Times* of 1 March carried a report on the lecture; *The Spectator* announced the forthcoming publication on 2 March; the *Sunday Times* reported on the lecture on 3 March; *The Spectator* published the text on 9 March. Snow suspected that Leavis had planned the publicity. In a postscript written for the American edition of 'Two Cultures?', Leavis said that he had excluded journalists because the Richmond lecture was always a private event, and he had not wanted the 'ugly kind of publicity' that the press would 'inevitably' have given it. Leavis was 'intent on ensuring that my actual theme and argument should be really attended to': it would have been foolish to think that admitting journalists would 'further that aim'. 'My purpose was to see the publication of the full text myself.' (F. R. Leavis, *Nor Shall My Sword: Discourses on Pluralism, Compassion, and Social Hope* [London: Chatto & Windus, 1972], 73–4.) Leavis must have recognized the Cambridge correspondent of *The Times* in his audience; he had been invited, though whether Leavis saw the guest list is not known. L. P. Wilkinson was the University Orator and a classicist at King's, the college whose Bloomsbury associations and values Leavis deplored, so not someone one would otherwise expect to be invited to a Downing event. Later, when the Syndics of the university press declined to publish the lecture in book form, Leavis wrote exasperatedly that there was no point in trying to explain his case better to 'the classics who are the resisters.... You can't educate Public Orators—or Syndics.' (MacKillop, *F. R. Leavis*, 317–18, 321–3, 438 n. 33.) Though it is curious that Leavis appears not to have objected to Wilkinson's presence, it would have been perverse for him to trust Wilkinson to pick out the important points for a report in the establishment's newspaper; and such a move would not have been in keeping with his persistent efforts not to let the press impose its terms on him.

Collier have drawn attention to the role of little magazines and their readerships in the ways poets and novelists conceived of the constituency of modernism and the generalizations and abstractions entailed in imagining a wider 'public' to write for.[24] Eliot and Woolf are understandably important figures in these arguments; I would contend that Leavis thought at least as seriously as either of them about the nature of the public and thus about the way intellectual life in Britain operated.[25]

Writing to Denys Harding in 1940, Leavis remarked: 'small as our public is its unusual quality makes it not negligible. A good proportion of it, anyway, is an unusually genuine article; it really reads & follows up, & has got from *Scrutiny* a useful common background.' Harding had put many 'Downing men (& others)' onto L. H. Myers's novels and 'made him a part of their currency'. They looked forward to Myers's next book and what Harding would say about it. Leavis reported that a Downing man had written to him drawing his attention to another's review of a Myers novel in *The Dublin Review*, a Catholic periodical. This was 'evidence, such as is always turning up, of a public active to a degree that offsets its smallness'.[26] Decades later, Leavis and Harding reflected on their public again. The occasion was Ronald Hayman's profile of Leavis for the *New Review* in 1975, a year after a BBC profile for which Harding had been interviewed, along with M. C. Bradbrook, William Walsh, Stuart Hall, Richard Hoggart, Raymond Williams, Roy Fuller, Christopher Ricks, and John Gross.[27] Leavis was unsurprisingly

---

[24] Jürgen Habermas, *The Structural Transformation of the Public Sphere: An Inquiry into a Category of Bourgeois Society*, trans. Thomas Burger (Cambridge, Mass.: MIT Press, 1989); Mark S. Morrisson, *The Public Face of Modernism: Little Magazines, Audiences, and Reception, 1905–1920* (Madison: University of Wisconsin Press, 2001); Patrick Collier, *Modernism on Fleet Street* (Aldershot: Ashgate, 2006).

[25] See Terry Eagleton, *The Function of Criticism* (1984; London: Verso, 2005), 78–9. For different interpretations of the theory and practice of 'minority culture', see Ross Alloway, 'Selling the Great Tradition: Resistance and Conformity in the Publishing Practices of F. R. Leavis', *Book History* 6 (2003): 232–42; D. L. LeMahieu, *A Culture for Democracy: Mass Communication and the Cultivated Mind between the Wars* (Oxford: Clarendon Press, 1988), 294–304.

[26] Leavis to Harding, 24 September [1940], F. R. Leavis papers, Col 9.59a, Emmanuel. Other letters in which Leavis comments on *Scrutiny*'s 'public' include: Leavis to Harding, n.d. ('after all, our public is an *élite*'); Leavis to Harding, n.d. (December 1951 or January 1952); Leavis to D. F. Pocock, 18 January 1950 ('Our centre, as you know, is literature, but we aim also at enlisting the man of specialist training who can write for an intelligent non-specialist public'), all in Leavis papers, Col 9.59a, Emmanuel. G. H. Bantock's comments on 'the *Scrutiny* reader' and the idiolect of '*Scrutiny* keywords' indicate that Leavis was not alone in the way he conceived of the journal's public. Bantock, 'Authority and Method in Education', *Scrutiny* 15/4 (December 1948): 289–90.

[27] Harding to Leavis, n.d. [June 1975], Leavis papers, Col 9.59a, Emmanuel; Philip French, 'Leavis at 80—What Has His Influence Been?' *The Listener*, 24 July 1974, 107–10.

concerned to exercise some control on the succession of summations of his career and what he stood for, and he was especially wary of Gross's attempts to co-opt his record. (The new editor of the *Times Literary Supplement*, Gross had previously attacked Leavis and *Scrutiny* in his celebratory history of literary journalism, *The Rise and Fall of the Man of Letters*.)[28] Telling Harding he would rather he did not speak to Hayman or cooperate further with the BBC, Leavis said that 'the boys'—figures such as Gross and Ian Hamilton, who had moved from *The Spectator* to the *New Review*—'command all the means of publicity, they feel, & yet we have survived, & now have a growing élite with us which, being real, is truly to be feared: that's their apprehension. I should like to believe that it's well-grounded. But... '[29] Harding reassured him: 'I'm glad the establishment figures want to make up to you, however firm you remain. I think what they fear is not only a committed élite but the better side of the people they have to recruit to their own ranks, even perhaps their own better side.'[30]

Leavis continued to address himself to this sort of 'élite' even as his work reached a steadily larger readership. (Chatto & Windus sold nearly 8,000 copies of *New Bearings in English Poetry* in the 1950s, far more than it sold in the 1930s when first published.)[31] Leavis undoubtedly was sceptical of the capacity of most people to read in a 'critically adult' fashion. He opposed university expansion partly on the grounds that 'only a limited proportion of any young adult age group is capable of profiting by, or enjoying, university education'—though his experience teaching at the new University of York in the late 1960s prompted him to modify his position somewhat.[32] In any case, there was more to the idea of 'minority culture' than pessimism about the general population's capacity to read and think: minority culture presupposed relationships between multiple publics.

The opening paragraphs of *Mass Civilisation and Minority Culture* bear returning to: 'In any period it is upon a very small minority that the discerning appreciation of art and literature depends: it is... only a few who are capable of unprompted, first-hand judgment. They are still a small minority, though a larger one, who are capable of endorsing such first-hand

---

[28] Collini, 'Critic as Journalist', 171 and n.; John Gross, *The Rise and Fall of the Man of Letters: Aspects of English Literary Life since 1800* (1969; Chicago: Ivan R. Dee, 1992), 285–301.

[29] Leavis to Harding, 23 June 1975, Leavis papers, Col 9.59a, Emmanuel (ellipsis in original). No mention was made of Leavis's former pupil Karl Miller, who was assistant editor of *New Review*.

[30] Harding to Leavis, n.d. (mid-1975), Leavis papers, Col 9.59a, Emmanuel.

[31] Chatto & Windus ledgers, 9/522, 10/399, 11/41, 11/435, 13/141, Reading.

[32] Leavis to *The Times*, 22 January 1968, in Leavis, *Letters in Criticism*, 128; MacKillop, *F. R. Leavis*, 364–5.

judgment by genuine personal response.'[33] What was envisaged here was
a constellation of publics with some ultimate connection to the 'critically
adult public', the critical centre of the culture. This was how the judgements of a tiny minority became 'standards' in past ages; it was why Johnson's unusually 'competent' and 'cultivated' reader could also be a
'common reader'.[34] The 'absence of an intelligent public' in a reciprocal
relationship with contemporary poets explained why Auden's talent went
undeveloped or became malformed, and why, once Auden was uncriti-
cally acclaimed by those who should have been able to enforce standards
of criticism, his name would become 'well-known to the *Listener* public'.
The standards of taste and sensibility obtaining among 'the *Listener* public'
were shaped by the performance or, in the twentieth century, the absence
of, a much smaller 'real public for poetry...capable of appreciating and
checking critically the editorial standards'.[35] Leavis was being hopeful as
well as gloomy: a public brought together around a little magazine or a
critical review such as *Scrutiny* could exert some indirect influence on 'the
Listener public' or the 'relatively large public that goes for guidance to the
Observer and the *Sunday Times*'.[36] In his 'Retrospect' to the Cambridge
University Press reprint of *Scrutiny* in 1963, Leavis said that the journal
had proved that 'even a very small public may...be disproportionately
influential'.[37]

Penguin Books was premised on a very different conception of intellectual life and the 'public'. As a mass-market publisher of 'serious' books,
it assumed that a writer with complicated things to say could communicate directly with a wide readership, rather than working indirectly
through a nucleus of active readers to try to shift the terms of discourse.
Leavis's position was unusual; Penguin's was orthodox.[38] In twentieth-
century Britain, the usual way intellectuals communicated with a large
non-specialist audience was by working in a new register or medium—
broadcasting, writing for national newspapers or weekly magazines, or
writing a Penguin. The Pelican Advisory Group—W. E. Williams, Krishna
Menon, Peter Chalmers-Mitchell, and H. L. Beales—would 'suggest how
to reach readers who had hardly been reached before; but, and this was

[33] F. R. Leavis, 'Mass Civilisation and Minority Culture' (1930), in *For Continuity* (Cambridge: Minority Press, 1933), 13–14.
[34] F. R. Leavis, *How to Teach Reading: A Primer for Ezra Pound* (Cambridge: Minority Press, 1932), 3–4; Leavis, 'What's Wrong with Criticism?', *Scrutiny* 1/2 (September 1932): 145–6.
[35] F. R. Leavis, '"This Poetical Renascence"', *Scrutiny* 2/1 (June 1933): 66, 68–9.
[36] Leavis, 'Mass Civilisation and Minority Culture', 32.
[37] F. R. Leavis, '"Scrutiny": A Retrospect', *Scrutiny*, vol. 20, *A Retrospect, Indexes, Errata* (Cambridge: Cambridge University Press, 1963), 24.
[38] Compare LeMahieu, *Culture for Democracy*, 303.

crucial, not by a fashionable intellectualism, nor by talking down or watering down, but by clear, firm speech. They all believed that it is important, in Forster's phrase, "to connect," and that connecting starts in respect for both the subject and the readers. Allen Lane asked authors to write to the top of their bent for the Judes, the Leonard Basts, the Paul Morels and the Gordon Comstocks.'[39] The quotation is from Richard Hoggart, and some of the touchstones are more his than Penguin's. But there was an identity of style and ambition between teachers and writers such as Hoggart and Penguin Books, which was one reason some of the important works of post-war social and cultural analysis—*The Uses of Literacy*, *Culture and Society*, the sociological best-sellers of the period by Michael Young and Peter Wilmot—reached their huge audiences in Penguin editions. The 'serious "common reader" or "intelligent layman" from any class' to whom Hoggart addressed the book he published with Chatto & Windus turned out to be a similar reader to Penguin's imagined Leonard Bast or Gordon Comstock.[40] What Lane asked of Penguin authors, Hoggart thought, was 'to bank on people's potentialities—the most important of all rules of thumb in a democracy'.[41]

The post-war BBC, too, banked on the potentialities of intelligent lay people, though not all the time, to be sure, and more often on the Home Service and in the programmes and talks produced by the regional studios than on the Light Programme. Even the Third Programme was more proselytizing than its reputation as a minoritarian cloister admits.[42] Leavis's followers, even those, like Denys Thompson, who put their names to endorsements of 'minority culture', usually accepted the BBC ethic of high-minded compromise or the Penguin strategy of working out a style that

[39] Richard Hoggart, *Imagined Life: Life and Times, Volume III, 1959–91* (1992: Oxford: Oxford University Press, 1993), 51.
[40] Richard Hoggart, *The Uses of Literacy: Aspects of Working-Class Life, with Special References to Publications and Entertainments* (London: Chatto & Windus, 1957), 11. Penguin decided to buy the paperback rights to *The Uses of Literacy* less than three months after its hardback publication by Chatto & Windus. The file on the book in the Penguin archives does not mention questions of style or tone. Peter Calvocoressi to Richard Hoggart, 25 May 1957, Hoggart papers, 3/11/9, Sheffield; Eunice Frost to Calvocoressi, 15 May 1957, Penguin archives, DM1107/A431, Bristol. Alan Glover was the book's champion at Penguin. Glover to Frost, 7 May 1957, Penguin archives, DM1107/A431, Bristol.
[41] Hoggart, *Imagined Life*, 51. For more on these issues, see Rick Rylance, 'Reading with a Mission: The Public Sphere of Penguin Books', *Critical Quarterly* 47/4 (2005): 48–66; Nicholas Joicey, 'A Paperback Guide to Progress: Penguin Books 1935–c.1951', *Twentieth Century British History* 4/1 (1993): 25–56.
[42] Humphrey Carpenter, *The Envy of the World: Fifty Years of the BBC Third Programme and Radio 3* (London: Weidenfeld & Nicolson, 1996), chs 1–9. This judgement is also based on my reading of the files on *First Reading*, which showcased new writing, and the Third Programme short story competition of 1948–9: Wain, John: Talks: File 1A: 1950–4; Ludovic Kennedy: Talks [Personal File] I: 1944–62; Short Story Competition, 1948–9, R51/554, BBC WAC.

could carry along an earnest general audience willing to persist with something new.[43] As well as editing *Discrimination and Popular Culture* for Penguin, Thompson was an active broadcaster. When he wrote scripts for school broadcasts in the 1940s and 1950s, the BBC officer he dealt with was John Scupham, who had read English at Emmanuel in the 1920s while Leavis was teaching there, and who had reviewed books for Thompson's *English in Schools*.[44] In 1949, Thompson presented the introductory talk in a Forces Educational Broadcasts series entitled 'Thinking for Yourself', which was 'designed to encourage a critical approach and sales resistance'.[45] The idea came from R. E. Keen of the BBC's Talks Department. Thompson obliged with a script beginning with a dramatization packaging *Scrutiny* messages in a most un-*Scrutiny* genre:

> the family filling up the weekly pools coupon; showing enjoyment, knowledge, some skill.... One or two other examples mentioned to prove that in some spheres we're ardent & competent judges. We enjoy these things because we're critics.... Transition to point that in most departments of life we'd get more out of it if we used judgment. Develop this with examples from Press, Books, Adverts. etc. and one more dramatic sketch: either (a) a series of bullying, whispering or insinuating voices—'Do you suffer from foot odour—even your best friends....' [...] 'Men of good taste....' etc. *or*/ (b) A single example: an advert for some home encyclopaedia, playing (insinuating whispers again) on theme: 'Are you doing enough for your children? .. the trust they place in you... You wouldn't let Your Children Down... Knowledge is the key .. to a place in a grammar school, a £1000 job etc...' The purchase of the thing... disillusion.... etc. etc.[46]

The most substantial exercise in broadcasting *Scrutiny* ideas was the *Pelican Guide to English Literature*, edited by Boris Ford and published in seven volumes between 1954 and 1961. Marilyn Butler has remarked that, through the *Guide*, Ford 'did more than anyone except Leavis himself to disseminate Leavisite views'.[47] The volumes of the *Guide*'s first edition had print runs of 30,000 and took the work of a team of *Scrutiny*

[43] Recalling debates with other pupils and admirers of Leavis during his time at Cambridge, David Matthews attributes to the future director Peter Wood the Reithian desire 'to raise the taste of the general public a little way [rather] than limit himself only to the best'. David Matthews, *Memories of F. R. Leavis* (Bishopstone: Brynmill Press, 2010), 18.

[44] John Cain, 'Scupham, John (1904–1990)', *Oxford Dictionary of National Biography*, <http://www.oxforddnb.com/view/article/39993>, accessed 1 December 2010; Asa Briggs, *The History of Broadcasting in the United Kingdom*, vol. 5, *Competition, 1955–1974* (Oxford: Oxford University Press, 1995), 468–9.

[45] R. E. Keen to Thompson, 29 June 1949, RCONT3: Denys Thompson: Talks Misc. 1943–56, BBC WAC (all ellipses in original except that in square brackets).

[46] Thompson to Kean, 4 July 1949, RCONT3: Denys Thompson: Talks Misc. 1943–56, BBC WAC.

[47] Marilyn Butler, 'Moments', *London Review of Books*, 2 September 1982, 10.

alumni and sympathizers to an audience far greater than those reached by books published by Chatto & Windus, let alone a precarious literary journal such as *Scrutiny* itself. However, a Leavisian approach to literature consisted of more than a collection of Leavisian 'views', and the enterprise of writing for readers outside the minority public Leavis envisioned opens up for analysis the relationships between Leavisian judgements ('views') and Leavisian modes of judging. Like school and adult-education teaching, the business of producing a Penguin version of *Scrutiny* criticism discloses some of the ways the movement's ideas, values, and styles could be rearticulated or reassembled in ways that Leavis himself could not have countenanced. The publishing history of the *Guide* also reveals something of the profile of the *Scrutiny* movement as the journal's own life was coming to an end.

The idea for what became the *Pelican Guide to English Literature* came from Allen Lane himself. At an editorial meeting in 1950, Lane proposed publishing a history of English literature. The simplest option, he thought, would be to reissue the *Concise Cambridge History of English Literature*, first published in 1941.[48] W. E. Williams persuaded Lane that the *Concise Cambridge History* had been badly outdated even when it first appeared.[49] George Sampson, the author of *English for the English*, had been engaged to distill the fourteen-volume *Cambridge History* published between 1907 and 1916 into a single volume and add updates on the intervening years, with predictably unsatisfactory results.[50] Lane told Williams to come up with a better idea. Williams returned from Harmondsworth to the Bureau of Current Affairs' offices and passed the assignment on to Ford, the bureau's chief editor. Ford produced an outline that Williams presented to Lane two weeks later. Because Lane 'worked on the astute principle of accepting ideas from anyone but commissioning the book from someone else', Williams said he would present the scheme as his own and then, if Lane approved of the outline, suggest that Ford be appointed editor. Unexpectedly, Lane suggested they recruit Bonamy Dobrée. (Telling the story many years later, Ford assumed that his audience would share, or at least expect, his horror at the prospect.[51] Although they were on quite

---

[48] Although Penguin published original non-fiction, its fiction list at this time still consisted of reprints, and in the 1930s and 1940s, the time lag between hardcover publication and a paperback edition was usually six or seven years. Stuart Laing, 'The Production of Literature', in Alan Sinfield (ed.), *Society and Literature 1945–1970* (London: Methuen, 1983), 128.

[49] Boris Ford, 'Round and about the *Pelican Guide to English Literature*', in Thompson (ed.), *The Leavises*, 104.

[50] Boris Ford, 'The Concise "C.H.E.L."', *Scrutiny* 10/2 (October 1941): 201, 202–3.

[51] Ford, 'Round and About', 107.

warm terms personally, Leavis took Dobrée to represent two cultural ills: the metropolitan literary world, and Eliot's *Criterion*, to which Dobrée had been a regular contributor.[52]) Williams convinced Lane to choose Ford instead. The fact that Williams would be able to keep an eye on Ford while he remained at the Bureau of Current Affairs was apparently a consideration.[53]

This was not altogether new territory for Ford. As a recent graduate nearly a decade earlier, he had reviewed the *Concise Cambridge History* for *Scrutiny*. In between the rather formulaic revelations of Sampson's faulty judgements of Donne, Milton, and Marvell, the gratuitous references to Pound and Sturt, and a dutiful disparaging of facts for the sake of facts were some reflections on the sorts of 'histories and manuals which one would be glad to have on the shelf'. There was 'an obvious need for an encyclopaedia of literary fact'; but it would also be valuable to have 'a critical history of English literature'. To use the phrase 'critical history' in *Scrutiny* in 1941 was to flirt with paradox. In the judgement of the Leavises and Knights, history, like other forms of scholarship, always threatened to substitute for criticism, not just in the work of E. M. W. Tillyard or Basil Willey, but also in the hands of those, like Bradbrook, who saw themselves primarily as critics. Ford envisaged two types of worthwhile critical history. One would be a history of the 'margin of contact' between society and literature: a 'history which could supply one with the material necessary to an understanding of, for instance, Jonson's satire, or the emergence of modern English prose, of Jane Austen's assurance'. The relevant facts would be 'open to dispute': the desiderated history would look less like a textbook than 'something of the kind supplied by L. C. Knights in relation to Jonson', or even, 'if it had a more specifically literary reference', Willey's work on the intellectual 'background' to the eighteenth and nineteenth centuries.[54]

The other type of valuable critical history would be a more 'internal' literary history that incorporated some original interpretation, enacting criticism rather than simply pronouncing judgement, as the *Concise Cambridge History* had (it contained 'virtually no quotations').[55] A 'critical survey' for a 'general reader' would seek to bring out the 'larger pattern' of a period or arc. Roger Fry's forty-page essay on the evolution of the visual arts was an unsurpassable model, Ford said, an uncharacteristic

[52] F. R. Leavis, ' "Antony and Cleopatra" and "All for Love": A Critical Exercise', *Scrutiny* 5/2 (September 1936): 158; F. R. Leavis to Bonamy Dobrée, 10 January 1944, 13 February 1944, 21 October 1944, 26 July 1948, Bonamy Dobrée correspondence, Leeds.
[53] Ford, 'Round and About', 107.
[54] Ford, 'The Concise "C.H.E.L." ', 204–5.
[55] Ford, 'Round and About', 105.

endorsement of a Bloomsbury product in *Scrutiny*. A student would need much the same as the general reader, 'with the difference that the pattern would be emphasized with minor rather than major talent. Second- and third-rate literature offers no doubt little intrinsic interest, but it reveals very accurately the general health of the artistic patient.'[56]

The *Guide* obviously did much more than implement the proposals Ford made in 1941, but the *Scrutiny* review did encapsulate some of the distinctive ambitions of the later series. Each volume of the *Guide* opened with a lengthy survey of the social setting of the period and a literary survey, providing that 'larger pattern' and an exploration of the 'margin of contact' between literature and society. The *Scrutiny* review and the idea of the *Guide* both presupposed, first, that the function of criticism could be reconciled with that of a survey of literary history; and, second, that criticism could be performed meaningfully for an audience outside the minute 'critically adult public' envisioned in *Mass Civilisation and Minority Culture*. The second assumption, as we shall see, was one F. R. Leavis could not accept; but others involved with *Scrutiny* did. When Ford took his outline to Knights, who had experience in extramural as well as 'internal' university teaching, he was enthusiastic but 'unnerved by the scale of the undertaking'.[57] Knights became a contributor. So did another *Scrutiny* editor, Harding; and so did many others who had written for the journal or studied with Leavis, including David Holbrook, G. H. Bantock, Seymour Betsky, Derek Traversi, L. G. Salingar, G. D. Klingopulos, R. G. Cox, R. C. Churchill, and Frank Whitehead.

Indeed, as they reviewed the typescript of the first volume, on 'the age of Chaucer', senior staff at Penguin came to the conclusion that the *Guide* was unduly dominated by Scrutineers and worried about how reviewers would respond. Alan Glover and others at Penguin were alarmed when they received a commentary they had solicited from Kenneth Allott, the poet and Professor of English at the University of Liverpool. (The Liverpool English department was 'in some ways...conservative', and the university library did not have a run of *Scrutiny*.)[58] Writing as a 'non-specialist', Allott reported that *The Age of Chaucer* was better than he had expected, and a marked improvement on 'an old-fashioned dry-as-dust literary history'. Publishing it would not harm Penguin. However, it was regrettable that 'the wide distribution of Penguins is going to spread the pure *Scrutiny*

---

[56] Ford, 'The Concise "C.H.E.L."', 204–5.

[57] Ford, 'Round and About', 108.

[58] Kenneth Muir, 'English Literature at Liverpool', *Critical Survey* 1/4 (summer 1964): 236; James D. Stewart, Muriel E. Hammond, and Erwin Saenger, *British Union-Catalogue of Periodicals: A Record of the Periodicals of the World, from the Seventeenth Century to the Present Day, in British Libraries*, vol. 4, *S–Z* (London: Butterworths, 1958), 63.

influence so strongly'. The text sported too much 'jargon' and 'some *Scrutiny* rudeness'.[59]

What most bothered Allott was the exclusivity and fixation on 'purity' that he detected in the book. Neither the text nor the notes credited critics who were not linked to *Scrutiny* 'except for purely editorial work. There *must* be some books & articles & viewpoints they could approve. I'm afraid many academic folk will take against the *Guide* because it is EXCLUSIVELY *Scrutiny*.' Other academics 'wouldn't mind a boost for Leavis & his friends if some other critics were mentioned e.g. Bateson & his group, [John Crowe] Ransom in USA (also C[leanth] Brooks & Yvor Winters), various contributors to *Essays in Criticism* etc... There is a lot of agreement now outside *Scrutiny* on the nature of close criticism, on avoiding the old kind of literary history, or dead-end antiquarianism, but you would not gather it from this volume.' Bad in itself, this exclusivity made the *Guide* 'uneven': 'This volume is exclusively written by *Scrutiny* folk & it even uses very inferior contributors on occasion to preserve this "purity" (& good candidates off their particular subjects).'[60] Several weeks after receiving Allott's report, Glover told Ford that he had consulted people outside the company and reported 'a very strongly held opinion in all quarters that to produce a Pelican Guide to English Literature which contains so very high a proportion of writers representing one particular school of criticism—and that a school which is by no means universally approved—might very well have unfortunate repercussions'.[61] Glover's solution was to hold back the medieval volume and publish the volumes out of order, beginning with a more ecumenical one.

'I know that many people regard Scrutineers much like Communists,' Ford retorted, 'and would insist that they dominate (and contaminate?) a literary Popular Front just as Communists do a political P.F.' He told Glover he thought it not entirely fair for Penguin to be 'surprised that the Guide has taken this Cambridge shape', since he had never hidden his intentions.[62] As early as April 1950 he had lent Eunice Frost—the Penguin editor who was formally Allen Lane's secretary and paid accordingly— a copy of *Scrutiny* containing an essay by John Speirs, evidently to give her an idea of what Speirs could do as the lead contributor to *The Age of Chaucer*.[63] Williams had worked in the same building while Ford planned the *Guide* and began recruiting contributors. And, as we have seen,

[59] Kenneth Allott to Glover, 21 February 1953, Penguin archives, 0290.0, Bristol.
[60] Ibid. Italicized capitals replace triple underlining in the original. Ellipsis in original.
[61] Glover to Ford, 12 March 1953, Penguin archives, 0290.0, Bristol.
[62] Ford to Glover, 27 March 1953, Penguin archives, 0290.0, Bristol.
[63] Eunice Frost to Ford, 18 April 1950, Penguin archives, 0290.0, Bristol. Frost thought Speirs's article 'very good and fresh'. On Frost see Lewis, *Penguin Special*, 123–6.

Williams had long been interested in *Scrutiny* and lent institutional support to its spin-offs, so clearly had an idea of what *Scrutiny* stood for. He must have been unaware of how divisive it could seem to university literary critics rather than the adult education tutors and schoolteachers who were his primary educational constituency.

Ford disputed the idea that an association with *Scrutiny* was a liability: not these days, anyway. By now, 'a book by a Scrutiny writer now receives as many favourable reviews as unfavourable'. Oxford dons might anathematize Leavis, Ford told Glover, but their undergraduates admired him. He also disputed the claim that the Chaucer volume was dominated by *Scrutiny* people: 'for some three or four of the contributors [out of a total of ten] are not Scrutineers and the essays of at least two that are Scrutineers are wholly un-Scrutiny-like'.[64] However, if one counts the number of *chapters* by *Scrutiny*-affiliated contributors, the proportions change markedly. Two *Scrutiny* regulars each wrote three chapters of the *Age of Chaucer*. John Speirs, who had covered the medieval angle for *Scrutiny*, wrote the fifty-page survey of poetry at the beginning of the volume as well as two other chapters.[65] Ford did not press the case for volume one strongly and instead emphasized the diversity of the second installment, *The Age of Shakespeare*. L. G. Salingar's contributions were 'brilliantly done, nothing Scrutinyish about them. And the same goes for the essays by Knights and Traversi, both Scrutiny writers, but here writing without any of the "revaluing" tone often associated with Scrutiny. Nearly all the other writers are not Scrutineers.'[66] Rather than issue the volumes out of sequence, Ford suggested, Penguin could publish the Chaucer and Shakespeare volumes simultaneously. After talking to Williams, Frost, and others on Penguin's Editorial Committee, Glover accepted Ford's proposal, and rushed the typescript of the Shakespeare volume to the printers.[67]

Publishing the first two volumes at the same time mitigated Glover's concern about excessive *Scrutiny* influence, but it did not dispel it. His worries issued in a rather comical letter to Salingar, the author of both the framing chapters of the Shakespeare volume.[68] While an undergraduate at

[64] Ford to Glover, 27 March 1953, Penguin archives, 0290.0, Bristol.
[65] John Speirs, 'A Survey of Medieval Verse', in Boris Ford (ed.), *A Guide to English Literature*, vol. 1, *The Age of Chaucer* (Harmondsworth: Penguin, 1954), 17–67. See also Leavis to the *New Statesman*, 13 December 1968, in Leavis, *Letters in Criticism*, 131; Boris Ford, 'John Hastie Speirs', *Emmanuel College Magazine* 62 (1979–80): 97.
[66] Ford to Glover, 27 March 1953, Penguin archives, 0290.0, Bristol.
[67] Glover to Ford, 11 May 1953, Penguin archives, 0290.0, Bristol.
[68] L. G. Salingar, 'The Social Setting', in Boris Ford (ed.), *A Guide to English Literature*, vol. 2, *The Age of Shakespeare* (Harmondsworth: Penguin, 1955), 15–47; Salingar, 'The Elizabethan Renaissance', in Ford (ed.), *Age of Shakespeare*, 51–116.

Trinity College, Salingar had managed to have Leavis take him for supervisions for one term. He knew Leavis 'fairly well' but 'never became one of his inner circle'.[69] When Glover reviewed the typescript of *The Age of Shakespeare*, however, he was suspected Salingar of being a 'Leavisite'. 'I see that in your notes there are a considerable number of references to something which is indicated simply by the use of Roman numerals; for example, "On Neo-Platinism [*sic*] see XLIV." You nowhere make it clear to what these references refer. Are they possibly issues of *Scrutiny*?'[70] Salingar hurriedly explained his cryptic system: the list of further reading was numbered, and the roman numerals in his footnotes were keyed to the numbers of the books in the list.[71]

'[W]e are still not altogether happy about the identification of the series with the Cambridge school', Glover told Ford, '(and one has to remember that it isn't by any means even a unanimous Cambridge school and there is a quite strong and permanent non/anti-Scrutiny element at Cambridge itself).'[72] The disquiet even extended to withdrawing the Pelican badge: 'we can't avoid the feeling that the use of the title "Pelican Guide to English Literature" may seem to suggest that we as a firm are identifying ourselves exclusively, or at any rate chiefly, with the Cambridge school and that this might not be a wise thing to do'. Glover therefore proposed that the first two volumes be issued as independent books 'without, for the moment, using the series title. If, as we hope will be the case, their reception is a favourable one and we do not get slanged by reviewers for having sold ourselves to Dr Leavis and his following, we would then from volume 3 go on with the series under the title *The Pelican Guide to English Literature*; and make it clear in our publicity that the two previous volumes had been part of it and in reprints of them add the series title to them.'[73]

This was, as Ford retorted, to propose 'bringing out a series as if it weren't one and as if it had never been planned as one'. Critics might assume anyway that the volumes would constitute a series. The book-buying public might be less likely to invest in the individual volumes if it did not see them as parts of a worthwhile whole, or suspect that some problem with the third volume had derailed the series. It did not 'seem sensible publishing behaviour', and it would make both Ford and Penguin

[69] L. G. Salingar, untitled essay, *Cambridge Quarterly* 25/4 (1996): 399–400.
[70] Glover to Salingar, 26 June 1953, Penguin archives, 02.0297.8, Bristol.
[71] Salingar to Glover, 27 June 1953, Penguin archives, 02.0297.8, Bristol.
[72] Glover to Ford, 11 May 1953, Penguin archives, 0290.0, Bristol. The original letter actually reads: 'non-anti-Scrutiny'. I have assumed that this was a secretarial error and that the first hyphen should be a slash.
[73] Glover to Ford, 11 May 1953, Penguin archives, 0290.0, Bristol.

'look a little foolish'. He succeeded in persuading Glover to issue the volumes as part of a series, with the general introduction Ford had already written, but the word 'Pelican' did not appear in the titles of the early volumes.[74] In the event, printing troubles undid the plan to publish the second volume alongside the first, and *The Age of Chaucer* appeared by itself in October 1954.[75] The *Times Literary Supplement* gave it a favourable notice.[76] Glover's response to Ford was probably as maddening as it was satisfying: '*TLS* leader an unexpected reaction to volume one [and] should certainly do good.'[77] From volume three onwards, the series was renamed *The Pelican Guide to English Literature*.

Though he sometimes hedged and claimed that the *Guide* represented a greater variety of perspectives than sceptics allowed, Ford acknowledged most of the contributors 'are Cambridge and would probably admit that Scrutiny has had a good deal of influence with them'. To 'throw in a few Oxford and Bloomsbury contributors' would only weaken the series, by unravelling its coherence. The Cambridge and *Scrutiny* orientation was a strength, even 'the *essence* of the Guide'. Right from the beginning, Ford said, 'the point that I have insisted on...and for which I have had apparent support, has been that it should be homogeneous, that it should be written from a consistent standpoint, that the contributors should share a certain general approach to literature and certain broad standards'.[78] Allott appears to have taken the homogeneity of the first volume as a sign of a concerted campaign to exert *Scrutiny*'s influence—the Scrutineer as communist agent. Though the result may have been the same, it makes more sense to see Ford's recruitment of *Scrutiny* people as a consequence of the way *Scrutiny* shaped Ford's literary sensibility and the sorts of criticism he valued.

Scrutiny had never been as uniform as its detractors alleged, but it was not a broad church. An editor who shared the Leavises' assumptions about the value of 'scholarship' would have had trouble regarding someone with a record of publication in the *Review of English Studies* or even *Essays in Criticism* as a good choice to write on medieval literature for the *Guide*. The 'Chaucerian period presents special and peculiar difficulties' for literary criticism, Ford wrote, 'the field being so much the preserve of the crusted academics'. Ford was more or less restating Leavis's judgement of the late 1930s that there was no body of genuine literary criticism of Chaucer, only linguistic, historical, and textual scholarship: there was

[74] Ford to Glover, 16 June 1953, Penguin archives, 0290.0, Bristol.
[75] Glover to Ford, 14 September 1954, Penguin archives, 0290.0, Bristol.
[76] John Speirs to Miss Swann (?), 30 October 1954, Penguin archives, 0290.0, Bristol.
[77] Glover to Ford, 17 November 1954, Penguin archives, 0290.0, Bristol.
[78] Ford to Glover, 27 March 1953, Penguin archives, 0290.0, Bristol.

'nothing' other than the articles Speirs was publishing in *Scrutiny*.[79] In recommending that Penguin have *The Age of Chaucer* checked by a medievalist, Allott acknowledged that there were not many 'with a taste for the critical analysis of literature'; there was 'mutual distrust' between 'scholars & critics'. But there were a few, remote from *Scrutiny*. Allott suggested C. S. Lewis, who was as strong a partisan for Oxford English as Leavis was for 'the essential Cambridge', and not a critic whose premises Ford could have endorsed.[80]

By the same token, *Scrutiny* credentials could substitute for other measures of expertise or aptitude. This is another way of putting Allott's observation that in order to preserve its *Scrutiny* 'purity', the *Guide* used second-rate contributors or 'good candidates off their particular subjects'.[81] Allott was commenting on the medieval volume, but the judgement applies most tellingly to the final instalment, *The Modern Age*. It made sense for Ford to choose G. H. Bantock to write on L. H. Myers, since along with Harding he was one of the novelist's advocates in *Scrutiny*; but only his status as a *Scrutiny* regular can explain Ford's selection of him to write the lengthy introduction on the social and intellectual background of twentieth-century literature.[82] (The two men had of course disagreed heatedly about educational philosophies in the journal's pages.) Not all of Bantock's claims were drawn from *Scrutiny* or consonant with Leavis's positions—unlike Leavis, he found a few reasons for optimism at the beginning of the 1960s[83]—but Leavis was quoted liberally (he got the chapter's last word), and the contentions about the psychological effects of mass culture align with those made in *Culture and Environment* and Denys Thompson's essays from that time. The 'mechanization' of social relationships and personality was the dominant tendency of modernity, and many significant developments in the art and thought of the twentieth century were responses to this challenge. '[T]he cinema and television foster a kind of escapist day-dreaming which is likely to be emotionally exhausting and crippling to apprehensions of the real world': like some of the contributors to *Discrimination and Popular Culture*, Bantock was able

[79] Leavis to Ian Parsons, 16 June 1946, Chatto & Windus archive, CW 100/33, Reading.
[80] Kenneth Allott to Glover, 21 February 1953, Penguin archives, 0290.0, Bristol. Allott wrote of Lewis: 'He is not sympathetic to Leavis, but he is a critic as well as a scholar.'
[81] Allott to Glover, 21 February 1953, Penguin archives, 0290.0, Bristol.
[82] G. H. Bantock, 'The Social and Intellectual Background', in Boris Ford (ed.), *The Pelican Guide to English Literature*, vol. 7, *The Modern Age* (1961; Harmondsworth: Penguin, 1964), 13–48; Bantock, 'L. H. Myers and Bloomsbury', in Ford (ed.), *Modern Age*, 270–9.
[83] Bantock, 'Social and Intellectual Background', 41.

English as a Vocation

to apply *Scrutiny*'s criticisms of interwar films and best-sellers to 1950s television.[84] Television programmes 'of inane triviality sterilize the emotions and standardize the outlook and attitudes of millions of people'. These millions, Bantock reminded his readers, were 'the "educated" and literate descendants of the people who produced the folk song and the folk tale, who built the parish churches and nourished Bunyan'.[85] It is not only the invocation of Bunyan and folk tales that recalls *Culture and Environment*, but also the lingering note of late-Victorian Liberal disillusionment with the achievement of universal literacy.[86] The familiar intertexts of *Scrutiny* cultural criticism were adduced in support of the argument. Bantock quoted I. A. Richards's comments in *Principles of Literary Criticism* about the tendency of 'bad art' to distort people's attitudes and perceptions, and Pound was brought in to pronounce that the debasement of language by the press and popular fiction caused 'the whole machinery of social and of individual thought and order' to go to pot.[87]

D. H. Lawrence loomed over the discussion, not only as a major novelist, but also as Bantock's pre-eminent interpreter of industrial society (Sturt was his authority on the modernization of rural England).[88] In other volumes of the *Guide*, these surveys of the 'margin' between literature and society were grounded in non-literary sources, preparing the way for the more strictly literary discussion in succeeding chapters. Bantock's survey used literature to illuminate society to illuminate literature; it exhibited the circularity of much *Scrutiny* commentary about literature and society. The creative writer, Bantock said, 'pursues his sense of the "real" beneath the level attainable (as yet, at least) by the scientific sociologist; where the latter conceptualizes, the former, at his best, attempts to employ a more unified interplay of feeling and intellect, one which defines itself through the emotive complexities of language. He *feels into* situations rather than subjects them to rational and therefore extraverted analysis. He is essentially the practitioner of *Verstehen*.'[89]

Thus Lawrence out-Webered Weber. Bantock was working with an essentially ethnographic conception of social science, as Thompson and the

[84] Charles Barr, a Lecturer in Film at St John's College, York, wrote in the NATE journal *English in Education* in 1968: 'Leavis has not been personally interested in cinema or television, but his authority has been such that his attitudes tend often to be carried over without re-thinking, even after more than thirty years.' Charles Barr, 'Film and Literature', *English in Education* 2/2 (1968): 58.

[85] Bantock, 'Social and Intellectual Background', 38.

[86] See, for instance, John Garrett Leigh, 'What Do the Masses Read?' *Economic Review* 14/2 (1904): 176, 177.

[87] Bantock, 'Social and Intellectual Background', 38–9.

[88] Ibid., 15–16, 20, 21, 32, 40.

[89] Ibid., 43 (emphasis in original).

Leavises had in the 1930s and as Raymond Williams, in their wake, had in the 1940s.[90] This was a conception of social science licensed, as we have seen, by *Middletown* rather than by Malinowski. The *Scrutiny* tendency to discern affinities between ethnography and literature can also be discerned in Brian Jackson's writings on the sociology of education and the working class in the 1960s. A pupil of Leavis's at Downing who then became involved with the Institute of Community Studies, Jackson was 'explicit in aligning social research with the tradition of the "creative artist"', a paradigmatic example of which was Lawrence.[91]

Andor Gomme's chapter on 'Criticism and the Reading Public' in the same volume was an even more partisan piece of mimicry than Bantock's. Gomme made no mention of William Empson's criticism, and *Essays in Criticism* was mentioned only to be compared unfavourably with *Scrutiny*. The 'essential difference' between the two publications was the difference 'between academic literariness uncontrolled by critical insight, and the benefit of working with a sense of relevance, always in sight of Arnold's "central, truly human point of view"'.[92] *Scrutiny* and Leavis himself were discussed at length. The inevitable Pound quotation about literature, language, thought, and order was reproduced in its entirety, and the first principles of *How to Teach Reading* and *Mass Civilization and Minority Culture* asserted as the basis for thinking about the function of criticism:

> The period has been one of a great general cultural upheaval, in which mass literacy and the enormous increase in the power and range of mass media have been accompanied by an apparently final decay and disintegration of traditional sanctions of belief and behaviour. Thus the literary tradition comes to have a greater importance than ever, as on it alone now depends the possibility of maintaining a link with the past by which we can draw on the collective experience of the race.[93]

> Only on the basis of a common reader who can be appealed to . . . who is part of a homogeneous culture with 'more-than-individual judgement, better than individual taste', can literature flourish and perform its function in the community.[94]

As well as paraphrasing Leavis and even quoting him without attribution, Gomme mimicked his word choices (though not his syntax, with its oral

---

[90] Compare Ortolano, *Two Cultures Controversy*, ch. 4. See also G. H. Bantock, 'Literature and the Social Sciences', *Critical Quarterly* 17/2 (1975): 99–127, esp. 120–4.

[91] Mike Savage, *Identities and Social Change in Britain since 1940: The Politics of Method* (Oxford: Oxford University Press, 2010), 180.

[92] Andor Gomme, 'Criticism and the Reading Public', in Ford (ed.), *Modern Age*, 362.

[93] Ibid., 351. Compare Leavis, 'Mass Civilisation and Minority Culture', 15.

[94] Gomme, 'Criticism and the Reading Public', 352. Compare Leavis, *How to Teach Reading*, 3–4.

pulse and frequent parentheses). The imitation can be seen in the use of
the phrase 'the race', surely archaic in this sense by the early 1960s, and in
the characterization of Auden and company as a 'gang'. Gomme reiterated Leavis's indictment of the backscratching and laxity of standards that
enabled Auden, Spender, Day Lewis, and MacNeice to amount to a 'poetical renascence' three decades earlier. Spender's autobiography, Gomme
remarked in a dismissal more reminiscent of Q. D. Leavis than her husband, was 'a revealing document of the operation of a metropolitan literary clique. It can hardly be recommended on other grounds.'[95]

Gomme had read Moral Sciences at Clare College in the early 1950s,
though when he won a three-year fellowship at the same college, he took
supervisions in English (one of his pupils was Fred Inglis). After some
years as an adult education tutor, he became a lecturer in English at the
new University of Keele.[96] He was not a pupil of Leavis's, nor a close
friend, but he was nevertheless one of 'the whole-hog admirers of later
years', to use Denys Thompson's phrase.[97] Reassessing *Scrutiny* in *Essays in
Criticism* in 1964, after Cambridge University Press had brought out its
reissue, Kenneth Trodd described Gomme's chapter as an 'out of
touch... piece of fossil-writing'. Gomme was so militant, Trodd went on,
that he could not see that 'part, at least, of the battle is won, that large
recognition for the movement arrived a while ago'.[98] Trodd's criticism
coincided with a point Allott made about the first volume of the *Guide*:
Scrutiny had persuaded many people working or studying in English departments that 'close criticism' mattered, and that 'the old kind of literary
history' and 'dead-end antiquarianism' were to be avoided, but the *Guide*'s
authors acted as if these were still embattled heterodoxies.[99]

There are, then, grounds for saying that the *Guide* did much to 'disseminate Leavisite views'. Yet the *Scrutiny* project is not altogether reduc-
ible to specific judgements or even to its critical principles and cultural
and historical assumptions. It was also a particular kind of intellectual act,
one substantially different from the act of assembling a critical history of

[95] Gomme, 'Criticism and the Reading Public', 351, 355, 374 n.
[96] Fred Inglis, 'Andor Gomme: Critic and Architectural Historian', *The Independent*, 30
October 2008; Andor Gomme, untitled essay, *Cambridge Quarterly* 25/4 (1996):
314–15.
[97] Gomme, untitled essay, 314; Denys Thompson, 'Teacher and Friend', in Thompson
(ed.), *The Leavises*, 48.
[98] Kenneth Trodd, 'Report from the Younger Generation', *Essays in Criticism* 14/1 (January 1964): 22–3. Trodd, an Oxford graduate, was teaching at the University of Ghana at
the time. He later worked for the BBC and produced many of Dennis Potter's television
plays. On Trodd's time at Oxford and as a university lecturer in Ghana and Nigeria, see
Humphrey Carpenter, *Dennis Potter: A Biography* (London: Faber & Faber, 1998), 48–50,
134, 158.
[99] Allott to Glover, 21 February 1953, Penguin archives, 0290.0, Bristol.

English literature for an audience of students and lay readers. The survey chapters by Salingar that Ford thought so highly of recalled *Scrutiny* in some of their content, but not in their performative force. Like Knights and Leavis before him, Salingar attributed a measure of Shakespeare's greatness to the interplay between pullulating popular and learned cultures in early modern England. The vitality of Elizabethan and Jacobean theatre was a product not only of Renaissance humanism but also its 'broad contact with popular entertainment and popular thinking, quickened by the Reformation. Above all, it was a vitality of the spoken language, and here, too, the Reformation contributed immensely.' From Tyndale's Bible to the Authorized Version, the Latin and Anglo-Saxon components of the language were hammered into a new medium fit for the word of God. 'Literature gained, in consequence, a vastly sharper sense of the relative values of words and idioms, popular and learned, which was nowhere more active than in the theatre. The drama flourished as long as humanist-trained poets remained closely in touch with popular speech and popular traditions; and as popular influence grew weaker the drama declined.'[100] Earlier in *The Age of Shakespeare*, in the survey of the social context, Salingar had flagged this linguistic conjuncture as one of the distinguishing qualities of the period.[101] The *Scrutiny* genealogy was clear to contemporary readers such as Stuart Hall and Paddy Whannel, who sandwiched the passage from the 'social setting' chapter between block quotations from *Culture and Environment* in one of the later chapters of *The Popular Arts*.[102] But for Salingar in the *Guide*, these ideas did not have what might be called the allegorical power they had had for Leavis and Knights (and, come to that, Hall and Whannel). Salingar was specifying what was distinctive and enabling about the cultural background of early modern England, in order to help readers make sense of the riches of its drama. There was no question of pressing further and presenting this moment as a model, *the* model, for thinking through the relationship between literature and culture.

At the end of the survey of the Elizabethan literary Renaissance, Salingar revisited Knights's version of the 'dissociation of sensibility' thesis. Bacon's *Advancement of Learning* (1605) 'presents the Renaissance view of poetry more arrestingly than Sidney or any other Elizabethan critic; but also, by tone and statement, it sharpens the latent conflict between active reason and the imagination'. The telling *Scrutiny* note was the reference to 'tone' as well as statement: the text, not simply the ideas it articulated, was

---

[100] Salingar, 'The Elizabethan Literary Renaissance', 54.
[101] Salingar, 'The Social Setting', 16.
[102] Hall and Whannel, *Popular Arts*, 376–7.

a motor of cultural change. Bacon's characterization of poetry as 'Feigned History' 'indicates Bacon's severance between the words of poetry and its matter'; of greater consequence for subsequent poetry was his generally 'utilitarian' judgement of poetry and his 'broader, and primary, distinction between the mind of man and the nature of things'. The growing authority of mathematics and the physical sciences appeared to leave no room 'for Nature to vie with fancy; and poetry was to reduce itself, for later neo-classicism, to a clear, neat, and decorative reflexion of the external world.' Salingar concluded: 'The problem of the relations between science and poetry had already been interposed between Bacon, Donne, and Jonson and the succeeding generation of Milton, Marvell, and Hobbes.'[103] The phrase 'dissociation of sensibility' was not used, nor Knights cited. The argument nevertheless traced the contours of Knights's *Scrutiny* essay of 1943 quite closely. Yet the implications for those living and writing after the early eighteenth century were not elaborated on: Salingar did not insist that this 'problem' was one from which 'we' had never recovered.[104] His use of the word 'utilitarian' may have associated Bacon with nineteenth-century calculation; but Knights explicitly made Mill's thought a logical consequence of Bacon's principles, and Bacon the origin of a pressing modern predicament.[105] The modern predicament was not part of Salingar's brief. Having made his point about the dissociation between imagination and reason, he provided a page-long overview of 'the prose of leisure' before bringing the chapter to a close.[106]

Knights's and Leavis's sense of what was at stake in Shakespeare criticism was expressed by Eliot in *The Sacred Wood*: the important critic was 'absorbed in the present problems of art, and…wishes to bring the forces of the past to bear upon the solution of these problems'.[107] For Leavis and Knights, any other approach to the literature of earlier times risked succumbing to the numbing tendencies of 'literary history'. Salingar's chapters, and Ford's scheme for the *Guide* as a whole, presupposed that literary history could be 'critical' and in touch with the living in more oblique ways than a dialogue with the past about how to remake the tradition in the modern age.

Ford told Alan Glover in 1953 that 'neither Dr nor Mrs Leavis are contributing to the Guide and they do not at present feel sympathetic

---

[103] Salingar, 'Elizabethan Literary Renaissance', 113–14.   [104] Ibid., 115.

[105] L. C. Knights, 'Bacon and the Seventeenth-century Dissociation of Sensibility', *Scrutiny* 11/4 (summer 1943): 282 and n.

[106] Salingar, 'Elizabethan Literary Renaissance', 114–15.

[107] T. S. Eliot, 'Imperfect Critics' in *The Sacred Wood: Essays on Poetry and Criticism* (1920; London: Methuen, 1932), 37–8; Leavis, *How to Teach Reading*, 38.

towards it'.[108] When Ford approached F. R. Leavis with a rough outline
for the *Guide*, Leavis expressed doubts that there were enough 'people of
the necessary calibre'. Moreover, the best of them 'wouldn't want, or be
able, to do that kind of writing'.[109] Three years later, when *Scrutiny*
stopped abruptly—several contributions did not materialize and there
were no articles in reserve—Leavis told Holbrook that the *Guide* had si-
phoned off his contributors: 'we couldn't afford to lose *one* essay a
year.... Ford's gain...was Scrutiny's loss. He approached all my main
people.'[110] Ian MacKillop has suggested a further reason for Leavis's reservations about the *Guide*. Judgements in a handbook for students and
readers informally seeking an education could take on a fixity. This was
'quite contrary to *Scrutiny*'s ambition for nimble, opportunistic response
to the present'.[111] This is an attractive explanation, though it runs up
against the fact that alongside the nimbly responsive reviews and sympo-
sia, *Scrutiny* published much that was not very provisional. The bulk of
several of Leavis's books appeared first in *Scrutiny*, and *Revaluation* (1936)
went to the printers not in typescript but as a bundle of annotated '*Scrutiny* galleys which I had saved.... For the last chapter I had no galleys, so
I tore the pages from *Scrutiny*.'[112] Back issues of *Scrutiny* functioned as
reference books. Michael Black recalled: 'many of my weekly essays were
written with the Faculty Library's copy of the relevant volume of *Scrutiny*
on the desk beside me...and I was one of many. Cambridge supervisors
must have sighed as they recognized this week's permutation of the word
from Downing.'[113]

After Leavis's death, Ford wrote that his abstention was 'an unworthy
act of pride'—or perhaps a sign of 'a strange temerity or caution, as if he
hesitated to move outside his role of "guardian" of a minority culture to a
wider and more general readership'. Perhaps Leavis worried that addressing that general readership would entail unacceptable simplification, even
'falsifying what he had to say'.[114] This is a judgement that made sense
within the parameters of Ford's democratic understanding of expertise
and communication, a position shared, with variations, by so many of
Leavis's collaborators and followers in adult education, teacher training,

[108] Ford to Glover, 27 March 1953, Penguin archives, 0290.0, Bristol.
[109] Ford, 'Round and About', 109.
[110] Leavis to Holbrook, 3 December 1953, F. R. Leavis papers, DCPP/LEA/4/8, Downing (emphasis in original).
[111] MacKillop, *F. R. Leavis*, 279–80.
[112] Leavis to Parsons, 3 July 1936, Chatto & Windus archive, CW 63/12, Reading.
Education and the University reached the publisher in a similar state: Leavis to Harold
Raymond, 2 June 1943, Chatto & Windus archive, CW 94/17, Reading.
[113] Michael Black, 'The Long Pursuit', in Thompson (ed.), *The Leavises*, 87.
[114] Ford, 'Round and About', 110.

schools, and even universities: those of his pupils and admirers who held academic teaching posts often taught extension or WEA classes as well, or had spent years as adult education tutors before securing an 'internal' lectureship—a generalization that holds for people as different as Knights, Salingar, and Gomme. The idea of minority culture was an element of Leavis's thinking that his collaborators and followers dispensed with easily. If Ford had been genuinely invested in the idea, he would surely have taken more pains with his logic than he did when he declared: 'I think I might even...suggest that one of the tests of a responsible "minority" concern for literature is its readiness to communicate with...the educated but critically less sophisticated reader who reads for enjoyment and for meaning.'[115] Leavis could not square this circle.

[115] Ford, 'Round and About', 111.

8

Scrutiny's Empire

Scrutiny's history is an international history. F. R. Leavis's conception of the function of criticism and his identification of its enemies inspired reforms and attempted reforms of university English teaching around the British empire. *Scrutiny* was also coupled with New Critical efforts to install criticism (rather than historical and linguistic scholarship) at the centre of English curricula in the United States. To the extent that *Scrutiny* mattered to Americans, it was as a body of bracing reassessments of particular authors and essays on genres: its arguments about contemporary culture and the idea of a university had little impact in the United States.[1] *Scrutiny*'s cultural criticism was pressed into colonial service, however. *Mass Civilisation and Minority Culture* enabled Australia's most important Leavisian thinker to frame the relationship between literature and colonial culture in terms other than those of national identity. And in places as different as India and New Zealand, *Fiction and the Reading Public* suggested ways of thinking about colonial literatures.

Scrutiny's impact outside Britain could be indirect, as students and teachers came across copies of *Scrutiny* or Leavis's books in shops remote from Cambridge. Of course, there were also Cambridge graduates around the world motivated to spread the word. Students of Leavis's got jobs in continental Europe (Freiburg, Nijmegen) and East Asia (Aichiken), but it was in the colonies or former colonies of the formal empire that they had the strongest footholds. A Leavisian presence in a colonial university was unusual, despite claims to the contrary.[2] Colonial English departments based their curricula on the Oxford and University of London models rather than Cambridge's example, a choice reflected in the frequent division of departments into 'literature' and 'language' (or early English) wings. University colleges in the empire were often formally or informally governed by the federal University of London, not an institution where *Scrutiny* made an unusually deep impact. Two important African university

---

[1] However, see R. J. Kaufmann's reflections in 'F. R. Leavis: The Morality of Mind', *Critical Quarterly* 1/3 (1959): 249–50.

[2] Simon Gikandi, 'Globalization and the Claims of Postcoloniality', *South Atlantic Quarterly* 100/3 (2001): 650–3; Derek Attridge, *Joyce Effects: On Language, Theory, and History* (Cambridge: Cambridge University Press, 2000), 1–2.

colleges of this type, Makarere and Ibadan in Nigeria, have been described as having 'Leavisite' English departments on the basis of only slight or problematic evidence.[3]

In the English department Derek Attridge entered as a University of Natal undergraduate in the early 1960s, however, Leavis was the 'guiding spirit': 'the curriculum was based, for poetry, on the winnowed canon he presented in *Revaluation* and *New Bearings*, for fiction, on the equally circumscribed list of writers celebrated in *The Great Tradition*, and, for methodology, on "close reading" or "practical criticism"'.[4] R. T. Jones, a Downing pupil of Leavis's, had taught at Natal since the mid-1950s, rising to senior lecturer by 1962.[5] Jones was a strong believer in Leavis's mission. His proposal to have an entire run of *Scrutiny* reprinted by the University of Natal Library ultimately led to the Cambridge University Press reissue in 1963, which brought complete sets of the journal to most British (and many Commonwealth) university and training college libraries for the first time.[6]

---

[3] Gikandi, 'Globalization and the Claims of Postcoloniality', 650 n. 57, says: 'The fact that Leavis's students and disciples ran the major centers of literary studies in the British colonial world should be taken as axiomatic', but for specific cases he refers the reader to Carol Sicherman, 'Ngugi's Colonial Education: "The Subversion ... of the African Mind"', *African Studies Review* 38/3 (1995): 11–41; and Robert M. Wren, *Those Magical Years: The Making of Nigerian Literature at Ibadan: 1948–1966* (Washington, DC: Three Continents Press, 1991). The interview-based profiles of Ibadan lecturers and professors in ch. 2 of Wren's book provide no evidence that I can discern of Leavisite commitments or styles. Sicherman suggests (16) that Ngugi's teachers at Makarere College 'took an Arnoldian, Leavisite approach to the texts', but this seems an overstatement. The grounds for the claim are the moralism of the teaching (not unique to Leavis, of course) and the premium placed on Dickens, Lawrence, and Conrad. This is to project Leavis's later dedication to Dickens back to the time of *The Great Tradition*; and there are other reasons why British lecturers might push Conrad in an African university. Gikandi's book on Ngugi also takes it as axiomatic that Ngugi's education at Makarere was 'Leavisite'; when he does cite an authority, it is Sicherman's article. Simon Gikandi, *Ngugi wa Thiong'o* (Cambridge: Cambridge University Press, 2000), 36, 47, 249, 300 n. 15. Ngugi himself has said that Leavis, Eliot, and Arnold 'dominated our daily essays' at Makarere in the late 1950s and early 1960s. However, a syllabus heavy on Spenser and Milton cannot have been organized on very Leavisian lines. Ngũgĩ wa Thiong'o, *Decolonising the Mind: The Politics of Language in African Literature* (London: James Currey, 1986), 90.

[4] Attridge, *Joyce Effects*, 1–2.

[5] 'Appointments and Awards, Etc.', *NL* (1957): 38; 'Appointments, Honours, Etc.', *NL* (1962): 28.

[6] Ian MacKillop, *F. R. Leavis: A Life in Criticism* (London: Allen Lane, 1995), 309; Leavis to R. T. Jones, 31 October 1959, F. R. Leavis papers, DCPP/LEA/15/28, Downing. Other Downing English graduates who taught in South Africa include J. C. F. (Roy) Littlewood at Stellenbosch, the pre-eminent Afrikaner university, in the 1950s before returning to Britain to teach at Leeds and then Bristol; and Michael Vaughan, who was teaching in the English department at the University of Natal's Durban campus in the 1980s. 'Appointments and Awards', *NL* (1955): 19; 'Obituaries', *NL* (1986): 19 (Littlewood); 'Appointments, Retirements and Distinctions', *NL* (1985): 13 (Vaughan). W. A. Edwards, an early *Scrutiny* contributor, taught at the University of Cape Town from 1934 to 1941. His time at the University of Western Australia is discussed briefly below, 229–30.

Getting access to *Scrutiny* and other critical periodicals bedevilled teachers in colonial universities. 'I have tried in vain to find any reference to the *Calendar of Modern Letters*, *The Criterion* or *Scrutiny* in the catalogues of many university libraries' in India, wrote C. D. Narasimhaiah. [7] The number of bookshops on the subcontinent handling *Scrutiny* subscriptions or ordering copies of issues as they came out could be counted on one hand.[8] When Narasimhaiah went from the state of Mysore and its university to study at Cambridge in the late 1940s, he had not even heard of Leavis. His tutor at Christ's College encouraged him to attend Leavis's seminars, and the experience left a deep imprint on his career. On his return to Mysore he attempted to reform university examination papers to make them more in tune with *Scrutiny* values. He also launched a journal of his own, to which Leavis generously contributed an essay.[9] The difficulty in acquiring recent books of British criticism in Ceylon was a chronic problem that the Second World War made acute. In 1944, when teachers preparing pupils for the university entrance examinations told E. F. C. Ludowyk, the professor of English at the University of Ceylon, that they could not get hold of the books he recommended, he decided the best thing he could do as a stopgap measure was to put together a *Scrutiny* primer. Asking Leavis for permission, Ludowyk stressed that he wanted only short excerpts—from *Scrutiny* and from *Education and the University*, *Revaluation*, and *Fiction and the Reading Public*—so as not to spoil the whole works for the students if they got the chance to read them later. Leavis gave his blessing and persuaded Chatto & Windus to give Ludowyk carte blanche.[10]

A member of Ceylon's Dutch community, Ludowyk was one of the students from the empire who mingled with Knights, Thompson, and other

---

[7] C. D. Narasimhaiah, *'N for Nobody': Autobiography of an English Teacher* (Delhi: B. R. Publishing Corporation, 1991), 60.

[8] The two surviving sales ledgers kept by *Scrutiny*'s distributors, Deighton, Bell, & Co., date from the second half of the 1940s and early 1950s. The first records three bookshops taking out subscriptions on behalf of clients. Those in Calcutta and Delhi bought a single subscription each; the Minerva Bookshop in Lahore bought five or six copies of each new issue between 1945 and 1948. (*Scrutiny* trade sales ledger, 1945–9, 7, 79, 87, Deighton, Bell, & Co. archives, Add. 9453, B5/1, CUL.) The ledger for the early 1950s records three subscriptions from bookshops or news agencies on the subcontinent: the same agency in Delhi, and two in Pakistan. (*Scrutiny* 'looseleaf ledger', Deighton, Bell, & Co. archives, Add. 9453, B5/2, CUL [pages unnumbered]: Euro-Pakistan News Agency, Narayangunj Dacca [1952–3]; Ideal Book House, Lahore [1951, 1953]; Newsco International, Delhi [1950, 1952].) It is possible that subscriptions taken out by London news agencies were destined for the subcontinent.

[9] Narasimhaiah, *'N for Nobody'*, 31–2, 55, 62, 128–31, 177–91, 256.

[10] Harold Raymond to F. R. Leavis, 28 August 1944, Chatto & Windus archive, CW 100/33, Reading.

research students at the Leavises' house on the eve of *Scrutiny*.[11] On his return to Colombo, he became 'a power in Ceylon education', in Leavis's words.[12] In the succeeding decades there was some further traffic in personnel between the two institutions. Leavis met, and thought well of, some of Ludowyk's students.[13] One of them, Upali Amarasinghe, went to Downing College as a research student in 1952 and completed a thesis about Augustan poetry before returning to the University of Ceylon as a lecturer.[14] Two Downing English graduates, David Craig and Robin Mayhead (the latter a *Scrutiny* contributor), lectured there in the 1950s and early 1960s.[15]

Like many colonial professors, Ludowyk was at once an ambassador for the metropole and someone who wanted to lose himself in a sustaining local or indigenous culture, on which he wrote several books. He pointedly used the first person plural when musing on the predicament of English in a colonial setting: 'English is studied as if it were the natural expression of the people of this country, when we should, if it is to be of any value to us, remember at all times that it is the expression of a culture very different from ours.' The challenges of that undertaking could be 'evaded as they so often are, by substituting for literary studies drill and dogma'.[16] Literary criticism of the sort Leavis practised was not only an alternative to 'drill and dogma', but a way of challenging dogmas of various kinds. Practical criticism was a species of the clear, unsettling reason that would be needed if Europeans were to chip away at their systematized misunderstanding of colonized peoples. 'The West has to unlearn a great deal it has come to believe about the East', he wrote in 1957; the training of practical criticism was among other things a training in unlearning. Richards's practical criticism lectures clarified the 'high destiny of Comparative Literature'.[17]

In his 1944 book *Marginal Comments*, Ludowyk sought to broker the work of Richards and Leavis to a local audience, and especially to teachers

[11] MacKillop. *F. R. Leavis*, 143–4; Percy Colin-Thomé, 'Memoir', in E. F. C. Ludowyk, *Those Long Afternoons: Childhood in Colonial Ceylon* (Colombo: Lake House Bookshop, 1989), xvii–xviii.

[12] Leavis to Raymond, 25 August 1944, Chatto & Windus archive, CW 100/33, Reading.

[13] F. R. Leavis to D. F. Pocock, 31 July 1953, F. R. Leavis papers, Col 9.59.121, Emmanuel.

[14] Amarasinghe moved to the University of Malaya shortly afterwards, before dying at the age of 30 in 1959. 'News of Members', *NL* (1960): 29–30; admissions book (archivist), Downing.

[15] 'Honours, Appointments, Etc.', *NL* (1960): 31; [Council for Academic Freedom and Democracy,] *The Craig Affair: Background to the Case of Dr David Craig and Others, Lancaster University* (London: Council for Academic Freedom and Democracy, 1972), 1.

[16] E. F. C. Ludowyk, *Marginal Comments* (Colombo: Ola Book Company, 1945), iv.

[17] E. F. C. Ludowyk, 'The East-West Problem in Sinhalese Literature', *Yearbook of Comparative and General Literature* 6 (1957): 35.

of the upper forms in high schools (English was the medium of secondary education before independence in 1947, and on into the 1950s).[18] In that respect, *Marginal Comments* complemented Ludowyk's *Scrutiny* primer for teachers. Ludowyk apologized to his readers for referring to Richards and Leavis 'in a way that might suggest to the reader unfamiliar with it that they were canonical authority', and he regretted treating their work 'as if it had been some handy general purposes drug': but since the book was written 'to make good an unhappy lack of information', the awkwardness was unavoidable.[19] Ludowyk praised Richards for his 'fine critical work' as well as for his theoretical contributions, and Leavis for the perceptiveness of his readings and his focus on 'the only material on which it is safe to base valuations of literature—the culture the literature articulates'. He added, however, that Leavis's interpretations were sometimes strained. 'The critical rigour and the brilliance of the intelligence seem sometimes deflected from their true end by the moralist's desire to hold fast to threatened values.'[20]

Although *Marginal Comments* was intended to introduce Cambridge English to teachers in Ceylon, it was not a survey of the main figures' writings. Instead, Ludowyk discussed a series of problems—imagery, symbols, myth, and so on—in a way that reflected what he had learned from the Cambridge school, sometimes referring in passing to their work. The chapter on 'The Sentimental, The Pathetic and the Sublime', for instance, mentioned Leavis's reading of Keats in *Revaluation* several times. Ludowyk also made frequent asides on the Singhalese and Tamil languages, and about the way in which the context of English and English teaching in Ceylon affected the issues at hand. The book's title may have alluded to its colonial predicament as well as the author's subordination to his canonical authorities.

In an excursus on examinees' responses to a poem, Ludowyk described the assumptions he sought to challenge. Some of the would-be undergraduates proved laughably guileless; others had clearly been drilled to respond as they did. 'Alliteration paid the biggest dividends. In most cases it worked its way into onomatopoeia and ultimately to a memory of Pope's "the sound must be the echo to the sense".... This was selected as the typical manifestation of the poet's power. What had been taught was repeated, and as it seemed to be the duty of the candidates to discover this mark of poetic power they speedily found it.' Candidates who had learned

---

[18] Robin Mayhead, 'Changing English in Two Young Dominions', *Universities Quarterly* 12/4 (August 1958): 428–9.

[19] Ludowyk, *Marginal Comments*, 1–2.

[20] Ibid., 2–3.

the rules of prosody duly identified caesuras. Others supplied 'history of literature lumber—the references to classical and romantic, metaphysical, etc'. Here Ludowyk nodded to his epigraph from Leavis's *Education and the University*: without first-hand judgement, the accumulation of facts about literature was just 'so much lumber'.[21] Ludowyk borrowed Leavis's diagnosis of the failings of existing approaches to the teaching of literature as well as his positive prescriptions.

Ludowyk sought Leavis's advice as he reorganized the Colombo curriculum along the principles of the Cambridge tripos.[22] The filtering down of 'the practical critical approach' into the schools had predictable unintended consequences as well as the desired ones. Too many students starting university, Mayhead reported in *Use of English* in the mid-1960s, arrived with only 'a muddled hash of notions culled from Leavis, Richards and Empson'. As a result, a 'new set of "stock responses"' had appeared. As Raymond Williams's adult students learned to hunt for objective correlatives, so did the Ceylon freshers agree reflexively that a poem's meaning was never on the surface; that Eliot's idea of impersonality meant that an overtly emotional poem was a poor one; and that metrical regularity was a bad thing and its converse a good thing. 'Clare's *My Early Home* and the banal song *Beneath the Lights of Home* on a "Criticism in Practice" Reading Sheet produced a large majority in favour of the latter purely on this score.'[23] Mayhead had been using the sixth-form exercises from *Use of English* on Ceylon undergraduates.

Cambridge English graduates who worked in universities characteristically found themselves at odds with custodians of an Oxford or London tradition of English studies that placed more emphasis on scholarship than criticism. The distinction can seem artificial, especially after mid-century, when, as Kenneth Allott told Penguin, a majority of English lecturers accepted the value of the sort of criticism practised in *Scrutiny*. As Francis Mulhern has observed, F. W. Bateson's journal *Essays in Criticism*, launched in 1951, was both a cause and a consequence of the accommodation between the scholarly and the critical.[24] Yet powerful academics such as Helen Gardner and C. S. Lewis continued to press the case for English-as-scholarship (notwithstanding Lewis's own accomplishments as a critic), and professors such as Knights and Empson worried

[21] Ludowyk, *Marginal Comments*, 23, 34; F. R. Leavis, *Education and the University: A Sketch for an 'English School'* (London: Chatto & Windus, 1943), 68.

[22] Alan Filreis, *Wallace Stevens and the Actual World* (Princeton: Princeton University Press, 1991), 328 n. 81.

[23] Robin Mayhead, 'English at the University of Ceylon', *Use of English* 7/4 (1965): 272–3.

[24] Francis Mulhern, *The Moment of 'Scrutiny'* (London: New Left Books, 1979), 324; F. W. Bateson, 'The Function of Criticism at the Present Time', *Essays in Criticism* 3/1 (1953): 26–7.

that the academic standing of literary scholarship threatened the prospects of critics whose careers they had a stake in.[25] Nowhere was the conflict between Leavisian critics and the adherents of a professedly Oxonian scholarly tradition more acute than in Australia, where for three years in the 1960s, a new professor much influenced by Leavis recast the University of Sydney's English department, leading to a schism in which, in effect, two rival departments would compete for students. The Australian case is one of the two foci of the following discussion of criticism and scholarship. The other, complementary case is the transatlantic moment of the 1940s and 1950s, when American critics made efforts to welcome *Scrutiny* as an ally or complement to the New Criticism.

In his last years, Leavis was very pessimistic about American intellectual life and the prospects for universities in the United States.[26] As late as the 1950s, though, he could still find succour in a belief in 'a small, real and decisive Cross-Atlantic community'.[27] The Americans Marius Bewley, Seymour Betsky, and John Farrelly had brought fresh perspectives and personal styles to the Downing English school, and Donald Culver's familiarity with American journals such as *Symposium* and *Hound and Horn* had decisively shaped the early *Scrutiny*. Culver's old teacher at Princeton, Willard Thorp, had given Culver and Knights advice as they planned the new journal, and he contributed to early numbers.[28] Leavis and *Scrutiny* had other admirers in the American academy. The critic H. M. McLuhan, later 'Marshall McLuhan', media guru, was an ardent admirer, though never a pupil. After graduating from the University of Manitoba, he read for a second BA at Trinity Hall with Lionel Elvin in the mid-1930s before taking up teaching positions in Wisconsin and St Louis. When he returned to Cambridge to begin a PhD it was under the supervision of M. C. Bradbrook. But he did visit the Doughty Society to speak on 'American Universities'. In the *Sewanee Review* in 1944, he set out a case for the superiority of Leavis's critical practice to Richards's and Empson's. McLuhan 'amplified the critical judgments of Leavis with the fervor of a true believer'. He modelled experimental classes at the University

---

[25] William Empson to [W. A.] Sanderson, 22 January 1958; Empson to L. C. Knights, 27 December 1966, William Empson papers, bMS Eng 1401, Houghton Library, Harvard University, both reprinted in John Haffenden (ed.), *Selected Letters of William Empson* (Oxford: Oxford University Press, 2006), 276–8, 423–4.

[26] F. R. Leavis, 'Élites, Oligarchies and an Educated Public', in *Nor Shall My Sword: Discourses on Pluralism, Compassion, and Social Hope* (London: Chatto & Windus, 1972), 206; Donald Davie, *These the Companions: Recollections* (Cambridge: Cambridge University Press, 1982), 159.

[27] Leavis to Lionel Trilling, 26 January 1952, Lionel Trilling papers, box 7, folder 3, Columbia.

[28] MacKillop, *F. R. Leavis*, 144–5; L. C. Knights, untitled essay, *Cambridge Quarterly* 25/4 (1996): 358 n.

of Wisconsin on *Culture and Environment*, and his first book, *The Mechanical Bride: The Folklore of Industrial Man* harked back to *Culture and Environment* in its analysis of advertisements and the (primarily American) tradition of commentary on the 'machine age' on which Leavis and Thompson drew heavily.[29]

American interest in Leavis and *Scrutiny* was concentrated in the late 1940s and early 1950s. The orders by American bookshops recorded in *Scrutiny*'s distribution ledgers tended to come, unsurprisingly, from shops located near universities (though two subscriptions were purchased from a Pittsburgh department store).[30] The largest cluster of bookshops stocking *Scrutiny* and managing subscriptions for clients was in Chicago. Two of these shops catered to the University of Chicago. One bought ten copies of each new issue from the end of 1948, and the other paid for five subscriptions the following year.[31] The Chicago English department did not have strong personal and disciplinary ties to *Scrutiny* or Cambridge. Academics and students at Chicago were most likely alerted to *Scrutiny* by the publication in 1948 of Eric Bentley's hefty anthology for American readers, *The Importance of Scrutiny*. Nearly all the American orders recorded in the *Scrutiny* sales ledger date from within a year of its appearance.

Bentley's publisher, George W. Stewart, had approached Leavis the year before. 'Partly because of Eric Bentley's enthusiastic comments about *Scrutiny*, Mr Knights & you... in the 1946 issue of the *Kenyon Review*, we recently published [Knights's] *Explorations* & hope to publish your *Revaluation* this fall. Bentley... now writes us suggesting the publication of a *Scrutiny Reader*.' Mindful of the success of a selection from *Partisan Review*, Stewart was keen to publish a *Scrutiny* anthology. He thought Bentley would make a good editor, but realized that Leavis might prefer to do it himself. Bentley had told Stewart he would edit the volume ' "if you get Leavis's approval. I don't know how much he approves of me, if at all" '.[32] He did: asking Harding what he thought of the idea, Leavis said that

---

[29] Philip Marchand, *Marshall McLuhan: The Medium and the Messenger* (1989; Cambridge, Mass.: MIT Press, 1998), 35–47, 49, 60–4, 116–19 (quotation from 40); Doughty Society minute book, unnumbered page, DCCS/4/4/1/1, Downing.

[30] Trade sales ledger, 24 (in Philadelphia near the University of Pennsylvania), 63, 103 (Princeton), 65, 90 (Harvard Square), 72 (Kenyon College, Gambier, Ohio), 74 (the Columbia University Bookstore), 93 (on the edge of the University of Minnesota campus), 116 (in Madison, a block away from the University of Wisconsin), 127 (New Haven, close to the Yale campus), Deighton, Bell, & Co. archives, Add. 9453, B5/1, CUL. The department store sales are recorded ibid., 105.

[31] Trade sales ledger, 26, 106, Deighton, Bell, & Co. archives, Add. 9453, B5/1, CUL. Dealings with bookshops elsewhere in the city are recorded ibid., 101, 116, 117.

[32] F. R. Leavis to D. W. Harding, 25 June [1947], F. R. Leavis papers, Col 9.59a, Emmanuel, quoting Stewart quoting Bentley. When Chatto & Windus reprinted Leavis's *New Bearings in English Poetry* in January 1950, the print order included '520 with Geo. Stewart imprint'. Chatto & Windus ledgers, 11/41, Reading.

Bentley 'seems very amenable & quite judicious'.[33] As Leavis told Harding, Bentley was English but had now 'settled in the American academic world'. The anthology was 'to be on a large scale, the idea being to make it (sets of *Scrutiny* being unobtainable) a classic in American "English Schools"'. Leavis felt confident in the book's success, given the appreciative comments about *Scrutiny* appearing in American journals and the volume of letters he received from Americans. He told Harding his feeling was that 'if we're to be introduced, it's best that it shall be a large selection, one that shows the general context & circumstances of our literary criticism'.[34]

Bentley did not know Leavis personally, and he had never been published in *Scrutiny*.[35] In two respects, he was an unlikely candidate for *Scrutiny*'s standard-bearer in the United States. He was a drama critic, not an area in which *Scrutiny* invested much, and he had been a pupil of C. S. Lewis at Oxford.[36] Lewis remained a mentor, but Bentley did devote the concluding section of his introduction to seeing off Lewis's defence in *Rehabilitations* ('note the anti-Leavisian title') of Anglo-Saxon studies and his dismissal of the idea that reading the work of one's contemporaries required any tuition. Bentley endorsed Leavis's case for the importance of modern literature and the necessity of critical training in order to be able to appreciate it.[37] Bentley did not belabour the deadening effects of a preoccupation with scholarship or 'learning' in his introduction—though the volume did reproduce Leavis's debate with Bateson over the place of scholarship—but he was recruiting *Scrutiny* to the cause of the New Criticism. Right from the beginning of the volume, Leavis and *Scrutiny* were brought under the umbrella of the New Criticism, alongside John Crowe Ransom, R. P. Blackmur, Cleanth Brooks, and Robert Penn Warren—and Empson.[38] Bentley even dedicated the book to Ransom, which rankled with Leavis, since the contents were not really Bentley's to give away as a sixtieth birthday present to Ransom.[39]

If, in these 'placing' moves, Bentley was using *Scrutiny* to shore up the authority of the New Criticism, as his introduction unfolded it identified qualities in Leavis and *Scrutiny* that he judged lacking in the New Criticism, or in the New Criticism as practised by the disciples rather than the

[33] Leavis to Harding, 25 June [1947], Leavis papers, Col 9.59a, Emmanuel.

[34] Leavis to Harding, 23 November 1947, Leavis papers, Col 9.59a, Emmanuel.

[35] Eric Bentley, 'Introduction' in Bentley (ed.), *The Importance of Scrutiny: Selections from 'Scrutiny: a Quarterly Review', 1932–1948* (New York: George W. Stewart, 1948), xxvi.

[36] Jonathan Kalb, 'A Critic Has Praise for a Playwright (Himself)', *New York Times*, 12 November 2006.

[37] Bentley, 'Introduction', xxiii–xxvi.

[38] Ibid., xiii.

[39] Bentley (ed.), *Importance of Scrutiny*, v; Leavis to Harding, 31 March 1965, Leavis papers, Col 9.59a, Emmanuel. Bentley had not asked Leavis's permission.

masters. Leavis was concerned with judgement as well as explication; *Scrutiny's* critique was a matter of sensibility as well as technique. After Brooks and Warren's textbook, *Understanding Poetry* (1938), introduced college freshmen to the rudiments of the New Criticism, there had been a boom in 'expounding and explaining', which was 'good as far as it goes'.[40] Leavis always went further. His insistence on revaluing authors and works and his aversion to joining clubs guaranteed *Scrutiny* clear-sightedness as well as independence.[41] While American critics, 'once they have accepted a modernist author, tend to be overawed by him', *Scrutiny* had been severe on authors it had championed. And while 'literary people in general waited till recently to discover that Lawrence was great, and that Aldous Huxley is not great, *Scrutiny* made the correct appraisals from the start'.[42] All these qualities—the insistence on judgement, if not rank-ing, the premium on sensibility as well as deft explication, and the break-ing of idols—were manifest in one of Bentley's selections, Leavis's 1937 essay on D. H. Lawrence's posthumous papers, which segued into an argument against Eliot's critical and cultural values as well as a valuation of Lawrence.

The Importance of Scrutiny treated *Scrutiny* as a fairly strictly literary journal. Bentley reproduced nothing by Thompson and the only cultural criticism that made it into the volume did so through the back door, via Q. D. Leavis's 'sociological note' on the values informing the dilettantish tradition of literary study exemplified by George Gordon, and a blazing essay on feminism, education, and women's careers that Bentley would not have anthologized if it had not also been a review of Woolf's *Three Guineas*.[43] Bentley headed one section '*Scrutiny* and Modern Culture', but it was mostly about the nature of criticism—this was the section that included the Leavis–Bateson debate of the 1930s, as well as the exchange between Leavis and René Wellek in 1937, in which Leavis famously or infamously declined to spell out the theoretical substructure of his criti-cism. The debates over Marxism in the 1930s registered in one of the editorials Bentley reproduced, but Leavis's fullest statement on Marxism, materialism, and culture, 'Under Which King, Bezonian?', was absent.

The *Scrutiny* legacy as conveyed by Bentley's volume to American crit-ics and graduate students consisted of a sequence of essays on the nature

[40] Bentley, 'Introduction', xii, xxii.
[41] 'My experience with the British Council abroad has I think some relevance here. It was felt as painfully bad to have *Scrutiny* stop publication, because foreigners felt so sure it was honest. Dr Leavis often seems to me very wrong-headed, but he both appears and is very incorruptible'. Empson to Sanderson, 22 January 1958, in Haffenden (ed.), *Selected Letters of William Empson*, 277–8.
[42] Bentley, 'Introduction', xxv.
[43] It appeared in the final section, 'A Modern Miscellany', paired with an essay on Woolf by W. H. Mellers, and after pieces on Eliot, Lawrence, Auden, Joyce, and others.

and function of criticism (the editorial manifestoes, the debates with Bateson and Wellek, essays on Richards and on Johnson, Coleridge, Arnold, and Eliot as critics by Leavis and D. W. Harding) and a body of literary judgements. The volume included six essays or short reviews about Shakespeare and Shakespeare criticism, along with neighbouring essays on genres, such as Leavis's 'Tragedy and the "Medium"' and Knights's 'Notes on Comedy'. Otherwise, there was very little relating to the seventeenth century, which was so important to *Scrutiny*—no dispatches from the Milton wars, for instance. Bentley included nothing on the eighteenth century except for the essay on Johnson as critic, and the novel before the twentieth century was served only by an essay on Dickens by R. C. Churchill, Bentley's anthology predating the Leavises' turn to Dickens. Nearly half the book was given over to *Scrutiny* takes on modern writers. Bentley reproduced eight essays or reviews concerning Eliot. Pieces by Leavis and Harding figured most prominently, but Bentley also published the work of more peripheral *Scrutiny* contributors, including a number of Downing College students. Godfrey Lienhardt, not Leavis, supplied the critical valuation of Auden.

Bentley had enlisted *Scrutiny* in a campaign to lever 'criticism' into the privileged position hitherto held by 'scholarship' in English departments in the United States. He was also a participant in another initiative in the same campaign, the summer school at Kenyon College. The college was the base of Ransom and, of course, the *Kenyon Review*. When Ransom applied to the Rockefeller Foundation for the grant that made the Kenyon school possible, he stressed that the better students were not satisfied with the accumulation of 'facts which are important but largely sub-literary, and which are not being consistently employed with intelligent purpose'. Those students knew that 'critics have a deeper and more enlightened interest in the creative process as a human adventure'. It was these students to whom the School of English—initially referred to as the 'School of Criticism'—would appeal, and it would 'bring literary criticism into the academy more rapidly, by teaching it to those who are going to be teachers'.[44] 'My view of the aim of the School', Lionel Trilling wrote after

---

[44] Gerald Graff, *Professing Literature: An Institutional History* (1987; Chicago: University of Chicago Press, 2007), 158; David H. Stevens to Gordon K. Chalmers, 29 January 1947, Trilling papers, box 12, folder 4, Columbia. The School of English removed to the University of Indiana in 1951, after the grant from the Rockefeller Foundation ran out. Renamed the School of Letters, it was run by Indiana professors with Ransom and Trilling remaining as senior fellows; Philip Rahv, Austin Warren, and Allen Tate were assigned this title too. No critic associated with *Scrutiny* or Downing College appears in the correspondent list in the finding aid for the Indiana University School of Letters Director's Records, 1947–79, at the Indiana University Office of University Archives and Records Management.

the first session, '. . . is that it should focus attention on criticism and shake up the English departments by its existence.'[45]

Most of the Kenyon school's instructors, and the 'fellows' who constituted its 'group of permanent advisors', worked in American universities.[46] Ransom, Trilling, and F. O. Matthiessen of Harvard, the third member of the executive council of 'senior fellows', also recruited some British critics as fellows: Knights, Empson, Herbert Read, and Basil Willey, with whom Trilling was friendly.[47] The organizers were keen to get critics from Britain over to Ohio to teach. 'I should like . . . to have us approach both Eliot and Leavis with a view to getting one of them over next summer', Ransom told Trilling in 1947.[48] Both men were approached. Neither cabled, as they had been asked to do if they accepted, and Ransom assumed neither would come.[49] They continued to pursue Eliot, but apparently not Leavis.[50] Knights accepted an invitation to teach, and spent the summer of 1950 in Gambier, the sole representative of the *Scrutiny* movement in the school's three years there.[51] When students and instructors played softball in off-hours, he captained the Scrutineers; Empson's team was the Ambiguities.[52] Ransom was elated by Empson's acceptance of an invitation to teach at the first session in 1948, when he would showcase parts of his forthcoming *Structure of Complex Words*. 'Empson has a magnificent subject, along his lines, and is all steamed up over the thing; and there's nobody, not even Eliot, who could advertise us better.' The students treated Empson as a cult figure during the two summers he spent at Kenyon.[53] Not for nothing did Leavis observe: 'Empson is a great power in America.'[54]

Empson's work was assigned in the 1950 Kenyon course on 'Philosophy of Criticism' alongside Eliot, Trilling, Brooks, and Richards, whose *Principles of Literary Criticism* was the one book students were especially

---

[45] Trilling to Ransom, 23 August 1949, Trilling papers, box 14, folder 2, Columbia.
[46] *The Kenyon School of English: At Kenyon College: Second Session Summer 1949* (Gambier; Kenyon College, n.d.), 3, copy in School of English papers, box 1, Kenyon, Brooks, Austin Warren, Yvor Winters, Kenneth Burke, Arthur Mizener, Allen Tate, R. P. Blackmur, and others served as fellows or instructors. Eric Bentley too was a fellow, and taught courses on drama at Kenyon.
[47] Basil Willey to Trilling, 1 November 1947, Trilling papers, box 13, folder 1; Willey to Trilling, 4 March 1948, Trilling papers, box 13, folder 3, Columbia.
[48] Ransom to Trilling, 5 November 1947, Trilling papers, box 8, folder 2, Columbia.
[49] Ibid.
[50] Ransom to Trilling, 4 October 1948, Trilling papers, box 8, folder 2, Columbia.
[51] L. C. Knights to Trilling, 12 July 1950, Trilling papers, box 14, folder 3, Columbia.
[52] Knights, untitled essay, 358 n.; John Haffenden, *William Empson*, vol. 2, *Against the Christians* (Oxford: Oxford University Press, 2006), 203.
[53] Haffenden, *Against the Christians*, 127, 200–3.
[54] He added: '—very much more so than Richards'. Leavis to Harding, 7 August 1951, Leavis papers, Col 9.59a, Emmanuel.

advised to purchase. No *Scrutiny* critic was mentioned.[55] Bentley might see Ransom, Empson, and Leavis as engaged in the same enterprise, but the critical procedures on display in *Scrutiny* were less assimilable to the increasingly formalist practices of the New Criticism than the bravura 'verbal analysis' of Empson's *Seven Types of Ambiguity* and *The Structure of Complex Words*—though in annexing Empson's work, the American critics glossed over his disagreement with their rejection of authorial intent as a matter worthy of critical attention (a disagreement Empson was happy to go on prosecuting).[56]

Knights, though no slouch as a close reader, did not offer anything as close to the New Critical project as Empson did. He taught a course on Shakespeare and gave a public lecture on 'Literature and the Study of Society' (his inaugural lecture at Sheffield in 1947 had the same title).[57] Knights's exploration of the interplay between literary works and their social and historical contexts had proved suggestive to Raymond Williams and other adult education tutors as they sought to relate literary studies to social transformations. Part of the appeal of his thinking may have been his conviction that the social could be 'read' through literature: criticism could incorporate historical considerations without surrendering to 'scholarship'. Trilling had thought that the contexts of literature were not attended to sufficiently in the summer school's offerings: 'I feel that graduate training in literature', he told Ransom in 1949, 'should include a large knowledge of the older literature with at least some—and I think a heavy—emphasis on historical and cultural matters; our tendency is not that at all: most of our courses are in modern and contemporary subjects and with a strong aesthetic or formal slant.'[58] Whether Trilling actually looked to Knights to supply this perspective at Kenyon is not disclosed by his correspondence with Ransom. In any case, Knights's contribution to the School of English was complementary or tangential: the *Scrutiny* tradition was not being harnessed to any great extent to the campaign to entrench the New Criticism in the American academy.

Australia was another site of friction between criticism and scholarship: but there students and admirers of Leavis were the chief actors. The University of Western Australia had appointed a Scrutineer to its chair in

[55] Typed information sheet for students and auditors at the 1950 session, School of English papers, box 1, Kenyon. The class was taught by Philip Blair Rice, a philosopher and the associate editor of the *Kenyon Review*.
[56] Frank Kermode, '"Disgusting"', in *Bury Place Papers: Essays from the London Review of Books* (London: London Review of Books, 2009), 244–5.
[57] 'Kenyon College: The School of English: Forum Program for 1950', School of English papers, box 1, Kenyon.
[58] Trilling to Ransom, 23 August 1949, Trilling papers, box 14, folder 2, Columbia.

English as early as the 1940s. This was W. A. Edwards, another of the postgraduate researchers who congregated at the Leavises' house in Chesterton Hall Crescent at the beginning of the 1930s.[59] Edwards was working on Jacobean drama and contributed a 'revaluation' of John Webster backing up Leavis and Wilson Knight on the need to read poetic drama as a genre radically different from the sorts of drama that had flourished since Ibsen. He also taught tutorial classes, and reflected on the challenges of adult education in an essay for *Scrutiny*.[60] He arrived in Perth, still only 31, after six years lecturing at the University of Cape Town. He brought with him a reputation for immense energy, some of which was channelled into reforming English studies at the university and training schoolteachers.[61]

The main Leavisian presence in Australia was at the University of Melbourne from the 1950s to the 1970s, a group that removed to the University of Sydney for several years in the 1960s, when its leading figure, S. L. (Sam) Goldberg, was appointed to a chair there. As an undergraduate at the University of Melbourne in the mid-1940s, Goldberg was exceptionally conscientious and conscientiously exceptional. With the support of his mentor, Professor Ian Maxwell, Goldberg left Melbourne for Oxford to study for a BLitt, as Maxwell himself had.[62] At Oxford his application to work on Joyce was rejected and he decamped to the sixteenth century to write on the historian Sir John Hayward under the supervision of David Nichol Smith. Like other Oxford students of this time, Goldberg began to read Leavis eagerly.[63] However, he did not adopt Leavis's judgements wholesale, and the abiding interest of the first decade and more of his career, Joyce, was never a pivotal figure in Leavis's 'tradition' or

[59] E. H. McCormick, 'In the 1930s: Cambridge to New Zealand', in Ian MacKillop and Richard Storer (eds), *F. R. Leavis: Essays and Documents* (Sheffield: Sheffield Academic Press, 1995), 229.

[60] W. A. Edwards, 'Revaluations (1): John Webster', *Scrutiny* 2/1 (June 1933): 12–23; Edwards, 'Ideals and Facts in Adult Education', *Scrutiny* 3/1 (June 1934): 91–101.

[61] Leigh Dale, *The English Men: Professing Literature in Australian Universities* (Toowoomba, Queensland: Association for the Study of Australian Literature, 1997), 114–16; Fred Alexander, *Campus at Crawley: A Narrative and Critical Appreciation of the First Fifty Years of the University of Western Australia* (Melbourne: F. W. Cheshire, 1963), 203. The campus bookshop handled only a single subscription to *Scrutiny* in the late 1940s. Trade sales ledger, 112, Deighton, Bell, & Co. archives, Add. 9453, B5/1, CUL.

[62] Jane Grant, 'A Critical Mind: On Sam Goldberg', *Meanjin* 69/1 (2010): 45–6. On the Oxford BLitt degree, see D. J. Palmer, *The Rise of English Studies: An Account of the Study of English Language and Literature from Its Origins to the Making of the Oxford English School* (London: Oxford University Press, 1965), 127.

[63] 'S. L. Goldberg', in Richard Freadman (ed.), *Literature, Criticism, and the Universities: Interviews with Leonie Kramer, S. L. Goldberg, and Howard Felperin* (Perth: International Specialized Book Services, 1983), 19, 20.

his conception of literature. The Joyce critics Goldberg argued with in *The Classical Temper*, his 1961 book on *Ulysses*, were mostly Americans, and Leavis was not an overt presence.[64] Goldberg has, however, been characterized as one of those 'who did their best to save Joyce for the Great Tradition, stressing the humanity and precision of his portrayals of human life and minimizing his games with the medium of representation'.[65] Quite a long time after reading Leavis, Goldberg met him. Q. D. Leavis described him in 1963 as 'a man we've met & know a good deal of & like'.[66]

When Goldberg returned to the Melbourne department as a lecturer in 1953, Vincent Buckley, who was also interested in Leavis, became his chief interlocutor. They came to perceive Leavis's criticism as inadequate for comprehending tragedy and the 'metaphysical' questions prompted by literature more generally.[67] Buckley, a poet and a liberal and politically active Catholic, was never a disciple, but he was sufficiently interested in Leavis as to write about him in depth, alongside Arnold and Eliot, in his book *Poetry and Morality*.[68] Buckley began writing the book as a thesis under Willey while at Cambridge from 1955 to 1957; in his autobiography he said he could not remember 'whether it was he or I who first suggested that I drop my thesis and write a book'.[69] Though he let his chance at a Cambridge PhD lapse, Buckley secured another credential as a critic: his book was published by Chatto & Windus in 1959. (Chatto published Goldberg's book too.)

Unlike Buckley and Goldberg, Maggie O'Keefe and T. B. (Jock) Tomlinson, who married in the mid-1950s, were unambiguously partisan admirers of Leavis and *Scrutiny*. Their commitment to Cambridge English was so strong that they both went off to Cambridge in the late 1950s, not to undertake doctorates, but to complete Part II of the English tripos, Maggie at Newnham College and Jock at St John's. Thus two people who

[64] See S. L. Goldberg, *The Classical Temper: A Study of James Joyce's 'Ulysses'* (London: Chatto & Windus, 1961), 18–19.

[65] Attridge, *Joyce Effects*, 3; see also 179.

[66] 'S. L. Goldberg', in Freadman (ed.), *Literature, Criticism, and the Universities*, 20; Q. D. Leavis to David Craig, 26 November 1963, Q. D. Leavis papers, GCPP Leavis 2/1/7, Girton.

[67] Grant, 'Critical Mind', 47; 'S. L. Goldberg', in Freadman (ed.), *Literature, Criticism, and the Universities*, 19–20.

[68] John M. Wright, 'Grasping the Cosmic Jugular: *Golden Builders* Revisited', *Journal of the Association for the Study of Australian Literature* (2010), <http://www.nla.gov.au/openpublish/index.php/jasal/article/view/1412/1939>, accessed 25 July 2011; Vincent Buckley, *Poetry and Morality: Studies on the Criticism of Matthew Arnold, T. S. Eliot and F. R. Leavis* (1959; London: Chatto & Windus, 1961).

[69] Vincent Buckley, *Cutting Green Hay: Friendships, Movements and Cultural Conflicts in Australia's Great Decades* (Melbourne: Allen Lane/Penguin, 1983), 93; Chris Wallace-Crabbe, 'Buckley, Vincent Thomas (1925–1988)', *Australian Dictionary of Biography*, vol. 17 (Melbourne: Melbourne University Press, 2007), 152–4.

had been teaching at Melbourne University from the early 1950s graduated BA from Cambridge in 1960 and 1961.[70] Even before their time in
Cambridge, the Tomlinsons acted as members of a Leavisian cell of which
Goldberg was the leader.

Its organ was the *Melbourne Critical Review*, a staff–student annual
launched in 1958 with Goldberg as the primary editor. He asked the
Leavises themselves for contributions. F. R. Leavis allowed the journal to
publish his Richmond lecture.[71] When Q. D. Leavis was unable, for
family reasons, to contribute, she wrote to a former Downing student—
David Craig, recently returned from Colombo—suggesting he do so. She
told him that the *Melbourne Critical Review* had been launched 'as a successor to *Scrutiny*' and now reached 'a serious university public in Australia, [the] U.S.A & other parts of the world'.[72] Essays by Melbourne
students and their teachers took *The Great Tradition* or the *Scrutiny* Shakespeare criticism of Leavis, Knights, and Derek Traversi as starting points;
a review of Neville Shute's novel *On the Beach* began by quoting Richards
on the way bad art fixed immature ways of thinking and perceiving.[73]
Philippa Moody echoed the verdicts of the Richmond lecture (Snow
'cannot be taken seriously as a writer') and borrowed its premise or gambit.
Leavis had said that Snow was 'a portent': what was worth considering
was not his thesis, but the fact that it could be taken seriously at the
present time.[74] Moody opened: 'I would suggest…that one very good
argument for the discussion of contemporary novels is this: that although,
with a few exceptions the novels themselves may not merit any very serious or prolonged consideration, their vogue, in which we all participate,
does.'[75]

Maggie Tomlinson could pastiche the fluent denunciations characteristic
of Q. D. Leavis's style:

> Dr Tillyard has said of the prose of *Henry IV*: 'Some of [it] has a perfect
> polish that may go beyond any similar quality in the verse. This prose is the
> property of the Prince and of Falstaff; it is derived from the best things in
> Lyly's plays; and it looks forward to the elegancies of Congreve.' It surely
> annihilates them. The qualities in *The Way of the World* that prompt the

[70] *The Cambridge University List of Members 1973–1974* (Cambridge: Cambridge
University Press, 1974), 1159.
[71] F. R. Leavis, 'Two Cultures? The Significance of C. P. Snow', *Melbourne Critical
Review* 5 (1962): 90–101.
[72] Q. D. Leavis to Craig, 26 November 1963, Q. D. Leavis papers, GCPP Leavis 2/1/7,
Girton.
[73] David Moody, 'Mr Shute's Apocalypse', *Melbourne Critical Review* 2 (1959): 100.
[74] F. R. Leavis, 'Two Cultures? The Significance of Lord Snow', in *Nor Shall My Sword*, 42.
[75] Philippa Moody, 'In the Lavatory of the Athenaeum: Post-war English Novels', *Melbourne Critical Review* 6 (1963): 83.

adjective 'brilliant' are obvious enough, but one has only to think of the comparison with Shakespeare to feel that the brilliance is dangerously febrile. There is a kind of nervous constriction about Congreve's wit...

The assertion that a textual quality was 'obvious enough' to an implied 'us' was characteristic of *Scrutiny* criticism, and the appeal to Shakespeare as the standard and the quasi-medical criticism of Congreve suggest an effort to sound like the Leavises. The foil was familiar too, of course. Tomlinson went on to make other criticisms of Tillyard: his 'scholarly' thesis that Hal was a study of 'the kingly type' 'insults Shakespeare's humanity and our intelligence. It is a particularly crude form of that historicist fallacy which asks us to suppress our own clear responses to literature in favour of shaky hypotheses about "what an Elizabethan audience would have thought."'[76]

Tillyard and his scholarship were regular targets of the *Melbourne Critical Review*. Wilbur Sanders regretted that Tillyard had used Sir John Davies's *Orchestra* (1596) to illustrate Elizabethan cosmology, 'not because the treatment is unscholarly', but because focusing on its representativeness obscured its 'solid, and therefore timeless, poetic achievement'.[77] The journal's appeal for contributions expressed the *Scrutiny* case for criticism over scholarship in Leavisian language: 'The only proviso—one implicit in our title—is that we seek *critical* essays, in which literary scholarship or history is absorbed and given relevance in a living response to literature *as* literature.'[78]

Yet the *Review* had room for heterodoxy and dissent. A. D. (David) Moody, a New Zealander who joined the Melbourne department in 1958 after studying at Oxford, contributed a probing essay on Gardner, Lewis, and Graham Hough, each of whom had mounted book-length attacks on the sorts of criticism for which Leavis stood. Moody worried not so much about the 'scholarism' of Lewis and Gardner's definition of proper literary study, but about the attendant notion that literature was something to be merely enjoyed. Moody preferred Leavis's argument—he quoted *Education and the University*—that exploring literature was an experience that could humanize. But Leavis and his epigones could be excessive, ideological, in their moralism. This fault was on display on the final volume of the *Pelican Guide to English Literature*, *The Modern Age*, which, as we have seen, included some 'fossilized' versions of *Scrutiny* contentions. Moody

---

[76] Maggie Tomlinson, '*Henry IV*', *Melbourne Critical Review* 6 (1963): 3–4.

[77] Wilbur Sanders, 'Philosophy and Sensibility in Poetry', *Melbourne Critical Review* 1 (1958): 32.

[78] 'Editorial', *Melbourne Critical Review* 4 (1961): 2. The editorial added that despite the variety of critics these days, they possessed a unity of interest: 'it is our common pursuit that a journal such as this may try to further'.

did not confine himself to a criticism of followers such as Bantock, but dissected some of Leavis's own writings that manifested these failures. Leavis's zeal, Moody suggested, made him insufficiently aware of the contexts in which critical faculties had to be exercised. Leavis had defended a swingeing judgement of Katherine Mansfield that Lawrence made in a letter to her. 'Lawrence's genius manifested itself in sympathetic insight and an accompanying diagnostic intelligence', Leavis said. The letter was 'no more to be called "cruel" than medicine would be'. Moody argued that Leavis's investment in Lawrence and evaluative 'diagnosis' led him to blur distinctions between what was legitimate in criticism or literature and what was humane in personal relationships. If the study of literature was to be humanizing, those pursuing it had to do their best to avoid warring factions; critics and scholars should cooperate.[79]

Critics and scholars did cooperate at Melbourne, though not without friction. Students became aware that Goldberg, the Tomlinsons, and others sympathetic to Leavis and *Scrutiny* had reservations about the critical permissiveness of Professor Maxwell and others in the department.[80] The ensuing disputes were mild, however. 'The establishment was rather vague about what it collectively and genteelly stood for', Moody has recalled, 'and the younger and newer just had some fairly strong and clear ideas about what should be on the syllabus and how they would teach it'.[81] Things were different when Goldberg moved to Sydney in 1963.[82]

Goldberg was appointed in the autumn of the 'god professor', as local usage had it. He was vested with the resources and, it appeared, the authority to reorganize its curriculum and culture as he saw fit. Q. D. Leavis told David Craig in 1963 that Goldberg was 'building up an English school... staffed by Cambridge Eng. Lit. products where possible'.[83] Two recent Downing College BAs were hired, John Wiltshire and Howard Jacobson (who would later mine his sojourn at Sydney University for comic material in his novels). Michael Wilding, an Oxford graduate, was recruited through the offices of Wallace Robson, an Oxford admirer of Leavis who contributed to the *Pelican Guide*.[84] Goldberg was also able to

---

[79] A. D. Moody, 'Retreating from Literature: Scholarism and Ideology', *Melbourne Critical Review* 6 (1963): 110–22 (quotation from 120–1).

[80] Grant, 'Critical Mind', 48–9.

[81] David Moody to Jane Grant, 28 August 2009, quoted in Grant, 'Critical Mind', 48–9.

[82] For a brief narrative, see W. F. Connell, G. E. Sherington, B. H. Fletcher, C. Turney, and U. Bygott, *Australia's First: A History of the University of Sydney*, vol. 2, *1940–1990* (Sydney: Hale & Iremonger, 1995), 140–2.

[83] Q. D. Leavis to Craig, 26 November 1963, Q. D. Leavis papers, GCPP Leavis 2/1/7, Girton.

[84] Michael Wilding, 'Among Leavisites', *Southerly* 59/3–4 (1999): 67; 'Professor W. W. Robson: Obituary', *The Times*, 5 August 1993.

import the Tomlinsons as lecturers and several other former Melbourne students (and in some cases *Review* contributors) as tutors: Wilbur Sanders, Andrew Deacon, Peter Nicholls, and Germaine Greer, who left to study for her doctorate at Cambridge soon afterwards.[85] In Australian academic folklore, Goldberg and his allies are usually cast in the role of 'the Leavisites'.[86] However, not all of the junior staff brought up from Melbourne identified strongly with Leavis and *Scrutiny*. Inasmuch as 'Professor Goldberg and his followers' were 'Leavisites', M. C. Bradbrook observed in 1971, having toured Australia several years earlier under the auspices of the British Council, they were 'Leavisites of a curious local brand'.[87]

At Sydney, Goldberg wielded an authority unusual for a 'Leavisite' (a label that he eventually gave up resisting).[88] The typical role of a university English department's 'usual resident Leavisite' was that of gadfly or 'conscience', unsettling the perceived complacency or concentration on 'scholarship' prevailing among the majority.[89] Looking back, Wilding remarked: 'Leavisism in power was not the same as Leavisism in opposition. In opposition it had a dialectical, leavening effect on the system within which it operated. In power it became totalitarian.'[90] That word is unhelpful, and it is doubtful whether Goldberg's critical convictions should be blamed for his leadership style, but the opportunity to reorder a large English department along Leavisian lines was indeed unprecedented.

The old dispensation, Wiltshire recalled, was 'a Sydney literary culture in which a combination of old-style Oxford scholarship with a loose laissez-faire cynicism had taken on the semblance of an adequate philosophy'.[91] What Wiltshire took for laissez-faire cynicism others perceived as tolerant pluralism.[92] That the Sydney English department was guided by a tradition of 'old-style Oxford scholarship' is less controversial. A faith in literary

[85] John Wiltshire, untitled essay, *Cambridge Quarterly* 25/4 (1996): 415–16, 417–18; Wilding, 'Among Leavisites', 82.
[86] Andrew Riemer, *Sandstone Gothic: Confessions of an Accidental Academic* (Sydney: Allen & Unwin, 1998); John Docker, *In a Critical Condition: Reading Australian Literature* (Melbourne: Penguin, 1984), 1–14. See also Wiltshire, untitled essay, 416, 420.
[87] M. C. Bradbrook, 'What Is Cambridge English?' (typescript, 1971), 3, M. C. Bradbrook papers, Bradbrook 47/429, Girton; and see also Peter Nicholls's recollections, quoted in Sophie Cunningham, 'Alien Star', *Meanjin* 62/1 (2003): 103.
[88] 'S. L. Goldberg', in Freadman (ed.), *Literature, Criticism, and the Universities*, 19.
[89] The phrase 'usual resident Leavisite' is Michael Bell's: Bell, untitled essay, *Cambridge Quarterly* 25/4 (1996): 305.
[90] Wilding, 'Among Leavisites', 82.
[91] Wiltshire, untitled essay, 420.
[92] Riemer, *Sandstone Gothic*, 29; Wilding, 'Among Leavisites', 80. See also John Docker, *Australian Cultural Elites: Intellectual Traditions in Sydney and Melbourne* (Sydney: Angus & Robertson, 1974), chs 6–8, esp. p. 130.

scholarship as exemplified by Oxford was diffused among academics who had been educated entirely in Australia as well as those who had been at Oxford. Promising Sydney graduates were encouraged to apply there rather than other British universities to continue their education. They could be helped on their way by members of the department who cultivated their ties to Oxford.[93] Thelma Herring epitomized the Sydney–Oxford complex. She had been the top MA student in English at the University of Sydney in 1941, and won a scholarship to Oxford for postgraduate study.[94] She was overpoweringly erudite about early modern English literature and had a command of Greek; she was more historicist than literary-critical; she believed in coverage rather than selectivity. Andrew Riemer came to respect Herring as a colleague, but as a student he had found her tedious. 'I...resented the relentless way in which she dealt with the ranks of minor writers and their work, most of which I had not read and had little intention, or indeed opportunity, of reading.' Herring believed in the sort of literary history Leavis had battled since *How to Teach Reading*: one concerned with the past for its own sake, not with what was living and capable of being brought to bear on the present.[95] 'An ossified Oxford English is everywhere', Bradbrook wrote of the Australian university scene in 1967 in a postcard to her colleagues back at Girton College; '—not only Oxford but Merton, & quite meaningless in the modern context. The Melburnian Leavisites became more explicable against this background...'[96]

As an Oxford graduate himself, Goldberg knew that tradition from within. His first move against the Sydney status quo was to overhaul the undergraduate syllabus. The details were thrashed out in a series of long meetings, but the curricular policy was set by the professor. No longer would the department offer 'a comprehensive survey of literature from the end of the sixteenth century onwards'. Close reading and discrimination were promoted at the expensive of scholarship and coverage.[97] Sydney students were introduced to the practical criticism and 'dating' classes that Goldberg and Jock Tomlinson had taught at Melbourne: Goldberg would hand out sheets of unattributed poems and ask the students to work out their provenance 'unaided by anything apart from the words on

[93] Riemer, *Sandstone Gothic*, 12, 34, 150, 151.
[94] Cassandra Pybus, *The Devil and James McAuley* (St Lucia, Queensland: University of Queensland Press, 1999), 23–4; 'Social News and Gossip', *Sunday Herald* (Sydney), 6 November 1949.
[95] Riemer, *Sandstone Gothic*, 114–15, 135, 143–5.
[96] M. C. Bradbrook to the members of the Combination Room, Girton College, 10 May 1967, Bradbrook papers, Bradbrook 36/418, Girton.
[97] Riemer, *Sandstone Gothic*, 134–5.

the page'.[98] More unusually, Jock Tomlinson would ask his Melbourne students to date passages from thrillers and westerns.[99] Goldberg also instituted a history-of-ideas course, something Cambridge English was known for (Leavis had sketched a replacement for Cambridge's 'nugatory' Literature, Life and Thought paper in *Education and the University*).[100] The range of authors and texts to be studied contracted dramatically. After the Goldberg curriculum was established in 1964, Riemer remarks, it was almost impossible to avoid Lawrence; English majors had to study both *The Rainbow* and *Women in Love* two years running.[101] The canon was rigid and some classes approximated the 'Leavisite' caricatures sketched by the movement's enemies. One student recalls a class on *Sons and Lovers*. Maggie Tomlinson gave the students notice that the following week her husband would be discussing Alan Sillitoe's *Saturday Night and Sunday Morning*, made to play the part of the inferior novel of Nottinghamshire working class. She said he had not read it yet, but knew it was no good.[102]

The Tomlinsons served as dependable lieutenants to Goldberg, but on critical questions the new staff did not form a unified bloc. A dissident group gathered around Jacobson and Wiltshire, who are said to have had doubts about some of Goldberg's positions, such as his stress on metaphysical over moral questions.[103] In the beginning, some of the locals were receptive to Goldberg's plans: paring back the syllabus would acknowledge the practical reality of what students could be expected to read thoughtfully in the time available. There was apprehension about what the new professor would do, but it was later that the department became irreparably divided, as a consequence of the manner in which Goldberg pursued his reforms. People were eventually forced, by overt confrontations in meetings as well as by the general pressure of the situation, to take sides.[104]

The leader of the other side was G. A. Wilkes, a Sydney insider whom many had expected to ascend to the Challis chair. Instead, he was appointed to a less prestigious professorship, the new chair in Australian literature. Wilkes quietly and adeptly gathered together and reassured

[98] June Factor, untitled essay in Hume Dow (ed.), *More Memories of Melbourne University: Undergraduate Life in the Years since 1919* (Melbourne: Hutchinson of Australia, 1985), 125.
[99] Cunningham, 'Alien Star', 103.
[100] Jane Grant, email to the author, 21 May 2011; Leavis, *Education and the University*, 48.
[101] Riemer, *Sandstone Gothic*, 150–1.
[102] Richard Waterhouse, conversation with the author, 13 March 2011.
[103] Docker, *In a Critical Condition*, 5; Wilding, 'Among Leavisites', 85. See also Nicholls's comments quoted in Cunningham, 'Alien Star', 103.
[104] Wilding, 'Among Leavisites', 90; Riemer, *Sandstone Gothic*, 141, 175–7.

those unhappy with the new order, and eventually exploited a clause in his contract to put forward a radical proposal. The terms of the chair in Australian literature stipulated that the professor would also have some responsibility for the teaching of 'English literature', which was generally regarded—certainly by Goldberg—as the province of the Challis Professor of English Literature.[105] The university administration's thinking seems to have been that anyone appointed to the Australian chair should also be competent to teach in the other areas the department covered.[106] In what a professor from another department described as 'a fantastic misinterpretation' of his conditions of appointment, Wilkes now proposed that he and sympathetic colleagues should offer an alternative suite of undergraduate courses in English.[107] Essentially, Wilkes was proposing that the English department split in two, with one staff and one curriculum led by Goldberg, and a second staff and a second curriculum led by him. Alongside the still fairly new courses reflecting Goldberg's conception of English, there would be non-Leavisian 'alternative courses'.

Wilkes's 'English B' offerings were at once an innovation and a restoration of the ancien régime. They provided 'for the study of particular literary periods in some depth, through the work of the major authors and with references to the literary genres and conventions of the time': periods and conventions over singular or transcendent texts. The scholarly allegiances of Wilkes's alternative courses were manifest in the prescription for the honours curriculum: 'Critical theory and literary criticism' was an elective course, but '*English Scholarship*: palaeography, bibliography, editorial procedure' was compulsory. Third-year students would now study 'the rise of the novel in the seventeenth and eighteenth centuries', reading Fielding, Richardson, Stern, and others whose novels Leavis told students to read in the bath, not wasting time on them.[108]

A majority of the English department supported the idea of running parallel curricula and the proposal went to a meeting of the Faculty of Arts, at which all tenured members of academic staff could vote. Wilkes said that the alternative courses 'were put forward not as a criticism of existing courses but as a way of diversifying the study of English'. Goldberg said that, 'in the interests of harmony in the department of English', he would not oppose Wilkes's motion, and then listed some objections,

[105] Faculty of Arts minute book, 55 (11 November 1965), G3/1/8, Sydney.
[106] Ibid., 56 (11 November 1965).
[107] Ibid. The professor quoted was R. N. Spann, Professor of Government and Public Administration. Spann had been a member of the committee that set up the chair in Australian literature.
[108] Faculty of Arts minute book, 28, 29 (29 September 1965), 58 (11 November 1965), G3/1/8, Sydney; Tony Inglis, untitled essay, *Cambridge Quarterly* 25/4 (1996): 35.

one of which was that the new arrangements would confuse the students.[109] Goldberg was making an unconvincing attempt to play the academic statesman, forsaking his customary role, the confident critic flushed with disciplinary authority. He did not say: my courses channel the energies of the discipline at its best; Wilkes's courses will ensure that Sydney remains a backwater.[110] Goldberg must have decided that he could not win at the faculty meeting and would resume the fight when the proposal went up to the university-wide Professorial Board. There, concerns about the alternative courses were expressed most forcefully by the Professor of Latin, who persuaded the Professorial Board to send it back to the Faculty of Arts to vote on again. No amendment was mooted: the board was in effect asking the faculty if it was really sure it wanted to do this.[111] When the Faculty of Arts met again to consider the English B courses, the Deputy Vice-Chancellor was invited along to clarify the remit of Wilkes's professorship and make it clear that the administration would tolerate the department schism. The meeting approved the alternative courses a second time by a comfortable margin.[112]

The faculty's decision was the beginning of the end of the Goldberg experiment. The duelling curricula remained in place for several years, but within months of the faculty vote Goldberg had successfully applied for a chair at Melbourne University. The Tomlinsons followed him back. Junior members of the Goldberg group left for further study overseas or positions elsewhere. Back at Melbourne, Goldberg exercised the control over teaching that he had been denied at Sydney. In their second year, students took classes and sat examinations in practical criticism.[113] The department gained a reputation as a Leavisian centre. When Goldberg left Melbourne for a research position at the Australian National University in Canberra in 1976, the appointment of his successor was, if anything, even more of a rupture than his own naming to the Challis chair had been. Howard Felperin had come from Yale, the centre of 'deconstruction in America'. Confronted by 'this last outpost of Leavisite imperialism', he was unimpressed by a 'literary puritanism...with its self-righteous scrupulosity and unflinching last judgements'. To the extent that 'the "plain style" I found in Melbourne had become the expression of an unconscious reflex rather than independent or considered or even informed

[109] Faculty of Arts minute book, 29, 30 (29 September 1965), G3/1/8, Sydney.
[110] The contrast with Leavis's directness in committee meetings is pointed. See Raymond Williams, 'Seeing a Man Running', in Denys Thompson (ed.), *The Leavises: Recollections and Impressions* (Cambridge: Cambridge University Press, 1984), 117–18.
[111] Professorial Board minute book, 103 (18 October 1965), G2/1/22, Sydney.
[112] Faculty of Arts minute book, 55–6, 58 (11 November 1965), G3/1/8, Sydney.
[113] Rita Erlich, untitled essay in Dow (ed.), *More Memories of Melbourne University*, 166–7.

reflection, it was more truly a jargon than anything I had ever heard on an ordinary evening in New Haven'.[114]

John Wiltshire has remarked that Leavisism's 'colonial outpost developed, as is the way of colonies, a certain parodic relation to its origins'.[115] The lateness of the Leavisian spring in Australia also calls to mind Pascale Casanova's claim that '[a]nachronism is characteristic of areas distant from the literary Greenwich meridian'.[116] Yet the belatedness and excesses of Australian Leavisism were not simply functions of distance from Cambridge. Teachers and writers in Britain not in direct or regular contact with Leavis could succumb to the same sorts of slavish imitation of the Leavises as some in the Goldberg circle. The styles and postures on display in the *Melbourne Critical Review* were not more 'parodic' than those of the *Pelican Guide to English Literature*. There was, moreover, scepticism and independence among Leavis's Australian admirers as well as whole-hog enthusiasm. A creaky centre-and-periphery model of imperial or international intellectual networks seriously weakens the force of Casanova's concept of a literary world system, and it cannot explain much about the *Scrutiny* movement in the British empire. What was distinctive about Goldberg's two English departments was not their colonial quality but the fact that they were exceptional instances of 'Leavisism in power'. A related question remains: how did *Scrutiny* ideas inform colonial critics' understanding of colonial cultures?

No core member of the Goldberg group was a major figure in the colonial cultural politics of the 1950s and 1960s, though Melbourne colleagues and former students such as Buckley and Chris Wallace-Crabbe were important participants in the contemporary debates on, and institutionalization of, 'Australian literature', as were Wilkes and many others at the University of Sydney.[117] Nevertheless, underwriting Goldberg's educational project was an interpretation of Australia's cultural predicament, an interpretation structured by Leavis's thinking. Goldberg elaborated on the colonial function of criticism in a long editorial in the *Melbourne Critical Review* three years before he left for Sydney.

---

[114] Howard Felperin, *Beyond Deconstruction: The Uses and Abuses of Literary Theory* (Oxford: Oxford University Press, 1985), 8, 9.

[115] Wiltshire, untitled essay, 417–18.

[116] Pascale Casanova, *The World Republic of Letters*, trans. M. B. DeBevoise (1999; Cambridge, Mass.: Harvard University Press, 2004), 100.

[117] This was more a matter of different priorities than principle. Goldberg wrote about Australian literature for the journal *Meanjin*. He objected to the emphasis on Australian literature in Wilkes's alternative courses because it was, like large tranches of English literature, of insufficient quality. Faculty of Arts minute book, 30 (29 September 1965), G3/1/8, Sydney; [S. L. Goldberg], 'Editorial: On Choosing Our Culture', *Melbourne Critical Review* 3 (1960): 4. See generally Dale, *English Men*, ch. 5.

This essay, 'On Choosing Our Culture', radiated the cultural confidence of literary critics in the *Scrutiny* tradition acting as cultural critics. Its point of departure was Raymond Williams's recently published argument with that tradition. Goldberg summarized Williams's contentions in the conclusion to *Culture and Society*, first, that culture should be seen as a 'whole way of life', and, secondly, that modern British culture was a matter of working-class traditions as well as the best that had been thought and said. Goldberg quickly juxtaposed this argument with Leavis's idea of minority culture, quoting a pivotal passage from *Mass Civilisation and Minority Culture*. Purporting to reconcile the two positions, Goldberg only nominally accepted Williams's claims. Yes, culture could be considered as a whole way of life, but that culture's progress could only be achieved by improving the quality and dissemination of culture in the restricted sense of art, literature, and thought. This was, as Goldberg acknowledged, essentially a 'brief gloss' on Leavis's 'attitudes to culture, literature, and education for the last thirty years: a brief glance at *Culture and Environment*, for example, shows it as relevant and as useful as it was when it first appeared in 1933'.[118]

Leavis's arguments, and Williams's too, acquired special inflections in the colonial context. The living working-class tradition identified variously by Williams and Richard Hoggart could be seen, Goldberg realized, as analogous to the 'Australian Tradition' that cultural nationalists were perpetually examining (or awaiting).[119] Goldberg did not believe that Australia had any 'really live and truly enriching indigenous traditions' (when intellectuals in settler colonies used the words 'indigenous', 'native', and 'autochthonous', they were usually thinking of an independent, self-sustaining *settler* culture or tradition).[120] This was not an uncommon position. More unusual was Goldberg's belief that searching for what was authentically Australian had deleterious effects on the culture. 'Instead of worrying about what our national "tradition" should lead us to think and feel and choose, we do better to leave the cultural chips fall where they may, and to get on with thinking and feeling and choosing in the world as we actually experience it.'

This required 'a combination of imaginative openness and critical self-knowledge'. Hence the importance of criticism in a colonial culture. But

[118] Goldberg, 'On Choosing Our Culture', 2.
[119] Ibid. The phrase 'Australian Tradition' may have been an allusion to A. A. Phillips's recent collection of essays, *The Australian Tradition: Studies in Colonial Culture* (Melbourne: F. W. Cheshire, 1958), or shorthand for the sorts of cultural criticism produced by Vincent Buckley, Nettie and Vance Palmer, Geoffrey Serle, Stephen Murray-Smith, and others.
[120] J. C. Beaglehole, 'The New Zealand Scholar' (1954), in Peter Munz (ed.), *The Feel of Truth: Essays in New Zealand and Pacific History* (Wellington: A. H. and A. W. Reed, 1969), 247.

Australia lacked any tradition of 'responsible cultural exploration and criticism by which we might partly redress our poverty'.[121] English teaching had a civic mission, and Goldberg hoped that his Sydney 'English school' would contribute to Australian culture through the training of sensibility.[122] However, in 'On Choosing Our Culture', Goldberg did not mount a case for university English teaching as the critical centre, as Leavis did in his *Scrutiny* manifestoes and *Education and the University*, and would do again in the public lectures of the 1960s. Instead Goldberg envisioned a critical 'minority' that included artists and academics (though not all of them) and bank clerks and wharf-labourers (though not all of them).[123]

This was more an ideal than a programme, and the ideal had more in common with schoolteachers' efforts to popularize discrimination than with Leavis's conception of a disproportionately influential 'critically adult public'. The terms of the argument were nevertheless Leavisian. 'The heart of the very existence of such a minority is the desire to discriminate, and it is here, in the discrimination of value, that the two aspects of culture'—'high culture' and culture as 'a whole way of life'—'meet together. Unless a culture, in both senses, finally encourages everybody, no matter who he is (for we are all members of "the masses") to see and to choose for himself, and to the very limit of his ability, what is of greater value rather than what is of less, then not only does art after art go out for the minority, but universal darkness buries us all.'[124] In this way the *Scrutiny* tradition framed Goldberg's conception of the colonial function of criticism.

Others sought to bring *Scrutiny* insights to bear on the texts actually produced by colonial cultures. In the mid-1960s, Narasimhaiah convened a symposium on 'Fiction and the Reading Public in India'. Introducing the conference, Narasimhaiah hit a succession of *Scrutiny* notes: the loss of the organic community, the degradation of leisure, day-dreaming, substitute-living, the threat posed by book societies and their 'choices', the need to inculcate standards.[125] How those standards were constituted was a very different question in India, however. The Mysore conference was

[121] Goldberg, 'On Choosing Our Culture', 5, 6.
[122] Wiltshire, untitled essay, 416; Docker, *In a Critical Condition*, 4–5.
[123] Goldberg, 'On Choosing Our Culture', 6.
[124] Ibid.
[125] C. D. Narasimhaiah, 'Introduction', in Narasimhaiah (ed.), *Fiction and the Reading Public in India* (Mysore: University of Mysore, 1967), vii–xv. See also Balagopal Varma, 'Some Thoughts on English Fiction and the Reading Public', ibid., 1–7. Narasimhaiah managed to work in the quotation from *Lady Chatterley's Lover* about how 'the way our sympathy flows and recoils' was what 'really determines our lives' that Leavis and Thompson had used to conclude a chapter of *Culture and Environment*. Narasimhaiah, 'Introduction', viii; F. R. Leavis and Denys Thompson, *Culture and Environment: The Training of Critical Awareness* (1933; London: Chatto & Windus, 1950), 55–6.

attended by speakers of Hindi, English, Kannada, Telugu, Tamil, and Malayalam, and Narasimhaiah hoped they could arrive at 'some sort of general agreement and shared assumptions among all of us reading fiction in different languages'.[126] Perhaps the contributor who took Q. D. Leavis's questions most seriously was one who made no mention of her—though the judgemental panache with which Ka Naa Subramanyam described the world of 'slick magazines in Tamil' strongly suggests familiarity with her work. A prolific short-story writer and novelist as well as a critic, Subramanyam surveyed the machinery of Tamil-language publishing and emphasized the unusual influence periodicals exerted on novels as well as short stories. The periodical production line and readers' relationship with it generated expectations that militated against standards: 'the reader expects his writer to be conscious of what he expects from him.... The reader-writer relationship deteriorates into a sort of fan-mail—"keep-me-pleased, I shall keep you" popular sort of attitude.'[127] Sheltered from criticism, authors came to believe their own publicity. Writers and the 'public' alike lacked 'a critical training in literature and literary appreciation'. The only solutions would be to 'insist... on standards'—though Subramanyam did not suggest how this might be done—and to expose Tamil readers to translated examples of 'the novel as practised in the other languages of the world'—something that 'Tamil insularity... militates against'.[128] Subramanyam's piece was by no means a direct application of a *Scrutiny* template to a different culture, but it did take as a first principle one of *Scrutiny's* premises, the importance of the relationship between creative writers and a critical public that articulated and enforced standards.

Elizabeth Smith made a similar point in her *History of New Zealand Fiction* of 1939. Referring explicitly to *Fiction and the Reading Public*, she closed her own book with a plea for standards, to turn a reading public into 'a reading and a thinking public'. Democracy depended on it, as did 'a possible literature in the future'.[129] New Zealand cultural criticism was a discourse of expectation: a national literature, even a national identity, was a thing of the future, a 'marvellous year'.[130] 'I know someone', Leavis

[126] Narasimhaiah, 'Introduction', xi.
[127] Ka Naa Subramanyam, 'Slick Magazines in Tamil: Their Literary Merit and Their Impact on Fiction', in Narasimhaiah (ed.), *Fiction and the Reading Public in India*, 121.
[128] Subramanyam, 'Slick Magazines', 122, 124, 125.
[129] E. M. Smith, *A History of New Zealand Fiction from 1862 to the Present Time with Some Account of Its Relation to the National Life and Character* (Dunedin: A. H. & A. W. Reed, 1939), 75–6.
[130] M. H. Holcroft, *The Deepening Stream: Cultural Influences in New Zealand* (Christchurch, NZ: Caxton Press, 1940); J. C. Beaglehole, *New Zealand: A Short History* (London: G. Allen & Unwin, 1936). The quotation is from Allen Curnow, 'Attitudes for a New Zealand Poet: III: The Skeleton of the Great Moa in the Canterbury Museum, Christchurch' (1943), in *Collected Poems, 1933–1973* (Wellington: A. H. & A. W. Reed, 1974), 142.

remarked in the first number of *Scrutiny*, 'who is enquiring why New Zealand has developed nothing in the nature of a distinctive literature.'[131] The someone was E. H. McCormick. Bored with, and insufficiently prepared for, his thesis on a Tudor topic, he sought advice, and Leavis suggested he revisit the master's thesis on New Zealand literature he had written in Wellington, placing more emphasis on 'cultural and historical forces'—making it 'anthropological' in the manner of *Fiction and the Reading Public*.[132]

What McCormick ended up writing was more a study of literature in its general social context than an examination of the business and institutions of literature, but the Leavsises' influence ran deeper than the questionnaire responses appended to the thesis.[133] *Fiction and the Reading Public* and *Culture and Environment* suggested ways of reading 'bad' or undistinguished texts as cultural documents, which meant that clumsy New Zealand novels could be examined with some explanatory and thus constructive purpose rather than subjected to summary dismissal. In the popular survey that he developed his Cambridge thesis into, McCormick identified signs of genuine literary life in the short stories Frank Sargeson wrote in the 1930s. Sargeson had a feel for the rhythms of demotic, masculine speech, McCormick argued, and his labourers drifting through shabby towns and scrubby countryside exemplified a genuinely New Zealand outlook. In contrast, the characters in most New Zealand fiction (especially in novels by women) were unreal transplants from the world of English fiction. Sargeson tapped into an 'unwritten' New Zealand identity developing since the mid-nineteenth century. 'Thus, paradoxical as it may seem, Frank Sargeson is traditional to a greater degree than any other New Zealand writer of to-day; he is the exponent of a local tradition that has hitherto been inarticulate.'[134] The gender politics were not the

[131] F. R. Leavis, '"Babbitt Buys the World"', *Scrutiny* 1/1 (May 1932): 82.
[132] E. H. McCormick, *An Absurd Ambition: Autobiographical Writings*, ed. Dennis McEldowney (Auckland: Auckland University Press, 1996), 115–19, 131–2; McCormick, 'In the 1930s', 229–31; Donal Smith, 'Eric McCormick's Cambridge', in James Ross, Linda Gill, and Stuart McRae (eds), *Writing a New Country: A Collection of Essays Presented to E. H. McCormick in His 88th Year* (Auckland: Ariel Books, 1993), 38–50; M. P. K. Sorrenson, 'The Making of *Letters and Art in New Zealand*' in Ross, Gill, and McRae (ed.), *Writing a New Country*, 58–80.
[133] E. H. McCormick, 'Literature in New Zealand: An Essay in Cultural Criticism' (Cambridge University thesis, 1935), copy in E. H. McCormick papers, MSX-4250, Alexander Turnbull Library, National Library of New Zealand, Wellington. The English Faculty appointed Willey, not Leavis, as supervisor. The examiners awarded the thesis the degree of MLitt, not the PhD McCormick had hoped for. McCormick, *Absurd Ambition*, 118, 132.
[134] E. H. McCormick, *Letters and Art in New Zealand* (Wellington: Department of Internal Affairs, 1940), 182.

Leavises', and Sargeson's labourers were not Sturt's: but McCormick's understanding of the relationship between literature, language, and a living culture derived from *Mass Civilisation and Minority Culture* and *Culture and Environment.*

Two decades later, the critical apparatus of *Fiction and the Reading Public* proved suggestive for an analysis of the apparent inadequacy of another 'national literature': Scotland's. David Craig came to Downing College from the University of Aberdeen as a research student, and Q. D. Leavis as well as her husband assumed the role of supervisor.[135] As Craig groped for a thesis topic, she encouraged him to consider why nineteenth-century Scottish literature was not like its American counterpart. Why did Walter Scott not 'turn the inherited theological seriousness into a comparable literary activity', as Nathaniel Hawthorne did? Why did no contemporary Scot manage to do what Mark Twain did with dialect? 'You will find yourself asking (& I hope answering) the most interesting & important questions in the field of the general question: What conditions are necessary to produce & maintain a literature?' Since it was such an important question, she hoped that Craig would 'have a shot at it, even though it means dealing with the Press, Religious institutions, Education, Printing & the visual arts, Political institutions, History, Economics, & the Autobiographies of Eminent Scots as well as Fiction, Poetry & Polite Letters'.[136] Craig did do research on the infrastructure of literature—the published version of the thesis included a chapter on 'Fiction and the Scottish reading public'—and one of the book's preoccupations was the effect on Scottish literature of changes in the vernacular and the social composition of urban centres: the echoes of the Elizabethan language community of early *Scrutiny* criticism were quite audible.[137] Craig's book was not avowedly or implicitly anthropological, but both the Leavises saw its terrain as 'the sociology of literature'.[138] They went as far as arranging for Craig to meet David Pocock, one of the Cambridge English undergraduates who went over to social anthropology, thinking that he would make a good examiner for the thesis.[139]

[135] 'Mrs Leavis...had been in effect my research supervisor when nobody in the English Faculty had had the sort of commitment I needed to seeing literature in its historical situation.' David Craig, letter to the editor, *London Review of Books*, 8 November 1990.
[136] Q. D. Leavis to Craig, 21 May [1955], Q. D. Leavis papers, GCPP Leavis 2/1/7, Girton.
[137] David Craig, *Scottish Literature and the Scottish People, 1680–1830* (London: Chatto & Windus, 1961), chs 1, 2, 7, 8.
[138] Q. D. Leavis to Craig, 21 May 1955, 24 May 1955, Q. D. Leavis papers, GCPP Leavis 2/1/7, Girton.
[139] Q. D. Leavis to Craig, 23 November 1955, Q. D. Leavis papers, GCPP Leavis 2/1/7, Girton; F. R. Leavis to Pocock, 1 December 1955 and 13 December 1955, F. R. Leavis papers, Col 9.59.121, Emmanuel.

That the Leavises provided the impetus for analyses of Scottish and Indian literatures as cultural formations is difficult to square with F. R. Leavis's reputation, which has been growing since the 1980s, as an ideologue of 'Englishness'. So is the role of an avowed 'Leavisite', William Walsh, in the institutionalization of the study of 'commonwealth literature' in Britain, starting with the University of Leeds. (After becoming the first Professor of Commonwealth Literature at Leeds in 1972, Walsh wrote books about R. K. Narayan and Patrick White—and another about Leavis.)[140] Leavis himself had little to say about the African, Indian, and Caribbean writing of the 1960s and 1970s. Although he 'did not have much interest in the transnational', Simon Gikandi writes in one of the most thought-provoking post-colonial reconsiderations of Leavis, 'he was not indifferent to the universality of Englishness'. In his handling of Conrad and James, Gikandi continues, 'Leavis had the uncanny ability to naturalize difference and to make it part of the pantheon of Englishness, and it is my contention that in the process of reading English texts according to the Leavisite grammar, colonial readers were being asked to leave their differences behind and join the common community of Englishness, denoted by literature *against* the logic of colonial governmentality.'[141]

Teaching English literature to colonized peoples is almost inescapably, at some level, an exercise in substitution, asserting the claims of a metropolitan literature and language at the expense of the indigenous (the promotion of English literary study in nineteenth-century India has become the exemplary case).[142] Gikandi's observation that Leavis's writings on the so-called English novel from *The Great Tradition* onwards 'naturalize difference' is a shrewd one, but it does not follow that his work was a major contribution to the literary project of imperialism. Leavis and his pupils were far less influential in the empire-commonwealth—and especially in Africa—than Gikandi's argument assumes.[143] He also projects the heightened interest in 'Englishness' of Leavis's later years back onto an earlier period when *Scrutiny* approaches were being embedded in English teaching in Britain and parts of the empire. Gikandi's supporting quotations are drawn from Leavis's 1967 Clark lectures. It would be harder to find comparable evidence in *Scrutiny*. There was a marked English accent to his comments on American culture and French poetry, to be sure, but, at

---

[140] See Angus Calder, 'Leads from Leeds', *Journal of Commonwealth Literature* 21/9 (1986): 9–11; Arthur Ravenscroft, 'The Origins', *Journal of Commonwealth Literature* 21/9 (1986): 2–4.

[141] Gikandi, 'Globalization and the Claims of Postcoloniality', 651.

[142] Gauri Viswanathan, *Masks of Conquest: Literary Study and British Rule in India* (New York: Columbia University Press, 1989).

[143] See above, 217–18.

least during his Cambridge teaching career, national questions were less integral to his thinking than they were for some of the other exponents of literary study with whom he is sometimes linked, such as Arnold (to say nothing of the Kiplingesque Henry Newbolt).[144] The modernity that concerned him was a 'Western process' that crossed national boundaries.

To emphasize Englishness is also to neglect the ways in which *Scrutiny* criticism seemed valuable in imperial contexts for reasons other than the *content* of its readings. After all, the Leavises and *Scrutiny* offered modes of reading as well as readings of texts that could function as avatars of a certain idea of England. *Fiction and the Reading Public* pointed to ways of analysing the literary cultures of colonists (as in New Zealand) and colonized peoples (as in India) alike. For Ludowyk, critical thinking, rather than the qualities of the texts to be read, was the cosmopolitan gift of literary study: difference was naturalized not through the peculiarities of Englishness, but through a putatively universal critical reason. For Goldberg, too, the distinctively colonial value of Leavisism lay in the unsettling qualities of its critical practice rather than its potentially anglicizing canon. And outside the British empire, in the United States, 'the importance of *Scrutiny*' rested in its critical judgements, not in its larger cultural project. Once again, what had been a unified praxis in Leavis's own work separated out into its constituent parts in other contexts.

---

[144] Stefan Collini, *Public Moralists: Political Thought and Intellectual Life in Britain, 1850–1930* (Oxford: Clarendon Press, 1991), 355–68, esp. 368.

Conclusion: The Project of *Scrutiny*

Scrutiny's life and afterlife overseas and the movement's history in Britain are intersecting stories, but the chronologies do not map onto each other. F. R. Leavis's criticism was the basis of a curriculum restructure in Ceylon in the 1940s and one in Australia in the 1960s. *Fiction and the Reading Public* provided cues for thinking about New Zealand literature in the 1930s and Scottish literature in the 1950s. These disjunctures clearly have more to do with differences in local contexts than positions relative to the Cambridge meridian—or an unfolding logic. The *Scrutiny* movement's history within Britain was also, of course, shaped by its social and cultural contexts, but the British history of the movement has a more consistent pattern. That history divides into three phases: the establishment of the movement in the 1930s; a period of consolidation and diffusion from the war years to the early 1960s; and its eclipse in the later 1960s and 1970s.

When *Scrutiny* was founded, Leavis and his collaborators were acutely concerned with how university literary studies could become, to borrow a phrase from the end of Leavis's life, 'a discipline of thought'.[1] In placing the encounter between the reader and the pattern and texture of the words on the page at the centre of English, Leavis was greatly indebted to I. A. Richards. It was Leavis, though, who developed practical criticism into an educational programme that could be translated from Cambridge teaching situations to sixth forms and evening classes. In these early years, as in the final phase of his career, Leavis's preoccupation with language pervaded his thinking about culture as well as his interpretative practice. Language, tradition, continuity, culture: these collectivities were sources of value and meaning. The movement back and forth between the collective and the individual, between the general and the concrete, a movement enacted in literature and the reading of literature, made intimacy with literature more than a matter of taste.

Leavis's thinking about tradition, continuity, and culture owed an initial debt, again, to Richards, but more to Eliot and Lawrence. Eliot's

---

[1] F. R. Leavis, *The Living Principle: English as a Discipline of Thought* (London: Chatto & Windus, 1975).

conception of tradition as a creative force to be wrestled with informed Leavis's understanding of criticism as engaged with the artistic challenges of the present; Eliot's *Four Quartets*, published between 1936 and 1942, proved to be the last twentieth-century literary work of real significance to Leavis. Lawrence's novels and his non-fiction, including his letters, became touchstones for Leavis and other *Scrutiny* contributors from Denys Thompson to G. H. Bantock. Lawrence was an exemplar of creative intelligence and an interpreter of the modern condition. Texts published in and around *Scrutiny* hopped from Lawrence to contemporary American social science, albeit social science that could be readily assimilated to literature. However, in contrast to the Lynds' *Middletown*, with its interest in finance and credit, the *Scrutiny* group's modernity was one whose pervasive logic was industrial. The machine was their coordinating metaphor for the culture of democracy. *Culture and Environment* presented these ideas unevenly ('chucking it at the reader'), but the quirks of format did not prevent its being reprinted often and taken up in schools and adult education. There was early interest from the WEA, and schools where Scrutineers taught, such as Gresham's and Dartington Hall, became beachheads of the movement's educational 'campaign'. But the institutionalization of *Scrutiny* approaches really belongs to the next phase, the years from the early 1940s to the early 1950s.

During this second period Leavis elaborated on his conception of English and education and wrote about fiction with more intensity than he had previously. *The Great Tradition* was preceded by a succession of *Scrutiny* essays on the novel, and it was at this point that Leavis came to be known for his criticism of fiction, having made his name writing about poetry. He remained a critic and teacher of poetry, though, and poetry more than prose oriented his teaching practice. Although the 1940s and 1950s witnessed a remarkable development of *Scrutiny*'s literary criticism, its initiatives in analysing contemporary culture were not renewed significantly. When 'left-Leavisites' updated, extended, and skewed this cultural criticism in the 1940s and 1950s, their reference points were books written in the early 1930s, *Culture and Environment* and *Fiction and the Reading Public*. Specimens of advertising reprinted in *Culture and Environment* still appeared pertinent enough for Richard Hoggart to use in his extension classes more than fifteen years later. It was Hoggart, Raymond Williams, and Stuart Hall and Paddy Whannel, rather than any member of the journal's 'connexion', who did the most with *Scrutiny*'s work on contemporary culture after the journal's early phase.

What the Leavises, Thompson, and L. C. Knights had written about the modern 'environment' and the conditions necessary for genuine 'culture' underpinned David Holbrook's widely influential vision for English

250 *English as a Vocation*

in secondary modern schools after the war, and coloured the ambitions of many university graduates who went into teaching. *Scrutiny* affected secondary education at this level of guiding assumptions, and at the level of particular teaching practices—above all practical criticism. Through the 1940s and 1950s, Scrutineers, pupils of Leavis, and supporters without direct connections to him rose to positions of authority in schools and within teachers' organizations. The journal *Use of English*, in which Thompson, Holbrook, Raymond O'Malley, and Frank Whitehead took leading roles, helped coordinate teachers' groups as well as functioning as a forum or platform for a form of English teaching in which *Scrutiny* was the chief inspiration.

Their standing with teachers made Thompson and Holbrook familiar to a larger public than the readership of *Scrutiny*. Boris Ford's editorship of the *Pelican Guide to English Literature* made *Scrutiny* authors and *Scrutiny* judgements known to some of the thousands of new students entering the university system in the 1950s and 1960s, as well as the adult education students, autodidacts, and multifarious 'general readers' reached by Penguin's non-fiction books. The *Pelican Guide*, like (on a much more modest scale) the broadcasting activities of Ford, Thompson, and Holbrook, was squarely within the British tradition of principled popularization. Hoggart and Williams, their breakthrough books rapidly paperbacked by Penguin, owed their national recognition to the same process. Leavis's own model of concatenated 'publics' was not the strategy his followers adopted.

The *Pelican Guide* was a characteristic product of the fifteen or so years after the Second World War. Academics and pre-war 'men of letters' (Cyril Connolly, for instance) now addressed much bigger and more variegated audiences—in the Sunday papers, on a newly diversified radio network, on television, in paperbacks that were inexpensive but stylishly and respectably produced. Younger and assertively provincial and working-class voices did too: novelists such as John Braine, academics such as Hoggart. This was a moment of democratization of both the audience and the contributor pool: but it depended on the persistence of older hierarchies and standards, older assumptions about the value and authority of art and seriousness.[2] This double helix of democratization and deference is one of the things that makes the years from the Second World War to the early 1960s such a distinctive conjuncture in modern British history.

[2] This interpretation of the post-war years derives from Stefan Collini, *Absent Minds: Intellectuals in Britain* (Oxford: Oxford University Press, 2006), esp. chs 6, 7, 16–18 and p. 421; Michael Bell, 'F. R. Leavis', in A. Walton Litz, Louis Menand, and Lawrence Rainey (eds), *The Cambridge History of Literary Criticism*, vol. 7, *Modernism and the New Criticism* (Cambridge: Cambridge University Press, 2000), 392.

That deference, to existing cultural norms and forms if not to class-derived authority, lent social sanction to the *Scrutiny* principle of 'discrimination' as an educational goal. Over the course of the 1960s the helix unwound. Holbrook and Whitehead lamented that discrimination was no longer a compelling ideal for younger teachers. Grammar schools were rolled into comprehensives. The idea of literature as relatively independent of power structures and enabling readers to transcend their 'environment' was disputed. With iconoclastic exceptions like the young Fred Inglis, progressive or radical English teachers were more likely to get their questions and the beginnings of answers from linguists and their interpreters in the institutes of education than from literary critics. *Scrutiny*-derived approaches to popular culture, even in the form of *The Popular Arts* rather than *Discrimination and Popular Culture*, no longer had much power to suggest original and persuasive ways of analysing a mass culture that was more aesthetically complex than, or certainly very different from, the interwar productions to which *Culture and Environment* was a response. By 1970, what remained of the *Scrutiny* movement had lost most of the left, which had been an important constituency in the schools and, in the phase of left-Leavisism, its major source of regeneration. The movement's decline was thus in part a consequence of the cultural changes of 'the sixties', which swept away so much else besides, and in part a result of the fact that many *Scrutiny* insights had been pushed as far as they practically could.

As this summary indicates, and the book as a whole shows, the movement was always more than an academic one. The university, in part a metaphorical term, held the centre of Leavis's thinking about culture and the minority who would take responsibility for it in modern times, but he addressed himself primarily to the undergraduates, the 'intelligent young men and women' who would 'go down from the Universities', not their lecturers.[3] Samuel Goldberg, reconstructing a university English department on Cambridge or *Scrutiny* lines, had as his horizon a critically sensitive Australian public. The British schoolteachers and adult education tutors doing *Scrutiny*'s work, or setting it to work for them, were also, in their different ways, concerned with a public rather than a profession. The movement's 'educational project' was not 'professionalization', in the way that it was for the American New Critics in the decade and more before the founding of the Kenyon School of English. Being 'Dr Leavis' when many other college fellows and English Faculty members at Cambridge did not have doctorates did not make Leavis a supporter of the idea of a research university. In the *Times Literary Supplement* in 1963 he took issue

[3] 'Scrutiny: A Manifesto', *Scrutiny* 1/1 (May 1932): 5.

with the idea of imposing 'American' definitions of research on English departments in the United Kingdom. Talk of contributions to knowledge was inadequate: a university should be a 'centre of human consciousness', not a congeries of specialist departments.[4]

All the same, the Leavises and their collaborators in the early years of *Scrutiny* were concerned to replace the belletrism and scholarship that they regarded as the complementary modes of conventional literary criticism. Although they believed in 'unspecialized intelligence', they also spoke, following Richards, of 'training' readers. 'Discrimination' was both an end and a means of a critical training. The most famous instance of the movement's discriminating tendency is F. R. Leavis's contraction of what has subsequently come to be called the canon. 'The great English novelists', he declared at the beginning of *The Great Tradition*, 'are Jane Austen, George Eliot, Henry James and Joseph Conrad—to stop for the moment at that comparatively safe point in history.' To appreciate Austen's distinction, he remarked a few pages later, 'is to feel that life isn't long enough to permit of one's giving much time to Fielding or any to Mr Priestley'.[5] There was an element of strategic provocation in this, and Leavis also told students to 'cultivate promiscuity' in their reading; his wife plied students and house guests with obscure books to read for the occasional gems buried deep inside.[6] Nevertheless, there is plenty of anecdotal evidence that the message undergraduates took was that they did not have to read widely. Leavis is often criticized for this, but he was being pragmatic as well as dogmatic. Since readers—and especially students—do not have world enough and time to read everything, is it more rewarding to read extensively or intensively, to give priority to breadth or to discrimination? Leavis's answer entailed costs as well as benefits, but it was a serious answer. It seems unlikely that Thelma Herring, cramming centuries' worth of authors into her Sydney University lectures, or the adult education tutor who proposed to cover Joyce's complete works in a single session, had devoted much reflection to this question. Significantly, Leavis's thinking about the canon mattered most to his followers when they were engaged in curricular reform—as with Goldberg at Sydney, and Williams when he argued for slimmer syllabi than was the norm in the Oxford Extra-Mural

---

[4] 'General Board of the Faculties: Committee on Post-graduate Instruction: Copied below is an article published in the *Times Literary Supplement* dated 26 July 1963. Research in English by F. R. Leavis', typescript in M. C. Bradbrook papers, folder labelled 'Brad S. Leavis, FR&QD 1', Girton.

[5] F. R. Leavis, *The Great Tradition: George Eliot, Henry James, Joseph Conrad* (1948; London: Chatto & Windus, 1960), 1, 3.

[6] Michael Tanner, 'Some Recollections of the Leavises', in Denys Thompson (ed.), *The Leavises: Recollections and Impressions* (Cambridge; Cambridge University Press, 1984), 133, 135, 137–8.

Delegacy. It was less common for Leavis's followers to insist as a matter of principle that such and such an author was not worth reading. Leavisian teachers such as Whitehead made catholic suggestions for reading in schools.[7] Discrimination did not necessarily mean a compact canon.

It has been suggested that pruning the canon made Leavis's model of English more accessible to 'students from unlettered backgrounds' than more traditional courses that assumed a lot of background reading.[8] Practical criticism exercises also downgraded the value of extensive reading. But 'dating' seminars, in which students had to place an unattributed passage in context on the basis of their practical criticism of it, did presuppose or necessitate a fairly high level of familiarity with literary history. As Leavis told Philip Brockbank at the University of York, a course based on 'Passages for assignment to period (etc), and for intelligent comment' was 'Literary History, Cultural History, Background, as much as it is "Practical Criticism"'.[9] When John Wiltshire began teaching at Sydney, he formed the opinion that Australian students lacked the breadth of reading a British sixth form provided, and that classes in practical criticism were less effective in consequence.[10]

The connection between Leavis's idea of a university and 'students from unlettered backgrounds' has, in any case, been exaggerated. Leavis worked at great personal cost to train a critical élite whose intellectual attainments were not simply a complement to upper-middle-class taste and *savoir faire*: but between the upper middle class that Leavis associated with Bloomsbury and King's College and the ranks of working-class and lower-middle-class scholarship children stood an enormous prosperous middle class. It was from this social stratum that the majority of Leavis's pupils were recruited. Many of them arrived from fee-paying schools rather than the post-Butler grammar schools that feature so prominently, in the mythology that has come to envelop Leavis's school. For all his aversion to writers and scholars whose public-school credentials were at least implicit in their personae—Auden, for instance—Leavis did not mount any substantial criticism of the public schools and their place in British society. This was not an unusual position, but it is indicative of the limits to the meritocratic reformism that others have claimed for him.

Calling into question the position of the public schools would have entailed an embrace of the state—proper 'meritocracies' are societies where the state monopolizes the education of élites—that Leavis would

[7] Frank Whitehead, *The Disappearing Dais: A Study of the Principles and Practice of English Teaching* (London: Chatto & Windus, 1966), ch. 2.
[8] Marilyn Butler, 'Moments', *London Review of Books*, 2 September 1982, 10.
[9] Leavis to Philip Brockbank, 12 May 1965, York.
[10] John Wiltshire, untitled essay, *Cambridge Quarterly* 25/4 (1996): 418.

have found unacceptable. He remained a supporter of the Liberal Party long after it had become a minor party at Westminster elections. However, he was often at odds with what became of the liberal tradition in the twentieth century (not least in Bloomsbury or King's, the Cambridge base of Noël Annan and E. M. Forster).[11] His decision not to be a defence witness in the *Lady Chatterley's Lover* trial had none of the resigned acceptance of the imperfect that was characteristic of other twentieth-century inheritors of Victorian liberalism, including some who testified on Penguin's behalf.[12] Emphasizing Leavis's moral strenuousness and his individualism, perhaps at the expense of his investment in collectivities such as 'tradition', Guy Ortolano characterizes Leavis's politics as a 'radical liberalism'.[13] I find more persuasive Peter Mandler's judgement that Leavis's thinking was 'too idiosyncratic to flow neatly into one of the main currents of social and political thought'.[14]

The project of *Scrutiny* was 'political' in the loose sense of the word. It sought to refine and extend the function of criticism and sensibility against the standardizing tendency of modern civilization, and this ambition took organizational form among teachers and educationalists. Some aspects of this educational campaign had a bearing on the policy questions that political parties and civil servants dealt with, such as the role of the secondary modern school, the merits of grammar schools, and English curricula. The movement's deeper concerns, however, were not amenable to prosecution through political institutions, whether formal or informal. To say this is to make a point different from, though compatible with, Francis Mulhern's claim that the logic of the *Scrutiny* opposition between 'culture' and 'civilization' entailed a depreciation and, 'at the limit', a dissolution of the category of *'politics as such'*.[15] The relation of many of the journal's contributors to Marxism illustrates Mulhern's point well. In the pages of *Scrutiny*, Soviet communism was not a real alternative

---

[11] On Bloomsbury and Liberalism, see Peter Stansky, *On or About December 1910: Early Bloomsbury and Its Intimate World* (Cambridge, Mass.: Harvard University Press, 1996).

[12] Leavis's choice contrasts sharply with Virginia Woolf's efforts on behalf of Radclyffe Hall three decades before when *The Well of Loneliness* was under legal assault for obscenity, despite her dissatisfaction with the novel and Hall herself. *The Letters of Virginia Woolf*, vol. 3, *1923–1928*, ed. Nigel Nicolson and Joanne Trautmann (New York: Harcourt Brace Jovanovich, 1977), 520, 529–30, 555, 559.

[13] Guy Ortolano, *The Two Cultures Controversy: Science, Literature and Cultural Politics in Postwar Britain* (Cambridge: Cambridge University Press, 2009), ch. 2, esp. pp. 85–9.

[14] Peter Mandler, review of *The Two Cultures Controversy: Science, Literature, and Cultural Politics in Postwar Britain* by Guy Ortolano, H-Albion, January 2010, <http://www.h-net.org/reviews/showrev.php?id=25388>, accessed 28 July 2011.

[15] Francis Mulhern, *The Moment of 'Scrutiny'* (London: New Left Books, 1979), 330–1. (emphasis in original).

to capitalism. Both were industrial civilizations.[16] Communism might make for a more just society, but it would not derail the logic of mass civilization. This position was at once radical and, for practical purposes, apolitical. It was radical at a level where there could be no operative political organization.

A less familiar example of that *Scrutiny* logic at or near its limits is David Holbrook's thinking after the phase represented by *English for Maturity* and *English for the Rejected*. By the early 1970s, Holbrook had pressed a *Scrutiny* conception of cultural and individual well-being further and further into the territory of psychoanalysis and what he called 'philosophical anthropology'. The sometime hero of secondary modern English teachers was being criticized as a reactionary for championing the exploration of the self at the expense of the exploration of contemporary social issues and a corresponding striving for social justice.[17] Reviewing Holbrook's recent work in 1973, Leavis's student A. A. H. (Tony) Inglis remarked that in castigating liberalism's failures, Holbrook sounded illiberal. (The review was one of two commissioned by *The Human World*, which had been hospitable to Holbrook although he did not share the Christian or Wittgensteinian concerns of other contributors.) Inglis protested that the ills of capitalist culture were at least in part 'economic and political in their nature', and a deeper probing of human interiority could not be a sufficient remedy. Holbrook conceded 'that our prospects of rich and secure lives depend not only on our experiences in infancy, but directly on the sort of society in which we live': but, Inglis said, the admission did not make as much difference as it should have to his cultural critique.[18] For Holbrook at this time, concerns other than the psychic were subsidiary or insignificant. 'Politics as such', one might say, was beside the point.

Most people working within the *Scrutiny* tradition did not push up against its meta-political or anti-political 'limits' as Holbrook did. Mulhern is right to say that the 'logic' of *Scrutiny* pointed that way, but that logic did not govern all the protean ways in which *Scrutiny* thought and practice were appropriated. Leavis's conceptions of criticism, its context, and its mission were mutually supportive, but the constituent elements remained meaningful and usable when they were extracted from the whole and redeployed. Thompson and Ford could articulate firmly

---

[16] Perry Anderson, 'Components of the National Culture', *New Left Review* 50 (1968): 54–5.

[17] Margaret Mathieson, *The Preachers of Culture: A Study of English and Its Teachers* (London: Allen & Unwin, 1975), 200.

[18] A. A. H. Inglis and Peter Abbs, 'Philosophical Anthropology: Two Views of Recent Work by David Holbrook', *The Human World* 11 (May 1973): 74.

Leavisian judgements without accepting the idea of 'minority culture'. And critics on the left who rejected Leavis's assessment of what was valuable and vital in modern culture depended on his analytical methods and criteria to make their dissenting evaluations.

Part of *Scrutiny*'s appeal to critics on the left was the fact that it offered a method—practical criticism, close reading—as well as a theory. The method was highly portable. A Leavisian training enabled Hoggart to 'read' generic stories and popular songs for working-class sensibilities. That training was more than technical instruction. Discriminating between the genuine and the artificial or unfelt was a moral as well as analytical undertaking. It was informed by the body of *Scrutiny* thinking on the relationship between art and society and the conditions for a living culture. Locating genuine communal emotions (rather than industrially produced ones) within working people's responses to sentimental songs, as Hoggart did, or seeing in music hall a sustaining 'tradition', as Hall and Whannel did, were judgements Q. D. Leavis could not have come to, but they shared some of her working assumptions.

The aspects of *Scrutiny*'s cultural criticism that left-Leavisites found most compelling were its arguments about art and society, the main sources of which were Knights and F. R. Leavis, and the analysis of the culture industry in *Culture and Environment* and *Fiction and the Reading Public*, with their exploration of the ways in which advertising and commercial art engineered coarsened, materialist desires. The romantic–radical critique of industrial capitalism, of which *Scrutiny* was one significant chapter, was less important to left-Leavisite literary critics, certainly to Hoggart and Hall and Whannel. That tradition, however, was central to E. P. Thompson's *The Making of the English Working Class*, which quoted Leavis for support. In the twentieth century, as Meredith Veldman has shown, the romantic anti-industrial tradition undergirded certain kinds of socialism (such as that of Thompson and R. H. Tawney), early forms of environmentalism, and staunchly English conservatism.[19] Bantock was *Scrutiny*'s most forceful such conservative, forthrightly defending hierarchies and condemning the vulgarized culture of the 'industrial-bureaucratic state'. The Black Papers, to which Bantock contributed, fed into Conservative thinking on education during the Thatcher years, but otherwise Scrutineers had little impact on organized conservatism, with or without an initial capital. As well as repudiating the idea that the market could be trusted to set values, *Scrutiny* was scathing about the forms of middle-class associationalism and 'service' so important to organized

---

[19] Meredith Veldman, *Fantasy, the Bomb, and the Greening of Britain: Romantic Protest, 1945–1980* (Cambridge: Cambridge University Press, 1994).

Conservatism after mid-century.[20] Thompson and O'Malley, the Scrutineers most invested in rural life, shared Bantock's hostility to the culture
industrialism had made, but not his belief in authority. Both were paci-
fists, and their writings occasionally gestured towards later environmen-
talist ideas.[21]

The romantic affiliations of *Scrutiny* certainly help situate the movement in a continuum that runs from Blake and Wordsworth, through
Ruskin and Morris, and on to some of Leavis's twentieth-century interlocutors. But, as I have argued, that tradition does not encompass all of
Scrutiny's programme, or even all of what was significant and germinal in
its cultural critique. This is one reason it is unconvincing to conclude, as
Mulhern does, that, strategically, *Scrutiny*'s programme was just 'a latter-
day variation on the romantic/utilitarian antinomy'.[22] A judgement at
this level of capaciousness has both the accuracy and the banality of Keynes's observation that 'in the long run' we will all be dead (Keynes was
playing with the banality, of course). At this resolution all the texture *and
all the conflict* of cultural life disappear.

All intellectual history is the history of unintended consequences, and
on closer examination any movement or group emerges as more complex
and varied than it appears at first.[23] Even so, the range of careers and enterprises that Leavis and *Scrutiny* enabled or supported is extraordinary,
and the movement matters for that variousness as well as for its impact on
education and its role in bringing popular culture within the purview of

---

[20] There is no reference to Leavis or *Scrutiny* in, for instance, E. H. H. Green, *Ideologies
of Conservatism: Conservative Political Ideas in the Twentieth Century* (Oxford: Oxford
University Press, 2002), or Lawrence Black, 'The Lost World of Young Conservatism',
Historical Journal 51/4 (2008): 991–1024. In *Cold Cream: My Early Life and Other Mistakes* (London: Bloomsbury, 2009), Ferdinand Mount, at different times a Conservative
party advisor and editor of the *Times Literary Supplement*, provides an insider's view of the
reconstruction of Conservative principles from Selwyn Lloyd to Thatcher that gives some
idea of the sorts of literary sensibility that were more attuned to Toryism than the *Scrutiny*
movement was.

[21] Raymond O'Malley, *One-Horse Farm: Crofting in the West Highlands* (London: Frederick Muller, 1948), 4, 7–10; R. O'Malley and D. Thompson, *English for the Living*
(London: Methuen, 1949), 36–7; Denys Thompson, 'Recent Pacifist Literature', *Scrutiny*
5/1 (June 1936): 71–4.

[22] Mulhern, *Moment of* '*Scrutiny*', 330. Mulhern claims that this antinomy constitutes
one of the enduring structures of modern British culture. I would argue instead that the
synthesis of the 'romantic' and the 'utilitarian' through commercial culture is one of the
defining features of British culture from the early twentieth century. Christopher Hilliard,
To Exercise Our Talents: The Democratization of Writing in Britain (Cambridge, Mass.: Harvard University Press, 2006).

[23] I poach David Blackbourn's epigram: 'All history is the history of unintended consequences, but that is especially true when we are trying to untangle humanity's relationship
with the natural environment.' David Blackbourn, *The Conquest of Nature: Water, Landscape and the Making of Modern Germany* (London: Jonathan Cape, 2006), 12.

the humanities in Britain. Leavis did not approve of many of these developments, but he had put himself in a position where he would have to bear them. Although he has a reputation for being insistent and unbending, he was, all his life, a teacher, and to teach, no matter how confidently, is to make oneself vulnerable. Teachers of literature often get repaid in ways they have not looked for.

APPENDIX

Schools and Fathers' Occupations
of Downing College Undergraduates
Reading English, 1932–62

The following table lists the schools and fathers' occupations of men admitted to Downing College to read English as undergraduates in F. R. Leavis's time there. (Including their names as well would evidently contravene the Data Protection Act 1998.) The table excludes research students but includes those university graduates taking a second bachelor's degree and Catholic priests studying for the English tripos after completing their seminary training (priests usually supplied the name of their seminaries rather than the schools they had attended earlier). The list is ordered by matriculation date. The names of men applying to read English were found in the agenda papers for the college's Governing Body's meetings (DCGB/M/3/1a, 2–5, Downing College archives) and the minute book of the college's 'Selection Committee' (DCAT 9/1/2). The names were then matched with the matriculation certificates in the college's admissions books (DCAT/5/1/6–13), which record a good deal of information about the matriculants but *not* the subjects they were reading (though two volumes from the 1930s were annotated by a college official to record subjects read). The admissions books from 1957 onwards were shielded by the Data Protection Act, and the information from them provided here was generously supplied by the college archivist, Kate Thompson. (The matriculation certificates can record more sensitive information than the categories relevant here.) In some cases further details have been drawn from the *Downing College Association News Letter*, 1934–2008; *The Cambridge University List of Members 1973–1974* (Cambridge: Cambridge University Press, 1974); and other archival and published sources.

Student	School	Father's Occupation
1932		
1	Dean Close School, Cheltenham	General Secretary, Church Missionary Society
2	Grantham Boys' National School; King's School, Grantham	Outfitter
3	Bradfield College, Chateau d'Oex, Switzerland	Judge
4	St Joseph College, Yokohama; St Columba's College, Dublin	Merchant
5	Ashampstead, Seaford; Eastbourne College	Gentleman
6	Southport College, Lancs; Merchant Taylors' School, Crosby	Electrical engineer
7	Clayesmore School, Winchester	Secretary, NTU
8	Clifton College, junior and senior schools	Inspector of Indian Police (retired)
1933		
9	St George's Road Council School; Oldershaw School for Boys	Superintendent of Customs and Excise (deceased)
10	Roundhay School, Leeds	Accountant
11	Gaisby Street School, Hull; Central School, Scarborough; High School, Scarborough	Railway clerk
12	Greenmount School, Tottington; King Edward VII School, Lytham	Assurance society district manager
13	Bridlington School, Yorkshire; International College, St Gallen, Switzerland	(Deceased)
14	Alleyn's School, Dulwich	Insurance clerk
15	Aldro School, Eastbourne; Wellington College	Far Eastern merchant (retired)
16	Beverley Grammar School	Retired bank manager
17	St Lawrence College Junior School; St Lawrence College, Ramsgate	Engineer
18	Leamington College	Assistant schoolmaster
19	Redland Hill House School, Bristol; Queen Elizabeth's Hospital, Bristol	Baptist minister
20	Sea Point Boys' High School, Cape Town; Buckingham County Secondary School	Guliador
21	March District Senior School; March Grammar School	Slate-layer (deceased)
1934		
22	Cambridge and County High School	Army
23	Westgate School, Warwick; Warwick School	Commercial traveller
24	Oberlin College, Ohio	Librarian
25	Parkside Preparatory School, Tottenham; Tottenham Grammar School; St Alban's School	Civil servant

26	Junior Mixed Elementary School; Senior Elementary School; March Grammar School	Chargeman tuner
27	Bishop Colton School, Simla; University of Bristol	Superintendent, railways (in India)
1935		
28	East Sheen County School	Schoolmaster
29	All Saints' Elementary School; Maidstone Grammar School	Journalist
30	Wheeler Street Elementary School; Boulevard Secondary School	Commercial traveller
31	Preparatory School for Boys, Ilminster; Ilminster Grammar School; Bristol University.	Retired
32	Salisbury Council School; Bishop Wordsworth's School, Salisbury	Accountant
33	Thorpe Hall Preparatory School; Bishops' Stortford College	Baptist minister and headmaster
34	St Agnes RC, Bow; Campion House, Osterly; St Edmund's Old Hall, Ware	Electrical engineer
35	Woodford House School, Birchington, Kent; Secondary School, Lowestoft; County Secondary School, Sandown, Isle of Wight	Auctioneer and estate agent
36	Salisbury School, Australia; National School, Wigan; Wigan Grammar School	Builder
1936		
37	Oldershaw School	Superintendent of Customs and Excise (deceased)
38	Forest School	Box and carton manufacturer
39	Wilson's Grammar School, Camberwell; St Bartholomew's (C. of E.) School, Sydenham	Electrical engineer
40	King's College Choir School; Gresham's School	Brigadier in Indian Army
41	Maidstone Grammar School; King's School, Rochester	Civil servant (retired)
42	Newport Secondary School	Tailor
1937		
43	Wednesbury Boys' High School	Clerk
44	St Andrews-on-Hudson, New York; Woodstock College, New York	(deceased)
45	St Albans School	Teacher
46	Wednesbury Boys' High School	Cashier
1938		
47	St Louis University, Missouri	Driver
48	Leamington College	Postman
49	Warwick School	Ex-officer, mercantile marine

(continued)

Student	School	Father's Occupation
50	Ratcliffe College, Leicester	Medical practitioner
51	Cheltenham College; Cheltenham Technical College	Aeronautical engineer
52	March Grammar School	Locomotive engine driver
53	Marlborough College	Colonel, Regular Army
1939		
54	Nether Edge Secondary School, Sheffield	Warehouseman
55	Seaford College, Sussex	Clergyman
56	Cotton College, Staffordshire	Clerk
57	Kingsmoor School, Glossop	Agent (deceased)
58	Trent College, Derbyshire	Company director
59	King's School, Rochester	Manager of assurance society and author
60	Batley Grammar School	Waste merchant (textiles)
61	Wallasey Grammar School	Coroner's clerk
62	Leeds Modern School	Insurance superintendent
1940		
63	Cheltenham Grammar School	Ironmonger
64	Scarborough Boys' High School	Incorporated accountant
65	Bishop Wordsworth's School, Salisbury	Barrack warden
66	University College School	Clerk
67	St Albans School	Master watchmaker
68	Queen Elizabeth's Grammar School	Tea merchant
69	Gresham's School	Invigilational engineer
70	St Michael's College, Hitchin; the English College in Lisbon	Railway employee
71	Warwick School	Medical practitioner
72	March Grammar School	Painter, decorator, and plumber (deceased)
1941		
73	City of Norwich School	Manager for Wholsesale Motor Fact[o]rs
74	King's School, Rochester	Civil servant
75	Salvatonian College, Harrow Weald	Army surgeon
76	Portsmouth Grammar School	Marine engineer
1942		
77	Downside School	Electrical engineer
78	St Mary's College, Crosby	Timber salesman
79	City Boys' Grammar School, Leicester	Recruiting officer, Royal Marines
80	Wycliffe College, Stonehouse, Gloucestershire	Representative of Messrs Wills
81	Bishop Wordsworth's School, Salisbury	Pharmaceutical chemist
82	Bolton School	Ironmonger and furnisher

83	East Ham Grammar School; Commonweal Secondary School, Swindon	General dealer
1943		
84	Batley Grammar School	Shoddy manufacturer's cashier
85	Haberdashers' Aske's School	Assurance clerk
86	Wallasey Grammar School	Licensed victualler, deceased (father); civil servant (stepfather)
87	March Grammar School	Signalman
88	Poole Grammar School	Optician
89	Forest School	Town Clerk, Solicitor and Civil Defence Controller of Hackney
90	King William's College, Isle of Man	Headmaster
1944		
91	Bristol Grammar School	Journalist
92	Aldershot County High School	Deceased
93	St. Mary's College, Blackburn	Cashier
94	Devonport High School	Gunner, Royal Navy (deceased)
95	March Grammar School	Headmaster
96	Ealing County School	Civil servant
97	Bishop Wordsworth's School, Salisbury	Upholsterer
98	Haberdashers' Aske's Hampstead School	Civil servant
99	Taunton School	Shipbroker
100	St Dunstan's College, Catford	Foreman shipwright
101	Presentation Brothers' College, Co. Cork; African Missions Dromantine College, Newry, Co. Down	Boiler mechanic
102	Holt High School, Liverpool	Hay and corn merchant
103	Poole Grammar School	Lieutenant, R.N.V.R.
104	Canton High School, Cardiff	Brewers' cellarman
105	Taunton School	Basket-maker
1945		
106	City of Norwich School	Sample room manager, boot and shoe factory
107	St Mary's College, Crosby	Manufacturer's agent
108	St Ignatius' College, London	Managing clerk
109	Saltley College, Birmingham	Schoolmaster
110	Central High School, Manchester	Shorthand typist and telephonist
111	Beverley Grammar School	Ironmonger
112	Lord Williams's School, Thame	Scientific instrument maker
1946		
113	Clapham Terrace School, Leamington Spa; Warwick School	Headmaster

(*continued*)

Student	School	Father's Occupation
114	St Columba's School, Greenock; Blair's College, Aberdeen; Gregorian University, Rome	(deceased)
115	Junior High School, Douglas; King William's College, Castletown	Architect and surveyor
116	King Edward VI School, Nuneaton; University College, Leicester	Civil servant
117	Cambridge and County High School; Bourneville Day Continuation School	Sales representative
118	Queen Elizabeth Grammar School, Carmarthen; University College of Wales, Aberystwyth	Mental nurse
119	Staincliffe C. of E. School; Batley Grammar School	Former power-loom tuner
120	Claremont Council School; Blackpool Grammar School	Civil servant
121	Manor House School	Dental surgeon (deceased)
122	Benwick Council School; March Grammar School	Agricultural labourer
123	Westminster City School; King's College London	
124	Rathfern Road School; St Dunstan's College	(deceased)
125	Eastsborough Council School, Dewsbury; Batley Grammar School	Shoddy merchant (textiles: compare the description provided by his brother, no. 60, above)
126	Park Avenue Council School, Nuneaton; King Edward VI Grammar School, Nuneaton	Head lampman, colliery
127	St Mary's College, Crosby	Master mariner
128	Dawson Primary School; City of Norwich School	Saw-mill labourer
1947		
129	Quarry Bank High School for Boys	Railway employee
130	Merchant Taylors' School, Northwood	Schoolmaster
131	Wallasey Grammar School	HM Inspector of Taxes
132	Poole Grammar School	Honorary archivist to Poole Corporation
133	King Edward School, Lichfield	Miner (shot firer) (deceased)
134	Manchester Grammar School	Accountant (deceased)
135	High Storr Grammar School, Sheffield	Commercial representative
136	Kettering Grammar School	Schoolmaster
137	Haberdasher's Aske's Hampstead School	Company secretary
138	Leamington College	Company secretary
1948		
139	Newport (Isle of Wight) County Grammar Secondary School	Aircraft mechanic

140	Haberdasher's Aske's Hampstead School	Schoolmaster
141	Armstrong Junior College	Agricultural advisor to Central Georgia Railway
142	Forest School	Life underwriter
143	St Dunstan's College	Accountant
144	Whitgift School, Croydon	Equipment Branch of the British Broadcasting Corporation
145	St Mary's College, Crosby	Accountant
146	Devonport High School	Gunner, Royal Navy
147	Wallasey Grammar School	Clerk
148	Wednesbury Boys' High School	Foreman, Edge Tool Trade
149	St Olave's Grammar School	Schoolmaster
150	St Dunstan's College	Foreman shipwright
151	Alderham School, Elstree	Director of equine research station of Veterinary Educational Trust
152	St Dunstan's College	Local government officer
153	West Hartlepool Grammar School	Owner and principal of North Eastern School of Motoring
154	March Grammar School	Farmer (retired)
155	Gresham's School	Pharmacist, company director
1949		
156	Ushaw College, Durham	Works foreman
157	Liverpool Institute High School	Shipwright
158	Queen Elizabeth's Grammar School, Gainsborough	Grocery manager
159	Lord Williams's School	Chartered civil engineer
160	Cheltenham Grammar School	Schoolmaster
161	Tiffin Boys' School, Kingston-on-Thames	Schoolteacher (retired)
162	Bolton School	Schoolteacher
1950		
163	St Albans School	Chief storeman, Hertfordshire County Council Hospital
164	Queen Elizabeth's Grammar School, Gainsborough	Foreman fitter
165	Downside School	Consulting engineer
166	Malvern College	Managing director, Engineers' Tools Company
167	Oswestry High School for Boys	Farmer
168	Maynooth College and Ushaw College	Factory manager
169	Greenford County Grammar School	Photographer

(*continued*)

Student	School	Father's Occupation
170	Framlingham College	Clerk
171	Queen Elizabeth's Grammar School, Wakefield	HM Inspector of Mines and Quarries
172	Blackpool Grammar School	Civil servant (clerical)
173	University of Southern California; University of California	Butcher
174	Hitchin Grammar School	Manufacturer
175	Farnborough Grammar School	Civil servant
176	Haileybury and Imperial Service College, Hertford	Information Officer and Control Commission
1951		
177	Brighton College	Lt-Col, Royal Artillery (retired)
178	Manchester Grammar School	Director, Manchester Art Galleries
179	Heath Grammar School, Halifax	Maintenance engineer
180	Chingford County High School	Civil servant
181	King Edward VII, Lytham	Bank cashier
182	Lord Williams's School	Engineer (retired)
183	Haberdashers' Aske's Hampstead School	Bank clerk
184	St Louis University High School	————
185	St Cuthbert's Grammar School	Superintendent, Great Northern Telegraph Company of Denmark (deceased)
186	Tiffin Boys' School	
187	Belle Vue Grammar School, Bradford	Executive Engineer, P.O. Telephones
188	King Edward VI Grammar School, Retford	Colliery banksman
189	Royal High School, Edinburgh	Commercial artist
190	Scarborough High School	Civil servant
191	Stationers' Company's School	Managing editor
192	Harrow County Grammar School	Accountant
193	Forest School	Clothier
194	Marlborough College	Director of a carpet factory
195	Wolverhampton Grammar School	Master butcher
196	Dromantine College, Newry, Northern Ireland	Charge-hand labourer, Mersey Dock and Harbour Board
197	John Fisher School, Purley	Assistant staff manager, bank
198	Queen's College, Taunton	Architect's assistant
199	Liverpool Institute High School	Police constable
1952		
200	Perse School	Heating engineer
201	Harrow County Grammar School	Customs and Excise officer

202	St Mary's Grammar School, Darlington	Head of Engineering Department, Technical College, Darlington
203	Oswestry High School	Surgical bootmaker
204	Hendon County School	Master hairdresser
205	Ratcliffe College	Medical practitioner
206	Queen Elizabeth's Grammar School, Crediton	Managing director
207	Crypt Grammar School, Gloucester	(Deceased)
208	Burnage High School, Manchester	Electrical engineer (chartered)
209	Queen Elizabeth's Grammar School, Wakefield	Colliery manager

1953

210	Forest School	School bursar
211	King's College School Wimbledon	Musician
212	Kettering Grammar	Upholsterer and cabinet maker
213	Chislehurst and Sidcup County Grammar School	Civil servant (clerical)
214	Greenford County Grammar School	Master tailor
215	Bedford School	Solicitors' managing clerk (retired)
216	West Leeds High School	Motor mechanic
217	Haberdashers' Aske's Hampstead School	Bank clerk
218	Sudbury Grammar	Representative, Eastern Electricity Board
219	Epsom College	Market clerk
220	John Fisher School	Importer
221	Chislehurst and Sidcup County Grammar School	Retail tobacconist and newsagent

1954

222	Framlingham	Veterinary surgeon
223	Haileybury and Imperial Service College	District commissioner, Nyasaland (retired)
224	Haberdashers' Aske's Hampstead School	Hairdresser
225	John Fisher School	Schoolmaster
226	East Ham Grammar School	Public house manager
227	Emmanuel School	Civil servant
228	Purley County Grammar	Unskilled labourer
229	Harrow County Grammar	Teacher
230	St Joseph's Seminary	Civil servant
231	Groton School, Massachusetts; University of the South, Tennessee (Sewanee)	Professor of Philosophy
232	King Edward VII, Lytham	Industrial chemist

(continued)

Student	School	Father's Occupation
233	The King's School, Peterborough	Employee of provision merchant
234	Neath County Grammar School and University College of Wales, Aberystwyth	Senior chemistry master, grammar school
1955		
235	Portsmouth Grammar School	WRA, HMS *Vernon*
236	Ushaw College	Deceased
237	Sir Joseph Williamson's Mathematical School, Rochester	Armaments fitter
238	St Illtyd's College, Cardiff	Welder
239	Christ's College, Brecon	Holy orders in Church of England
240	University of Toronto	Physician
241	St Olave's Grammar School	Watchmaker
242	Royal High School, Edinburgh	Master mariner, merchant navy
243	Christ's Hospital	Builder and farmer
244	Chislehurst and Sidcup Grammar School	Intertype operator
245	St Illtyd's College	Schoolmaster
246	West Leeds High School	Baker (retired)
247	City Boys' Grammar School, Leicester	Music hall artiste
248	Roundhay School, Leeds	Textile dealer
249	Lycée de Tourcoing	Headmaster of École Michelet, Tourcoing
250	Highgate School	Teacher
251	King Edward VI, Retford	Signwriter and decorator
252	John Fisher School	Civil servant (retired)
253	Ratcliffe College	Steel representative
1956		
254	Sir Joseph Williamson's Mathematical School	Schoolmaster
255	———	———
256	St Alban's School	Railway clerk
257	———	Chartered accountant
258	Queen Elizabeth Grammar School, Darlington	Leathercraft instructor
259	Royal Liberty School	Printer's machine minder
260	St George's College, Weybridge and Cambridgeshire Technical College	Adviser and buyer in antique furniture etc.
261	Barnsley and District Holgate Grammar School	Coal merchant
262	Haberdashers' Aske's Hampstead School	Chartered quantity surveyor
263	Woodhouse Grammar School	Headmaster of secondary technical school
264	Ushaw College and Cambridgeshire Technical College	Retired

| 265 | Sir Joseph Williamson's Mathematical School | Ironmonger and house furnisher |
| 266 | Sir Joseph Williamson's Mathematical School | Motor trader and garage proprietor |

1957

267	Scarborough Boys High	Retired bank official
268	King Edward VI, Pontefract	Agent for British Transport Commission, British Waterways
269	The King's School, Pontefract	Surface labourer, Prince of Wales Colliery, Pontefract
270	Sir Joseph Williamson's Mathematical School	Bookseller
271	King Edward VII, Lytham	Chiropodist
272	Mill Hill School, London	Salesman
273	Chingford County High School	—————
274	City of Norwich School	Audit clerk
275	Dulwich College	Clerk in Bank of England
276	St George's School, Harpenden	Industrial artist
277	St Alban's County Grammar School for Boys	Fitter in aircraft factory (chargehand)
278	St Paul's School, London	General Secretary of the Labour Party
279	University College, Ghana	Weaving
280	Highgate School	Lecturer, University of Exeter
281	John Fisher School	Bank official
282	King Edward VII, Lytham	Clerk

1958

283	Huddersfield New College	Headmaster
284	Perse School	Editor
285	Royal High School, Edinburgh	Greengrocer (shop manager)
286	John Fisher School	Insurance surveyor
287	City Boys' School, Leicester	Regional fuel inspector
288	St Dunstan's College	Pharmacist
289	Wolstanton Grammar School, Newcastle-under-Lyme	Master grocer
290	Bablake School, Coventry, and the University of Exeter	Motor mechanic
291	Quintin School, London	Artist
292	Tiffin Boys' School	Bank manager
293	John Fisher School	Insurance official
294	Perse School	Retired
295	City of London School	Journalist
296	Sir Joseph Williamson's Mathematical School	Cost accountant
297	Liverpool Institute High School	Progress clerk

(continued)

Student	School	Father's Occupation
1959		
298	St George's College, Weybridge	Bank of England
299	Sir Joseph Williamson's Mathematical School	Motor and electrical engineer, HM Dockyard
300	Stand Grammar School, Whitefield	Sales representative
301	John Fisher School	Senior editor (Pitman)
302	Farnborough Grammar School	Major (quartermaster), RAMC
303	Dulwich College	Warrant officer, Metropolitan Police
304	Haberdashers' Aske's Hampstead School	History master
305	Northgate Grammar School for Boys, Ipswich	Cabinet maker (reproduction furniture)
306	Finchley Catholic Grammar School	Civil servant (retired)
307	Palmer's School for Boys, Grays, Essex	Solicitor (former profession)
308	Bristol Cathedral School	Manager of men's outfitting shop
309	The King's School, Macclesfield	Bank cashier
310	Carmel College, Wallingford	Tool factor
311	Tiffin Boys' School	Retired police sergeant (and telephonist)
1960		
312	Ashby-de-la-Zouch Grammar	Head teacher
313	Merchant Taylor's, Northwood	Civil servant
314	Belmont Abbey School, Hereford, and the University of Exeter	Medical officer of health
315	Perse School	Headmaster
316	Bournemouth School	Motor engineer
317	City of Leicester Boys' Grammar School	Hosiery warehouse manager
318	Forest School	Telephone engineer
319	Stowe School	Barrister-at-law
320	Northgate Grammar School for Boys, Ipswich	————
321	Bemrose School, Derby	Pattern-maker
1961		
322	Perse School	Chartered municipal treasurer
323	Bemrose Grammar School	Businessman
324	Stand Grammar School	Market trader
325	St Bede's College, Manchester	Turner
326	Judd School, Tonbridge	Civil servant
1962		
327	Brighton College	Colonial police officer
328	High Pavement Grammar School, Nottingham	Chartered accountant
329	Tiffin Boys' School	Company director

330	Royal High School, Edinburgh and Edinburgh University	Chef
331	St Patrick's College, Wellington, New Zealand	Salesman (deceased)
332	John Fisher School	Solicitor to the Board of Trade
333	St Cuthbert's Grammar School, Newcastle-on-Tyne	Company director, roofing felt manufacturer
334	Portsmouth Grammar School	Farmer
335	King's School, Macclesfield	Professional civil servant

References

A. PRIMARY SOURCES

I. Manuscripts and Archives
Borthwick Institute, University of York.
Leavis, F. R. Papers.
BBC Written Archives Centre, Reading.
Ford, Boris. Contributor Files.
Holbrook, David. Contributor Files.
Kennedy, Ludovic. Contributor Files.
Third Programme Short Story Competition, 1948–9. Files.
Thompson, Denys. Contributor Files.
Wain, John. Contributor Files.
Brotherton Library, University of Leeds.
Dobrée, Bonamy. Papers.
Knight, G. Wilson. Papers.
Cambridge University Library.
Deighton, Bell, & Co. Archives.
[R. B. Ford, I. Watt, C. Barber, L. Salingar, F. Whitehead, and H. E. Poole.]
  'Report of a Committee of Enquiry into the Problems of Teaching in the English Faculty: February–April 1937'.
Columbia University Library, New York.
Trilling, Lionel. Papers.
Downing College, Cambridge.
Admissions Books.
Doughty Society. Minute Book.
Governing Body Records.
Leavis, F. R. Papers.
Emmanuel College, Cambridge.
Harding, D. W. Papers.
Leavis, F. R. Papers.
Girton College, Cambridge.
Bradbrook, M. C. Papers.
Diggle, Margaret. Papers.
Leavis, Q. D. Papers.
Harry Ransom Humanities Research Center, University of Texas at Austin.
Wesker, Arnold. Papers.
Houghton Library, Harvard University, Cambridge, Massachusetts.
Empson, William. Papers.
Leavis, F. R. Papers.

Kenyon College Archives, Gambier, Ohio.
School of English Papers.
King's College Archive Centre, Cambridge.
Annan, N. G. Papers.
Rylands, G. H. W. Papers.
Library of Congress, Washington, DC.
Chase, Stuart. Papers.
The National Archives, Kew.
Board of Education and Successors: Private Office. Files and Papers (Series II).
University of Bristol Library.
Penguin Archive.
University of Oxford Archives.
Department of Continuing Education. Papers.
University of Reading Library.
Chatto & Windus Archive.
The Group Papers.
University of Sheffield Library.
Hoggart, Richard. Papers.
University of Sussex Library.
Madge, Charles. Papers.
University of Sydney Archives.
Faculty of Arts Minute Books.
Professorial Board Minute Books.

II. Periodicals and Series
Calendar of Modern Letters.
Clare Association Annual.
Critical Quarterly.
Critical Survey.
Downing College Association Newsletter and College Record.
Emmanuel College Magazine.
English in Education.
English in Schools.
Examination Papers for Scholarships and Exhibitions in the Colleges of the University of Cambridge.
Girton Review.
The Human World.
Melbourne Critical Review (later *Critical Review*).
Newnham College Roll Letter.
NATE Bulletin.
Our Time.
Scrutiny.
The Teaching of English: Issued by the Incorporated Association of Assistant Masters in Secondary Schools.
Use of English.

III. Recorded Interviews

Brokensha, David. Interview with Alan Macfarlane, 25 August 2006. Available at <http://www.alanmacfarlane.com/DO/filmshow/brokensha1_fast.htm>, accessed 8 August 2011.

Goody, Jack. Interview with Eric Hobsbawm, 18 May 1991. Available at <http://www.dspace.cam.ac.uk/handle/1810/268>, accessed 4 July 2011.

Ruel, Malcolm. Interview with Alan Macfarlane, 15 December 2002. Available at <http://www.dspace.cam.ac.uk/handle/1810/756>, accessed 8 August 2011.

IV. Unpublished Thesis

E. H. McCormick, 'Literature in New Zealand: An Essay in Cultural Criticism', Cambridge University thesis, 1935 (copy in E. H. McCormick Papers, MSX-4250, Alexander Turnbull Library, National Library of New Zealand, Wellington).

V. Books and Articles

Alvarez, A., *Where Did It All Go Right? A Memoir* (New York: William Morrow, 1999).

Amis, Kingsley, *Memoirs* (London: Hutchinson, 1991).

Anderson, Perry, 'Components of the National Culture', *New Left Review* 50 (1968): 3–57.

—— *Considerations on Western Marxism* (London: New Left Books, 1976).

Arnold, Matthew, *The Complete Prose Works of Matthew Arnold*, ed. R. H. Super, 11 vols (Ann Arbor: University of Michigan Press, 1960–77).

Bantock, G. H., *Education, Culture and the Emotions* (London: Faber & Faber, 1967).

—— *Education in an Industrial Society* (London: Faber & Faber, 1963).

Bateson, F. W., 'The Alternative to *Scrutiny*', *Essays in Criticism* 14/1 (1964): 10–20.

—— 'Contributions to a Dictionary of Critical Terms: II. Dissociation of Sensibility', *Essays in Criticism* 1/3 (1951): 302–12.

—— 'The Function of Criticism at the Present Time', *Essays in Criticism* 3/1 (1953): 1–27.

Batsleer, Janet, Tony Davis, Rebecca O'Rourke, and Chris Weedon, *Rewriting English: Cultural Politics of Gender and Class* (London: Methuen, 1985).

Beaglehole, J. C., *New Zealand: A Short History* (London: G. Allen & Unwin, 1936).

—— 'The New Zealand Scholar' (1954), in Peter Munz (ed.), *The Feel of Truth: Essays in New Zealand and Pacific History* (Wellington: A. H. & A. W. Reed for Victoria University of Wellington, 1969), 237–52.

Bennett, E. A., *Fame and Fiction: An Enquiry into Certain Popularities* (London: Grant Richards, 1901).

Bentley, Eric (ed.), *The Importance of Scrutiny: Selections from 'Scrutiny: a Quarterly Review', 1932–1948* (New York: George W. Stewart, 1948).

Biaggini, Ernest Gordon, *English in Australia: Taste and Training in a Modern Community* (Melbourne: Melbourne University Press in association with Oxford University Press, 1933).

—— *The Reading and Writing of English* (London: Hutchinson, 1936).

Blishen, Edward, *Roaring Boys: A Schoolmaster's Agony* (1955; Bath: Chivers, 1974).

Blyth, John A., *English University Adult Education, 1908–1958: The Unique Tradition* (Manchester: Manchester University Press, 1983).

Bradbrook, M. C., *Themes and Conventions of Elizabethan Tragedy* (Cambridge: Cambridge University Press, 1935).

Britton, James, 'How We Got Here', in Nicholas Bagnall (ed.), *New Movements in the Study and Teaching of English* (London: Maurice Temple Smith, 1973), 13–28.

—— 'Professor P. Gurrey', *ELT Journal* 35/3 (1981): 352–3.

—— *Prospect and Retrospect: Selected Essays of James Britton*, ed. Gordon M. Pradl (Montclair, NJ: Boynton/Cook, 1982).

Brooke, Stopford, *English Literature* (1876; Toronto: James Campbell & Son, 1877).

Buckley, Vincent, *Cutting Green Hay: Friendships, Movements and Cultural Conflicts in Australia's Great Decades* (Melbourne: Allen Lane/Penguin, 1983).

—— *Poetry and Morality: Studies on the Criticism of Matthew Arnold, T. S. Eliot and F. R. Leavis* (1959; London: Chatto & Windus, 1961).

[Centre for Contemporary Cultural Studies], *Culture, Media, Language: Working Papers in Cultural Studies, 1972–79* (London: Hutchinson, 1980).

Chadwick, H. Munro and N. Kershaw Chadwick, *The Growth of Literature*, vol. 1, *The Ancient Literatures of Europe* (Cambridge: Cambridge University Press, 1932).

Chase, Stuart and F. J. Schlink, *Your Money's Worth: A Study in the Waste of the Consumer's Dollar* (New York: Macmillan, 1927).

Churchill, R. C., *Disagreements: A Polemic on Culture in the English Democracy* (London: Secker and Warburg, 1950).

Clements, Simon, John Dixon, and Leslie Stratta, *Reflections: An English Course for Students Aged 14–18* (1963; Oxford: Oxford University Press, 1966).

Collinson, Patrick, *The History of a History Man: Or, the Twentieth Century Viewed from a Safe Distance: The Memoirs of Patrick Collinson* (Woodbridge: Boydell Press, 2011).

Constable, John (ed.), *Selected Letters of I. A. Richards, CH* (Oxford: Clarendon Press, 1990).

[Council for Academic Freedom and Democracy,] *The Craig Affair: Background to the Case of Dr David Craig and Others, Lancaster University* (London: Council for Academic Freedom and Democracy, 1972).

Cox, Brian, *The Great Betrayal: Memoirs of a Life in Education* (London: Chapman, 1992).

—— and A. E. Dyson (eds), *Black Paper Two: The Crisis in Education* (London: Critical Quarterly Society, n.d. [1969]).

———— (eds), *Fight for Education: A Black Paper* (London: Critical Quarterly Society, n.d. [1969]).

Craig, David, letter to the editor, *London Review of Books*, 8 November 1990.

—— *Scottish Literature and the Scottish People, 1680–1830* (London: Chatto & Windus, 1961).

Curnow, Allen, 'Attitudes for a New Zealand Poet: III: The Skeleton of the Great Moa in the Canterbury Museum, Christchurch' (1943), in *Collected Poems, 1933–1973* (Wellington: A. H. & A. W. Reed, 1974), 142.

Davie, Donald, *These the Companions: Recollections* (Cambridge: Cambridge University Press, 1982).

Dawson, S. W., '*Scrutiny* and the Idea of a University', *Essays in Criticism* 14/1 (January 1964): 1–9.

Dixon, John, *Growth through English: A Report Based on the Dartmouth Seminar 1966* (1967; [Reading]: National Association for the Teaching of English, 1969).

Dow, Hume (ed.), *More Memories of Melbourne University: Undergraduate Life in the Years Since 1919* (Melbourne: Hutchinson of Australia, 1985).

Duncan, Ronald, *All Men Are Islands: An Autobiography* (London: Rupert Hart-Davis, 1964).

Eliot, T. S., *The Sacred Wood: Essays on Poetry and Criticism* (1920; London: Methuen, 1932).

——*Selected Essays* (London: Faber & Faber, 1951).

Elvin, Lionel, *Encounters with Education* (London: Institute of Education, University of London, 1987).

Empson, William, *Some Versions of Pastoral* (London: Chatto & Windus, 1935).

Enright, D. J., *Conspirators and Poets* (London: Chatto & Windus, 1966).

——*Memoirs of a Mendicant Professor* (London: Chatto & Windus, 1969).

Felperin, Howard, *Beyond Deconstruction: The Uses and Abuses of Literary Theory* (Oxford: Oxford University Press, 1985).

Findlater, Richard, *What Are Writers Worth?* (London: Society of Authors, 1963), reproduced in Peter Davison, Rolf Meyersohn, and Edward Shils (eds), *Literary Taste, Culture and Mass Communication*, 14 vols (Cambridge: Chadwyck-Healey and Teaneck, NJ: Somerset House, 1978–80), 10: 279–309.

Ford, Boris, *The Bureau of Current Affairs, 1946–1951* (London: Bureau of Current Affairs, 1951).

——'David Holbrook: A Portrait', in Edwin Webb (ed.), *Powers of Being: David Holbrook and His Work* (Madison, NJ: Fairleigh Dickinson University Press, 1995), 27–50.

——*Liberal Education in a Technical Age: A Survey of the Relationship of Vocational and Non-Vocational Further Education and Training* (London: Parrish, 1955).

——'Obituary: Professor L. C. Knights', *The Independent*, 15 March 1997.

——(ed.), *The Pelican Guide to English Literature*, 7 vols (Harmondsworth: Penguin, 1954–61).

French, Philip, 'Leavis at 80—What Has His Influence Been?' *The Listener*, 24 July 1974.

Glanville, Brian, *Football Memories: Over 50 Years of the Beautiful Game* (London: Robson Books, 2004).

Goldberg, S. L., *The Classical Temper: A Study of James Joyce's 'Ulysses'* (London: Chatto & Windus, 1961).

Gordon, George, *The Discipline of Letters* (Oxford: Clarendon Press, 1946).

Greenfield, George, *Scribblers for Bread: Aspects of the English Novel since 1945* (London: Hodder & Stoughton, 1989).

——*A Smattering of Monsters: A Kind of Memoir* (Columbia, SC: Camden House, 1995).

Grierson, H. J. C. and G. Bullough (eds), *The Oxford Book of Seventeenth Century Verse* (Oxford: Oxford University Press, 1934).

Groombridge, Brian, *Television and the People: A Programme for Democratic Participation* (Harmondsworth: Penguin, 1972).

Gross, John, *The Rise and Fall of the Man of Letters: Aspects of English Literary Life since 1800* (1969; Chicago: Ivan R. Dee, 1992).

Haffenden, John (ed.), *Selected Letters of William Empson* (Oxford: Oxford University Press, 2006).

Hall, Stuart and Paddy Whannel, *The Popular Arts* (London: Hutchinson, 1964).

Hawkins, T. H. and L. J. F. Brimble, *Adult Education: The Record of the British Army* (London: Macmillan, 1947).

Hayman, Ronald (ed.), *My Cambridge* (1977; London: Robson Books, 1986).

Higher Education: Report of the Committee Appointed by the Prime Minister under the chairmanship of Lord Robbins, 1961–1963 (London): HM Stationery Office, 1963.

Himmelweit, Hilde T., A. N. Oppenheim, and Pamela Vince, *Television and the Child: An Empirical Study of the Effect of Television on the Young* (London: Oxford University Press, 1958).

Hobsbawm, Eric, 'Diary', *London Review of Books*, 27 May 2010, 41.

Hoggart, Richard, *An Imagined Life: Life and Times, Volume III, 1959–91* (1992; Oxford: Oxford University Press, 1993).

——*A Sort of Clowning: Life and Times, Volume II, 1940–59* (London: Chatto & Windus, 1990).

——*Speaking to Each Other: Essays*, Vol. 1, *About Society;* Vol. 2, *About Literature* (London: Chatto & Windus, 1970).

——*The Uses of Literacy: Aspects of Working-Class Life, with Special References to Publications and Entertainments* (London: Chatto & Windus, 1957).

Holbrook, David, *English for Maturity: English in the Secondary School* (Cambridge: Cambridge University Press, 1961; 2nd edn, 1967).

——*English for the Rejected: Training Literacy in the Lower Streams of the Secondary School* (1964; Cambridge: Cambridge University Press, 1968).

——(ed.), *The Case against Pornography* (London: Tom Stacey, 1972).

Holcroft, M. H., *The Deepening Stream: Cultural Influences in New Zealand* (Christchurch, NZ: Caxton Press, 1940).

Inglis, Fred, *The Englishness of English Teaching* (London: Longman, 1969).

Jackson, Brian and Dennis Marsden, *Education and the Working Class: Some General Themes Raised by a Study of 88 Working-Class Children in a Northern Industrial City* (1962; Harmondsworth: Penguin, 1966).

Jackson, Brian (ed.), *English versus Examinations: A Handbook for Teachers* (London: Chatto & Windus, 1965).

——and Denys Thompson (eds), *English in Education: A Selection of Articles on the Teaching of English at Different Levels from Infant School to University* (London: Chatto & Windus, 1962).

Jameson, Storm, *Journey from the North II* (London: Collins & Harvill Press, 1970).

Jenkinson, A. J., *What Do Boys and Girls Read? An Investigation into Reading Habits with Some Suggestions about the Teaching of Literature in Secondary and Senior Schools* (1940; London: Methuen, 1946).

Kermode, Frank, *Not Entitled: A Memoir* (New York: Farrar, Straus, & Giroux, 1995).

Knight, G. Wilson, *The Wheel of Fire* (1930; London: Routledge, 2001).

Knights, L. C., *Explorations: Essays in Criticism Mainly on the Literature of the Seventeenth Century* (London: Chatto & Windus, 1946).

Kracauer, Siegfried, *The Salaried Masses: Duty and Distraction in Weimar Germany*, trans. Quintin Hoare (London: Verso, 1998).

Leavis, F. R., *Anna Karenina and Other Essays* (London: Chatto & Windus, 1967).

——*Education and the University: A Sketch for an 'English School'* (London: Chatto & Windus, 1943).

——*English Literature in Our Time and the University: The Clark Lectures 1967* (1969; Cambridge: Cambridge University Press, 1979).

——*For Continuity* (Cambridge: Minority Press, 1933).

——*The Great Tradition: George Eliot, Henry James, Joseph Conrad* (1948; London: Chatto & Windus, 1960).

——*How to Teach Reading: A Primer for Ezra Pound* (Cambridge: Minority Press, 1932).

——*Letters in Criticism*, ed. John Tasker (London: Chatto & Windus, 1974).

——*The Living Principle: English as a Discipline of Thought* (London: Chatto & Windus, 1975).

——*New Bearings in English Poetry: A Study of the Contemporary Situation* (London: Chatto & Windus, 1932).

——*Nor Shall My Sword: Discourses on Pluralism, Compassion, and Social Hope* (London: Chatto & Windus, 1972).

——(ed.), *Determinations: Critical Essays* (London: Chatto & Windus, 1934).

——(ed.), *Towards Standards of Criticism: Selections from the Calendar of Modern Letters, 1925–7* (1933; London: Lawrence & Wishart, 1976).

——and Denys Thompson, *Culture and Environment: The Training of Critical Awareness* (1933; London: Chatto & Windus, 1950).

Leavis, Q. D., *Fiction and the Reading Public* (1932; London: Chatto & Windus, 1965).

Leigh, John Garrett, 'What Do the Masses Read?', *Economic Review* 14/2 (1904): 166–77.

Lewis, C. S., *Rehabilitations and Other Essays* (London: Oxford University Press, 1939).

Lindsay, Jack, *Fanfrolico, and After* (London: Bodley Head, 1962).

Ludowyk, E. F. C., 'The East-West Problem in Sinhalese Literature', *Yearbook of Comparative and General Literature* 6 (1957): 31–5.

——*Marginal Comments* (Colombo: Ola Book Company, 1945).

——*Those Long Afternoons: Childhood in Colonial Ceylon* (Colombo: Lake House Bookshop, 1989).

Lynd, Robert S., *Knowledge for What? The Place of Social Science in American Culture* (1939, Princeton: Princeton University Press, 1948).

——and Helen Merrell Lynd, *Middletown: A Study in American Culture* (New York: Harcourt, Brace, & Co., 1929).

MacCabe, Colin, 'An Interview with Stuart Hall, December 2007', *Critical Quarterly* 50/1–2 (2008): 12–42.

McCormick, E. H., *An Absurd Ambition: Autobiographical Writings*, ed. Dennis McEldowney (Auckland: Auckland University Press, 1996).

——*Letters and Art in New Zealand* (Wellington: Department of Internal Affairs, 1940).

Macherey, Pierre, *A Theory of Literary Production*, trans. Geoffrey Wall (1966; London: Routledge & Kegan Paul, 1978).

McIlroy, John and Sallie Westwood (eds), *Border Country: Raymond Williams in Adult Education* (Leicester: National Institute of Adult Continuing Education, 1993).

Marshall, Sybil, *An Experiment in Education* (1963; Cambridge: Cambridge University Press, 1966).

Mathieson, Margaret, *The Preachers of Culture: A Study of English and Its Teachers* (London: Allen & Unwin, 1975).

Matthews, David, *Memories of F. R. Leavis* (Bishopstone: Brynmill Press, 2010).

Mayhead, Robin, 'Changing English in Two Young Dominions', *Universities Quarterly* 12/4 (August 1958): 426–56.

Mellers, Wilfrid, *Twilight of the Gods: The Beatles in Retrospect* (London: Faber & Faber, 1973).

Miller, Karl, 'Cambridge Diary', *New Statesman*, 28 May 1965.

——*Dark Horses: An Experience of Literary Journalism* (London: Picador, 1999).

——*Rebecca's Vest: A Memoir* (London: Hamish Hamilton, 1993).

Mount, Ferdinand, *Cold Cream: My Early Life and Other Mistakes* (London: Bloomsbury, 2009).

Narasimhaiah, C. D., *'N for Nobody': Autobiography of an English Teacher* (Delhi: B. R. Publishing Corporation, 1991).

——(ed.), *Fiction and the Reading Public in India* (Mysore: University of Mysore, 1967).

O'Brien, Edward J., *The Dance of the Machines: The American Short Story and the Industrial Age* (London: Jonathan Cape, 1929).

O'Malley, Raymond, *One-Horse Farm: Crofting in the West Highlands* (London: Frederick Muller, 1948).

——and D. Thompson, *English for the Living* (London: Methuen, 1949).

————*English for the Living: Part II* (London: Methuen, 1952).

Orwell, George, *The Collected Essays, Journalism and Letters of George Orwell*, ed. Sonia Orwell and Ian Angus, 4 vols (Boston: Nonpareil Books, 2000).

Phillips, A. A., *The Australian Tradition: Studies in Colonial Culture* (Melbourne: F. W. Cheshire, 1958).

Pinto, Vivian de Sola (ed.), *The Teaching of English in Schools: A Symposium Edited for the English Association* (London: Macmillan, 1946).

Popular Culture and Personal Responsibility: A Conference of Those Engaged in Education Together with Parents, Those Directly or Indirectly Concerned with the Welfare of Children and Young People, and People Involved in the Mass Media Themselves, to Examine the Impact of Mass Communications on Present-Day Moral and Cultural Standards: Held at Church House, Westminister, 26th to 28th October 1960: Verbatiom Report (London, n.d.).

Pound, Ezra, *A B C of Reading* (New Haven: Yale University Press, 1934).

——*How to Read* (London: Desmond Harmsworth, 1931).

Priestley, J. B., *English Journey: Being a Rambling but Truthful Account of What One Man Saw and Heard and Felt during a Journey through England during the Autumn of the Year 1933* (1934; Harmondsworth: Penguin, 1977).

Pryce-Jones, Alan, untitled memoir in William Plomer et al., *Coming to London* (London: Phoenix House, 1957), 118–27.

The Public Schools and the General Education System: Report of the Committee on Public Schools Appointed by the President of the Board of Education in July 1942 (London: HM Stationery Office, 1944).

Raybould, S. G. (ed.), *Trends in English Adult Education* (London: Heinemann, 1959).

Richards, I. A., *Practical Criticism: A Study of Literary Judgment* (London: Kegan Paul, Trench, Trubner, 1929).

——*Principles of Literary Criticism* (1924; London: Kegan Paul, Trench, Trubner, 1926).

Rickword, Edgell (ed.), *Scrutinies: By Various Writers*, 2 vols (London: Wishart, 1928–31).

Riemer, Andrew, *Sandstone Gothic: Confessions of an Accidental Academic* (Sydney: Allen & Unwin, 1998).

Sampson, Anthony, *Anatomy of Britain* (London: Hodder & Stoughton, 1962).

Sampson, George, *English for the English: A Chapter on National Education*, ed. Denys Thompson (1921; Cambridge: Cambridge University Press, 1970).

Smith, A. E., *English in the Modern School* (London: Methuen, 1954).

Smith, E. M., *A History of New Zealand Fiction from 1862 to the Present Time with Some Account of Its Relation to the National Life and Character* (Dunedin: A. H. & A. W. Reed, 1939).

Stevens, Frances, *The Living Tradition: The Social and Educational Assumptions of the Grammar School* (1960; London: Hutchinson, 1972).

Summerfield, Geoffrey, *Topics in English: For the Secondary School* (London: B. T. Batsford, 1965).

Thiong'o, Ngũgĩ wa, *Decolonising the Mind: The Politics of Language in African Literature* (London: James Currey, 1986).

Thomas, T. W., 'Practical Criticism and the Literature Class', *Adult Education* 24/2 (1951): 20–9.

Thompson, Denys, *Reading and Discrimination* (London: Chatto & Windus, 1934).

——(ed.), *Directions in the Teaching of English* (Cambridge: Cambridge University Press, 1969).

——(ed.), *Discrimination and Popular Culture* (Harmondsworth: Penguin, 1964).

—— (ed.), *The Leavises: Recollections and Impressions* (Cambridge: Cambridge University Press, 1984).

Thompson, E. P., *The Making of the English Working Class* (1963; Harmondsworth: Penguin, 1980).

Tillyard, E. M. W., *The Elizabethan World Picture* (London: Chatto & Windus, 1943).

—— *The Muse Unchained: An Intimate Account of the Revolution in English Studies at Cambridge* (London: Bowes & Bowes, 1958).

Trodd, Kenneth, 'Report from the Younger Generation', *Essays in Criticism* 14/1 (January 1964): 21–32.

Truscot, Bruce [pseud. E. Allison Peers], *Redbrick University* (London: Faber & Faber, 1943).

Vaizey, John, 'The Public Schools', in Hugh Thomas (ed.), *The Establishment: A Symposium* (London: Anthony Blond, 1959).

—— 'Scrutiny and Education', *Essays in Criticism* 14/1 (1964): 36–42.

Vaughan, Paul, *Exciting Times in the Accounts Department* (London: Sinclair Stevenson, 1995).

Veblen, Thorstein, *The Theory of the Leisure Class: An Economic Study in the Evolution of Institutions* (New York: Macmillan, 1899).

Walsh, William, *D. J. Enright: Poet of Humanism* (Cambridge: Cambridge University Press, 1974).

—— *F. R. Leavis* (London: Chatto & Windus, 1980).

—— *The Use of Imagination: Educational Thought and the Literary Mind* (London: Chatto & Windus, 1960).

Warburg, Fredric, *An Occupation for Gentlemen* (1959; Cambridge, Mass.: Riverside Press, 1960).

Whitehead, Frank, *The Disappearing Dais: A Study of the Principles and Practice of English Teaching* (London: Chatto & Windus, 1966).

Wilding, Michael, 'Among Leavisites', *Southerly* 59/3–4 (1999), 67–93.

Willey, Basil, *Cambridge and Other Memories, 1920–1953* (London: Chatto & Windus, 1970).

—— *The Seventeenth-Century Background: Studies in the Thought of the Age in Relation to Poetry and Religion* (London: Chatto & Windus, 1934).

Williams, Raymond, *Culture and Society, 1780–1950* (1958; Harmondsworth: Penguin, 1963).

—— *Politics and Letters: Interviews with New Left Review* (London: New Left Books, 1979).

—— *Reading and Criticism* (London: Frederick Muller, 1950).

Woolf, Virginia, 'Mr. Bennett and Mrs. Brown' (1924), in *Collected Essays*, vol. 2 (London: Hogarth Press, 1966), 319–37.

—— *The Letters of Virginia Woolf*, vol. 3, *1923–1928*, ed. Nigel Nicolson and Joanne Trautmann (New York: Harcourt Brace Jovanovich, 1977).

Woolford, Jack, 'Tony McLean: A Memoir', in Workers' Educational Association South Eastern District, *Adult Education and Social Change: Lectures and Reminiscences in Honour of Tony McLean* (n.p., n.d. [1984?]), 4–5.

Young, Allan and Michael Schmidt, 'A Conversation with Edgell Rickword', *Poetry Nation* 1 (1973): 73–89.

B. SECONDARY SOURCES

I. Published

Abravanel, Genevieve, 'English by Example: F. R. Leavis and the Americanization of Modern England', *Modernism/modernity* 15/4 (2008): 685–701.

Alexander, Fred, *Campus at Crawley: A Narrative and Critical Appreciation of the First Fifty Years of the University of Western Australia* (Melbourne: F. W. Cheshire, 1963).

Allen, David, *English Teaching since 1965: How Much Growth?* (London: Heinemann, 1980).

Alloway, Ross, 'Selling the Great Tradition: Resistance and Conformity in the Publishing Practices of F. R. Leavis', *Book History* 6 (2003): 227–50.

Ascherson, Neal, 'Great Brain Spotter', *Independent on Sunday*, 28 February 1993.

Attridge, David, *Joyce Effects: On Language, Theory, and History* (Cambridge: Cambridge University Press, 2000).

Baker, William, Maurice Kinch, and John Kimber, *F. R. Leavis and Q. D. Leavis: An Annotated Bibliography* (NewYork: Garland, 1989).

Baldick, Chris, *The Modern Movement*, vol. 10 of *The Oxford English Literary History*, ed. Jonathan Bate (Oxford: Oxford University Press, 2004).

—— *The Social Mission of English Criticism, 1848–1932* (Oxford: Clarendon Press, 1983).

Barber, Michael, *Anthony Powell: A Life* (London: Duckworth Overlook, 2004).

Barrs, Myra, 'Obituary: Martin Lightfoot', *The Independent*, 1 June 1999.

Beauchamp, Christopher, 'Getting *Your Money's Worth*: American Models for the Remaking of the Consumer Interest in Britain, 1930s–1960s', in Mark Bevir and Frank Trentmann (eds), *Critiques of Capital in Modern Britain and America Transatlantic Exchanges 1800 to the Present Day* (Basingstoke: Palgrave Macmillan, 2002), 127–50.

Beauman, Sally, *The Royal Shakespeare Company: A History of Ten Decades* (Oxford: Oxford University Press, 1982).

Bell, Michael, *F. R. Leavis* (Abingdon: Routledge, 1988).

—— 'F. R. Leavis', in A. Walton Litz, Louis Menand, and Lawrence Rainey (eds), *The Cambridge History of Literary Criticism*, vol. 7, *Modernism and the New Criticism* (Cambridge: Cambridge University Press, 2000), 389–422.

Bergonzi, Bernard, *Exploding English: Criticism, Theory, Culture* (Oxford: Clarendon Press, 1990).

Bilan, R. P., *The Literary Criticism of F. R. Leavis* (Cambridge: Cambridge University Press, 1979).

Black, Lawrence, 'The Lost World of Young Conservatism', *Historical Journal* 51/4 (2008): 991–1024.

—— *Redefining British Politics: Culture, Consumerism and Participation, 1954–70* (Basingstoke: Palgrave Macmillan, 2010).

Blackbourn, David, *The Conquest of Nature: Water, Landscape and the Making of Modern Germany* (London: Jonathan Cape, 2006).

Bradford, Richard, *Lucky Him: The Life of Kingsley Amis* (London: Peter Owen, 2001).

Briggs, Asa, *The History of Broadcasting in the United Kingdom*, 5 vols (Oxford: Oxford University Press, 1961–95).

Britton, John, 'A. C. Bradley and Those Children of Lady Macbeth', *Shakespeare Quarterly* 12/3 (summer 1961): 349–51.

Brooke, Christopher N. L., *A History of the University of Cambridge*, vol. 4, *1870–1990* (Cambridge: Cambridge University Press, 1993).

Brooke, Stephen, 'Gender and Working Class Identity in Britain during the 1950s', *Journal of Social History* 34/4 (summer 2001): 773–95.

Brower, Reuben, Helen Vendler, and John Hollander (eds), *I. A. Richards: Essays in His Honor* (New York: Oxford University Press, 1973).

Brown, Callum G., *The Death of Christian Britain: Understanding Secularisation, 1800–2000* (2001; Abingdon: Routledge, 2009).

Burk, Kathleen (ed.), *The British Isles since 1945* (Oxford: Oxford University Press, 2003).

Butler, Marilyn, 'Moments', *London Review of Books*, 2 September 1982.

Calder, Angus, 'Leads from Leeds', *Journal of Commonwealth Literature* 21/9 (1986): 9–11.

Cambridge Quarterly 25/4: Special Issue on F. R. Leavis, ed. D. C. Gervais, R. D. Gooder, A. P. Newton, F. M. Rosslyn, and G. C. Ward (1996).

The Cambridge University List of Members 1973–1974 (Cambridge: Cambridge University Press, 1974).

Campbell, Flann, *Eleven-Plus and All That: The Grammar School in a Changing Society* (London: Watts, 1956).

Carey, Hugh, *Mansfield Forbes and His Cambridge* (Cambridge: Cambridge University Press, 1984).

Carpenter, Humphrey, *Dennis Potter: A Biography* (London: Faber & Faber, 1998).

—— *The Envy of the World: Fifty Years of the BBC Third Programme and Radio 3* (London: Weidenfeld & Nicolson, 1996).

Casanova, Pascale, *The World Republic of Letters*, trans. M. B. DeBevoise (1999; Cambridge, Mass.: Harvard University Press, 2004).

Clausen, Christopher, 'The Palgrave Version', *Georgia Review* 34 (1980): 273–89.

Collier, Patrick, *Modernism on Fleet Street* (Aldershot: Ashgate, 2006).

Collini, Stefan, *Absent Minds: Intellectuals in Britain* (Oxford: Oxford University Press, 2006).

—— 'Cambridge and the Study of English', in Sarah J. Ormrod (ed.), *Cambridge Contributions* (Cambridge: Cambridge University Press, 1998), 42–64.

—— 'The Critic as Journalist: Leavis after *Scrutiny*', in Jeremy Treglown and Bridget Bennett (eds), *Grub Street and Ivory Tower: Literary Journalism and Literary Scholarship from Fielding to the Internet* (Oxford: Clarendon Press, 1998), 151–76.

—— 'Enduring Passion: E. P. Thompson's Reputation', in *Common Reading: Critics, Historians, Publics* (Oxford: Oxford University Press, 2008), 175–86.

Collini, Stefan, *English Pasts: Essays in History and Culture* (Oxford: Oxford University Press, 1999).

—— 'The Literary Critic and the Village Labourer: "Culture" in Twentieth-Century Britain', *Transactions of the Royal Historical Society* 14 (2004): 93–116.

—— 'On Highest Authority: The Literary Critic and Other Aviators in Early Twentieth-Century Britain' in Dorothy Ross (ed.), *Modernist Impulses in the Human Sciences, 1870–1930* (Baltimore: Johns Hopkins University Press, 1994), 152–70.

—— *Public Moralists: Political Thought and Intellectual Life in Britain, 1850–1930* (Oxford: Clarendon Press, 1991).

—— 'Where Did It All Go Wrong? Cultural Critics and "Modernity" in Inter-War Britain', in E. H. H. Green and D. M. Tanner (eds), *The Strange Survival of Liberal England: Political Leaders, Moral Values and the Reception of Economic Debate* (Cambridge: Cambridge University Press, 2007), 247–74.

Connell, W. F., G. E. Sherington, B. H. Fletcher, C. Turney, and U. Bygott, *Australia's First: A History of the University of Sydney*, vol. 2, *1940–1990* (Sydney: Hale & Iremonger, 1995).

Court, Franklin E., *Institutionalizing English Literature: The Culture and Politics of Literary Study, 1750–1900* (Stanford: Stanford University Press, 1992).

Cunningham, Sophie, 'Alien Star', *Meanjin* 62/1 (2003): 100–13.

Cunningham, Valentine, 'F. W. Bateson: Scholar, Critic, and Scholar-Critic', *Essays in Criticism* 29/2 (1979): 139–55.

Dale, Leigh, *The English Men: Professing Literature in Australian Universities* (Toowoomba, Queensland: Association for the study of Australian Litrature, 1997).

Davis, Madeleine, 'The Marxism of the British New Left', *Journal of Political Ideologies* 11/3 (2006): 335–58.

Day, Gary, *Re-reading Leavis: 'Culture' and Literary Criticism* (Basingstoke: Macmillan, 1996).

Deresiewicz, William, 'The Business of Theory', *Nation*, 16 February 2004.

Diggins, John Patrick, *Thorstein Veblen: Theorist of the Leisure Class* (Princeton: Princeton University Press, 1999).

Diggle, Margaret, 'Mansfield Forbes on the Romantic Revival', *Cambridge Quarterly* 6/2 (1973): 107–15.

Docker, John, *Australian Cultural Elites: Intellectual Traditions in Sydney and Melbourne* (Sydney: Angus & Robertson, 1974).

—— *In a Critical Condition: Reading Australian Literature* (Melbourne: Penguin, 1984).

Doyle, Brian, *English and Englishness* (London: Routledge, 1989).

—— 'The Invention of English', in Robert Colls and Philip Dodds (eds), *Englishness: Politics and Culture, 1880–1920* (Beckenham: Croom Helm, 1986), 89–115.

Dworkin, Dennis L., *Cultural Marxism in Postwar Britain: History, the New Left, and the Origins of Cultural Studies* (Durham, NC: Duke University Press, 1997).

Dyhouse, Carol, *Students: A Gendered History* (London: Routledge, 2006).

Dykes, David, *The University College of Swansea: An Illustrated History* (Stroud: Alan Sutton, 1992).

Eagleton, Terry, *Criticism and Ideology: A Study in Marxist Literary Theory* (1976; London: Verso, 1978).

——*Literary Theory: An Introduction* (1983; Minneapolis: University of Minnesota Press, 1996).

Esty, Jed, *A Shrinking Island: Modernism and National Culture in England* (Princeton: Princeton University Press, 2003).

Filreis, Alan, *Wallace Stevens and the Actual World* (Princeton: Princeton University Press, 1991).

French, Stanley, *The History of Downing College Cambridge* (Cambridge: Downing College Association, 1978).

——et al., *Aspects of Downing History*, vol. 2 (Cambridge: Downing College Association, 1989).

de Garis, Brian (ed.), *Campus in the Community: The University of Western Australia, 1963–1987* (Perth: University of Western Australia Press, 1988).

Gervais, David, *Literary Englands: Versions of 'Englishness' in Modern Writing* (Cambridge: Cambridge University Press, 1993).

Gikandi, Simon, 'Globalization and the Claims of Postcoloniality', *South Atlantic Quarterly* 100/3 (2001): 627–58.

——*Ngugi wa Thiong'o* (Cambridge: Cambridge University Press, 2000).

Goldman, Lawrence, *Dons and Workers: Oxford and Adult Education since 1850* (Oxford: Oxford University Press, 1995).

Goldstein, Jan, *The Post-Revolutionary Self: Politics and Psyche in France, 1750–1850* (Cambridge, Mass.: Harvard University Press, 2005).

Graff, Gerald, *Professing Literature: An Institutional History*, (1987; Chicago: University of Chicago Press, 2007).

Grant, Jane, 'A Critical Mind: On Sam Goldberg', *Meanjin* 69/1 (2010): 43–52.

Gray, J. M., *A History of the Perse School Cambridge* (Cambridge: Bowes & Bowes, 1921).

Green, E. H. H., *Ideologies of Conservatism: Conservative Political Ideas in the Twentieth Century* (Oxford: Oxford University Press, 2002).

Gross, Richard E. (ed.), *British Secondary Education: Overview and Appraisal* (London: Oxford University Press, 1965).

Habermas, Jürgen, *The Structural Transformation of the Public Sphere: An Inquiry into a Category of Bourgeois Society*, trans. Thomas Burger (Cambridge, Mass.: MIT Press, 1989).

Haffenden, John, *William Empson*, 2 vols (Oxford: Oxford University Press, 2005–6).

Hall, Stuart, 'Life and Times of the First New Left', *New Left Review*, n.s. 61 (2010): 177–96.

Halsey, A. H., and A. F. Heath, and J. M. Ridge, *Origins and Destinations: Family, Class and Education in Modern Britain* (Oxford: Clarendon Press, 1980).

Hart-Davis, Duff, *The House the Berrys Built: Inside The Telegraph, 1928–1986* (1990; Sevenoaks: Hodder and Stoughton, 1991).

Hawkes, Terence, *That Shakespeherian Rag: Essays on a Critical Process* (London: Methuen, 1986).

Hayman, Ronald, *Leavis* (London: Heinemann, 1976).

Hewison, Robert, *Too Much: Art and Society in the Sixties, 1960–75* (London: Methuen, 1986).

Hilliard, Christopher, 'Modernism and the Common Writer', *Historical Journal* 48/3 (September 2005): 769–87.

—— *To Exercise Our Talents: The Democratization of Writing in Britain* (Cambridge, Mass.: Harvard University Press, 2006).

Hilton, Matthew, *Consumerism in Twentieth-Century Britain: The Search for a Historical Movement* (Cambridge: Cambridge University Press, 2003).

—— 'The Polyester-Flannelled Philanthropists: The Birmingham Consumers' Group and Affluent Britain', in Lawrence Black and Hugh Pemberton (eds), *An Affluent Society? Britain's Post-war 'Golden Age' Revisited* (Aldershot: Ashgate, 2004), 149–66.

Hobday, Charles, *Edgell Rickword: A Poet at War* (Manchester: Carcanet Press, 1989).

Hodson, William Alan and John Carfora, 'Stuart Chase: Brief Life of a Public Thinker: 1888–1985', *Harvard Magazine*, September–October 2004, 38–9.

Holderness, Graham (ed.), *The Shakespeare Myth* (Manchester: Manchester University Press, 1988).

Holland, Steve, *The Trials of Hank Janson* (Tolworth: Telos, 2004).

Hollis, Patricia, *Jennie Lee: A Life* (1997; Oxford: Oxford University Press, 1998).

Hopkins, Harry, *The New Look: A Social History of the Forties and Fifties in Britain* (London: Secker & Warburg, 1963).

Hunter, Ian, *Culture and Government: The Emergence of Literary Education* (Basingstoke: Macmillan, 1988).

Igo, Sarah E., *The Averaged American: Surveys, Citizens, and the Making of a Mass Public* (Cambridge, Mass.: Harvard University Press, 2007).

Inglis, Fred, 'Andor Gomme: Critic and Architectural Historian', *The Independent*, 30 October 2008.

—— 'Professor Ian MacKillop', *The Independent*, 3 June 2004.

—— *Radical Earnestness: English Social Theory 1880–1980* (Oxford and Cambridge, Mass.: Martin Robertson with Basil Blackwell, 1982).

—— *Raymond Williams* (London: Routledge, 1995).

Jacobs, Eric, *Kingsley Amis: A Biography* (1995; London: Hodder & Stoughton, 1996).

Joicey, Nicholas, 'A Paperback Guide to Progress: Penguin Books 1935–c.1951', *Twentieth Century British History* 4/1 (1993): 25–56.

Jorgensen, Elizabeth Watkins and Henry Irvin Jorgensen, *Thorstein Veblen: Victorian Firebrand* (Armonk, NY: M. E. Sharpe, 1999).

Joyce, Chris, 'The Idea of "Anti-Philosophy" in the Work of F. R. Leavis', *Cambridge Quarterly* 38/1 (2009): 24–44.

Kermode, Frank, *Bury Place Papers: Essays from the London Review of Books* (London: London Review of Books, 2009).

—— 'The Shakespearian Rag', *New York Review of Books*, 24 September 1964.

Kinch, M. B., William Baker, and John Kimber, *F. R. Leavis and Q. D. Leavis: An Annotated Bibliography* (New York: Garland, 1989).

Laing, Dave, '*Scrutiny* to Subcultures: Notes on Literary Criticism and Popular Music', *Popular Music* 13/2 (May 1994): 179–90.

Lawrence, Jon, 'The British Sense of Class', *Journal of Contemporary History* 35 (April 2000): 307–18.

Lepenies, Wolf, *Between Literature and Science: The Rise of Sociology*, trans. R. J. Hollingdale (1985; Cambridge: Cambridge University Press, 1988).

Leventhal, F. M., ' "The Best for the Most": CEMA and State Sponsorship of the Arts in Wartime, 1939–1945', *Twentieth Century British History* 1/3 (1990): 289–317.

Lewis, Jeremy, *Penguin Special: The Life and Times of Allen Lane* (London: Viking, 2005).

Lowe, John, *Adult Education in England and Wales: A Critical Survey* (London: Michael Joseph, 1970).

Mackenzie, S. P., *Politics and Military Morale: Current-Affairs and Citizenship Education in the British Army, 1914–1950* (Oxford: Clarendon Press, 1992).

MacKillop, Ian, *F. R. Leavis: A Life in Criticism* (London: Allen Lane, 1995).

—— and Richard Storer (eds), *F. R. Leavis: Essays and Documents* (Sheffield: Sheffield Academic Press, 1995).

Mandler, Peter, *The English National Character: The History of an Idea from Edmund Burke to Tony Blair* (New Haven: Yale University Press, 2006).

—— Review of *The Two Cultures Controversy: Science, Literature, and Cultural Politics in Postwar Britain* by Guy Ortolano, H-Albion, January 2010, <http://www.h-net.org/reviews/showrev.php?id=25388>, accessed 28 July 2011.

Marchand, Philip, *Marshall McLuhan: The Medium and the Messenger* (1989; Cambridge, Mass.: MIT Press, 1998).

Massey, Anne, *The Independent Group: Modernism and Mass Culture in Britain, 1945–59* (Manchester: Manchester University Press, 1995).

Matthews, Sean, 'The Responsibilities of Dissent: F. R. Leavis after *Scrutiny*', *Literature and History* 13/2 (2004): 49–66.

May, Derwent, *Critical Times: The History of the Times Literary Supplement* (London: HarperCollins, 2001).

McAleer, Joseph, *Popular Reading and Publishing in Britain, 1914–1950* (Oxford: Clarendon Press, 1992).

McGovern, Charles, 'Consumption and Citizenship in the United States, 1900–1940', in Susan Strasser, Charles McGovern, and Matthias Judt (eds), *Getting and Spending: European and American Consumer Societies in the Twentieth Century* (Cambridge: Cambridge University Press, 1998), 37–58.

McGurl, Mark, *The Program Era: Postwar Fiction and the Rise of Creative Writing* (Cambridge, Mass.: Harvard University Press, 2009).

McIlroy, John, 'Teacher, Critic, Explorer', in W. John Morgan and Peter Preston (eds), *Raymond Williams: Politics, Education, Letters* (Basingstoke: Macmillan, 1993), 14–46.

McKenzie, D. F. and M. P. Allum, *F. R. Leavis: A Check-list 1924–1964* (London: Chatto & Windus, 1966).

McKibbin, Ross, *Classes and Cultures: England, 1918–1951* (Oxford: Oxford University Press, 1998).

McMurtry, Jo, *English Language, English Literature: The Creation of an Academic Discipline* (London: Mansell, 1985).

McSweeney, Kerry, 'Scrutiny', in Alvin Sullivan (ed.), *British Literary Magazines*, vol. 4, *The Modern Age, 1914–1984* (New York: Greenwood Press, 1986), 121–5.

Melman, Billie, *Women and the Popular Imagination in the Twenties: Flappers and Nymphs* (Basingstoke: Macmillan, 1988).

Mencher, M. B. (ed.), *Leavis, Dr MacKillop and 'The Cambridge Quarterly': A Brynmill Special Issue* (Denton, Norfolk: Brynmill Press, 1998).

Minihan, Janet, *The Nationalization of Culture: The Development of State Subsidies to the Arts in Great Britain* (New York: New York University Press, 1977).

Mitchell, Donald, 'Obituary: Professor Boris Ford', *The Independent*, 27 May 1998.

Mitchell, Leslie, *Maurice Bowra: A Life* (Oxford: Oxford University Press, 2009).

Montefiore, Jan and Kate Varney, 'A Conversation about Q. D. Leavis', *Women: A Cultural Review*, 19/2 (2008): 172–87.

Morrisson, Mark S., *The Public Face of Modernism: Little Magazines, Audiences, and Reception, 1905–1920* (Madison: University of Wisconsin Press, 2001).

Mulhern, Francis, 'Culture and Authority', *Critical Quarterly* 37/1 (1995): 77–89.
—— *The Moment of 'Scrutiny'* (London: New Left Books, 1979).

Naylor, Gillian, 'Good Design in British Industry 1930–56', in Peter Draper (ed.), *Reassessing Nikolaus Pevsner* (Aldershot: Ashgate, 2004), 177–94.

Neill, Heather, 'My Best Teacher', *Times Education Supplement*, 2 March 2001.

Newton, John, 'Between Vision and Enquiry', *Times Higher Education Supplement*, 25 August 1995.

Ortolano, Guy, 'F. R. Leavis, Science, and the Abiding Crisis of Modern Civilization', *History of Science* 43 (2005): 161–85.
—— *The Two Cultures Controversy: Science, Literature and Cultural Politics in Postwar Britain* (Cambridge: Cambridge University Press, 2009).

Osterwold, Tilman, *Pop Art* (Köln: Taschen, 2003).

Owen, Sue, '*The Abuse of Literacy* and the Feeling Heart: The Trials of Richard Hoggart', *Cambridge Quarterly* 34/2 (2005): 147–76.
—— (ed.), *Richard Hoggart and Cultural Studies* (Basingstoke: Palgrave Macmillan, 2008).

Oxford Dictionary of National Biography (Oxford: Oxford University Press, 2004).

Palmer, D. J., *The Rise of English Studies: An Account of the Study of English Language and Literature from Its Origins to the Making of the Oxford English School* (London: Oxford University Press, 1965).

Pittock, Malcolm, 'Richard Hoggart and the Leavises', *Essays in Criticism* 60/1 (2010): 51–69.

Pollentier, Caroline, '"Everybody's Essayist": On Middles and Middlebrows', in Kate Macdonald (ed.), *The Masculine Middlebrow, 1880–1950: What Mr Miniver Read* (Basingstoke: Palgrave Macmillan, 2011), 119–34.

Pybus, Cassandra, *The Devil and James McAuley* (St Lucia, Queensland: University of Queensland Press, 1999).

Ravenscroft, Arthur, 'The Origins', *Journal of Commonwealth Literature* 21/9 (1986): 2–4.

Raybould, S. G., *University Extramural Education in England, 1945–62: A Study in Finance and Policy* (London: Michael Joseph, 1964).

Rée, Harry, *Educator Extraordinary: The Life and Achievement of Henry Morris, 1889–1961* (London: Longman, 1973).

Richmond, John, 'Harold Rosen', *The Guardian*, 4 August 2008.

Rose, Jonathan, *The Intellectual Life of the British Working Class* (New Haven: Yale University Press, 2001).

Ross, James, Linda Gill, and Stuart McRae (eds), *Writing a New Country: A Collection of Essays Presented to E. H. McCormick in His 88th Year* (Auckland: Ariel Books, 1993).

Russo, John Paul, *I. A. Richards: His Life and Work* (London: Routledge, 1989).

Savage, Mike, *Identities and Social Change in Britain since 1940: The Politics of Method* (Oxford: Oxford University Press, 2010).

Schwartz, Leonard, 'Professions, Elites, and Universities in England, 1870–1970', *Historical Journal* 47 (2004): 941–62.

Scruton, Roger, *England: An Elegy* (London: Chatto & Windus, 2000).

Shayer, David, *The Teaching of English in Schools, 1900–1970* (London: Routledge & Kegan Paul, 1972).

Sicherman, Carol, 'Ngugi's Colonial Education: "The Subversion...of the African Mind"', *African Studies Review* 38/3 (1995): 11–41.

Simon, Brian (ed.), *The Search for Enlightenment: The Working Class and Adult Education in the Twentieth Century* (1990; Leicester: National Institute of Adult Continuing Education, 1992).

Silber, Norman, 'Chase, Stuart', in John A. Garraty and Mark C. Carnes (eds), *American National Biography*, 24 vols (New York: Oxford University Press, 1999), 4: 745–7.

Sinclair, Andrew, *Arts and Cultures: The History of the Fifty Years of the Arts Council of Great Britain* (London: Sinclair Stevenson, 1995).

Sinfield, Alan (ed.), Society and Literature 1945–1970 (London: Methuen, 1983).

Sirinelli, Jean-François, *Génération intellectuelle: khâgneux et normaliens dans l'entre-deux-guerres* (Paris: Fayard, 1988).

Smith, Dai, *Raymond Williams: A Warrior's Tale* (Cardigan: Parthian Books, 2008).

Spindler, Michael, *Veblen and Modern America: Revolutionary Iconoclast* (London: Pluto Press, 2002).

Spitz, Bob, *The Beatles: The Biography* (New York: Little, Brown, & Co., 2005).

Stanfield, Peter, 'Maximum Movies: Lawrence Alloway's Pop Art Film Criticism', *Screen* 49/2 (2008): 179–93.

Stansky, Peter, *On or About December 1910: Early Bloomsbury and Its Intimate World* (Cambridge, Mass.: Harvard University Press, 1996).

Steedman, Carolyn, *Childhood, Culture, and Class in Britain: Margaret McMillan, 1860–1931* (London: Virago Press, 1990).

—— 'State-sponsored Autobiography', in Becky Conekin, Frank Mort, and Chris Waters (eds), *Moments of Modernity: Reconstructing Britain, 1945–1964* (London: Rivers Oram Press, 1999), 41–54.

Steele, Tom, *The Emergence of Cultural Studies, 1945–65: Cultural Politics, Adult Education, and the English Question* (London: Lawrence & Wishart, 1997).

Stewart, James D., Muriel E. Hammond, and Erwin Saenger, *British Union-Catalogue of Periodicals: A Record of the Periodicals of the World, from the Seventeenth Century to the Present Day, in British Libraries*, vol. 4, *S-Z* (London: Butterworths, 1958).

Storer, Richard, *F. R. Leavis* (Abingdon: Routledge, 2009).

Tucker, Nicholas, 'Obituary: Edward Blishen', *The Independent*, 16 December 1996.

Veldman, Meredith, *Fantasy, the Bomb, and the Greening of Britain: Romantic Protest, 1945–1980* (Cambridge: Cambridge University Press, 1994).

Viswanathan, Gauri, *Masks of Conquest: Literary Study and British Rule in India* (New York: Columbia University Press, 1989).

Wallace-Crabbe, Chris, 'Buckley, Vincent Thomas (1925–1988)', *Australian Dictionary of Biography*, vol. 17 (Melbourne: Melbourne University Press, 2007), 152–4.

Waters, Chris, 'Beyond "Americanization": Rethinking Anglo-American Cultural Exchange between the Wars', *Cultural and Social History* 4/4 (2007): 451–9.

Welch, Edwin, *The Peripatetic University: Cambridge Local Lectures, 1873–1973* (Cambridge: Cambridge University Press, 1973).

Whitehead, Kate, *The Third Programme: A Literary History* (Oxford: Clarendon Press, 1989).

Woodhams, Stephen, 'Adult Education and the History of Cultural Studies', *Changing English* 6/2 (1999): 237–49.

Woolridge, Paul, 'The *Calendar* and the Modern Critical Essay' *Cambridge Quarterly* 40/2 (2011): 121–40.

Wren, Robert M., *Those Magical Years: The Making of Nigerian Literature at Ibadan: 1948–1966* (Washington, DC: Three Continents Press, 1991).

Wright, Iain, 'F. R. Leavis, the *Scrutiny* Movement and the Crisis', in Jonathan Clark et al. (eds), *Culture and Crisis in Britain in the Thirties* (London: Lawrence & Wishart, 1979).

Wright, John M., 'Grasping the Cosmic Jugular: Golden Builders Revisited', Journal of the Association for the Study of Australian Literature, Vincent Buckley Special Issue (2010), <http://www.nla.gov.au/openpublish/index.php/jasal/article/view/1412/1939>, accessed 25 July 2011.

II. Unpublished

Todd, Selina, 'From Scholarship Boys to Comprehensive Kids: Education, Getting on and Getting out of the Working-Class, c.1945–1970', unpublished paper, March 2009.

Index

292		*Index*

Cardinal Langley School 83
Cardinal Vaughan Grammar School 83
Carlyle, Thomas 55
Casanova, Pascale 240
Catholicism, 82–4
Catley, Peter 91 n. 75
Centre 42 172
Centre for Contemporary Cultural
	Studies, *see* University of
	Birmingham
Ceylon 219–22
Chadwick, H. Munro 28
Chadwick, N. Kershaw 28
Chaplin, Charlie 182, 184
Charlesworth, John 118–19
Chase, James Hadley 171
Chase, Stuart 49, 57, 61, 64–5, 66, 113,
	155, 180
Chatto & Windus 48, 114, 171, 202,
	219, 231
Chaucer, Geoffrey 29, 208–9
Chingford County High School 77
Chislehurst and Sidcup Grammar
	School 110, 115
Churchill, R. C. 83, 120, 204, 227
Churchill, Winston 23
City Boys' School (Leicester) 110
Clark, Charles 177–8
class 5, 78, 102, 107, 140, 145–6, 189
	middle 74–5, 77, 82
	upper and upper-middle 82, 102,
		193, 253
	working 12, 79–82, 168, 170, 241
Clegg, Eric 107
Clements, Simon 136, 137 n. 126
Clifton College 76
close reading 1, 27–8, 36, 135, 149,
	150, 218, 236
	see also practical criticism
Cobbett, William 55
Coleman, John 101
Coleridge, Samuel Taylor 37, 48, 72, 121
Collini, Stefan 53, 54–5, 168–9, 193, 195
Collins, Clifford 158
Coltham, Stephen 151
communism 59, 93, 175, 254–5
Communist Party 127
comprehensive schools, *see* schools
comprehensivization 119, 139, 193
	see also schools
Conquest, Robert 123
Conservative Party 122, 175, 256–7
consumption 58, 59, 60, 62, 65, 66
Cook, H. Caldwell 132
Cooper, Dorothy 115
Cox, C. B. 117, 118, 121, 122

Cox, Gordon 73, 90 n. 74
Cradock, Robert 87, 96
Craig, David 93, 220, 232, 245
creative writing 103, 126, 128, 130
	Downing College graduates and 101–4
Criterion 219
Critical Quarterly 117, 121, 122–3
Critical Survey 10, 11
criticism, *see* literary criticism
Crowther, R. H. 91 n. 74
cultural studies 11, 186, 187, 190
	see also University of Birmingham
culture 12, 43, 47, 51, 160, 185, 190,
	241–2
	decline of 69, 120, 165, 168, 169,
		172–3, 210, 242
	see also mass culture; popular culture
Culver, Donald 6, 223
Cuttle, Bill 4–5

Daily Mail 63
Dalglish, Jack 85, 109 n. 3
Dartington Hall 110, 124 n. 61, 249
Dartmouth College seminar on English
	teaching 119, 134–5
Davies, Hugh Sykes 126
Dawson, S. W. 42, 92
Delta 85, 103
democracy 112, 120, 121, 122, 144,
	243, 250
Dickens, Charles 55, 64, 227
Dicks, Terrance 99
discrimination 25, 36, 41, 43, 64, 115,
	123, 139–40, 150, 153, 177,
	181–2, 226, 236–7, 242
	examples of 1, 21, 22, 24, 132, 165
Dixon, John 119, 134–6, 137 n. 126
	Growth through English 119, 134–5,
		137–8
Dobrée, Bonamy 162 n. 95, 202–3
Doctor Who 99
Donne, John 25, 26, 53, 116–17
Dos Passos, John 56, 71, 113
Doughty Society 72, 100, 103, 121, 223
Downing College, Cambridge 4–5,
	106–7, 118, 122
	details of F. R. Leavis's students
		at 72–108
	examinations 5, 20–6, 30, 32, 43
Downside School 82, 84
Doyle, Ian 73, 83, 97
drama 31–3, 41, 105, 136, 154, 159,
	160–1, 184, 213, 225, 230
	see also theatre
Dryden, John 25, 30, 41
Dudman, B. S. 152